345 Yummy White Wine Recipes

(345 Yummy White Wine Recipes - Volume 1)

Mary Walter

Copyright: Published in the United States by Mary Walter/ © MARY WALTER

Published on September, 22 2020

All rights reserved. No part of this publication may be reproduced, stored in retrieval system, copied in any form or by any means, electronic, mechanical, photocopying, recording or otherwise transmitted without written permission from the publisher. Please do not participate in or encourage piracy of this material in any way. You must not circulate this book in any format. MARY WALTER does not control or direct users' actions and is not responsible for the information or content shared, harm and/or actions of the book readers.

In accordance with the U.S. Copyright Act of 1976, the scanning, uploading and electronic sharing of any part of this book without the permission of the publisher constitute unlawful piracy and theft of the author's intellectual property. If you would like to use material from the book (other than just simply for reviewing the book), prior permission must be obtained by contacting the author at author@rutabagarecipes.com

Thank you for your support of the author's rights.

Content

345 AWESOME WHITE WINE RECIPES .. 9

1. 3 Ingredient Mussels With White Wine And Pesto 9
2. Angel Hair With Fennel Pesto 9
3. Anise Cookie Baskets With Riesling Ice Cream And Fresh Fruit 10
4. Anniversary Punch 11
5. Autumn Apple Strudel 11
6. Baked Flounder Rolls With Tomato, Bell Pepper, And Bacon 12
7. Baked Pears With Sauternes Custard Sauce 13
8. Baked Rigatoni With Sausage And Mushrooms 14
9. Baked Sardines In Pepperonata 15
10. Blood Orange Roast Pork Loin 15
11. Blue Cheese Souffles With Grape Syrup On Fig And Walnut Brioche 16
12. Bolognese Sauce 17
13. Boneless Pork Chops With Ginger, Fig, And Lemon Compote 18
14. Braised Chicken Thighs With Squash And Mustard Greens 19
15. Braised Chicken In Sun Dried Tomato Cream 20
16. Braised Chicken With Garlic And White Wine 20
17. Braised Chicken With Leeks And Morels . 21
18. Braised Duck Legs With Leeks And Green Olives 21
19. Braised Lamb Shanks With Tomatoes And Rosemary 22
20. Braised Spareribs With Rigatoni 23
21. Braised Truffled Turkey 24
22. Braised Veal Breast With Bulb Vegetables 24
23. Braised Veal With Gremolata 25
24. Braised And Roasted Pork Shanks With Prosciutto And Porcini Mushrooms 26
25. Brandied Onion Soup With Croque Monsieur Croutons 27
26. Brie And Wild Mushroom Fondue 27
27. Brie, Roquefort And Wild Mushroom Fondue 28
28. Broiled Salmon Steaks With Horseradish Crust 29
29. Buttermilk Cake With Blackberries And Beaumes De Venise 29
30. Butternut Squash And Sage Orzo 30
31. Caneton Au Muscadet 30
32. Caramelized Onion And Wine Braised Brisket With Glazed Vegetables 31
33. Cauliflower Soup With Hazelnuts And Bacon 32
34. Cheese Fondue With Beer And Bourbon . 33
35. Cheesy Sausage And Sage Stuffing 34
36. Chicken Breasts Stuffed With Goat Cheese And Basil 34
37. Chicken Cacciatora 35
38. Chicken Francaise 36
39. Chicken Sausage 37
40. Chicken Sauté With White Wine 37
41. Chicken Stock 38
42. Chicken Under A Skillet With Lemon Pan Sauce 38
43. Chicken And Artichoke Stew 39
44. Chicken And Root Vegetable Stew 40
45. Chicken In Dill Mustard Sauce 40
46. Chicken In Riesling 41
47. Chicken With Prosciutto, Rosemary, And White Wine 42
48. Chicken With Sun Dried Tomato Cream Sauce 43
49. Chicken With Sweet And Hot Red Peppers 43
50. Chicken With Vegetables And Parsley Dumplings 44
51. Chicken With White Wine And Garlic 45
52. Chicken, Shrimp And Sausage Stew 45
53. Chili Lime Cream Sauce 46
54. Chilled Blueberry Soup 46
55. Chilled Grape Soup 47
56. Chilled Herbed Tomato Soup With Citrus And Spice 47
57. Chilled Watermelon Mint Soup 48
58. Choucroute Garnie 49
59. Choucroute With Caramelized Pears 49
60. Cider Braised Pheasant With Pearl Onions And Apples 50
61. Cipolline With Bay Leaf And Golden Raisins 51

62. Coconut Curry Sauce 52
63. Coniglio Pizzaiola 52
64. Coquilles St. Jacques 53
65. Coquilles St. Jacques With Beurre Blanc ... 53
66. Corn And Potatoes With Heirloom Tomatoes 54
67. Crab Bisque 55
68. Cranberry Rosemary Wine Jelly 55
69. Cream Of Artichoke And Jerusalem Artichoke Soup 56
70. Creamed Crab With Artichokes 57
71. Creamy Chinese Celery Soup 57
72. Crispy Chicken Thighs With Kale, Apricots, And Olives 58
73. Crispy Chicken Thighs With Spring Vegetables 59
74. Dried Fruit Compote With Vanilla And Orange 60
75. Dried Fruit Compote With White Wine ... 60
76. Duck Two Ways With Clementine Fig Relish 61
77. Escargot With Garlic Parsley Butter 62
78. Farfalle With Forest Mushrooms, Peas, And Parsley 63
79. Fish Fillets With Grapefruit Tarragon Beurre Blanc 63
80. Fish Fillets With Olives And Oregano 64
81. Fish Soup With Aïoli Croutons 65
82. Fish Stock 65
83. Fish In Foil With Sweet Onions, Tomatoes, And Mojo Verde 66
84. Fontina Risotto Cakes With Fresh Chives 67
85. Franks And Beans 67
86. French Potato Salad 68
87. Garlic Cheese Fondue 69
88. Garlic Orange Pork Chops 69
89. Garlic Roasted Chicken Breasts 69
90. Garlic And Herb Braised Squid 70
91. Garlicky Black Pepper Shrimp And Black Eyed Peas 71
92. Gemelli With Cheese And Quick Arrabbiata Sauce 71
93. Gemelli With Zucchini, Tomatoes, And Bacon 72
94. Gingered Beet Risotto 72
95. Glazed Sea Bass With Ginger Butter Sauce 73

96. Gratin Of Potatoes With White Cheddar And Tarragon 74
97. Greek Style Shrimp 74
98. Green Grape Sangria 75
99. Greens And Beans With Fried Bread 75
100. Grilled Cheese With Sauteed Mushrooms 76
101. Halibut With Capers, Olives, And Tomatoes 76
102. Halibut With Spicy Sausage, Tomatoes, And Rosemary 77
103. Hazelnut, Sage, And Mushroom Stuffing . 77
104. Herb Braised Ham 78
105. Herb Roasted Leg Of Lamb With Vegetables And Jus 79
106. Herb Rubbed Steaks With Olives Provencal 80
107. Herbed Fish Rolls In White Wine With Grapes 81
108. Holiday Ham With Riesling And Mustard 82
109. Holiday Punch 82
110. Honey Poached Pears With Mascarpone .. 83
111. Horseradish Crusted Salmon With Beet Sauce 83
112. If It Ain't Broke, Don't Fix It Stuffing 84
113. Instant Pot Shrimp Scampi 85
114. Italian Chicken With Mushroom And Wine Sauce 86
115. Italian Fish Soup 86
116. John Dory With Fried Fennel And Anchovy Butter Sauce 87
117. Kir 88
118. Kir II 88
119. Kris Kringle 88
120. Lamb Shanks With Tomatoes And Fresh Herbs 88
121. Lamb Shoulder With Citrus Fennel Salad . 89
122. Lavender And Thyme Roasted Poussins .. 90
123. Leg Of Lamb Poached In White Wine Court Bouillon 91
124. Lemon Chicken 91
125. Lemon Risotto 92
126. Lemon Dill Sauce 92
127. Lemony Mushroom Risotto 93
128. Lima Beans With Clams 93
129. Linguine With Mussels And Arugula Cream Sauce 94
130. Linguine With Salmon And Arugula 94

131. Lobster Pasta With Herbed Cream Sauce 95
132. Lobster Shepherd's Pie 96
133. Lobster Stock 97
134. Lobster And Shrimp Cioppino 97
135. Make Ahead Gravy 99
136. Mango Wine Cooler 99
137. Manhattan Seafood Chowder 100
138. Melon And Blueberry Coupe With White Wine, Vanilla And Mint 101
139. Mexican Chicken Sauté 101
140. Michael Lewis's Cassoulet De Canard 102
141. Minestrone With Cabbage And Spinach . 103
142. Mini Meatballs In Saffron Sauce 104
143. Mixed Mushroom Risotto 104
144. Monkfish Saganaki 105
145. Monkfish And Clam Bourride 105
146. Moules Marinière 106
147. Muscovy Duck Breasts With Pomegranate Wine Sauce 107
148. Mushroom And Leek Soup 108
149. Mussel Chowder 108
150. Mussels And Fries With Mustard Mayonnaise 109
151. Mussels And Zucchini Marinière 110
152. Mussels In Green Peppercorn Sauce 110
153. Mussels In Romesco Sauce 111
154. Mussels In Saffron And White Wine Broth 111
155. Mussels On The Half Shell With Pesto ... 112
156. Mussels With Fennel And Roasted Red Pepper Butter 113
157. Mussels With Garlic And Fines Herbes .. 113
158. Mussels With Roasted Potatoes 114
159. Mussels À La Marinière 115
160. Mustard Seed Crusted Salmon With Mustard Cream Sauce 115
161. Mustard Watercress Sauce 116
162. Mykonos Fillet Of Sole 116
163. Nectarine And Blueberry Clafouti 117
164. New Coq Au Vin 117
165. Oka Cheese Fondue 118
166. Orange Spice Fruit Compote 118
167. Oranges Poached In Riesling And Rosemary Syrup 119
168. Orecchiette With Rabbit, Tomato, And Basil Sauce 119
169. Paccheri With Shellfish, Squid, And Tomatoes 120
170. Pan Fried Trout With Green Onions 121
171. Pan Seared Swordfish Steaks With Shallot, Caper, And Balsamic Sauce 122
172. Pappardelle With Chicken Ragù, Fennel, And Peas 122
173. Parmesan Monkfish With Pastina Pasta And White Clam Sauce 123
174. Parsley Soup 124
175. Pasta With Roasted Romanesco And Capers 125
176. Pastry Twists With Spiced Sugar Honey Glaze 126
177. Peach White Wine Sangria 127
178. Peaches And Raspberries In Spiced White Wine 127
179. Pear Butter With Cardamom And Cinnamon 127
180. Pear Ice Cream With Spiced Pear Compote 128
181. Penne With Shrimp, Asparagus, And Sun Dried Tomatoes 129
182. Pineapple Sangria 129
183. Pink Gooseberry, Peach, And Elderflower Soup With Vanilla Ice Cream 130
184. Poached Artichokes 130
185. Poached Asian Pears With Star Anise And Tropical Fruit 131
186. Poached Oranges With Candied Zest And Ginger 131
187. Poached Pears In Phyllo Overcoat With Madeira Zabaglione `21' Club 132
188. Poached Pears With Chocolate Pear Sauce 133
189. Poached Salmon In Aspic 134
190. Poached Salmon With Tarragon Sauce And Fingerling Potatoes 135
191. Poached Wild Salmon With Peas And Morels 136
192. Pomegranate Aperitif 136
193. Porcini Mushroom Risotto 137
194. Pork Chops Scarpariello 137
195. Pork Loin Roast With Fennel Garlic Rub 138
196. Pork Medallions With Mustard Chive Sauce 139
197. Pork With Gorgonzola Sauce 139

198. Potato Gnocchi With Pork And Wild Mushroom Ragù 140
199. Pots De Crème With Riesling Poached Grapes 141
200. Provencal Fish Soup With Saffron Rouille 142
201. Provençal Braised Lamb Chops 143
202. Puerto Rican Crab 143
203. Pumpkin Cannelloni With Clams And Sage Brown Butter 144
204. Pumpkin And Shrimp Bisque 145
205. Pumpkin Seed Crusted Trout 146
206. Quick Cioppino 146
207. Quince Compote 147
208. Rabbit, Carrot, Leek, And Green Bean Ragoût 147
209. Rack Of Lamb With Red Currant Wine Sauce 148
210. Raspberry Syllabub 149
211. Rhubarb Sabayon With Strawberries 149
212. Riesling Poached Trout With Thyme 150
213. Rigatoni With Braised Lamb Ragù 150
214. Risotto Milanese Style (Risotta Alla Milanese) 151
215. Roast Chicken Provençale 152
216. Roast Chicken Stuffed With Fennel And Garlic 152
217. Roast Chicken With Lemon And Fresh Herbs 153
218. Roast Chicken With White Bean Stew And Pancetta 154
219. Roast Fillet Of Beef With Cornichon Tarragon Sauce 154
220. Roast Pork With Fruit Stuffing And Mustard Sauce 155
221. Roasted Asparagus And Wild Mushroom Fricassée 156
222. Roasted Asparagus With Brazil Nuts 156
223. Roasted Chicken, Ramps, And Potatoes. 157
224. Roasted Double Veal Chops 158
225. Roasted Farm Raised Barramundi With Fennel And Orange 158
226. Roasted Lamb Shoulder (Agnello De Latte Arrosto) 159
227. Roasted Pork Loin With Poached Plums 160
228. Roasted Red Snapper With Olives 161
229. Roasted Shellfish With Coriander, Fennel, And Meyer Lemon 161
230. Roasted Spiced Pork Loin With Root Vegetables 162
231. Roman Bortsch 163
232. Roman Style Fish Soup (Zuppa Di Pesce Alla Romana) 163
233. Romano Risotto With Radishes 164
234. Rotini With Roasted Peppers, Spinach And Pine Nuts 165
235. Rustic Pear Tart With Late Harvest Riesling 165
236. Sage Roasted Chicken With Madeira Sauce 166
237. Salmon Burgers With Lemon And Capers 167
238. Salmon Chowder 168
239. Salmon Fillets With Lemon Thyme Sauce 168
240. Salmon Rillettes 169
241. Salmon Trout Poached In White Wine .. 169
242. Salmon In Saffron Mussel Sauce 170
243. Salmon With Sesame And Orange Ginger Relish 170
244. Sauerkraut With Apples 171
245. Sauteed Baby Artichokes With Oven Dried Tomatoes And Green Olive Dressing 172
246. Sauteed Chicken With White Wine And Tomatoes 172
247. Sauteed Fresh Chanterelles 173
248. Sauteed Langoustine With Chardonnay Reduction 173
249. Sauteed Pasta With Lobster 175
250. Sautéed Pork Tenderloin With Prunes ... 176
251. Scallops Verde 176
252. Scallops With Mushrooms In White Wine Sauce 177
253. Sea Bass Amandine On Watercress 178
254. Sea Bass With Tomatoes And Onions ... 179
255. Sea Bream With Artichokes And Caper Dressing 179
256. Sea Scallops With Ham Braised Cabbage And Kale 180
257. Seafood Cannelloni 181
258. Seafood Stew With Fennel And Thyme . 182
259. Seared Scallops With Tarragon Butter Sauce 183
260. Seared Sea Scallops With Lemongrass Sauce

And Basil, Mint And Cilantro Salad 184
261. Seckel Pear Tart With Poire William Cream 185
262. Set It And Forget It Roast Pork Shoulder 186
263. Shellfish With Carrot Ginger Purée 187
264. Shrimp Risotto 187
265. Shrimp And Leek Linguine In White Wine Sauce 188
266. Shrimp And Mushroom Quinoa Risotto 189
267. Shrimp And Pea Risotto 190
268. Shrimp With Orange Dust 191
269. Skillet Stuffing With Italian Sausage And Wild Mushrooms 192
270. Slow Cooked Pork Shoulder With Braised White Beans 192
271. Sluggers' Strawberry Slushies 194
272. Smoked Salmon Benedict 194
273. Smoked Salmon Pasta Verde 195
274. Sole Piccata With Grapes And Capers ... 195
275. Spaghetti With Chorizo And Almonds ... 196
276. Spaghetti With Fresh Clams, Parsley, And Lemon 196
277. Spaghetti With Lobster And Mussels 197
278. Spanish Style Rice With Chicken And Seafood (Riz À La Valencienne) 198
279. Spice Rubbed Chicken Breasts With Lemon Shallot Sauce 199
280. Spiced Fruit Compote 200
281. Spiced Orange Wine 200
282. Spiced Pear Butter 201
283. Spicy Mussels In White Wine 201
284. Spicy Tomato Basil Sauce 202
285. Spiked Blackberry Coulis 202
286. Spinach, Pear And Green Bean Salad With Riesling Dressing 203
287. Spring Onion Soup With Garlic Croutons 203
288. Spring Vegetable Risotto With Poached Eggs 204
289. Steamed Cod With Cauliflower And Saffron 205
290. Steamed Fingerling Potatoes In White Wine 206
291. Steamed Mussels In White Wine 206
292. Steamed Mussels With Curry And Lemongrass 207

293. Steamed Mussels With Lemon Saffron Sauce 207
294. Steamed Mussels With Orange, Fennel, And Garlic 208
295. Steamed Mussels With Sausages And Fennel 209
296. Strawberry Mosel Cup 209
297. Strawberry And Cream Cake With Cardamom Syrup 210
298. Strawberry And Peach Sangria 211
299. Summer Fruit Terrine 211
300. Summer Punch 212
301. Sun Dried Tomato Onion Jam 212
302. Sunflower Seed "Risotto" With Squash And Mushrooms 213
303. Swiss Cheese And Porcini Fondue 214
304. Swiss Fondue 214
305. Swordfish Kebabs 215
306. Tagliatelle With Mussels, Clams And Pesto 215
307. Taglierini With Morels, Asparagus, And Nasturtiums 216
308. Tamarind Mango Sangria 217
309. Ten Minute Ravioli With Tomato Cream Sauce 217
310. Thanksgiving Dinner For One 218
311. Tom Valenti's Lamb Shanks 219
312. Tomato Mushroom Bisque 219
313. Tortelloni With Mushroom Sage Sauce .. 220
314. Triple Whammy Saffroned Tomato Fennel Soup 221
315. Tropical Fruit Compote With Mango Sorbet 221
316. Tropical Sparkling Sangria 221
317. Trout In Riesling 222
318. Turkey Breast Braciola 223
319. Turkey Cutlets With Springtime Vegetables 224
320. Turkey Giblet Stock 224
321. Turkey Tonnato 225
322. Twelve Fruit Compote 226
323. Vanilla Panna Cotta With Mixed Berry Compote 226
324. Vanilla Pear Clafoutis 227
325. Vanilla Poached Pineapple 227
326. Veal Piccata With Capers And Pine Nuts 228

327. Veal Scallops With Creamy Mushroom Sauce 229
328. Veal Scallops With Lemon And Capers ..229
329. Veal And Tomato Ragoût With Potatoes, Cinnamon, And Cream 230
330. Vegan "Tofurkey" With Mushroom Stuffing And Gravy 230
331. Vin D'orange (Orange Wine) 232
332. Walnut Risotto With Roasted Asparagus 232
333. Watermelon Sorbet With Wine Basil Gelée 233
334. White Chocolate Tiramisu Trifle With Spiced Pears 234
335. White Clam Sauce Dip 235
336. White Wine And Peach Sangria................236
337. White Zinfandel Sangria.............................236
338. Whole Snapper...237
339. Wild Mushroom Ravioli In Porcini Broth 237
340. Wild Mushroom Soup With Sherry 238
341. Wild Striped Bass With Charred Leeks And Squid Vinaigrette 239
342. Wine Baked Halibut Steaks With Mustard Fennel Butter..239
343. Wine Baked Onions With Herbed Crumb Topping 240
344. Yellow Tomato Soup 240
345. Ziti With Kielbasa And Sauerkraut 241

INDEX 242

CONCLUSION............................ 247

345 Awesome White Wine Recipes

***

1. 3 Ingredient Mussels With White Wine And Pesto

Serving: 4 appetizer servings | Prep: 10mins | Ready in:

Ingredients

- 1 cup dry white wine
- 2 pounds mussels, debearded, scrubbed
- 1/2 cup fresh store-bought pesto
- Kosher salt, freshly ground pepper

Direction

- Place wine in a big pot and bring to a boil. Add mussels. Cover the pot and return to heat. When it starts to boil again, reduce heat to simmer and continue cooking for about 4 minutes or until mussels begin to open up. Add in the pesto, stir, and season with pepper and salt.
- Discarding the liquid, spoon the mussels into individual bowls topped with broth. Serve hot.

Nutrition Information

- Calories: 557
- Cholesterol: 74 mg(25%)
- Protein: 33 g(66%)
- Total Fat: 39 g(60%)
- Saturated Fat: 7 g(34%)
- Sodium: 1307 mg(54%)
- Fiber: 2 g(6%)
- Total Carbohydrate: 13 g(4%)

2. Angel Hair With Fennel Pesto

Serving: 4 servings as a main, 6 as a starter | Prep: | Ready in:

Ingredients

- 2 tablespoons fennel seeds
- 1/2 teaspoon crushed red pepper flakes
- 6 tablespoons olive oil, divided
- 1 yellow onion, finely chopped
- 2 fennel bulbs, trimmed, cored, and finely chopped (core, outer layers, and fronds reserved; stalks discarded)
- 1/2 cup store-bought tomato sauce
- 1/2 cup white wine
- 1/2 teaspoon salt
- 1/2 cup currants
- 1/2 cup unseasoned bread crumbs, lightly toasted
- 1/2 cup finely chopped fennel fronds (from fennel above)
- 1 tablespoon dried oregano
- 1 pound angel hair pasta (capellini)

Direction

- Turn the oven to 375°F to preheat.
- In a heavy-duty saucepot, dry-toast fennel seeds over medium-high heat for 30-60 seconds until they smell nutty and turn light brown. Add crushed red pepper and toss once or twice. Make sure not to burn the flakes.
- Add onion and 4 tablespoons of olive oil. Sauté for 3-5 minutes until the onion starts to get tender. Add chopped fennel. Sauté for 5 minutes longer. Add salt, wine, and tomato sauce; and toss. Put a cover on and remove into the oven. Bake for 20-30 minutes.
- In the meantime, in 6-qt. salted water, put fennel outer layers and cores and boil it.
- Take the pot out of the oven (the vegetables will be very tender), and use an immersion blender to coarsely purée the sauce. Add

currants, whisk, and place the pot on the stovetop again over low to medium-low heat, and simmer without a cover for 10 minutes longer. In the meantime, prepare to garnish. In a bowl, mix together oregano, fennel fronds, bread crumbs, and the leftover 2 tablespoons olive oil, and mix to combine.

- Once the water boils, take out and dispose of the fennel, and add angel hair. Cook the pasta for 1 minute until slightly al dente and strain, saving 1 cup or so of the cooking water. Put the angel hair back into the pot and heat to medium heat. Pour the fennel sauce over the pasta and mix to blend. If necessary, add some of the reserved cooking water to help the sauce blend and complete cooking the pasta. Enjoy in shallow bowls, put a "halo" of garnish on top.

Nutrition Information

- Calories: 793
- Saturated Fat: 3 g(17%)
- Sodium: 615 mg(26%)
- Fiber: 12 g(49%)
- Total Carbohydrate: 125 g(42%)
- Protein: 20 g(41%)
- Total Fat: 24 g(36%)

3. Anise Cookie Baskets With Riesling Ice Cream And Fresh Fruit

Serving: Serves 4 | Prep: | Ready in:

Ingredients

- 1 1/2 cups cream
- 1/2 cup half and half
- 2/3 cup sugar
- 4 large egg yolks
- 1 cup late harvest Riesling wine
- 1/4 cup sugar
- 3 tablespoons unsalted butter, room temperature
- 2 tablespoons powdered sugar
- 1 teaspoon finely chopped aniseed
- 1/2 teaspoon vanilla extract
- 1/4 teaspoon grated orange peel
- 3 tablespoons egg whites
- 1/4 cup all purpose flour
- 1 1-pint basket strawberries, stemmed, quartered
- 1 cup small pineapple wedges
- 1 kiwi fruit, peeled, cut into wedges
- Fresh mint leaves

Direction

- To make the ice cream: Let 1/2 cup of half and half and 1/2 cup of cream simmer in a heavy medium-sized saucepan. In a medium-sized bowl, mix yolks and sugar together until well combined. Add in the hot cream mixture and mix. Put the mixture back into the saucepan and cook and stir for about 4 minutes over medium-low heat until the custard is thick enough to leave a trace of a finger run through the back of a spoon; don't bring it to a boil. Strain the custard mixture into a bowl. Stir in 1 cup of cream and wine. Keep the custard in the fridge until cold.
- Follow the manufacturer's directions in churning the custard in an ice cream maker. Place the ice cream mixture (ice cream is soft) in a covered container and keep it in the freezer. (You can prepare it 1 week in advance.)
- To make the cookies: Preheat the oven to 325°F. Coat a big, heavy non-stick baking sheet slightly with flour and butter. In a medium-sized bowl, combine the first 6 ingredients together. Mix in the flour and egg whites.
- On the middle of half of the prepared baking sheet, put in a slightly rounded tablespoon of the batter. On the middle of the other half of the prepared baking sheet, put in another slightly rounded tablespoon of the batter. Use the back of a spoon to slightly spread each rounded tablespoon of batter into 6-inch

circles. Put in the preheated oven and bake for about 8 minutes until the edges are browned, the centers of the cookies will be a little bit pale.
- Use a metal spatula to quickly remove the first cookie off the baking sheet. Flip the cookie over immediately and place on an inverted custard cup. Lightly flatten the cookie on the bottom of the custard cup then form crimps on the sides of the cookie. Do the same for the second cookie. Remove the cookies from the bottom of the cups. Wash the baking sheet on cold water and wipe to dry. Do the whole process again for the rest of the batter; first washing and drying then buttering and flouring the baking sheet between each batch of cookies. (You can prepare the cookies 3 days in advance. Keep it in a tightly covered container at room temperature.)
- Transfer the cookie baskets on plates. Put 3 small scoops of ice cream into each cookie basket.
- Garnish with mint leaves and fruit on top.

Nutrition Information

- Calories: 811
- Total Carbohydrate: 75 g(25%)
- Cholesterol: 341 mg(114%)
- Protein: 9 g(17%)
- Total Fat: 50 g(77%)
- Saturated Fat: 30 g(149%)
- Sodium: 80 mg(3%)
- Fiber: 3 g(12%)

4. Anniversary Punch

Serving: Makes about 16 servings | Prep: | Ready in:

Ingredients

- 1 package (15-ounce) frozen strawberries in sugar, thawed
- 2 teaspoons grated lime peel
- Juice of 1 lime
- 1 (750-ml) bottle Pinot Noir
- 1 (750-ml) bottle Sauternes
- 1 (750-ml) bottle dry Champagne

Direction

- Mix altogether lime peel, lime juice and strawberries in a saucepan. Simmer for 10 minutes; strain with a sieve. Let it cool. Put the fruit mixture on top of the block of ice in a punch bowl. Pour the wines before serving. Top with lime slices or whole strawberry, if desired.

Nutrition Information

5. Autumn Apple Strudel

Serving: Makes 6 to 8 servings | Prep: | Ready in:

Ingredients

- 1 cup apple juice
- 4 ounces bittersweet (not unsweetened) or semisweet chocolate, chopped
- 1 tablespoon brandy
- 1/2 teaspoon vanilla extract
- 1 cup plus 2 tablespoons apple juice
- 1/2 cup dry white wine
- 3 whole star anise*
- 1 cinnamon stick
- 1 vanilla bean, split lengthwise
- 1/3 cup (packed) dried Bing cherries
- 1/3 cup (packed) pitted prunes, halved
- 1 1/4 pounds Braeburn apples, peeled, cored, cut into 1/2-inch cubes
- 1/3 cup (packed) golden brown sugar
- 1 1/2 tablespoons cornstarch
- 2/3 cup hazelnuts, toasted, husked
- 1/2 cup graham cracker crumbs
- 3 tablespoons sugar

- 9 17x12-inch sheets fresh phyllo pastry or frozen, thawed
- 1/2 cup unsalted butter, melted
- Vanilla ice cream

Direction

- Sauce: Boil juice for 6 minutes till reduced to 1/2 cup in small saucepan; take off heat. Add chocolate; stand for 1 minute; whisk till smooth and melted. Mix in vanilla and brandy; you can make sauce 4 days ahead, chilled and covered. Before serving, rewarm.
- Filling: Mix cinnamon, star anise, wine and 1 cup juice in big saucepan; scrape in vanilla bean seeds then add bean. Simmer; take off heat. Cover; stand for 10 minutes. Add prunes and cherries; cover. Simmer for 5 minutes till fruit is plump; discard vanilla bean, cinnamon and star anise. Mix in sugar and apples; simmer for 45 minutes till liquid reduces to 3 tbsp. and apples are tender yet hold shape, occasionally mixing.
- Mix 2 tbsp. apple juice and cornstarch then add to filling; mix on medium high heat for 3 minutes till filling boils and thickens. You can make this 3 days ahead; slightly cool, cover then chill.
- Strudel: Preheat an oven to 375°F; butter big heavy baking sheet lightly. Blend initial 3 ingredients till nuts are ground finely in processor.
- On work surface, put dry kitchen then put 1 phyllo sheet over; use plastic wrap then damp towel to cover leftover phyllo. Lightly brush melted butter on phyllo. Put 2nd phyllo sheet over; brush butter. Sprinkle scant 3 tbsp. nut mixture; continue using 6 extra phyllo sheets, brushing butter on each then sprinkle scant 3 tbsp. nut mixture. Put leftover phyllo sheet over; brush butter. Put filling over phyllo stack in 12x3-in. log, beginning 2 1/2-in. from each short side and 2-in. from 1 long side. Fold short edges over filling. Roll strudel up jellyroll style, beginning at edge near filling and using towel as aid. Put strudel on prepped baking sheet, seam side down; brush butter on strudel. You can make this 4 hours ahead, chilled.
- Bake strudel for 45 minutes till golden, uncovered; cool for 30 minutes minimum. Cut room temperature or warm strudel to slices; put on plates. Serve with warm chocolate sauce and ice cream.

Nutrition Information

- Calories: 654
- Saturated Fat: 14 g(72%)
- Sodium: 183 mg(8%)
- Fiber: 7 g(28%)
- Total Carbohydrate: 87 g(29%)
- Cholesterol: 41 mg(14%)
- Protein: 7 g(13%)
- Total Fat: 33 g(51%)

6. Baked Flounder Rolls With Tomato, Bell Pepper, And Bacon

Serving: Serves 6 | Prep: | Ready in:

Ingredients

- 6 slices of lean bacon, chopped fine
- 1/4 cup finely chopped shallot
- 2/3 cup minced green bell pepper
- 1/2 cup dry white wine
- a 28-ounce can tomatoes including the juice, chopped
- 1/2 teaspoon crumbled dried basil
- six 1/2-pound flounder fillets, halved lengthwise and seasoned with salt and pepper
- 1/2 cup fine fresh bread crumbs
- 2 tablespoons finely chopped fresh parsley leaves
- 1 tablespoon olive oil

Direction

- Cook bacon in skillet on medium heat till crisp, turn onto paper towels to let drain, and throw all except 2 tablespoons fat. Cook bell pepper and shallot in fat left in skillet on medium low heat for 3 minutes, mixing, pour in wine, and let mixture boil for a minute, scratching up brown bits. Put in basil, pepper and salt to taste and tomatoes including juice, and let sauce simmer for 10 minutes, mixing from time to time, till thicken.
- Place halves of flounder fillet, skinned sides facing up, on a work counter, starting with narrow end, roll up every half of fillet like jelly-roll, and seal every roll using wooden pick.
- Place fish rolls in a flameproof, greased, 15-inch by 10-inch by 2-inch baking pan, seam sides facing down and without touching one another, evenly top with sauce, and let the mixture bake for 10 minutes in the center of a prepped 400°F. oven. Mix pepper and salt to taste, bacon, parsley and bread crumbs in bowl and scatter top of rolls with topping. Sprinkle oil on fish rolls and let the mixture bake till fish just flakes, for 10 minutes. Broil cooked mixture below a prepped broiler for 1 to 2 minutes, approximately 4-inch away from heat to have a crisper topping. Turn fish rolls onto a warm platter and scoop topping and sauce on top.

Nutrition Information

- Calories: 556
- Sodium: 1861 mg(78%)
- Fiber: 3 g(14%)
- Total Carbohydrate: 14 g(5%)
- Cholesterol: 240 mg(80%)
- Protein: 67 g(134%)
- Total Fat: 24 g(36%)
- Saturated Fat: 6 g(32%)

7. Baked Pears With Sauternes Custard Sauce

Serving: Makes 8 servings | Prep: | Ready in:

Ingredients

- 8 firm-ripe Bartlett pears
- 1/2 cup raisins, chopped
- 1/2 cup packed light brown sugar
- 1/2 teaspoon finely grated fresh orange zest
- 1/2 teaspoon finely grated fresh lemon zest
- 1 cup plus 2 tablespoons Sauternes or other white dessert wine
- 6 large egg yolks
- 1/4 cup granulated sugar
- Accompaniment: Madeleines

Direction

- Set the oven to 375°F for preheating.
- Peel the pears and leave the stems attached. Core the pears from the bottom using the sharp small knife or a melon-ball cutter. Mix the brown sugar, 2 tbsp. of Sauternes, zests, and raisins. Fill the cavities of the pear with the mixture. Arrange the pears into the buttered baking dish upright. Make sure that the baking dish used is large enough to hold all of them. Drizzle pears with the remaining cup of Sauternes.
- Use a foil to cover the dish. Let it bake in the middle of the oven for 30-45 minutes until tender. Use a metal spatula to transfer the pears into the serving plates or dish to hold the filling in place. Pour the cooking liquid into a bowl through the sieve.
- In a large metal bowl, mix the granulated sugar and yolks. In a stream, pour in the hot cooking liquid while whisking often. Set the bowl over the pan filled with barely simmering water. Whisk or beat the mixture using the handheld electric mixer for 3-5 minutes until the mixture's volume has tripled and the instant-read thermometer reads 160°F.
- Serve the pears together with the sauce while warm.

- Note: The pears can be baked a day in advance. Just let them cool, and then keep them chilled while covered. Cover and reheat the cooking liquid inside the 350°F oven for 15 minutes until heated through before preparing for the sauce.

Nutrition Information

- Calories: 289
- Sodium: 14 mg(1%)
- Fiber: 6 g(25%)
- Total Carbohydrate: 58 g(19%)
- Cholesterol: 138 mg(46%)
- Protein: 3 g(6%)
- Total Fat: 4 g(6%)
- Saturated Fat: 1 g(6%)

8. Baked Rigatoni With Sausage And Mushrooms

Serving: Makes 25 servings | Prep: | Ready in:

Ingredients

- 4 ounces dried porcini mushrooms
- 4 cups hot water
- 4 tablespoons olive oil
- 4 large onions, finely chopped
- 5 pounds hot Italian sausages, casings removed
- 4 pounds button mushrooms, sliced
- 4 teaspoons chopped fresh rosemary
- 2 cups dry white wine
- 4 bay leaves
- 2 14-ounce cans beef broth
- 4 cups half and half
- 4 pounds rigatoni
- 6 cups freshly grated Parmesan cheese
- Additional grated Parmesan cheese
- Fresh rosemary sprigs (for garnish)

Direction

- To prepare: Wash the porcini mushrooms, then put it in a medium bowl. Pour in 4 cups of hot water, put on cover, and allow to stand for around 20 minutes, until mushrooms become soft. Let drain and set aside the soaking liquid. Chop the porcini.
- In each of the 2 heavy big pots, heat the 2 tbsp oil on medium heat. Split the onions between the pots, then sauté for around 10 minutes, until they become tender. Split the sausage between the pots. Turn up the heat to high and cook for about 12 minutes, until it has no visible pink color, using the back of a fork to break it up into small pieces. Split the chopped rosemary and button mushrooms between the pots and mix for about 8 minutes, until the mushrooms start to soften. Split the bay leaves, wine and porcini between the pots and let it boil for about 6 minutes, until nearly all the liquid has evaporated, mixing often. Split the porcini soaking liquid between the pots and leave the sediment behind. Split the beef broth between the pots. Let it boil for about 20 minutes, until the sauce becomes syrupy, stirring from time to time. Split the half and half between the pots, then boil for about 5 minutes, until it becomes a bit thick, stirring from time to time. (The sauce can be prepared 1 day in advance. Let it cool a bit, then put on cover and let it chill. Reheat prior to continuing.)
- Brush oil on four 3 1/2-qt. porcelain or glass baking dishes. In the two big pots with boiling salted water, cook the pasta until it becomes just tender yet still firm to the bite, stirring from time to time, then drain. Split the pasta between the sauce in the pots, then mix until coated. Stir 3 cups of cheese into each pot, then sprinkle pepper and salt is to season the pasta. Distribute among the prepped baking dishes. (This can be made 1 day in advance. Cover and chill in the fridge. Bring them to room temperature prior to continuing.)
- Set an oven to 375 degrees F to preheat. Use foil to cover the dishes. Bake the pasta for around 25 minutes, just until it becomes hot yet not bubbly. Sprinkle extra cheese on top.

Put on rosemary sprigs to garnish and serve with extra cheese.

Nutrition Information

- Calories: 810
- Total Carbohydrate: 66 g(22%)
- Cholesterol: 102 mg(34%)
- Protein: 37 g(73%)
- Total Fat: 44 g(67%)
- Saturated Fat: 18 g(90%)
- Sodium: 1182 mg(49%)
- Fiber: 4 g(16%)

9. Baked Sardines In Pepperonata

Serving: Makes 8 servings | Prep: | Ready in:

Ingredients

- 4 red bell peppers
- 1/2 cup olive oil, plus more for drizzling
- 1/2 medium red onion, thinly sliced
- 2 garlic cloves, thinly sliced
- Kosher salt, freshly ground pepper
- 2 tablespoons tomato paste
- 1 tablespoon sugar
- 1/2 cup dry white wine
- 1/2 cup white wine vinegar
- 2 tablespoons chopped fresh flat-leaf parsley
- 2 tablespoons drained capers
- 1/2 teaspoons dried oregano
- 8 whole fresh sardines, scaled, gutted, deboned
- Chopped fresh dill and grilled crusty bread (for serving)

Direction

- Preheat the broiler. On a rimmed, broiler-proof baking sheet, let peppers broil for 8 to 10 minutes, flipping from time to time, till entirely blistered. Turn onto a medium size bowl, use plastic wrap to cover, and rest for 15 minutes. Remove peel, seed, and cut to make half-inch wide strips.
- Lower the oven heat to 450°F. In a big skillet, heat quarter cup of oil on moderate heat. Put in garlic and onion; add pepper and salt to season and cook for 8 to 10 minutes, mixing from time to time, till soft. Raise heat to moderately-high, put in sugar and tomato paste and cook for a minute, mixing, till tomato paste is starting to deepen in color. Pour in vinegar and wine and cook for 2 minutes, mixing frequently, till partially cooked down. Stir in oregano, capers, parsley and roasted peppers. Cook for 5 minutes, mixing from time to time, till thickened a bit. Turn pepperonata into a 3-quart, shallow baking dish.
- Season in and out of sardines using pepper and salt; place over pepperonata. Sprinkle oil over and bake for 15 to 20 minutes, till sardines are starting to brown and firm. Put dill on top, sprinkle with additional oil, and serve along with bread.

Nutrition Information

- Calories: 175
- Saturated Fat: 2 g(10%)
- Sodium: 287 mg(12%)
- Fiber: 2 g(7%)
- Total Carbohydrate: 7 g(2%)
- Cholesterol: 6 mg(2%)
- Protein: 3 g(6%)
- Total Fat: 14 g(22%)

10. Blood Orange Roast Pork Loin

Serving: Makes 6 servings | Prep: | Ready in:

Ingredients

- blood oranges
- 1 3-pound boneless pork loin, rolled and tied
- 3 tablespoons extra-virgin olive oil, divided

- 1 large onion, cut into 8 wedges
- 2 fresh rosemary sprigs, leaves stripped from stems, plus additional sprigs for garnish
- 1/2 cup dry white wine
- 1/2 cup low-salt chicken broth
- 1 large garlic clove, pressed
- Blood orange slices

Direction

- Place rack in the middle of oven; preheat the oven to 450°F. Peel 3 blood oranges in strips just the orange portion with vegetable peeler. Put the pork in big roasting pan. Massage with 2 tablespoons of olive oil; scatter pepper and salt over. In medium size bowl, toss leftover tablespoon of oil, rosemary leaves, onion and orange peel; scatter pepper and salt over. Surround pork with onion mixture. Roast for 25 minutes, till onion and pork are starting to brown.
- Meantime, juice oranges, sufficient to get 3/4 cup; put the juice to small saucepan. Put in broth, garlic and wine. Boil for 7 minutes, till cooked down to 1 1/4 cups.
- Put to roasting pan with half cup of orange juice mixture. Baste the pork using juices from pan. Lower the oven heat to 350°F; keep on roasting the pork till inserted thermometer into chunkiest portion of pork reads 150°F, basting frequently and putting in additional orange juice mixture as necessary, for an additional of 30 minutes.
- Put the pork on platter and use foil to loosely cover. Put the roasting pan on moderately-high heat; put to pan with leftover 3/4 cup orange juice mixture. Boil for 3 minutes, till thickened partially. Take strings off roast. Cut the pork; put on the platter. Top and surround around pork onion mixture and sauce. Jazz up using orange slices and rosemary sprigs.

Nutrition Information

---

11. Blue Cheese Souffles With Grape Syrup On Fig And Walnut Brioche

Serving: Makes 6 cheese course servings | Prep: 1.5hours | Ready in:

Ingredients

- 2 tablespoons warm water (105-115°F)
- 1 1/2 teaspoons active dry yeast (from a 1/4-oz package)
- 3 tablespoons sugar
- 2 cups plus 2 tablespoons all-purpose flour
- 1 1/2 teaspoons salt
- 3 large eggs
- 2 sticks (1 cup) unsalted butter, softened
- 1/2 lb dried Mission figs, stems discarded and figs chopped (1 1/2 cups)
- 1/2 cup walnuts (2 oz), chopped
- 2 cups white grape juice
- 1 cup dry fruity white wine such as Riesling
- 2 tablespoons unsalted butter, plus 1 tablespoon melted
- 3 tablespoons finely chopped walnuts
- 1/2 cup whole milk
- 2 tablespoons all-purpose flour
- 2 large eggs, separated
- 1/4 lb Maytag Blue cheese, crumbled (1 cup)
- a stand mixer fitted with paddle attachment; a 9- by 5- by 3-inch loaf pan; 6 (2-oz) heatproof baba au rhum molds or metal condiment cups

Direction

- Making the brioche dough: In a small bowl, mix together 1 tbsp sugar, yeast and water, until the sugar dissolves, then allow to stand for around 5 minutes, until it becomes foamy. (Get rid and begin again with the new yeast if the mixture does not foam.)
- In a bowl of a mixer, mix together the 1 tbsp sugar, salt and flour. Add eggs and yeast mixture and beat it on medium speed, until blended. Add butter and beat it for 5-8 minutes, until the dough becomes silky and smooth. (The dough will get sticky and very

soft.) Add nuts and figs and stir until blended. Sprinkle leftover tablespoon of sugar on top of the dough, then use clean kitchen towel and plastic wrap to cover the bowl and allow the dough to rise at warm room temperature in a draft-free area for about 2 hours, until nearly doubles in bulk.
- Grease the loaf pan with butter, then flour and shake off the excess. Use wooden spoon to mix the dough to release the air and evenly spread in the loaf pan. Use kitchen towel and plastic wrap to loosely cover the pan and allow the dough to rise at warm room temperature in a draft-free area for 1 to 1 1/2 more hours, until it nearly fills the pan (the dough will not reach the surface of the pan).
- Make the grape syrup as the dough rises: In a 2 to 3-qt. saucepan, boil the wine and juice on medium-high heat for about 30 minutes, until it reduces to approximately half a cup and becomes syrupy. Allow to cool to room temperature.
- Baking the brioche: Place the oven rack in the center position and set the oven to preheat to 375 degrees F.
- Let it bake for 35-45 minutes, until an inserted skewer or wooden pick in the middle exits clean and turns golden brown in color. Flip out the brioche on the rack, then flip it right side up and let it fully cool for around 1 1/2 hours.
- Making the soufflés and assembling the dish: Keep the oven rack in the center position and set the oven to preheat to 400 degrees F.
- Brush melted butter (1 tbsp) on the molds and put in nuts until coated and knock off the excess.
- In a 1-qt. heavy saucepan, boil the leftover 2 tbsp butter and milk. Whisk in the flour until it becomes smooth and put it back into a boil on medium heat. Take it out of the heat and whisk it forcefully for 1 minute, then whisk into the yolks in a big bowl.
- In a separate bowl, beat the whites using an electric mixer until it just holds stiff peaks.
- Mix 1/2 of the cheese into the yolk mixture and fold in 1/3 of the whites to make it light, then gently fold in the leftover whites yet thoroughly. Distribute among the molds and let it bake for about 30 minutes in a water bath, until it turns brown and puffed. Take out the molds from the water bath and let it cool for 5 minutes on a rack.
- As the soufflés cool, slice three half an inch-thick pieces from the brioche loaf, then slice each into half to make a total of six 2-inch squares. Set aside the rest of the loaf for later use.
- To loosen the soufflés, run a thin knife around the molds' edge. Distribute the brioche squares among the six plates and drizzle some grape syrup on top, then put soufflé on top of each. Sprinkle leftover cheese on top and serve right away.
- Notes: The brioche can be prepared a day in advance and completely cooled. Keep it at room temperature, well wrapped in plastic wrap. The grape syrup can be prepared 2 days in advance and keep it at room temperature in an airtight container. The cheese soufflés can be crumbled a day in advance and kept chilled in the fridge with cover.

Nutrition Information

- Calories: 893
- Protein: 19 g(39%)
- Total Fat: 53 g(82%)
- Saturated Fat: 29 g(145%)
- Sodium: 946 mg(39%)
- Fiber: 5 g(20%)
- Total Carbohydrate: 79 g(26%)
- Cholesterol: 265 mg(88%)

12. Bolognese Sauce

Serving: 9 | Prep: 10mins | Ready in:

Ingredients

- 2 tablespoons olive oil

- 4 slices bacon, cut into 1/2 inch pieces
- 1 large onion, minced
- 1 clove garlic, minced
- 1 pound lean ground beef
- 1/2 pound ground pork
- 1/2 pound fresh mushrooms, sliced
- 2 carrots, shredded
- 1 stalk celery, chopped
- 1 (28 ounce) can Italian plum tomatoes
- 6 ounces tomato sauce
- 1/2 cup dry white wine
- 1/2 cup chicken stock
- 1/2 teaspoon dried basil
- 1/2 teaspoon dried oregano
- salt and pepper to taste
- 1 pound pasta

Direction

- Warm oil over medium heat in a large skillet; sauté garlic, onion and bacon until bacon is crisp and turns brown; put aside.
- Brown pork and beef in a large saucepan. Drain off excess fat. Stir in pepper, salt, oregano, basil, stock, wine, tomato sauce, tomatoes, celery, carrots, mushrooms and bacon mixture to saucepan. Cover and lower the heat; simmer while stirring occasionally for 1 hour.
- Bring a large pot of lightly salted water to boiling. Add pasta; cook until al dente or for 8-10 minutes; drain.
- Serve the sauce over hot pasta.

Nutrition Information

- Calories: 471 calories;
- Total Carbohydrate: 46.5
- Cholesterol: 59
- Protein: 23.4
- Total Fat: 19.7
- Sodium: 463

13. Boneless Pork Chops With Ginger, Fig, And Lemon Compote

Serving: Serves 2. | Prep: | Ready in:

Ingredients

- 1 lemon
- 1 medium shallot
- 4 dried figs (preferably Calimyrna)
- two 1 1/4-inch-thick boneless pork loin chops (about 3/4 pound)
- 1 tablespoon olive oil
- 1 teaspoon grated peeled fresh gingerroot
- 1/3 cup water
- 2 tablespoons dry white wine
- 1 tablespoon unsalted butter
- Garnish: lemon slices

Direction

- Slice 3 zest strips lengthwise from lemon using vegetable peeler and slice strips crosswise to make enough extremely thin pieces to get a packed teaspoon. Squeeze lemon to get 2 tablespoons of juice. Mince the shallot and slice figs to quarter-inch-thick pieces.
- Blot the pork dry and add pepper and salt to season. Heat oil in skillet on medium high heat till hot yet not smoking and sauté pork for a minute per side till browned. Turn the pork onto plate and cook gingerroot and shallot in fat left in skillet, mixing, till aromatic, for half a minute. Put in figs, lemon juice, zest, wine, water and pork, and simmer for 10 minutes, with cover, or till pork is barely cooked completely.
- Turn the pork onto 2 plates and in case fig mixture is very liquid, boil for a minute, till cooked down to a consistency like a sauce. Mix into fig mixture with butter till blended.
- Jazz pork up using compote and serve along with slices of lemon.

Nutrition Information

- Calories: 159
- Fiber: 2 g(6%)
- Total Carbohydrate: 10 g(3%)
- Cholesterol: 36 mg(12%)
- Protein: 11 g(23%)
- Total Fat: 9 g(13%)
- Saturated Fat: 3 g(15%)
- Sodium: 37 mg(2%)

14. Braised Chicken Thighs With Squash And Mustard Greens

Serving: Serves 8 | Prep: | Ready in:

Ingredients

- 4 pounds skin-on, bone-in chicken thighs (about 12), patted dry
- Kosher salt, freshly ground pepper
- 2 tablespoons vegetable oil
- 8 scallions, white and pale green parts sliced into 1-inch pieces, dark green parts thinly sliced
- 4 dried chiles de árbol
- 1 (2-inch) piece ginger, peeled, thinly sliced
- 1 cup dry white wine
- 1/2 cup low-sodium soy sauce
- 3 tablespoons dark brown sugar
- 2 tablespoons toasted sesame oil
- 2 cups low-sodium chicken broth, divided
- 1 acorn squash, halved lengthwise, seeds removed, sliced 1/2-inch thick
- 1 bunch mustard greens, tough stems removed, leaves torn
- 2 tablespoons unseasoned rice vinegar
- 2 teaspoons toasted sesame seeds
- Cooked white rice (for serving)

Direction

- Season light the chicken thighs with pepper and salt all over. In a big Dutch oven or any heavy pot, heat vegetable oil on medium high heat. Work in two batches and take the fat out but leave 2 tablespoons in the pot between batches; cook chicken for 8-10 minutes, skin side down, till skin is crisp and brown. Move the chickens to a plate, placing it side up; at this point, chicken won't be cooked through.
- Cook ginger, chiles, pale green and white parts of scallions in same pot for 3 minutes till ginger and scallions are golden, mixing often. Pour in wine; simmer and cook for 5 minutes till reduced to 3 tbsp. Add 1 cup broth, sesame oil, brown sugar and soy sauce; simmer, stir to dissolve sugar. Put the chicken back in the pot, place the skin side up, overlapping if necessary. Cover pot partially and lower the heat; simmer for 25-30 minutes till chicken cooks through. Put chicken onto plate.
- Pour leftover 1 cup broth and add squash in pot; push in squash so the squash is mostly submerged. Place greens over; simmer. Cover pot partially; cook for 10-12 minutes till greens are wilted and squash becomes barely fork-tender; uncover. Put heat on medium; cook for 10-15 minutes till liquid has thin gravy consistency and reduces by 2/3.
- Take off heat; drizzle vinegar on veggies. Taste sauce; should be quite salty, but if needed, season with extra salt. Put chicken in pot, turning to coat it in sauce; sprinkle on sesame seeds and dark green parts of scallions. Serve it with rice.
- You can braise chicken 2 days in advance; cool. Cover; chill. Reheat on low heat, covered.

Nutrition Information

- Calories: 644
- Saturated Fat: 11 g(56%)
- Sodium: 962 mg(40%)
- Fiber: 2 g(7%)
- Total Carbohydrate: 14 g(5%)
- Cholesterol: 222 mg(74%)
- Protein: 41 g(82%)
- Total Fat: 45 g(70%)

15. Braised Chicken In Sun Dried Tomato Cream

Serving: Makes 2 Servings; can be doubled | Prep: | Ready in:

Ingredients

- 2 skinless boneless chicken breast halves
- 1 tablespoon oil from oil-packed sun-dried tomatoes
- 3 large garlic cloves, thinly sliced
- 1/2 cup dry white wine
- 1/3 cup whipping cream
- 1/4 cup drained oil-packed sun-dried tomatoes, thinly sliced
- 3 tablespoons thinly sliced fresh basil

Direction

- Scatter pepper and salt on chicken. In medium, heavy skillet, heat the oil on moderately-high heat. Put with chicken to skillet and sauté for 4 minutes on each side, till golden. Put in garlic and mix for half a minute. Put in cream, tomatoes and white wine, and boil. Put on skillet cover, lower heat to moderately-low and simmer for 3 minutes, till chicken is barely cooked completely. Turn the chicken onto plates. Put the basil to the sauce in skillet. Raise the heat and boil for 2 minutes till sauce is thick enough that it can coat a spoon. Season sauce with pepper and salt to taste; scoop on chicken to serve.

Nutrition Information

- Calories: 300
- Total Carbohydrate: 9 g(3%)
- Cholesterol: 108 mg(36%)
- Protein: 22 g(44%)
- Total Fat: 17 g(26%)
- Saturated Fat: 9 g(43%)
- Sodium: 102 mg(4%)
- Fiber: 1 g(5%)

16. Braised Chicken With Garlic And White Wine

Serving: Makes 8 servings | Prep: | Ready in:

Ingredients

- 2 3 1/2-pound whole chickens, each cut into 8 pieces
- 5 whole heads of garlic, cloves separated (about 70), unpeeled
- 6 tablespoons extra-virgin olive oil, divided
- 2 cups dry white wine
- 6 very large fresh thyme sprigs

Direction

- Cut off excess fat from chicken. Scatter pepper and salt on chicken. Mash garlic cloves lightly barely to flatten a bit, keeping cloves as whole as can be and peel intact.
- In big, heavy pot, heat 4 tablespoons of extra-virgin olive oil on moderately-high heat. Put in the chicken in 2 batches and cook till brown on every side, for 12 minutes every batch. Turn the chicken onto plate. Put to pot the garlic and leftover 2 tablespoons of olive oil. Mix for 4 minutes, till golden brown. Put in thyme and wine; boil. Put chicken back to pot. Lower heat to moderate, and simmer with cover for 20 minutes till chicken is cooked completely, move the pieces of chicken from top to bottom in 5 minutes interval, chicken will not submerge in sauce. Season with pepper and salt to taste.
- Turn the chicken onto platter. Surround chicken with scoop of garlic cloves and sprinkle sauce on top.

Nutrition Information

- Calories: 749
- Sodium: 197 mg(8%)
- Fiber: 1 g(4%)
- Total Carbohydrate: 12 g(4%)

- Cholesterol: 202 mg(67%)
- Protein: 52 g(105%)
- Total Fat: 51 g(78%)
- Saturated Fat: 13 g(65%)

17. Braised Chicken With Leeks And Morels

Serving: Makes 4 servings | Prep: | Ready in:

Ingredients

- 1/2 ounce dried morel mushrooms*
- 1 cup hot water
- 4 chicken leg-thigh pieces
- 1 tablespoon olive oil
- 3/4 cup dry white wine
- 4 leeks (white and pale green parts only), sliced (about 4 cups)
- 1 cup low-salt chicken broth
- 1 tablespoon chopped fresh thyme

Direction

- In a small bowl, place the morels. Pour in 1 cup of hot water and let morels sit to soften, around 45 minutes. Remove the morels from the water and set aside. Using a fine sieve, strain the liquid and set aside.
- Add salt and pepper to the chicken to season. In a heavy large pot, heat oil over medium-high heat. Sauté chicken in the pot for 6 minutes per side, until browned. Remove the chicken and add wine to the pot. Bring to a boil and scrap up the brown bits. Stir in the reserved morel liquid, morels, thyme, broth, and leeks. Place the chicken back into the pot. Return to a boil, reduce the heat and cover, and simmer for 40 minutes, until the sauce is thick and the chicken is cooked through. Turn the chicken once while simmering. Season with salt and pepper to taste. If preparing a day ahead, allow to slightly cool, then refrigerate until cold, uncovered. Cover and keep refrigerated until serving. Before serving, rewarm.

Nutrition Information

- Calories: 834
- Protein: 59 g(117%)
- Total Fat: 59 g(90%)
- Saturated Fat: 16 g(78%)
- Sodium: 319 mg(13%)
- Fiber: 1 g(5%)
- Total Carbohydrate: 11 g(4%)
- Cholesterol: 320 mg(107%)

18. Braised Duck Legs With Leeks And Green Olives

Serving: Makes 4 servings | Prep: | Ready in:

Ingredients

- 4 duck legs (drumsticks and thighs, attached)
- Salt
- Fresh-ground black pepper
- 2 tablespoons olive oil
- 2 leeks, white and pale green parts only, washed and coarsely chopped
- 1 carrot, peeled and coarsely chopped
- 6 thyme sprigs, leaves only
- 6 parsley sprigs, leaves only
- 1 bay leaf
- 1 cup green olives
- 1/2 cup white wine
- 1 1/2 cups chicken broth
- 1 strip of lemon zest

Direction

- Trim all the excess fat from the duck legs. Season the duck legs with salt and pepper a night before or several hours ahead. Cover the duck legs and keep refrigerated.
- Set the oven to 425°F for preheating.

- Heat the olive oil in an ovenproof skillet that is huge enough to hold the duck legs comfortably. Add the carrot and leeks. Cook the mixture over medium heat for 3 minutes. Mix in bay leaf, olives, parsley sprigs, additional salt, and thyme. Cook the mixture for 3 more minutes. Add the duck legs into the skillet, skin-side down. Add white wine into the skillet together with the lemon zest and chicken broth.
- Aware that the liquid should measure 1-inch deep, adding more liquid if necessary. Increase the heat and bring the mixture to a simmer. Put the skillet immediately into the oven. Remove the skillet from the oven after 30 minutes and flip the legs, skin-side up. If necessary, pour off the liquid, reserving some of it so that the duck skins are exposed. Adjust the oven's heat to 325°F. Continue to cook for 1-1 1/2 more hours until the skins of the duck are browned and the knife's tip slips in and out of the meat easily.
- Put the duck legs aside. Transfer the vegetables and braising juices into the small bowl. Let the liquid settle then skim off and discard the fat on the. The duck legs are going to make a startling amount of fat. If necessary, add salt, and then adjust the seasoning if you like. You can reduce the braising liquid to concentrate it if it's too thin. Place the vegetables and liquid back into the skillet. Place the duck legs on top. Just before serving, simmer the mixture and reheat for a few minutes.
- Variations: The pitted olives can be replaced, but use less amount of it, about 1/2 cup, and do not add them to the braise until the last 15 minutes of cooking.
- Also, you can use dry sherry instead of half of the wine.
- Substitute dried fruit for olives; you can use either prunes or figs. You can use red wine instead of white wine and mix together a piece of bacon or pancetta then braise. Leave out the zest of lemon.
- You can also use chicken legs instead of the duck legs, but you need to reduce the cooking time by half an hour.

Nutrition Information

- Calories: 1106
- Total Carbohydrate: 15 g(5%)
- Cholesterol: 174 mg(58%)
- Protein: 30 g(60%)
- Total Fat: 102 g(156%)
- Saturated Fat: 32 g(159%)
- Sodium: 1021 mg(43%)
- Fiber: 3 g(13%)

19. Braised Lamb Shanks With Tomatoes And Rosemary

Serving: Serves 6 | Prep: | Ready in:

Ingredients

- 6 lamb shanks (about 1 pound each)
- 2 tablespoons olive oil
- 4 cups chopped onion
- 4 garlic cloves, minced
- two 28-to-32-ounce cans tomatoes, drained and chopped
- 1 1/2 cups dry white wine
- 1 1/2 cups chicken broth
- 1 1/2 teaspoons crumbled dried rosemary
- 3/4 teaspoon ground allspice
- 1 tablespoon minced fresh parsley leaves
- 1 tablespoon minced fresh rosemary leaves

Direction

- Pat the lamb shanks dry. Season the lamb shanks with salt and pepper. Brown them in a large heavy kettle with oil over moderately high heat, 3 pieces at a time. Transfer the browned pieces into the roasting pan that is large enough to hold the pieces in one layer. Add onion into the kettle and cook it over moderate heat, stirring often until it is softened. Mix in garlic and cook for 3 minutes. Mix in broth, wine, dried rosemary, salt and pepper to taste, tomatoes, and allspice. Bring the sauce into a boil. Spoon the sauce all over the lamb shanks. Cover the shanks with foil tightly. Braise them inside the preheated 350°F oven for 1 1/2 hours, positioning them in the middle of the oven until tender. Transfer the shanks into the heatproof platter and cover to keep them warm. Pour the sauce into the cleaned kettle and boil it for 10 minutes until the sauce is reduced to 4 cups. Take note that the sauce and the lamb shanks can be prepared 2 days ahead. Just let them cool to room temperature and place them in a roasting pan, covered and chilled. Preheat the oven to 350°F and heat the lamb shanks with sauce inside the preheated oven until they are hot. Transfer the shanks into the heatproof platter. Mix 2 tsp. of parsley and 2 tsp. of fresh rosemary into the sauce. Distribute the shanks among the 6 heated plates. Spoon the sauce all over the shanks and sprinkle them with the remaining fresh rosemary and parsley.

Nutrition Information

- Calories: 941
- Sodium: 701 mg(29%)
- Fiber: 7 g(30%)
- Total Carbohydrate: 24 g(8%)
- Cholesterol: 250 mg(83%)
- Protein: 75 g(150%)
- Total Fat: 57 g(88%)
- Saturated Fat: 25 g(125%)

20. Braised Spareribs With Rigatoni

Serving: Makes 4 to 6 servings | Prep: | Ready in:

Ingredients

- 1/4 cup olive oil
- 4 pounds pork spareribs, cut into individual ribs
- 1 pound onions, thinly sliced
- 10 large garlic cloves, chopped
- 8 cherry peppers from jar, drained, seeded, chopped
- 3/4 teaspoon dried crushed red pepper
- 3 28-ounce cans Italian-style tomatoes in juice
- 1 cup canned low-salt chicken broth
- 1 cup dry white wine
- 4 large fresh thyme sprigs
- 2 bay leaves
- 1 pound rigatoni
- 1 1/2 cups freshly grated Parmesan
- 1/3 cup chopped fresh Italian parsley

Direction

- In big, heavy pot, heat the oil on high heat. Scatter pepper and salt on spareribs. Put the ribs onto pot in batches and brown every side, for 6 minutes. Turn ribs onto bowl. Put to pot with crushed red pepper, cherry peppers, garlic and onions. Sauté for 10 minutes, till onions barely start to brown. Put in tomatoes including their juices. Mash tomatoes coarsely with potato masher or back of a fork. Put the spareribs including the juices back to pot. Put in bay leaves, thyme, wine and broth and boil. Lower the heat to moderately-low. Simmer with no cover for 2 hours, till spareribs are extremely soft and sauce is thick, mixing from time to time. Add pepper and salt to season. May be done 2 days in advance. Cool partially. Chill till cold, then keep refrigerated with cover. Get rid of cold fat from surface of sauce, if wished. Reheat before proceeding.
- In big pot with salted boiling water, let pasta cook till just tender yet remain firm to bite. Strain and put pasta back to the same pot. Put in parsley, some sauce from spareribs and cheese and toss till coated. Turn the pasta onto a big bowl. Put spareribs and the rest of the sauce on top to serve.

Nutrition Information

- Calories: 2200
- Fiber: 21 g(82%)
- Total Carbohydrate: 132 g(44%)
- Cholesterol: 392 mg(131%)
- Protein: 110 g(220%)
- Total Fat: 135 g(208%)
- Saturated Fat: 44 g(219%)
- Sodium: 1691 mg(70%)

21. Braised Truffled Turkey

Serving: Makes 8 to 10 servings | Prep: | Ready in:

Ingredients

- 8 to 10 pound turkey
- Truffles, as many as possible, fresh if available
- 2 pounds ground pork
- 1 1/2 pounds ground veal
- 8 shallots
- Butter
- Salt, pepper to taste
- 3/4 cup cognac
- 2 cups fine bread crumbs
- 1/2 cup chopped parsley
- 3 carrots, cut in fine julienne
- 3 leeks, cut in fine julienne
- 3 stalks celery, cut in fine julienne
- White wine
- Beurre manié
- Freshly ground white pepper

Direction

- The night prior to cook the rinse turkey, cut some truffles, and inset them beneath the skin. Insert a few truffles into cavity also, loosely wrap turkey with foil, and refrigerate overnight.
- The following day, have the stuffing ready. In 8 tablespoons of butter, sauté shallots, veal and pork, and mix thoroughly with salt to taste and half cup of cognac. Do not cook fully, just mix on heat and put parsley and crumbs. Put seasonings to taste. Mix with truffles in turkey and lightly fill. Stich up the opening and truss the turkey.
- In butter or oil and butter combined, brown the turkey thoroughly and in a big braising pan, put the turkey on layer of celery, julienne leeks and carrots. Put 1 1/2 cups white wine and butter or oil and butter and set the heat to high. Place cover on pan, lower the heat, and allow to cook for 2 1/2 to 3 hours, basting turkey from time to time with even amounts of white wine and melted butter. Once turkey is soft, transfer onto hot platter and filter off pan juices. Cook juices down to 2 cups and thicken with beurre manié. Season with freshly ground white pepper and salt to taste and put leftover quarter cup cognac.
- Serve along with braised celery and potatoes Anna.

Nutrition Information

22. Braised Veal Breast With Bulb Vegetables

Serving: Makes 4 servings | Prep: | Ready in:

Ingredients

- 3-pound veal breast
- Coarse salt and white pepper, to taste
- 2 tablespoons corn oil
- 2 large shallots, peeled
- 1 onion, quartered
- 1 leek, split and cleaned
- 12 cloves of garlic, unpeeled
- 2 bay leaves
- 1/3 cup diced celery root
- 4 whole cloves
- 1/2 teaspoon white peppercorns
- 1/2 teaspoon ground cumin
- 1/2 cabbage, quartered
- 2 cups dry white wine
- 1 1/3 cups apple cider

- 1/3 cup snipped chives

Direction

- Preheat an oven to 250°F. Add white pepper and salt to season the veal. In a big Dutch oven, heat oil over medium-high heat. Put the veal; brown thoroughly on every side. Turn onto a plate.
- To pan, put the following 9 ingredients and let cook, mixing, till onion starts to brown. Put the cabbage; allow to cook till wilted and slightly browned. Put a cup each of cider and wine. Put veal back to pot. Add salt to season, place cover and let braise in oven for 2 1/2 to 3 hours till meat is really soft.
- Take vegetables and veal off juices and retain warmth. Drain and defat juices; put back to pot. Put the rest of the cider and wine; boil. To thicken, cook down for 15 minutes. Fix seasonings. Put veal back to pot; allow to simmer, basting with the sauce till syrupy and meat is well glazed.
- To serve, put the vegetables on platter; cut veal along the bones and put on top. Scoop sauce over everything and scatter chives on top.

Nutrition Information

23. Braised Veal With Gremolata

Serving: Makes 6 servings | Prep: 40mins | Ready in:

Ingredients

- 2 cups boiling water
- 1 ounce dried porcini
- 1 (4 1/2- to 5-pounds) boneless veal shoulder roast, rolled and tied by butcher
- 2 large garlic cloves, cut lengthwise into 20 thin slices
- 1 tablespoon olive oil
- 1 cup dry white wine
- 1 tablespoon potato starch dissolved in 1 1/2 tablespoons cold water
- 2 tablespoons finely chopped fresh flat-leaf parsley
- 1 tablespoon finely chopped fresh basil
- 1 tablespoon finely grated fresh lemon zest
- 2 teaspoons minced garlic
- Accompaniment: porcini matzo polenta wedges

Direction

- Put boiling water on porcini in bowl; stand for 10-20 minutes till soft. Lift porcini out; squeeze extra liquid into bowl. Rinse to remove grit. Put soaking liquid through dampened paper towel-lined sieve into separate bowl. Chop porcini; keep for polenta.
- Pat dry veal; cut 20 one and a half-inch deep slits with thin-bladed knife all over. Use garlic slice to stuff each slit; season veal with pepper and salt.
- Heat oil in 4-6-quart heavy pot on medium high heat till hot yet not smoking; brown all sides of veal for 10 minutes. Add wine; boiling on high heat to deglaze pot, keeping veal in pot, for 5 minutes, mixing and scraping brown bits up, till wine is cooked down by 1/2. Mix porcini-soaking liquid in; gently simmer for 2 hours till meat is tender, with cover, flipping veal every 30 minutes. Put veal on cutting board; fully cool.
- Skim froth and fat from pan juices surface; boil till reduced to 2 cups. Put through very fine sieve into saucepan; simmer. Mix dissolved potato starch; whisk into pan juices and simmer till slightly thick.
- Gremolata: Mix gremolata ingredients.
- Mix 1/2 gremolata into sauce; season with pepper and salt. Chill, with cover, the leftover gremolata.
- Heat and serve veal: Preheat an oven to 350°F.
- Discard veal strings; slice meat across grain to quarter-inch thick slices. In 13x9-inch glass/ceramic baking dish, arrange the slices overlapping; put sauce on meat. Use foil to

cover dish; heat for 30 minutes in middle of oven.
- Sprinkle leftover gremolata.
- Veal can be made 1 day ahead, cooled on cutting board yet not sliced, covered and chilled. While cold, slice meat; reheat in sauce.
- You can make sauce 1 day ahead; fully cool. Chill, covered.

Nutrition Information

- Calories: 513
- Saturated Fat: 7 g(37%)
- Sodium: 256 mg(11%)
- Fiber: 1 g(3%)
- Total Carbohydrate: 7 g(2%)
- Cholesterol: 216 mg(72%)
- Protein: 72 g(144%)
- Total Fat: 20 g(31%)

24. Braised And Roasted Pork Shanks With Prosciutto And Porcini Mushrooms

Serving: Makes 4 servings | Prep: | Ready in:

Ingredients

- 1 ounce dried porcini mushrooms
- 1 cup boiling water
- 4 whole fresh pork shanks with rind (each 1 1/4 to 1 1/2 pounds)
- 4 tablespoons olive oil, divided
- 1 large onion, chopped
- 1 cup chopped carrots
- 1 cup chopped leek (white and pale green parts only)
- 1/2 cup chopped celery
- 2 ounces prosciutto, chopped
- 6 garlic cloves, chopped
- 1 cup dry white wine
- 1 cup low-salt chicken broth
- 3 teaspoons chopped fresh sage, divided
- 2 teaspoons chopped fresh rosemary, divided
- Chopped fresh Italian parsley

Direction

- In a small bowl, put porcini mushrooms. Put a cup of boiling water on top and allow to sit for a minimum of half an hour till mushrooms soften. Let drain and slice the mushrooms; set aside soaking water.
- Preheat the oven to 325°F. Scatter pepper and salt on pork. In a heavy big wide pot, heat 3 tablespoons oil over medium-high heat. Put in batches pork, if needed, and sauté for 15 minutes till brown on every side. To a rimmed baking sheet, put the pork.
- Scoop off and throw all except 2 tablespoons of fat from the pot. Turn the heat to medium. Put prosciutto, celery, leek, carrots and onion. Put cover and allow to cook for 10 minutes till vegetables are tender and starting to color, mixing from time to time. Add in chopped porcini and garlic. Put wine and boil, scratching up some browned bits. Put broth and leftover mushroom soaking water, retaining some sediment in the bowl. Add in a teaspoon rosemary and a teaspoon sage. Put pork and any accumulated juices back to the pot, set in 1 layer.
- Boil pork mixture, cover the pot, and put in the oven. Braise pork for 1 hour 30 minutes till really soft, flipping over after every half an hour. Can be prepared 2 days in advance. Slightly cool. Chill without cover till cold, then put cover and remain refrigerated. Let simmer till just warm prior proceeding.
- Preheat the oven to 425°F. To a rimmed baking sheet, put the pork. Brush with leftover 1 tablespoon of oil; scatter leftover black pepper, a teaspoon rosemary and 2 teaspoons sage on top. Roast pork for 20 minutes till browned.
- In the meantime, swirl the pan and scoop off some fat from the surface of the sauce. Let boil for 7 minutes till sauce slightly coats spoon. Put pepper and salt to season.

- Ladle sauce onto a big shallow platter or distribute between 4 shallow bowls. Put pork on top of sauce, scatter parsley over, serve.

Nutrition Information

- Calories: 497
- Total Carbohydrate: 20 g(7%)
- Cholesterol: 84 mg(28%)
- Protein: 31 g(61%)
- Total Fat: 30 g(47%)
- Saturated Fat: 8 g(38%)
- Sodium: 503 mg(21%)
- Fiber: 4 g(16%)

25. Brandied Onion Soup With Croque Monsieur Croutons

Serving: Makes 6 servings | Prep: | Ready in:

Ingredients

- 3 tablespoons butter
- 2 1/2 pounds onions, thinly sliced
- 4 14 1/2-ounce cans beef broth
- 3/4 cup dry white wine
- 2 teaspoons Dijon mustard
- 1 to 2 tablespoons brandy
- 18 1/3-inch-thick slices of French bread baguette
- 2 cups grated Swiss cheese
- 1 cup coarsely chopped ham

Direction

- In big, heavy pot, liquify the butter on moderately-high heat. Put in and sauté onions for half an hour, till dark brown yet not charred, mixing from time to time. Put in wine, mustard and broth, and boil. Lower the heat to moderate and simmer for 15 minutes, to meld the flavors. Pour in brandy to taste and simmer for five minutes. Add pepper and salt to season soup.
- Meantime, preheat the broiler. On a baking sheet, place the bread. Broil for a minute, till starting to color. Pile a ham and cheese on bread; scatter with pepper. Broil for 2 minutes, till cheese has melted, flipping sheet for equal cooking.
- Scoop the soup in deep bowls. Put 3 croutons on top of each to serve.

Nutrition Information

- Calories: 455
- Fiber: 4 g(16%)
- Total Carbohydrate: 37 g(12%)
- Cholesterol: 71 mg(24%)
- Protein: 24 g(49%)
- Total Fat: 21 g(33%)
- Saturated Fat: 12 g(59%)
- Sodium: 1646 mg(69%)

26. Brie And Wild Mushroom Fondue

Serving: Serves 4 to 6 | Prep: | Ready in:

Ingredients

- 1 cup water
- 1 ounce dried porcini mushrooms*
- 2 tablespoons (1/4 stick) butter
- 8 ounces fresh shiitake mushrooms, stemmed, finely chopped
- 2 tablespoons chopped shallot
- 1 pound ripe Brie cheese, well chilled, rind trimmed, cheese cut into 1/2-inch pieces (about 2 cups)
- 2 tablespoons cornstarch
- 1 cup dry white wine
- Bite-size pieces of cooked chicken, steamed quartered small red-skinned potatoes, steamed asparagus or green beans, and bite-size pieces of French bread or focaccia

- *Dried porcini mushrooms are available at Italian markets, specialty foods stores and many supermarkets.

Direction

- In small saucepan, boil a cup of water. Put in porcini mushrooms. Take off heat and rest for 20 minutes, till mushrooms are soft. Turn porcini onto work counter with slotted spoon. Chop porcini coarsely. Put soaking liquid and porcini aside.
- In big, heavy saucepan, liquify butter on moderate heat. Put in and sauté shiitake mushrooms for 3 minutes, till tender. Put in and sauté shallot for a minute. Put in porcini including soaking liquid, keeping any sediment behind. Raise the heat to high. Simmer for 3 minutes, till liquid vaporizes. May be done 8 hours in advance. Refrigerate with cover.
- In big bowl, toss cornstarch and Brie till coated. Put into mushrooms with wine. Simmer on moderate heat. Put cheese in 3 batches to mushrooms, mixing after every increment till cheese melts prior putting in additional. Keep mixing till mixture is just starts to simmer and smooth, avoid boiling. Season with pepper and salt to taste.
- Turn fondue onto pot of fondue. Place pot above canned heat burner or candle. Serve along with vegetables, bread and chicken.

Nutrition Information

27. Brie, Roquefort And Wild Mushroom Fondue

Serving: Serves 6 to 8 | Prep: | Ready in:

Ingredients

- 1 1/2 teaspoons olive oil
- 4 ounces fresh shiitake mushrooms, stemmed, caps diced
- 1 shallot, minced
- 1 teaspoon chopped fresh thyme
- 1 1/2 tablespoons all purpose flour
- 12 ounces chilled 60% (double crème) Brie cheese (do not use triple crème)
- 2 ounces chilled Roquefort cheese
- 1 cup dry white wine
- 1 13-ounce loaf crusty white bread, cut into 1 1/2-inch cubes
- Vegetables (such as carrot sticks, blanched broccoli, cauliflower and boiled small potatoes)

Direction

- In medium, heavy skillet, heat the oil on moderately-high heat. Put in shallot, thyme and mushrooms; sauté for 2 minutes, till mushrooms barely start to soften.
- Put flour in big bowl. Slice off Brie rind; throw the rind. Slice Brie to make cubes; put in flour. Toss till coated; separate the cubes of cheese. Break Roquefort up to the same bowl; toss till coated. In medium, heavy saucepan, pour wine and simmer on moderate heat. Put in handfuls of cheese, mixing till liquified after every increment. Keep mixing till smooth.
- Mix into fondue with mushroom mixture. Add a liberal amount of pepper to season. Turn onto fondue pot. Place pot on top of canned heat burner or candle. Serve along with vegetables and bread.

Nutrition Information

- Calories: 439
- Sodium: 844 mg(35%)
- Fiber: 3 g(13%)
- Total Carbohydrate: 35 g(12%)
- Cholesterol: 65 mg(22%)
- Protein: 21 g(43%)
- Total Fat: 22 g(34%)
- Saturated Fat: 12 g(62%)

28. Broiled Salmon Steaks With Horseradish Crust

Serving: Serves 2 | Prep: | Ready in:

Ingredients

- two 3/4-inch-thick salmon steaks
- 2 tablespoons unsalted butter, melted
- 1/4 cup dry white wine
- 1/2 cup coarse dry bread crumbs
- 2 tablespoons well-drained bottled horseradish
- 1 scallion, minced

Direction

- Place salmon steaks in flame-safe baking dish that is buttered, barely big enough to accommodate them in single layer, lightly brush some of butter on them, and add pepper and salt to season. Add wine on the surrounding of steaks and let steaks broil for 4 to 5 minutes, below preheated broiler approximately 4-inch away from heat, till nearly cooked completely. Meanwhile, thoroughly mix the rest of the scallion, horseradish, bread crumbs and leftover butter, evenly pat mixture of crumb on steaks, and let steaks broil for an additional of 2 to 4 minutes, or till they are barely cooked completely and crumbs turn golden in color.

Nutrition Information

- Calories: 645
- Total Fat: 40 g(61%)
- Saturated Fat: 14 g(68%)
- Sodium: 381 mg(16%)
- Fiber: 2 g(8%)
- Total Carbohydrate: 22 g(7%)
- Cholesterol: 139 mg(46%)
- Protein: 44 g(89%)

29. Buttermilk Cake With Blackberries And Beaumes De Venise

Serving: Makes 8 servings | Prep: | Ready in:

Ingredients

- 2 cups cake flour (not self-rising)
- 1 teaspoon baking powder
- 1 teaspoon baking soda
- 3/4 teaspoon salt
- 1 stick (1/2 cup) unsalted butter, softened
- 1 cup sugar
- 1 teaspoon vanilla
- 2 large eggs
- 1 cup well-shaken buttermilk
- 3/4 cup Beaumes-de-Venise or other white dessert wine
- 4 tablespoons sugar
- 1 (3- by 1-inch) strip fresh orange zest
- 1/3 cup seedless blackberry preserves or 1/2 cup blackberry preserves with seeds, strained
- 4 cups fresh blackberries (1 1/2 lb)

Direction

- Prepare cake: Preheat the oven to 350 °F.
- Line a wax paper round on bottom of a buttered round, 9-inch by 2-inch cake pan, then grease paper with butter.
- Sift baking powder and soda, salt and flour. In a big bowl, whip sugar and butter using electric mixer till fluffy and pale, then whip vanilla in. Put in eggs, 1 by 1, whipping thoroughly after every increment, then whip in all buttermilk using mixer on low speed till barely incorporated. Put in the mixture of flour in 3 additions, combining after every increment till barely incorporated.
- Scoop the batter to cake pan, evening the surface, and bake for 40 to 50 minutes in center of the oven till golden and a tester gets out clean. Cool for 10 minutes in pan on rack, then trace a sharp, thin knife on surrounding of

cake edge to detach. Flip on rack, slip the cake to cake plate.
- Prepare topping: in a heavy, small saucepan, boil 3 tablespoons sugar, zest and wine, mixing till sugar dissolves. Boil for a minute to two, till syrup is cooked down to approximately 2/3 cup. Throw the zest.
- Put 2 tablespoons of syrup aside and add the remaining evenly and gently on top of cake, cake will soak in the syrup.
- Mix in small saucepan the preserves, leftover tablespoon of sugar and reserved syrup and simmer for a minute, mixing from time to time, till partially thickened, consistency should be of a thick syrup. In big bowl, put in the blackberries, then top berries with preserves mixture. Use rubber spatula to slowly mix berries till coated, then add on top of cake, piling blackberries over.
- Serve at room temperature or while warm.
- Note: Cake may be done, with no topping and syrup, a day in advance; fully cool, then wrap with plastic wrap to store at room temperature.

Nutrition Information

- Calories: 468
- Saturated Fat: 8 g(40%)
- Sodium: 505 mg(21%)
- Fiber: 5 g(21%)
- Total Carbohydrate: 79 g(26%)
- Cholesterol: 78 mg(26%)
- Protein: 7 g(14%)
- Total Fat: 14 g(21%)

30. Butternut Squash And Sage Orzo

Serving: Makes 4 servings | Prep: | Ready in:

Ingredients

- 3 tablespoons butter
- 1 cup chopped onion
- 1 garlic clove, minced
- 1 2-pound butternut squash, peeled, seeded and cut into 1/2-inch pieces (about 4 cups)
- 4 cups canned low-salt chicken broth
- 1/2 cup dry white wine
- 1 cup orzo (rice-shaped pasta)
- 1/2 cup freshly grated Parmesan cheese
- 2 tablespoons chopped fresh sage

Direction

- In a big, heavy skillet, liquify butter on moderate heat. Put in and sauté onion for 6 minutes, till soft. Put in and sauté garlic for a minute, till aromatic. Put in butternut squash and mix till coated. Put in wine and half cup chicken of broth. Simmer for 10 minutes, till liquid is soaked in and squash is nearly tender. Meantime, in a heavy saucepan, boil 3 1/2 cups of broth. Put in orzo. Boil for 8 minutes, till tender yet remain firm to bite. Strain orzo if need be.
- Turn the orzo into a big bowl. Mix in mixture of butternut squash, then sage and Parmesan. Add pepper and salt to season.

Nutrition Information

- Calories: 383
- Fiber: 7 g(28%)
- Total Carbohydrate: 52 g(17%)
- Cholesterol: 33 mg(11%)
- Protein: 15 g(30%)
- Total Fat: 14 g(22%)
- Saturated Fat: 8 g(42%)
- Sodium: 235 mg(10%)

31. Caneton Au Muscadet

Serving: Serves 4 | Prep: | Ready in:

Ingredients

- 4 to 5 pound Long Island duckling
- Salt, ground ginger, ground cloves
- 1/3 cup cognac
- 1 pint Muscadet
- 2 or 3 small onions stuck with cloves
- 2 or 3 tiny carrots
- 2 tablespoons beurre manié
- 5 or 6 medium sized potatoes
- 5 tablespoons butter
- Freshly ground pepper
- 2/3 cup sultana raisins

Direction

- Rub duckling well with ground cloves, little ground ginger and salt; put onto rack in roasting pan. Roast for 1 1/4 hours in 325°F oven. Take duck from oven; put into deep iron casserole. Put warmed cognac over; ignite. Add beurre manie, carrots, onions stuck with cloves and Muscadet; blend. Put in oven; cook for 30 minutes, occasionally basting duck with liquid in the casserole.
- Meanwhile, peel potatoes; slice. Brown well in butter till crisp outside and around edges yet soft. Shake pan to keep potatoes from sticking on bottom occasionally. Season with pepper and salt to taste.
- Put raisins in duck mixture in casserole; cook for 10 minutes, basting 1 time. Put duck on hot platter to serve; surround with potatoes. Put little sauce on duck; serve leftover sauce in a sauce boat.

Nutrition Information

32. Caramelized Onion And Wine Braised Brisket With Glazed Vegetables

Serving: Serves 8 to 10 | Prep: | Ready in:

Ingredients

- 4 cups canned low-salt chicken broth
- 1 750-ml bottle dry white wine
- 1/2 cup brandy
- 1/3 cup vegetable oil
- 2 pounds meaty beef neck bones
- 3 1/2 pounds onions, thinly sliced
- 4 large celery stalks, sliced
- 1 1/2 teaspoons whole allspice
- 6 garlic cloves, chopped
- 2 teaspoons dried thyme
- 1 4 1/2- to 5-pound flat-cut brisket
- 3/4 cup chopped canned tomatoes
- 1 tablespoon tomato paste
- 2 1/2 pounds mixed baby vegetables (such as zucchini, crookneck and pattypan squashes, turnips, carrots and new potatoes)
- 8 red boiling onions
- 1/4 cup (1/2 stick) margarine
- 1/4 cup honey
- 1 teaspoon dried thyme
- 10 ounces cherry tomatoes
- 4 ounces asparagus tips or sugar snap peas

Direction

- Boil in pot with the initial 3 ingredients for 25 minutes, till cooked down to 4 cups.
- Preheat the oven to 325°F. In a big Dutch oven, heat the oil on high heat. Put in and sauté bones for 12 minutes, till nicely browned, flipping from time to time. Turn the bones onto bowl. Put to Dutch oven with celery, allspice and onions. Add salt to season; cook for 25 minutes, till onions turn golden, mixing frequently. Keep cooking for an additional of 15 minutes, till onions turn deep dark brown, scratching Dutch oven bottom and mixing frequently. Put in thyme and garlic; sauté for five minutes. Turn the mixture of onion into big roasting pan. Put in a cup broth mixture to Dutch oven. Boil, scratching up browned bits; turn onto the roasting pan.
- Liberally season brisket using pepper and salt. Put into Dutch oven and brown for 5 minutes on each side on high heat. Put the brisket over mixture of onion in roasting pan, fat side facing up; place bones around. Put to Dutch

oven with tomatoes and the rest of broth mixture; boil, scratching up browned bits. Pour on brisket with mixture.

- Use a heavy-duty foil to tightly cover the roasting pan and set in the oven. Bake for 3 hours 45 minutes, till brisket is soft. Take off foil. Let brisket cool for two hours. Chill for 3 hours with no cover. Tightly cover the brisket and keep in refrigerator for a day to 3 days maximum.
- Skim fat from pan juices surface; throw fat. Turn brisket onto chopping board, scraping off the gelled juices from brisket back to roasting pan. Simmer the roasting pan contents. Throw the bones. Use a coarse strainer place on top of a big bowl to pass the contents of the roasting pan. Force on solids to release as much liquid as there is. Use processor to purée the solids, with on/off switches. Stir sufficient purée to juices in a bowl till a thick sauce form. Put in tomato paste and mix to incorporate. Put the sauce to a medium size saucepan and simmer till heated completely. Add pepper and salt to season.
- Thinly cut brisket, slightly diagonal, across the grain. In a glass baking dish, place the slices. Sprinkle half cup of sauce on top; use foil to cover.
- Boil big pot with salted water. Put in turnips, carrots and all squashes and cook for 6 minutes, till tender-crisp. Turn onto big bowl with slotted spoon. Put potatoes into boiling water and cook for 12 minutes, till barely tender. Turn the potatoes into the same bowl with slotted spoon. Put in boiling water with onions and cook for 4 minutes, till nearly tender. Strain and cool partially. Remove onions peel; put into the same bowl.
- Preheat the oven to 350°F. Let brisket bake for half an hour, till heated completely.
- Meantime, in big, heavy skillet, boil honey, thyme and margarine on high heat for 5 minutes, till syrup is cooked down to 1/3 cup, mixing frequently. Put in tomatoes, asparagus and cooked vegetables; toss for 5 minutes, till heated. Add pepper and salt to season.

- Place the brisket on a platter. Simmer the rest of the sauce. Surround brisket with vegetables. Serve, separately passing the rest of the sauce.

Nutrition Information

- Calories: 1325
- Cholesterol: 284 mg(95%)
- Protein: 77 g(154%)
- Total Fat: 73 g(112%)
- Saturated Fat: 25 g(124%)
- Sodium: 458 mg(19%)
- Fiber: 13 g(53%)
- Total Carbohydrate: 68 g(23%)

33. Cauliflower Soup With Hazelnuts And Bacon

Serving: 6 servings | Prep: | Ready in:

Ingredients

- 1/2 cup blanched hazelnuts
- 1 medium head of cauliflower (about 2 pounds), cut into small florets
- 2 tablespoons extra-virgin olive oil, plus more for drizzling
- Kosher salt, freshly ground pepper
- 4 slices thick-cut bacon (about 4 ounces)
- 1 small fennel bulb, chopped
- 1 small onion, chopped
- 1 garlic clove, finely chopped
- 1/3 cup dry white wine or water
- 6 cups low-sodium chicken broth
- 3/4 cup heavy cream
- 2 bay leaves

Direction

- Preheat an oven to 350°F. On rimmed baking sheet, toast hazelnuts, occasionally tossing, for 10-12 minutes till golden brown. Cool; chop coarsely.

- Increase oven to 400°F as nuts cool. Toss 2 tbsp. oil and cauliflower on another baking sheet and season with pepper and salt; roast, tossing once, for 30-35 minutes till florets are tender and brown all over.
- Meanwhile, crosswise cut bacon to 1/2-in. pieces. Heat heavy pot on medium heat; cook bacon, mixing occasionally, for 10-12 minutes till crisp and brown. Put onto paper towels.
- Cook garlic, onion and fennel in drippings in pot, occasionally mixing, for 8-10 minutes till fennel and onion are very soft. Add wine; cook for 5 minutes till mostly evaporated. Add bay leaves, cream, broth and roasted cauliflower; season with pepper and salt. Boil; lower heat. Simmer for 20-25 minutes till cauliflower is tender. Pluck bay leaves out; discard. Slightly cool mixture.
- Puree cauliflower mixture in batches till very smooth; strain into pot. Season with pepper and salt.
- Put soup into bowls before serving; put nuts and bacon over. Drizzle oil.
- You can make soup 3 days ahead. Cool; cover. Separately chill bacon and soup.

Nutrition Information

- Calories: 390
- Saturated Fat: 11 g(56%)
- Sodium: 1175 mg(49%)
- Fiber: 5 g(21%)
- Total Carbohydrate: 17 g(6%)
- Cholesterol: 53 mg(18%)
- Protein: 13 g(26%)
- Total Fat: 32 g(49%)

34. Cheese Fondue With Beer And Bourbon

Serving: Serves 4 | Prep: | Ready in:

Ingredients

- 2 garlic cloves, halved lengthwise
- 1/2 cup Belgian beer (such as Duvel)
- 2 cups dry white wine, divided
- 3 tablespoons cornstarch
- 1 pound Gruyère, coarsely grated
- 1 pound Babybel cheese, grated
- 2 tablespoons bourbon or brandy
- 1/4 teaspoon baking soda
- 1 tablespoon fresh lemon juice
- Kosher salt
- 4 cups (1-inch pieces) country-style bread, preferably day-old
- Assorted ham and salumi, pickles, and crudités (for serving)

Direction

- Spread cut sides of garlic inside a big pot; finely grate garlic into the pot. On medium heat, pour in and boil 1 1/2 cup wine and beer. Stir leftover half cup of wine and cornstarch together in a small bowl until there are no lumps; incorporate the mixture into the pot. Boil while stirring regularly then lower heat to maintain a low simmer. Gradually put in Babybel and Gruyere; stir until smooth. Make sure to fully blend each batch of cheese before mixing another batch.
- In a small bowl, combine baking soda and bourbon. Stir the mixture into the fondue; add salt and lemon juice. Move the mixture on a fondue pot. Serve with crudités, bread, pickles, ham, and salumi to dip.

Nutrition Information

- Calories: 1122
- Sodium: 1177 mg(49%)
- Fiber: 2 g(7%)
- Total Carbohydrate: 35 g(12%)
- Cholesterol: 229 mg(76%)
- Protein: 69 g(138%)
- Total Fat: 70 g(107%)
- Saturated Fat: 42 g(210%)

35. Cheesy Sausage And Sage Stuffing

Serving: Serves 12 | Prep: | Ready in:

Ingredients

- 2 tablespoons unsalted butter, plus more
- 1 medium boule sourdough, cut into 1-inch pieces (9–10 cups), dried out overnight
- 2 tablespoons olive oil
- 1 pound sweet or spicy Italian sausage, casings removed
- 2 large onions, finely chopped
- 3 celery stalks, chopped
- 1/4 cup finely chopped sage
- Kosher salt, freshly ground pepper
- 1 cup dry white wine
- 2 large eggs, beaten to blend
- 1 cup low-sodium chicken broth
- 2 cups half-and-half
- 1 pound aged cheddar, grated (about 5 cups), divided

Direction

- Preheat an oven to 300 °F. With butter, grease a big foil piece and a shallow baking dish, 13x9-inch in size. In a big bowl, put 9 cups of bread.
- In a big skillet, heat the oil over moderately-high. Let sausage cook for 7 to 10 minutes, mixing from time to time and using wooden spoon, crumbling into small portions, till browned and cooked completely. Turn onto bowl with the bread.
- In same skillet, put 2 tablespoon butter, sage, celery and onions; add pepper and salt to season. Cook for 10 to 12 minutes, mixing frequently, till onions turn soft and golden brown. Put in wine and cook for 5 minutes, mixing from time to time, till nearly completely vaporized; scoop into bowl with sausage and bread.
- In medium bowl, beat broth and eggs till smooth, then add on top of bread mixture. Add in half-and-half and put in 3 cups of cheese; mix by tossing. Add pepper and salt to season. Turn onto prepped baking dish and cover in foil, buttered side facing down. Bake for 40 to 50 minutes till paring knife pricked into the middle gets out hot.
- Heat the broiler. Remove stuffing cover and put the rest of the cheese on top. Broil for 4 minutes till surface turn golden and bubbly. Allow to rest for a minimum of 10 minutes to half an hour maximum prior to serving.
- Do Ahead: Stuffing may be assembled a day in advance; cover in foil and refrigerate. Stuffing may be baked yet not broiled for 3 hours in advance. Keep at room temperature securely wrapped till set to broil.

Nutrition Information

- Calories: 565
- Cholesterol: 128 mg(43%)
- Protein: 24 g(49%)
- Total Fat: 39 g(60%)
- Saturated Fat: 19 g(93%)
- Sodium: 865 mg(36%)
- Fiber: 3 g(10%)
- Total Carbohydrate: 28 g(9%)

36. Chicken Breasts Stuffed With Goat Cheese And Basil

Serving: Serves 4 | Prep: | Ready in:

Ingredients

- 4 boneless chicken breast halves, skinned
- 1/2 cup fresh goat cheese (such as Montrachet) (about 4 ounces)
- 2 green onions, thinly sliced
- 3 basil leaves, shredded or 1 teaspoon dried, crumbled
- Salt and freshly ground pepper

- 1 egg, beaten to blend
- 1/2 cup dry breadcrumbs
- 2 tablespoons (1/4 stick) unsalted butter melted
- 1/4 cup (1/2 stick) unsalted butter
- 1/2 pound mushrooms, sliced
- 1/4 cup dry white wine
- 2/3 cup chicken stock or canned low-salt broth
- 4 tablespoons chilled unsalted butter (1/2 stick), cut into 4 pieces
- Salt and pepper

Direction

- Chicken: Preheat the oven to 350°F. Use meat mallet to pound the chicken among waxed paper sheets till thickness is quarter-inch. Blot dry the chicken. In small bowl, mix green onions, basil and cheese. Add pepper and salt to season. Smear mixture of cheese lengthwise on top of 1/2 of every piece of chicken. Fold in the short ends. Roll up chicken, beginning at a long side, to make tight logs. Use string to bind ends to seal. Dunk the chicken into egg, letting excess drip back to bowl. Turn in breadcrumbs, shake excess off. May be prepped 4 hours in advance. Chill.
- Put the chicken in a square, 8-inch baking dish. Add 2 tablespoons of liquified butter on top. Bake for 20 minutes, till cooked completely.
- Sauce: Meantime, in big, heavy skillet, liquify quarter cup of butter on moderate heat. Put in and sauté mushrooms for 8 minutes, till tender. Pour in wine and let boil for 3 minutes. Pour in stock and let boil for 6 minutes, till liquid is cooked down by 1/2. Take off heat and tilt 4 tablespoons of cold butter in, 1 by 1. Add freshly ground pepper and salt to season the sauce. Take string off chicken. Slice rolls crosswise to make rounds, half-inch-thick. Fan the slices on plates. Serve right away, separately passing the sauce.

Nutrition Information

- Calories: 559
- Protein: 28 g(56%)
- Total Fat: 44 g(67%)
- Saturated Fat: 24 g(122%)
- Sodium: 657 mg(27%)
- Fiber: 2 g(7%)
- Total Carbohydrate: 14 g(5%)
- Cholesterol: 182 mg(61%)

37. Chicken Cacciatora

Serving: Makes 4 main-course servings | Prep: | Ready in:

Ingredients

- 1 (3 1/2- to 4-lb) chicken, cut into 8 serving pieces
- 1 1/4 teaspoons salt
- 1 teaspoon black pepper
- 3 tablespoons olive oil
- 1 medium red onion, finely chopped
- 1 medium carrot, cut into 1/4-inch dice
- 2 celery ribs, cut into 1/4-inch dice
- 2 garlic cloves, finely chopped
- 1/4 teaspoon coarsely chopped fresh rosemary
- 1 cup Italian dry white wine (preferably Roero Arneis)
- 1 cup chopped drained canned whole tomatoes (from a 28- to 32-oz can tomatoes in juice)
- 1 cup water

Direction

- Pat the chicken dry and dust with 1/2 teaspoon each of pepper and salt. In a deep 12-inch heavy skillet over moderately high heat, put oil until hot yet not smoking then add the chicken and brown in 2 batches, with skin sides down first, flipping over once, about 10 minutes each batch. Place chicken once browned onto a plate.
- Add a pinch of salt, rosemary, celery, garlic, carrot, and onion to the skillet then lower the heat to moderate and cook for about 8

minutes, stirring occasionally, until onion is softened. Pour in the wine and boil for 3-5 minutes to deglaze, stirring and scraping up brown bits, until most of the wine is vaporized. Mix in the rest 1/2 teaspoon pepper, 3/4 teaspoon salt, water, and tomatoes then add the chicken back with any accumulated juices to the skillet and flip over to coat with the sauce. Flip the chicken with skin sides up and simmer for 25-30 minutes, covered, until chicken is cooked through.

- Cook's note: The flavor of chicken improves after one day. Cover and cool then chill it, covered.

Nutrition Information

- Calories: 776
- Fiber: 3 g(10%)
- Total Carbohydrate: 9 g(3%)
- Cholesterol: 217 mg(72%)
- Protein: 55 g(110%)
- Total Fat: 54 g(83%)
- Saturated Fat: 14 g(70%)
- Sodium: 1031 mg(43%)

38. Chicken Francaise

Serving: Makes 4 servings | Prep: 1hours | Ready in:

Ingredients

- 4 large skinless boneless chicken breast halves (2 pounds total)
- 1/2 cup vegetable oil
- 1 cup all-purpose flour
- 3/4 teaspoon salt
- 1/2 teaspoon black pepper
- 3 large eggs
- 1/2 stick (1/4 cup) unsalted butter
- 1/2 cup dry white wine
- 1/2 cup low-sodium chicken broth
- 3 tablespoons fresh lemon juice plus 1 whole lemon, thinly sliced
- 1 lemon
- 1/4 cup chopped fresh flat-leaf parsley

Direction

- Put the chicken breasts among 2 plastic wrap sheets and use a rolling pin or meat pounder's flat side to softly pound the chicken to make quarter-inch thick.
- In a heavy, 12-inch skillet, heat the oil on medium heat till hot yet not smoking.
- In shallow bowl, mix half teaspoon of salt, quarter teaspoon of pepper and flour while heating the oil. Dip 2 chicken pieces, 1 by 1, in mixture of flour, shaking extra off. In a separate shallow bowl, whip eggs lightly. Once oil is hot, dunk the floured chicken in beaten eggs till coated, allowing the excess to drip off, then fry, flipping over one time, till just cooked completely and golden brown, for a total of 4 minutes. Turn onto paper towels-lined-plate and cover loosely in foil to retain warmth. Fry the rest of the chicken in the exact same manner.
- Drain off and throw the oil, then wipe clean the skillet and let butter heat on low heat till froth settles. Put in broth, lemon juice and wine, and boil for 6 minutes, with no cover, mixing from time to time, till sauce is cooked down to roughly half cup. Mix in parsley and quarter teaspoon of pepper and leftover quarter teaspoon of salt. Top chicken with scoop of sauce and put lemon slices over.

Nutrition Information

- Calories: 676
- Total Carbohydrate: 28 g(9%)
- Cholesterol: 249 mg(83%)
- Protein: 34 g(67%)
- Total Fat: 47 g(72%)
- Saturated Fat: 11 g(55%)
- Sodium: 553 mg(23%)
- Fiber: 2 g(7%)

39. Chicken Sausage

Serving: Makes about 2 pounds/900 grams sausage | Prep: | Ready in:

Ingredients

- 1 1/2 pound/675 grams chicken thigh meat, diced and thoroughly chilled
- 225 grams schmaltz, frozen (or a scant cup if you don't have a scale, but shame on you)
- 1 tablespoon/10-12 grams kosher salt
- 3/4 cup roughly chopped fresh sage
- 2 large garlic cloves, finely minced
- 2 tablespoons finely chopped ginger
- 1 teaspoon freshly ground pepper
- 1/2 cup/120 milliliters dry white wine, chilled

Direction

- Mix all ingredients except for the wine in a big bowl; freeze for 20-30 minutes. Measure wine; put into freezer. Freeze grinder attachment if you're using the metal one and your mixing bowl. Prep your grinder. Take chicken mixture out from freezer; grind through medium/small die into freezing-cold mixing bowl. Put meat back into freezer for 10 minutes; set up the stand mixer.
- Take sausage mixture out from freezer; mix for 60 seconds with paddle attachment at medium high, adding very cold white wine while doing so. Paddling helps to bind the sausage well and distributes the seasonings rather than crumbling. In order to be sure that the seasoning is right, fry small sausage portion, refrigerating mixing bowl while cooking test piece; taste test piece. Add more salt, ginger, sage or pepper if needed then repaddle it. Repeat till you get your preferred seasoning amount.
- In plastic wrap, wrap sausage in a shape of 7.5-cm/2 1/2-in. diameter cylinder; in plastic bag, put wrapped sausage. Keeps for 1 week in the fridge/frozen for 3 months. (It gets unpleasant freezer odors/freezer burn the longer you freeze the meat. Label bag with the date to avoid leaving it for too long.)

Nutrition Information

- Calories: 278
- Cholesterol: 52 mg(17%)
- Protein: 13 g(26%)
- Total Fat: 22 g(35%)
- Saturated Fat: 7 g(36%)
- Sodium: 222 mg(9%)
- Fiber: 3 g(13%)
- Total Carbohydrate: 6 g(2%)

40. Chicken Sauté With White Wine

Serving: Serves 4 | Prep: | Ready in:

Ingredients

- 3 1/2 to 4 pound chicken, quartered
- Flour (optional)
- 4-6 tablespoons butter
- Salt, freshly ground pepper
- 1 cup white wine (Pouilly Fuissé or White Pinot)
- Garnish: chopped parsley or chives

Direction

- Heat butter in a skillet and brown the chicken pieces. Turn each piece so it colors evenly. Season with pepper and salt. Add white wine (about 1/2 - 3/4 cup). Reduce heat, cover the pan and allow to cook until chicken becomes tender. Add any other desired flavorings while cooking. Turn the chicken pieces a couple of times to absorb the flavorings and the juices. When cooked and tender, transfer the chicken to a warmed platter. Add a little wine into the pan and allow it to cook along with the juices. After the juices have cooked for several minutes, pour on the chicken and serve garnished with chives or parsley or as desired.

- Serve with any one of these wines: White Pinot, Meursault or Pouilly Fuisse.

Nutrition Information

- Calories: 1072
- Total Carbohydrate: 1 g(0%)
- Cholesterol: 357 mg(119%)
- Protein: 79 g(159%)
- Total Fat: 78 g(121%)
- Saturated Fat: 27 g(137%)
- Sodium: 1116 mg(46%)

41. Chicken Stock

Serving: 14 | Prep: | Ready in:

Ingredients

- 4 pounds chicken
- 7 cups water
- 1 large onion, halved
- 3 stalks celery
- 3 carrots, cut into 2 inch pieces
- 1 bay leaf
- 1 teaspoon grated fresh ginger
- salt to taste

Direction

- Add the chicken to a big pot over high heat. Pour in water to cover and boil them up; lower to medium-low heat and let simmer for 60 minutes.
- Take the chicken out from the pot, leave water there. Let chicken cool. Take out bones and skin out from the meat. Take the skins and bones back to the pot. Add salt, ginger, bay leaf, celery, carrots and onions. Keep simmering for 3 to 4 hours.
- Filter the stock through a strainer and let cool, uncovered.
- The chicken meat can be used for sandwiches, salads, soups or whatever needs chicken.

Remove any fat from the stock then use or store in freezer right away. Store it in one-cup amounts and replace water while making gravy, vegetables or rice.

Nutrition Information

- Calories: 252 calories;
- Total Fat: 14.4
- Sodium: 101
- Total Carbohydrate: 2.5
- Cholesterol: 87
- Protein: 26.6

42. Chicken Under A Skillet With Lemon Pan Sauce

Serving: 4 servings | Prep: | Ready in:

Ingredients

- 1 (3 1/2–4-lb.) chicken, patted dry
- Kosher salt, freshly ground pepper
- 2 Tbsp. extra-virgin olive oil
- 1 medium shallot, finely chopped
- 1/2 tsp. crushed red pepper flakes
- 1/4 cup dry white wine
- 1/4 cup fresh lemon juice
- 2 Tbsp. unsalted butter, cut into pieces
- 1/4 cup chopped parsley

Direction

- On a working surface, position chicken and snip off wing tips with kitchen shears (they get in the way of the breasts' cooking process, reserving them for stock). Turn chicken breast side down and cut along both sides of the backbone with shears to remove it (reserve for stock along with those wing tips).
- Open up the chicken and cut a shallow line along either side of the rectangular bone and strip of cartilage in the center of breast with the tip of a knife. Turn the chicken skin side up

and press down on the middle of breast to flatten it, you should hear the breastbone crack. Season both sides liberally with pepper and salt, then allow to sit at room temperature for a minimum of 20 minutes and maximum of an hour.

- Set the oven to 350°F. Heat a dry big cast-iron skillet on medium heat. Use paper towels to pat dry chicken, then season all over one more time with a light sprinkling of salt. Put into the skillet with oil then chicken with skin side down. Use foil to cover the bottom of another smaller cast-iron skillet and put over the chicken to weigh it down. Cook for 15 to 18 minutes while peeking under foil and lifting chicken a little to check until it is crisp overall and the skin turns deep golden brown. Remove the skillet on top and rotate the chicken skin side up. Turn the skillet to oven to roast chicken for 15 to 20 minutes, until cooked through. An instant-read thermometer tucked into the thickest part of breast should reach 160°F. Take the skillet out of the oven carefully and place the chicken on a plate to rest, skin side up (to save that crispness).
- Set skillet on medium low heat and put in red pepper flakes and shallot. Cook for 3 minutes while stirring frequently, until shallot is golden and tender. Put in lemon juice and wine, then swirl the skillet to emulsify. Lower heat to low and put in butter, then cook while swirling to mix, until melted. Add in juices that have pooled under the chicken on the plate, then blend in parsley. Turn the chicken back to skillet to serve.

Nutrition Information

- Calories: 756
- Fiber: 1 g(3%)
- Total Carbohydrate: 4 g(1%)
- Cholesterol: 232 mg(77%)
- Protein: 54 g(109%)
- Total Fat: 56 g(86%)
- Saturated Fat: 17 g(85%)
- Sodium: 1122 mg(47%)

43. Chicken And Artichoke Stew

Serving: Makes 4 servings | Prep: | Ready in:

Ingredients

- 3 tablespoons olive oil
- 2 medium onions, chopped
- 1 4 1/2-pound chicken, cut into 8 pieces
- 2 tablespoons all purpose flour
- 1 cup dry white wine
- 3 garlic cloves, chopped
- 6 medium artichokes, trimmed, halved, chokes removed according to recipe for Trimmed Artichokes
- 2 large tomatoes, peeled, seeded, chopped
- 2 cups canned low-salt chicken broth

Direction

- Heat 2 tbsp. oil on medium heat in big heavy pot. Add onions; sauté for 8 minutes till golden. Put onions into bowl.
- Heat leftover 1 tbsp. oil on medium high heat in same pot. Sprinkle pepper and salt on chicken. Put into pot; cook for 10 minutes till golden on all sides. Pour extra fat from pot off. Sprinkle flour on chicken in pot; flip chicken. Cook for 2 minutes till flour lightly browns. Put garlic, white wine and sautéed onions in chicken. Lower heat; simmer for 5 minutes till wine reduces by half.
- Drain artichoke halves. Put into chicken. Add broth and tomatoes; boil. Lower heat to low; cover. Simmer for 30 minutes till artichokes are tender and chicken is cooked through. From stew's surface, spoon fat off. Put artichoke and chicken onto big platter using slotted spoon; tent with foil. Boil the sauce in pot for 4 minutes till slightly thick. Season with pepper and salt to taste. Put sauce on artichokes and chicken.

Nutrition Information

- Calories: 969
- Protein: 71 g(142%)
- Total Fat: 63 g(98%)
- Saturated Fat: 17 g(83%)
- Sodium: 348 mg(15%)
- Fiber: 5 g(22%)
- Total Carbohydrate: 21 g(7%)
- Cholesterol: 260 mg(87%)

44. Chicken And Root Vegetable Stew

Serving: Makes 6 servings | Prep: | Ready in:

Ingredients

- 2 tablespoons olive oil
- 12 chicken thighs, well trimmed
- 2 cups chopped onions
- 6 garlic cloves, chopped
- 1 cup dry white wine
- 1/4 cup plus 2 tablespoons chopped fresh marjoram
- 2 large boiling potatoes, peeled, each cut into 12 pieces
- 3 large carrots, peeled, cut into 1/2-inch-thick rounds
- 2 large parsnips, peeled, cut into 1/2-inch-thick rounds
- 2 medium rutabagas, peeled, cut into 1 1/2-inch pieces
- 2 medium turnips, peeled, cut into 1 1/2-inch pieces
- 5 cups canned low-salt chicken broth
- 3/4 cup whipping cream
- 2 tablespoons cornstarch

Direction

- In a heavy big pot, heat oil on medium-high heat. In batches, cook chicken for 8 minutes per batch until all sides are brown. Put browned chicken in a big bowl. Pour off drippings from the pot but keep 2 tablespoons. Sauté onions in pot for 8 minutes on medium heat until they're golden. Add garlic then sauté for a minute. Add 1/4 cup marjoram and wine. Simmer for 4 minutes until wine evaporates. Put chicken again in the pot. Put veggies on chicken. Pour chicken broth on it. Boil, covered. Lower heat. Simmer for 30 minutes until chicken is cooked through and veggies are tender.
- Transfer veggies and chicken carefully with a slotted spoon in a big clean bowl. In pot, boil liquid for 10 minutes until it is reduced to 3 cups. In a medium bowl, mix cornstarch and cream. Mix into the liquid in the pot. Simmer for 5 minutes until thickened like a sauce. Put veggies and chicken back in the pot. Can make this 2 days in advance. Slightly cool, keep in fridge until cold and uncovered. Then cover and keep in fridge. Simmer stew, gently stirring. Add remaining 2 tbsp. marjoram. Serve.

Nutrition Information

- Calories: 1048
- Fiber: 11 g(44%)
- Total Carbohydrate: 54 g(18%)
- Cholesterol: 325 mg(108%)
- Protein: 59 g(118%)
- Total Fat: 65 g(100%)
- Saturated Fat: 20 g(102%)
- Sodium: 395 mg(16%)

45. Chicken In Dill Mustard Sauce

Serving: Makes 4 servings | Prep: | Ready in:

Ingredients

- 1/4 cup all-purpose flour
- 1/2 teaspoon salt
- 1/2 teaspoon black pepper
- 4 whole chicken legs (2 lb total)

- 3 tablespoons vegetable oil
- 3/4 cup chopped shallots (2 large)
- 1/2 cup dry white wine
- 1 cup low-sodium chicken broth
- 2 teaspoons whole-grain or coarse-grain mustard
- 1/4 cup chopped fresh dill

Direction

- Mix in a shallow bowl or pie plate the quarter teaspoon salt, quarter teaspoon pepper and flour. Blot dry the chicken, then dip legs, 1 by 1, in flour, shaking excess off. Turn onto wax paper sheet, placing chicken in single layer.
- In a heavy, 12-inch skillet, heat oil on medium high heat till hot yet not smoking, then let chicken brown for a total of 6 to 8 minutes, initially skin sides facing down, flipping over one time. Turn the chicken onto plate, then drain all except a tablespoon of skillet fat.
- Put shallots into skillet and sauté for 2 to 3 minutes, mixing from time to time, till golden brown. Pour in wine and boil, mixing and scratching brown bits up to deglaze the skillet. Put in mustard, broth, and leftover pepper and quarter teaspoon of salt. Simmer, then put chicken back to skillet, skin sides facing up, including any juices from the plate, and cook on medium heat for 25 minutes, with cover, till chicken is cooked completely. Turn the chicken onto platter and let boil for 3 to 5 minutes, till cooked down to a cup and thickened a bit. Take off heat and mix dill in, then top chicken with sauce.

Nutrition Information

- Calories: 906
- Saturated Fat: 16 g(79%)
- Sodium: 630 mg(26%)
- Fiber: 1 g(5%)
- Total Carbohydrate: 13 g(4%)
- Cholesterol: 320 mg(107%)
- Protein: 59 g(118%)
- Total Fat: 66 g(101%)

46. Chicken In Riesling

Serving: Makes 4 servings | Prep: 30mins | Ready in:

Ingredients

- 1 whole chicken (about 3 1/2 pound), backbone discarded and chicken cut French style into 8 pieces (see cooks' note, below)
- 1 tablespoon vegetable oil
- 3 tablespoons unsalted butter, divided
- 4 medium leeks (white and pale green parts only), finely chopped (2 cups)
- 2 tablespoons finely chopped shallot
- 4 medium carrots, halved diagonally
- 1 cup dry white wine (preferably Alsatian Riesling)
- 1 1/2 pound small (2-inch) red potatoes
- 2 tablespoons finely chopped flat-leaf parsley
- 1/2 cup crème fraîche or heavy cream
- Fresh lemon juice to taste

Direction

- Preheat an oven with rack in center to 350°F.
- Pat dry chicken; sprinkle rounded 3/4 tsp. pepper and 1 tsp. salt. Heat 1 tbsp. butter and oil in 3 1/2-5-qt. wide heavy ovenproof pot on medium high heat till foam subsides. Working in 2 batches, brown chicken for 10 minutes total for each batch, flipping once. Move onto plate.
- In the meantime, wash leeks then pat them dry.
- Pour fat from pot off; cover and cook shallot, leeks with 1/4 tsp. salt in leftover 2 tbsp. butter on medium low heat for 5-7 minutes till leeks are pale golden, occasionally stirring. Place chicken skin side up with juices from plate, add in wine and carrots; boil for 3-4 minutes till liquid reduces by half. Cover pot; braise chicken in oven for 20-25 minutes till cooked through.
- Peel potatoes as chicken braises; cover in cold water generously in a 2-3-qt. saucepan. Add 1 1/2 tsp. salt; boil. Simmer for 15 minutes till

- potatoes are tender; drain in a colander. Put potatoes back into saucepan then add parsley; shake till coated.
- Mix crème fraiche into the chicken mixture; season with lemon juice, pepper and salt. Add potatoes.
- The French style of cutting a chicken would yield two breast halves with wings attached, slice in half crosswise to get a total of four pieces from the breast, two thighs and two drumsticks. You may use 3-lb. chicken parts if you do not wish to butcher a whole chicken.

Nutrition Information

- Calories: 1205
- Fiber: 5 g(21%)
- Total Carbohydrate: 38 g(13%)
- Cholesterol: 335 mg(112%)
- Protein: 79 g(158%)
- Total Fat: 78 g(120%)
- Saturated Fat: 26 g(131%)
- Sodium: 372 mg(16%)

47. Chicken With Prosciutto, Rosemary, And White Wine

Serving: Makes 6 servings | Prep: | Ready in:

Ingredients

- 2 tablespoons extra-virgin olive oil
- 3 large chicken breast halves with ribs and skin, cut crosswise in half
- 3 chicken drumsticks with skin
- 3 chicken thighs with skin
- 1 cup 1/4-inch cubes prosciutto (about 5 ounces)
- 6 garlic cloves, thinly sliced
- 2 tablespoons chopped fresh rosemary
- 1 1/4 cups dry white wine
- 1 cup low-salt chicken broth
- 1 cup canned crushed tomatoes with added puree
- Fresh rosemary sprigs

Direction

- Preheat the oven to 325°F. In big heavy ovenproof pot, heat extra-virgin olive oil on moderately-high heat. Scatter pepper and salt on chicken. Sauté chicken in 2 batches till golden, for 4 minutes each side. Turn chicken onto platter. To the same pot, put in chopped rosemary, sliced garlic and prosciutto. Mix for a minute. Put in crushed tomatoes including puree, chicken broth and dry white wine. Boil, scratching up browned bits. Boil for five minutes. Put in chicken back to pot, placing in one pile. Bring back to boil. Place pot cover and put in in oven. Bake for 20 minutes till chicken breasts are cooked completely. Take chicken breasts out. Keep baking till thighs and drumsticks are cooked completely, for an additional of 10 minutes. Take pot out of oven. Put chicken breasts back to pot. May be done a day in advance. Slightly cool. Chill with no cover till cold, then put in cover and keep in refrigerator.
- Simmer chicken mixture. Turn the chicken onto platter; tent in foil. Boil for 5 minutes till glazes back of spoon and sauce is cooked down to 2 cups. Season sauce with pepper and salt to taste. Add sauce on top of chicken. Jazz up with rosemary sprigs then serve.

Nutrition Information

- Calories: 501
- Saturated Fat: 8 g(39%)
- Sodium: 891 mg(37%)
- Fiber: 1 g(4%)
- Total Carbohydrate: 6 g(2%)
- Cholesterol: 186 mg(62%)
- Protein: 44 g(88%)
- Total Fat: 30 g(47%)

48. Chicken With Sun Dried Tomato Cream Sauce

Serving: | Prep: | Ready in:

Ingredients

- 3 tablespoons Olive Oil
- 4 Boneless Chicken Breasts, pounded to tenderized
- 1 1/2 cups Heavy Cream
- 4 ounces Mascarpone Cheese
- 6 ounces Spicy Red Pesto
- 8 Sun-dried Tomatoes, drained and cut in quarters
- 2 tablespoons Basil, chopped
- 4 ounces Penne, cooked

Direction

- Use pepper and salt to season chicken. Grill. Slice to make bite-size portions.
- Put cream into a big saucepan and heat on moderately-low heat. Put in mascarpone and mix till blended and liquified.
- Mix pesto in and let cook for two minutes.
- Put in sun-dried tomatoes and chicken and cook to meld the flavors, for five minutes.
- Add pepper and salt to season. Put on top of cooked pasta.
- Jazz up using chopped basil.

Nutrition Information

49. Chicken With Sweet And Hot Red Peppers

Serving: Makes 4 servings | Prep: | Ready in:

Ingredients

- 8 small chicken thighs with skin and bones (2 1/2 lb)
- 3/4 teaspoon salt
- 2 tablespoons extra-virgin olive oil
- 3 red bell peppers, cut lengthwise into 1/3-inch-wide strips
- 1 onion, sliced
- 2 garlic cloves, smashed and peeled
- 1/4 to 1/2 teaspoon dried hot red pepper flakes
- 1/4 cup dry white wine

Direction

- Blot dry the chicken and scatter half teaspoon of salt over. In a heavy, 12-inch, ovenproof skillet, heat the oil on medium high heat till just starting to smoke, then let chicken cook for 5 minutes, skin sides facing down, till browned. Flip the chicken and cook for an additional of 2 minutes, then turn onto plate.
- Drain all except 2 tablespoons of skillet fat and cook leftover quarter teaspoon of salt, red pepper flakes to taste, garlic, onion and bell peppers on medium heat for 10 minutes, mixing, till softened. Pour in wine and boil for a minute. Put the chicken into the mixture of pepper, skin sides up, and cook with cover for 15 minutes, on medium heat till cooked completely.
- Switch broiler on. Uncover skillet and let chicken broil for 1 1/2 minutes, 4 to 6-inch away from heat till skin crisps.

Nutrition Information

- Calories: 604
- Cholesterol: 219 mg(73%)
- Protein: 38 g(77%)
- Total Fat: 44 g(68%)
- Saturated Fat: 11 g(55%)
- Sodium: 623 mg(26%)
- Fiber: 2 g(10%)
- Total Carbohydrate: 10 g(3%)

50. Chicken With Vegetables And Parsley Dumplings

Serving: Makes 6 servings | Prep: | Ready in:

Ingredients

- 3 tablespoons olive oil
- 4 whole leg-thigh chicken pieces
- 2 celery stalks, cut into 1-inch pieces
- 1 onion, cut into 1-inch pieces
- 1 large carrot, peeled, cut into 1-inch pieces
- 1 bay leaf
- 1/2 cup dry white wine
- 4 cups low-salt chicken broth
- 1 cup sugar snap peas, trimmed
- 1/2 cup chopped celery
- 1 cup baby carrots
- 12 pearl onions
- 3 tablespoons butter
- 4 skinless boneless chicken breast halves, cut into 1-inch cubes
- 3 tablespoons all purpose flour
- 1/4 cup whipping cream
- 1 tablespoon chopped fresh Italian parsley
- 1 teaspoon chopped fresh thyme
- Parsley dumplings

Direction

- Preheat the oven to 400 °F. In ovenproof, big skillet, heat the oil on moderate heat. Scatter pepper and salt on pieces of chicken leg-thigh. Put the chicken into skillet and cook for 5 minutes on each side, till golden brown. Put in bay leaf and an-inch pieces of onion, carrot, and celery. Cook for 8 minutes, till vegetables start to become soft, mixing from time to time. Pour in wine and mix for a minute, scratching browned bits up. Pour in broth, and braise for 40 minutes in oven with cover till chicken is soft.
- Turn the chicken onto a plate. Drain broth to medium size bowl, forcing on solids till liquid is extracted. Throw solids in the strainer. Take the meat from pieces of leg-thigh chicken and turn onto bowl. Throw bones and skin. Chicken and broth may be done a day in advance. Separately cover chicken and broth and chill.
- In big saucepan with salted boiling water, cook chopped celery and sugar snap peas till tender-crisp, for a minute. Turn the vegetables onto bowl with ice water with slotted spoon till cool. In the same water, let baby carrots cook for 5 minutes, till tender-crisp. Turn onto the same bowl with ice water with slotted spoon till cool. In the same water, let pearl onions cook for 8 minutes, till tender. Turn onto bowl with ice water with slotted spoon till cool. Clip onions root end; remove peel. Turn the pearl onions, baby carrots, celery and sugar snap peas onto medium size bowl. May be done a day in advance. Refrigerate with cover.
- In big pot or huge, heavy skillet, liquify butter on moderately-high heat. Scatter pepper and salt on pieces of chicken breast; put in and sauté the chicken into skillet for 2 minutes. Dust with flour and mix on moderately-low heat for 8 minutes, till chicken is barely cooked completely. Mix in thyme, parsley, cream, pearl onions, carrots, celery, sugar snap peas, chicken broth and reserved meat from chicken leg-thigh. Mix for 5 minutes, till vegetables are heated and sauce partially thickens. Season vegetables and chicken with pepper and salt to taste. Mix dumplings in and simmer for a minute, till dumplings are heated completely.

Nutrition Information

- Calories: 431
- Total Carbohydrate: 15 g(5%)
- Cholesterol: 113 mg(38%)
- Protein: 29 g(59%)
- Total Fat: 27 g(42%)
- Saturated Fat: 10 g(49%)
- Sodium: 165 mg(7%)
- Fiber: 3 g(11%)

51. Chicken With White Wine And Garlic

Serving: Serves 2 | Prep: | Ready in:

Ingredients

- 2 tablespoons olive oil
- 1 cup sliced mushrooms (about 3 ounces)
- 1 tablespoon minced garlic
- 1 whole boneless chicken breasts (about 12 ounces), halved
- Salt and pepper
- 3 tablespoon dry white wine
- 1 tablespoon lemon juice
- 1 tablespoon minced fresh parsley

Direction

- In medium, heavy skillet, heat the oil on moderate heat. Put in garlic and mushrooms and sauté for 5 minutes, till mushrooms start to brown. Turn the mushrooms onto plate; retain warmth. Add pepper and salt to season chicken. Put the chicken into skillet and cook for 6 minutes, till brown on each side, flipping one time. Pour lemon juice and wine into skillet and keep cooking for 2 minutes, till liquid is cooked down to 2 tablespoons. Top mushrooms with chick. Sprinkle pan juices on chicken. Scatter parsley over to serve.

Nutrition Information

- Calories: 396
- Saturated Fat: 6 g(28%)
- Sodium: 610 mg(25%)
- Fiber: 0 g(1%)
- Total Carbohydrate: 6 g(2%)
- Cholesterol: 87 mg(29%)
- Protein: 29 g(58%)
- Total Fat: 26 g(40%)

52. Chicken, Shrimp And Sausage Stew

Serving: Serves 6 | Prep: | Ready in:

Ingredients

- 1 pound andouille sausage,* cut into rounds
- 6 large chicken thighs (about 2 1/4 pounds)
- 3 cups chopped onions
- 2 1/3 cups chopped green bell peppers
- 1 1/4 cups chopped red bell pepper
- 6 large garlic cloves, chopped
- 3 tablespoons chopped fresh oregano
- 2 tablespoons chopped fresh thyme
- 1 tablespoon paprika
- 1 28-ounce can diced tomatoes with juices
- 1 14 1/2-ounce can low-salt chicken broth
- 1 cup dry white wine
- 3/4 cup sliced pimiento-stuffed green olives
- 1 pound uncooked large shrimp, peeled, deveined
- *A smoked pork and beef sausage, available at specialty foods stores. Hot links, smoked bratwurst, kielbasa or smoked Hungarian sausage can be substituted.

Direction

- Sauté sausage for 4 minutes till brown in big heavy pot on medium heat; put into big bowl. Sprinkle pepper and salt on chicken. Put chicken in pot; cook for 3 minutes per side till brown. Put chicken in bowl with the sausage. Pour all pan drippings off but 1 tbsp.
- Put bell peppers and onions in pot; sauté for 15 minutes till golden brown. Add paprika, thyme, garlic and oregano; sauté for 2 minutes. Put accumulated juices with chicken and sausage in pot. Add wine, chicken broth and tomatoes with juices; boil. Lower heat; cover. Simmer for 25 minutes till chicken cooks through.
- Uncover pot then add olives; simmer for 40 minutest till liquid reduces to thin sauce consistency and chicken is very tender. Add shrimp; simmer for 5 minutes till cooked

through. Season with pepper and salt to taste. You can prep stew 1 day ahead. Refrigerate till cold. Tightly cover; refrigerate. Rewarm on medium low heat before serving.

Nutrition Information

- Calories: 746
- Protein: 46 g(91%)
- Total Fat: 49 g(76%)
- Saturated Fat: 15 g(74%)
- Sodium: 1574 mg(66%)
- Fiber: 8 g(33%)
- Total Carbohydrate: 27 g(9%)
- Cholesterol: 264 mg(88%)

53. Chili Lime Cream Sauce

Serving: Makes about 2/3 cup | Prep: | Ready in:

Ingredients

- 1/4 cup dry white wine
- 1/4 cup fresh lime juice
- 1 tablespoon chopped peeled fresh ginger
- 1 tablespoon minced shallot
- 1/3 cup whipping cream
- 2 tablespoons chili-garlic sauce*
- 6 tablespoons (3/4 stick) unsalted butter, room temperature, cut into 1/2-inch pieces

Direction

- Mix in small, heavy saucepan with the initial 4 ingredients. Boil for 3 minutes on high heat till cooked down by half. Put in cream and boil for 2 minutes, till cooked down by 1/2. Lower the heat to low. Stir chili-garlic sauce in. Put in butter, a piece at one time, mixing barely till liquified before putting the next piece.

Nutrition Information

- Calories: 681
- Total Fat: 70 g(108%)
- Saturated Fat: 44 g(222%)
- Sodium: 32 mg(1%)
- Fiber: 1 g(3%)
- Total Carbohydrate: 10 g(3%)
- Cholesterol: 204 mg(68%)
- Protein: 3 g(5%)

54. Chilled Blueberry Soup

Serving: Makes 6 servings | Prep: 20mins | Ready in:

Ingredients

- 1/2 cup sugar
- Juice of 1 orange (or 1/4 cup store-bought orange juice)
- 1 cup fruity white wine (or white grape juice)
- 2 cups fresh blueberries (or frozen ones, thawed, with their juice)
- 1 cup plain yogurt

Direction

- 1. Bring together 1 cup of water, grape juice or wine, orange juice and sugar in a deep saucepan to a boil. Boil about a minute while stirring.
- 2. Put in berries and cook about 1 minute longer.
- 3. Take away from the heat and allow to cool thoroughly.
- 4. Puree the mixture and use a fine sieve to strain the mixture through, then refrigerate. Transfer the mixture into bowls and whisk in yogurt right before serving.

Nutrition Information

- Calories: 148
- Cholesterol: 5 mg(2%)
- Protein: 2 g(4%)
- Total Fat: 2 g(2%)
- Saturated Fat: 1 g(4%)

- Sodium: 21 mg(1%)
- Fiber: 2 g(7%)
- Total Carbohydrate: 29 g(10%)

55. Chilled Grape Soup

Serving: Makes 6 dessert servings | Prep: 20mins | Ready in:

Ingredients

- 1 (2-inch) cinnamon stick
- 2 whole cloves
- 10 black peppercorns
- 2 (2- by 1-inch) strips fresh lemon zest
- 2 (2- by 1-inch) strips fresh orange zest
- 1/2 teaspoon unflavored gelatin (from one 1/4-oz envelope)
- 1 1/2 cups plus 1 tablespoon white grape juice
- 1 cup dry white wine
- 1/2 cup sugar
- Pinch of freshly grated nutmeg
- 1 teaspoon finely grated fresh lemon zest
- 2 cups mixed grapes, stemmed, seeded if necessary, and sliced (lengthwise or crosswise)
- a 5-inch square of cheesecloth; kitchen string

Direction

- Put on cheesecloth the zest strips, peppercorns, cloves and cinnamon stick and bind it sealed.
- In small cup, scatter top of a tablespoon grape juice with gelatin and soften for a minute.
- In 1- to 2-quart saucepan, boil cheesecloth bag, nutmeg, sugar, leftover 1 1/2 cups of white grape juice and wine, then take off heat and put in the mixture of gelatin, mixing using metal spoon till it dissolves.
- Turn the soup onto bowl and chill with cover, in bigger bowl with cold water and ice inside the refrigerator for no less than 8 hours.
- Barely prior to serving, throw cheesecloth bag and to soup, put grapes and grated zest.
- Notes: Soup, with no added grapes and grated zest, may be refrigerated for 12 hours maximum. Put in grapes and zest barely prior to serving.
- Use a metal spoon to stir gelatin; since wooden may release oils, and whisk may blend small bubbles.

Nutrition Information

- Calories: 161
- Sodium: 9 mg(0%)
- Fiber: 1 g(4%)
- Total Carbohydrate: 37 g(12%)
- Protein: 1 g(1%)
- Total Fat: 0 g(0%)
- Saturated Fat: 0 g(0%)

56. Chilled Herbed Tomato Soup With Citrus And Spice

Serving: Makes 6 servings | Prep: | Ready in:

Ingredients

- 2 tablespoons olive oil
- 5 14-ounce cans diced tomatoes in juice
- 1/2 cup chopped shallots
- 2 tablespoons minced lemongrass
- 1 tablespoon minced fresh ginger
- 1 tablespoon chopped garlic
- 2 tablespoons honey
- 2 cups chicken stock or canned low-salt broth
- 1 cup dry white wine
- 1/2 cup fresh lime juice
- 1/4 cup chopped fresh cilantro
- 2 tablespoons chopped fresh mint
- 2 teaspoons grated lime peel
- 2 tablespoons fresh lemon juice
- 2 tablespoons aquavit or vodka
- 1/2 cup thinly sliced fresh arugula

Direction

- In a heavy big pot, heat oil on medium-low heat. Put in garlic, ginger, lemongrass, shallots and tomatoes with their juice; simmer for about 12 minutes until the liquid is evaporated. Put in honey and simmer for about 8 minutes until the mixture is very thick, frequently stirring. Put in the next 5 ingredients and chicken stock. Simmer for half an hour.
- Working in batches, strain the soup into a big bowl, pressing the solids to release the juices. Get rid of solids. Season soup with pepper and salt. Let the soup chill for at least 8 hours.
- Stir aquavit and lemon juice to the soup. Use arugula as a garnish.

Nutrition Information

- Calories: 167
- Saturated Fat: 1 g(4%)
- Sodium: 50 mg(2%)
- Fiber: 7 g(28%)
- Total Carbohydrate: 24 g(8%)
- Protein: 3 g(7%)
- Total Fat: 5 g(8%)

57. Chilled Watermelon Mint Soup

Serving: Makes 8 servings | Prep: | Ready in:

Ingredients

- 12 cups 1-inch pieces seeded or seedless watermelon (from about 7 pounds)
- 2 tablespoons cornstarch
- 2 cups Johannisberg Riesling wine
- 1/3 cup (or more) sugar
- 2 cups (lightly packed) fresh mint leaves (from about 1 large bunch)
- 1/2 teaspoon salt
- 1/4 teaspoon cayenne pepper
- 1 cup 1/4-inch cubes seeded or seedless watermelon
- 1/2 cup crème fraîche or sour cream, stirred to loosen
- Fresh mint sprigs

Direction

- In a processor, puree 12 cups of watermelon in batches, until smooth. Strain the puree into a big bowl. Remove 1 cup of the puree to a small bowl, then refrigerate, covered. Whisk into the rest of puree with cornstarch. In a big pot, bring 1/3 cup of sugar with wine to a simmer while stirring until sugar is dissolved. Simmer for about 3 minutes. Put in watermelon-cornstarch mixture and bring to a boil while whisking. Remove the soup to a bowl and stir in 2 cups of mint. Allow the mixture to a cool to room temperature for an hour, while whisking sometimes.
- Strain soup into a separate bowl while pressing on solids to draw out as much liquid as you can. Stir in cayenne and salt, then put in additional sugar if wanted. Refrigerate for a minimum of 4 hours and for a maximum of one day, until chilled.
- Whisk into the soup with reserved 1 cup of watermelon puree, then divide soup into 8 bowls. Mound in the center of each bowl with 2 tbsp. of cubed watermelon, then use crème fraiche to drizzle over soup. Use mint sprigs to decorate the soup bowl.

Nutrition Information

- Calories: 201
- Saturated Fat: 2 g(8%)
- Sodium: 165 mg(7%)
- Fiber: 3 g(10%)
- Total Carbohydrate: 33 g(11%)
- Cholesterol: 7 mg(2%)
- Protein: 3 g(5%)
- Total Fat: 3 g(5%)

58. Choucroute Garnie

Serving: Makes 8 servings | Prep: | Ready in:

Ingredients

- 1 3/4 pounds smoked meaty ham hocks
- 1 pound fully cooked bratwurst
- 8 ounces thick-sliced bacon strips, cut crosswise into 1-inch pieces
- 2 large onions, chopped
- 1 teaspoon juniper berries (optional)
- 1 teaspoon whole black peppercorns
- 10 whole cloves
- 8 whole allspice
- 3 bay leaves
- 3 Red Delicious apples, unpeeled, cored, cut into 1-inch pieces
- 2 2-pound jars sauerkraut, squeezed dry
- 2 pounds fully cooked kielbasa, cut diagonally into 1-inch pieces
- 1 pound fully cooked knockwurst
- 2 cups Alsatian Pinot Blanc or other dry white wine
- 2 pounds small red-skinned potatoes
- 2/3 cup chopped fresh parsley
- Assorted mustards
- Prepared white horseradish

Direction

- Cover ham hocks by 2-in. water in big saucepan; boil. Lower heat; cover. Simmer for 2 hours till meat is very tender. Put hocks in medium bowl. Boil broth for 15 minutes till reduced to 2 cups. From bones, remove meat; discard bones. In medium bowl, put hock meat. You can make it 1 day ahead. Separately cover broth and hock meat; chill.
- Preheat an oven to 350°F. Heat big heavy pot on medium high heat. Add bacon and bratwurst; sauté for 10 minutes till bratwurst is brown and bacon is crisp. Put into bowl with the hock meat.
- Put bay leaves, spices and onions in same pot; sauté for 5 minutes till onions are tender. Add apple; sauté for 2 minutes. Stir in sauerkraut.
- Add all the meats; to submerge, press. Add wine and reserved broth; boil for 10 minutes. Cover choucroute; bake for 1 1/2 hours.
- Meanwhile, cook the potatoes for 18 minutes till tender in pot with boiling salted water; drain. Slightly cool. Halve potatoes. In parsley, dip cut sides. On platter, put meats and sauerkraut; surround with potatoes then serve with horseradish and mustards.

Nutrition Information

59. Choucroute With Caramelized Pears

Serving: Makes 4 servings | Prep: | Ready in:

Ingredients

- 3 tablespoons butter
- 1 1/4 pounds (total) smoked pork chops and precooked assorted sausages (such as bratwurst and chicken-apple)
- 1 large onion, coarsely chopped
- 2 large firm pears, cored, thickly sliced
- 1 pound sauerkraut, rinsed, drained
- 1 cup dry white wine
- 1/8 teaspoon ground allspice
- Freshly ground black pepper
- 2 tablespoons minced fresh parsley

Direction

- In a big skillet, let the butter melt over medium-high heat setting. Put in the meats and let them cook in the melted butter for about 1 minute on every side until they turn brown in color. Put in the onion and let it cook for about 5 minutes until it turns brown in color. Put in the pears and let them cook for about 5 minutes until the pears have softened. Use tongs to put the cooked meats onto a plate. Put the wine, allspice and sauerkraut into the skillet and mix it while scraping off the browned bits of food. Put the cooked meats back into the skillet and place them over the sauerkraut mixture. Let the mixture boil. Lower the heat setting to medium-low heat then cover the skillet and allow the mixture to simmer for 10 minutes. Add in pepper to taste. Top it off with parsley then serve.

Nutrition Information

- Calories: 607
- Total Carbohydrate: 26 g(9%)
- Cholesterol: 122 mg(41%)
- Protein: 24 g(48%)
- Total Fat: 44 g(68%)
- Saturated Fat: 16 g(82%)
- Sodium: 1805 mg(75%)
- Fiber: 7 g(29%)

60. Cider Braised Pheasant With Pearl Onions And Apples

Serving: Makes 8 servings | Prep: | Ready in:

Ingredients

- 1/2 cup extra-virgin olive oil
- 5 tablespoons fresh ginger, peeled and roughly chopped
- 3 tablespoons fresh tarragon leaves, whole
- 1/2 cup freshly squeezed orange juice (from 1 1/2 oranges)
- 3 tablespoons finely grated orange zest (from 1 1/2 oranges)
- Large pinch kosher salt
- 1/4 teaspoon freshly ground black pepper
- 3 (3-pound) pheasants, each rinsed inside and out, patted dry, cut into 6 pieces
- 1 teaspoon kosher salt
- 1 teaspoon freshly ground black pepper
- 3 tablespoons extra-virgin olive oil
- 1 tablespoon unsalted butter
- 3 large yellow onions, halved and thinly sliced (about 6 cups)
- 1 bay leaf
- 1 teaspoon fennel seeds
- 1 teaspoon table salt
- Pinch sugar
- 2 to 3 cups low-sodium chicken broth, plus additional, if necessary
- 2 cups apple cider
- 1 cup dry white wine
- 3 Granny Smith apples, peeled, cored, and diced
- 10 ounces pearl onions, root ends trimmed
- 1 tablespoon extra-virgin olive oil
- 1 Granny Smith apple, peeled, cored, and cut into 1-inch cubes
- 2 teaspoons sugar
- Pinch kosher salt
- Pinch freshly ground black pepper
- 3 tablespoons apple cider
- Fresh tarragon leaves, chopped

Direction

- Making marinade: Mix together salt, pepper, zest, orange juice, tarragon, ginger, and olive oil in a blender and puree until smooth. Toss together pheasant with the marinade then mix to coat in a large bowl. Cover the bowl and refrigerate overnight to a maximum of 48 hours.
- In a very large Dutch oven, heat olive oil over moderately high heat until hot but not smoking to braise pheasant. Remove the pheasant pieces from the marinade and scrape off any excess. Sprinkle pheasant with 1/2 teaspoon of pepper and salt. Sear the pheasant in batches for 5 minutes per side, until thoroughly browned. Transfer the pheasant to a platter lined with paper towels to drain.
- Preheat oven to 325°F. Leave the browned bits and 1 tablespoon of oil in the pan, skim off the rest of the oil. Over moderately low heat, add butter and heat until melts. Stir in sugar, the leftover 1/2 teaspoon of pepper, salt, fennel seeds, bay leaf, and onions. Cook for 30 to 40

minutes, stirring occasionally, until the onions are caramelized thoroughly.

- Place the pheasant back into the pot and add wine, cider, and chicken broth. If the liquid does not cover half of the pheasant pieces, add more chicken broth as needed. Bring to a simmer over high heat. Add apples into the pot and cover. Transfer the pot into the oven and braise for 45 minutes to 1 hour until meat is tender and cooked through; turn pheasant occasionally.
- Transfer the pheasant pieces to a platter using either a slotted spoon or tongs. Keep warm by covering with foil. Over high heat, bring the pan juices in the pot to a boil. Boil for 25 minutes, uncovered, until the sauce has thickened and well reduced. Taste and if needed, add more salt and pepper.
- While waiting for the juices to reduce, prepare apples and caramelized onions, fill a medium pot with water and bring to a boil. Add pearl onions. Boil for 1 minute, uncovered. Drain, then run the pearl onions under cold water to cool. Once cool enough to handle, slip off the skins.
- In a small skillet, heat oil over moderately high heat until hot but not smoking. Put in salt, pepper, sugar, apples, and onions and mix until combined. Sear for 10 minutes, until apples and onions are dark golden; shake pan occasionally. Stir in apple cider and scrape up any browned bits from the pan. Cook on low heat, covered, for another 2 minutes, until the onions are fork tender.
- Over the pheasant, spoon some sauce and garnish with chopped tarragon, apples, and onions. Serve alongside extra sauce.

Nutrition Information

- Calories: 1184
- Fiber: 6 g(24%)
- Total Carbohydrate: 42 g(14%)
- Cholesterol: 315 mg(105%)
- Protein: 104 g(208%)
- Total Fat: 64 g(98%)
- Saturated Fat: 16 g(79%)
- Sodium: 770 mg(32%)

61. Cipolline With Bay Leaf And Golden Raisins

Serving: Makes 4 (hors d'oeuvre) servings | Prep: 30mins | Ready in:

Ingredients

- 1/4 cup golden raisins
- 1 tablespoon sugar
- 1 tablespoon unsalted butter
- 3/4 pound cipolline or small (1 1/2-inch) white boiling onions, peeled
- 1/3 cup dry white wine
- 1/2 fresh or dried bay leaf
- Crisp Rosemary Flatbread

Direction

- Let raisins immerse in hot water till set to use.
- Cut out a round parchment paper, 10-inch in size.
- In the middle of a heavy, 10-inch skillet, heat the sugar on moderate heat till it begins to liquify. Cook till golden brown, leaning skillet from time to time for even melting. Mix butter in, then put in and cook onions for 3 minutes, mixing from time to time, till starting to brown. Put in drained raisins, quarter teaspoon of pepper, quarter teaspoon of salt, bay leaf, and wine.
- Lower heat to low and use parchment to cover the onions, then the lid. Simmer slowly for 18 to 20 minutes, shake the skillet from time to time, till onions are soft.
- Take the lid and the parchment, then simmer for 3 minutes, mixing from time to time, till liquid is cooked down into glaze. Throw bay leaf. Serve at room temperature or while warm.
- Note: Cipolline may be done 2 days in advance and refrigerate.

62. Coconut Curry Sauce

Serving: Makes about 2 cups | Prep: | Ready in:

Ingredients

- 1/2 cup mirin*
- 1/4 cup chopped fresh lemongrass**
- 1 tablespoon chopped peeled fresh ginger
- 1/4 cup dry white wine
- 2 cups whipping cream
- 3/4 cup canned unsweetened coconut milk*
- 2 teaspoons Thai green or red curry paste*
- *Available at Asian markets and in the Asian foods section of some supermarkets.
- **Fresh lemongrass can be found in the produce section (not Asian foods section) of some supermarkets.

Direction

- Boil lemongrass, ginger and mirin in a heavy medium pot for six minutes or until it lessens to 1/4 cup. Add wine and continue boiling for another six minutes until it reduces to 1/4 cup. Add the coconut milk and the cream and boil on high heat. Reduce heat to medium and let simmer for 12 minutes, stirring occasionally. When the mixture is slightly thickened, stir in the curry paste and season to taste with pepper and salt. Keep aside to cool and refrigerate if you plan to use the next day. Before serving, warm on medium heat.

Nutrition Information

63. Coniglio Pizzaiola

Serving: Makes 4 servings | Prep: | Ready in:

Ingredients

- 1 2 1/2-3-pound rabbit, quartered
- Kosher salt and freshly ground black pepper
- 4 tablespoons olive oil, divided
- 1 small onion, thinly sliced
- 1 small red onion, thinly sliced
- 4 garlic cloves, minced
- 3 sprigs oregano
- 2 sprigs basil
- 1 cup white wine
- 1 14-ounce can whole, peeled tomatoes, preferably San Marzano

Direction

- Preheat the oven to 350°F. Add pepper and salt to season rabbit. In a big ovenproof pot, heat 2 tablespoons of olive oil over medium-high heat. Cook rabbit in batches for 2 to 3 minutes each side till golden brown. Turn rabbit onto plate. To pot, put the leftover 2 tablespoons oil. Put the onions; sauté for 4 minutes till starting to soften. Put the basil, oregano and garlic; lower the heat to medium and let cook for 3 minutes, mixing frequently, till tender. Put the wine; allow to simmer for 2 minutes till slightly cooked down. By hand, mash the tomatoes; put to the pot along with juices from can. Put half cup of water; boil. Lightly season with pepper and salt. Put rabbit back to pot; place cover.
- Turn the pot onto oven and let braise for 1 1/4 hours till meat is soft and nearly falling off the bone. Turn meat onto a platter. Over medium-high heat, cooked sauce down in pot for 10 minutes till thickened. Add pepper and salt to season. Top rabbit with sauce.

Nutrition Information

- Calories: 605
- Total Carbohydrate: 8 g(3%)

- Cholesterol: 178 mg(59%)
- Protein: 64 g(127%)
- Total Fat: 31 g(48%)
- Saturated Fat: 7 g(36%)
- Sodium: 1011 mg(42%)
- Fiber: 2 g(8%)

64. Coquilles St. Jacques

Serving: Makes 6 servings | Prep: | Ready in:

Ingredients

- 1 3/4 cups water
- 3/4 cup dry white wine
- 1 small onion, chopped
- Bouquet garni (see Mom's Tip)
- 1 teaspoon lemon juice
- 1 pound very fresh scallops
- 8 ounces mushrooms, washed and chopped
- 6 tablespoons butter
- 4 tablespoons flour
- 1/2 cup heavy cream
- Salt and freshly ground pepper
- N/A freshly ground pepper
- Bread crumbs
- Grated Swiss or Gruyère cheese

Direction

- Bring the wine, lemon juice, bouquet garni, water, and onion to a boil in a saucepan. Add the scallops. Cover the pan and simmer it over very low heat for 5 minutes until cooked through. Use a slotted spoon to remove the scallops from the pan; put aside.
- Combine the mushrooms with the scallop poaching liquid. Simmer the mushrooms for 10 minutes while uncovered. Strain the mushrooms and reserve them separately with the liquid. Discard the bouquet garni.
- Slice the scallops into 1/2-inch thick pieces. You can cut them in half horizontally if the scallops are too long.
- Place the butter in a medium saucepan and melt it. Mix in flour. Make sure you won't let it turn dark. Add 2-3 tbsp. of scallop liquid and stir until combined. Whisk the flour mixture and scallop liquid over very low heat until well-blended. Add the cream. Simmer the mixture while stirring it until thickened and blended. Season the mixture with pepper and salt to taste. Add the mushrooms and scallops; mix.
- Fill the 6-inches shallow ramekins or 6 scallop shells almost up to the top with the scallop mixture. Sprinkle bread crumbs lightly on top of the mixture. Sprinkle over the grated cheese. (Use plastic wrap to cover the scallops and refrigerate them until ready to serve.)
- Set the broiler to preheating. Broil the scallops until the cheese has melted and appears golden brown and the mixture is bubbling.
- Tips on making the bouquet garni: Wrap the 2 bay leaves, a sprig of fresh thyme (or 1/2 tsp. of dried thyme leaves), and 1-2 sprigs of parsley in a cheesecloth. Use a clean string or thread to tie the cheesecloth neatly.

Nutrition Information

65. Coquilles St. Jacques With Beurre Blanc

Serving: Makes 4 servings | Prep: | Ready in:

Ingredients

- 1 1/2 pounds medium sea scallops (24 to 28), tough muscle removed from sides if necessary
- 1/4 cup dry vermouth
- 1 1/2 tablespoons minced shallot
- 1 1/2 tablespoons white-wine vinegar
- 1 1/2 tablespoons dry white wine
- 1 tablespoon cold water
- 9 tablespoons cold unsalted butter, cut into tablespoon pieces

- 1 1/2 teaspoons finely chopped fresh tarragon

Direction

- Marinate scallops for 15 minutes in vermouth.
- Beurre blanc: Simmer wine, vinegar and shallot in a small heavy saucepan till liquid reduces to 1 tbsp. Take off from the heat; add water. Lower the heat to low; cook, 1 tbsp. at a time, whisking 6 tbsp. butter in, adding every new piece before last one fully melts, lifting the pan off from heat occasionally to cool mixture. Sauce should not get too hot to liquefy; should have thin hollandaise consistency. Take off from heat; whisk pepper and salt to taste and tarragon in. Keep, covered, warm off heat.
- Cook scallops: drain scallops; between paper towels, pat dry. Heat 1 1/2 tbsp. of leftover butter in a 12-in. nonstick skillet till foam subsides on medium high heat. Season 1/2 scallops with pepper and salt as butter heats. Sauté scallops for 4 minutes total till just cooked through, turning once. Wipe skillet out; sauté leftover scallops in leftover 1 1/2 tbsp. butter in the same way.
- Serve beurre blanc with scallops.

Nutrition Information

- Calories: 368
- Cholesterol: 110 mg(37%)
- Protein: 21 g(42%)
- Total Fat: 27 g(41%)
- Saturated Fat: 17 g(83%)
- Sodium: 672 mg(28%)
- Fiber: 0 g(1%)
- Total Carbohydrate: 7 g(2%)

66. Corn And Potatoes With Heirloom Tomatoes

Serving: Makes 6 (first course or side dish) servings | Prep: 30mins | Ready in:

Ingredients

- 1/4 pound bacon (4 slices), chopped
- 1 shallot, minced
- 1 teaspoon kosher salt, divided
- 1/4 cup dry white wine
- 1/2 pound Yukon Gold potatoes, peeled and cut into 1/3-inch dice (1 1/2 cups)
- 1 1/4 cups plus 1 tablespoon water, divided
- 4 cups corn (from 8 ears), divided
- 1 1/2 teaspoons sweet Spanish smoked paprika
- 1/4 teaspoon chopped fresh thyme
- 1/2 pound heirloom or cherry tomatoes, chopped or halved

Direction

- Cook bacon till crisp and brown in a medium heavy saucepan on medium heat, occasionally mixing. Put onto paper towels with a slotted spoon; drain. Keep fat in pan.
- Cook 1/4 tsp. kosher salt and shallot in fat in pan on medium heat till soft, occasionally mixing. Add wine; boil on high heat for 3 minutes till reduced by half, scraping brown bits up, mixing. Mix in 1/2 tsp. kosher salt, 1/2 cup water and potatoes; simmer for 10 minutes till liquid thickens and reduces to by 3 quarters, occasionally mixing, uncovered.
- Meanwhile, puree 1 tbsp. water and 1 cup corn in a blender. Through fine-mesh sieve, force into a bowl; press on solids hard then discard.
- Put leftover 3 cups corn kernels, leftover 1/4 tsp. kosher salt, leftover 3/4 cup water, thyme and paprika into potato mixture; simmer for 10-12 minutes till most liquid evaporates and potatoes and corn are tender, occasionally mixing, partially covered.
- Take off heat; mix in kosher salt to taste, 1/4 tsp. pepper, corn liquid and tomatoes. Sprinkle bacon; serve.

Nutrition Information

- Calories: 211
- Protein: 7 g(14%)

- Total Fat: 9 g(14%)
- Saturated Fat: 3 g(14%)
- Sodium: 460 mg(19%)
- Fiber: 4 g(15%)
- Total Carbohydrate: 29 g(10%)
- Cholesterol: 12 mg(4%)

67. Crab Bisque

Serving: 4 | Prep: 5mins | Ready in:

Ingredients

- 1 (10.75 ounce) can condensed tomato soup
- 1 (10.75 ounce) can condensed cream of mushroom soup
- 1 1/4 cups milk
- 1 1/4 cups imitation crabmeat
- salt to taste
- ground black pepper to taste
- 1 pinch curry powder

Direction

- Mix milk and soups till smooth. Add crabmeat and curry powder, pepper and salt to taste. Heat, don't boil, till steaming; serve.

Nutrition Information

- Calories: 197 calories;
- Total Carbohydrate: 25.5
- Cholesterol: 15
- Protein: 8.4
- Total Fat: 7.4
- Sodium: 1316

68. Cranberry Rosemary Wine Jelly

Serving: Makes 8 servings | Prep: 30mins | Ready in:

Ingredients

- 4 (12-ounce) bags fresh or frozen cranberries (14 cups; do not thaw)
- 3 cups sugar
- 2 cups dry white wine
- 2 (5-inch) fresh rosemary sprigs
- 3 2/3 cups cold water
- 1 tablespoon plus 2 teaspoons unflavored gelatin (from three 1/4-ounce envelopes)
- a 6-cup nonreactive mold (see cooks' note, below) or glass loaf pan

Direction

- In 6- to 8-quarts pot, boil 2 2/3 cups water, rosemary, wine, sugar and cranberries, mixing till sugar dissolves, then lower the heat and cover slightly, simmer for 8 to 10 minutes, mixing from time to time, till all the berries popped. Pass in dampened paper towels-lines-big colander lined place in deep bowl, then rest for 10 to 15 minutes, till all the juices have strained through, and throw the solids. Boil cranberry liquid in small saucepan till cooked down in case you have over 4 cups; in case less, pour in water to measure 4 cups total.
- Mix in small, clean saucepan with leftover cup of water and gelatin and rest for a minute till soften. Heat on medium heat, mixing, till gelatin dissolves. Mix into cranberry liquid with gelatin mixture till incorporated. Put the mixture of cranberry in a slightly greased mold, scooping off any froth. Let come to room temperature, then use plastic wrap to cover and refrigerate till set firmly, not less than half a day.
- Trace a thin knife tip between mold edge and jelly to remove from mold. Lean the mold sideways and knock mold side on a work counter, flipping it, to break seal evenly and detach the cranberry jelly. Maintaining the mold leaned, invert one plate on top of mold, then flip cranberry sauce over to plate.
- Notes: Glass, enameled cast iron and stainless steel are non-reactive, however do not use uncoated iron and pure aluminum, which may give an unpleasant color and taste to recipes that have acidic ingredients.

- • Use a serving plate 2-inches to 3-inches wider than mold to unmold the jelly to have allowance for expanding. Brush mold with a flavorless vegetable oil prior to filling.
- • Cranberry jelly may be refrigerated in mold for 2 days maximum.

Nutrition Information

- Calories: 415
- Saturated Fat: 0 g(0%)
- Sodium: 31 mg(1%)
- Fiber: 8 g(33%)
- Total Carbohydrate: 99 g(33%)
- Protein: 2 g(5%)
- Total Fat: 0 g(1%)

69. Cream Of Artichoke And Jerusalem Artichoke Soup

Serving: Makes 6 servings | Prep: | Ready in:

Ingredients

- 1 lemon, halved
- 1 1/2 lb artichokes (2 or 3)
- 1/2 lb Jerusalem artichokes
- 1 cup chopped onion
- 1 tablespoon chopped garlic
- 3 tablespoons unsalted butter
- 3/4 teaspoon salt
- 1/2 cup dry white wine
- 3 1/2 cups chicken broth
- 3/4 cup heavy cream
- Garnish: sliced almonds, toasted

Direction

- Clip the regular artichokes: press juice from a half of lemon right in a big bowl with water, then put the same half in water.
- Trim stem from an artichoke, then cut off quarter-inch from stem end to reveal the inner core. Cut off sides of stem going down to light inner core, then rub with another half of lemon. Put the stem in acidulated water.
- Use serrated knife to slice off an-inch from top of the same artichoke. Lean outer leaves back top snap off near to base, then throw a few additional layers of leaves in exactly the same manner till you reach light yellow leaves that has light green tips. Trim green tips.
- Use a sharp paring knife to cut off fibrous, dark green portions from sides and base of artichoke, then rub half of lemon on cut surfaces.
- Slice artichoke to make 8 wedges, then using paring knife, trim purple leaves and fuzzy choke. Rub half of lemon on every cut surface, then put the artichoke to the acidulated water. Prep the rest of the artichokes in exactly the same manner.
- Clip Jerusalem artichokes: use sharp paring knife to remove peel from Jerusalem artichokes and slice to make quarter-inch-thick pieces.
- Make soup: in a heavy, 4-quart pot, cook onion, garlic and Jerusalem artichokes in butter with cover on medium low heat for 5 minutes, mixing from time to time. Strain the regular artichokes and put into pot including salt. Cook with cover for 5 minutes, mixing from time to time, till Jerusalem artichokes are tender-crisp. Pour in wine and boil for 3 minutes, with no cover, till cooked down by 1/2. Pour in broth and simmer for 20 to 25 minutes, with cover, till vegetables are extremely tender.
- Use blender to purée soup in batches for 2 minutes, till extremely smooth, be careful once processing hot liquids. Put soup back to pot and mix in pepper to taste and cream. Rewarm soup, mixing.
- Note: Soup can be stored for 3 days. Cool fully, with no cover, and refrigerate with cover.

Nutrition Information

- Calories: 310

- Fiber: 7 g(30%)
- Total Carbohydrate: 28 g(9%)
- Cholesterol: 60 mg(20%)
- Protein: 9 g(18%)
- Total Fat: 19 g(29%)
- Saturated Fat: 11 g(55%)
- Sodium: 613 mg(26%)

70. Creamed Crab With Artichokes

Serving: Serves 8 | Prep: | Ready in:

Ingredients

- 1/2 cup butter
- 1/2 cup flour
- 1/4 cup onion, grated
- 1/2 cup green onion, chopped
- 2 tablespoons parsley, chopped
- 2 cups whipping cream
- 3/4 cup dry white wine
- 2 1/2 teaspoons salt
- 1/2 teaspoon white pepper
- 1/4 teaspoon Cayenne pepper
- 2 tablespoons lemon juice
- 2 pounds crab meat
- 1 14-ounce can artichoke hearts, drained and sliced
- 1/2 pound mushrooms, sliced

Direction

- Liquify butter, mix in and cook flour for 5 minutes on moderate heat. Put in parsley and onions and cook for 2 minutes to 3. Slowly mix in cream and heat thoroughly. Put in salt, peppers and wine. Combine thoroughly and simmer mixing continuously. Take off heat. Put in lemon juice once mixture is lukewarm.
- Put the meat in base of baking dish, 18 X 28-inch in size. Top with 1/3 of sauce. Top sauce with layer of artichokes, then put 1/3 of sauce to cover. Put in mushrooms, and put the rest of the sauce on top. Bake for 30 to 40 minutes in 350°F oven.

Nutrition Information

- Calories: 446
- Protein: 25 g(51%)
- Total Fat: 31 g(48%)
- Saturated Fat: 19 g(96%)
- Sodium: 710 mg(30%)
- Fiber: 4 g(14%)
- Total Carbohydrate: 16 g(5%)
- Cholesterol: 207 mg(69%)

71. Creamy Chinese Celery Soup

Serving: Makes 6 servings | Prep: 30mins | Ready in:

Ingredients

- 1 medium leek (white and pale green parts only), chopped
- 1 medium russet (baking) potato
- 1/2 cup chopped shallot
- 2 tablespoons unsalted butter
- 1 tablespoon olive oil
- 2 bunches Chinese celery (1 1/2 lb total), top leaves discarded and stalks cut into 2-inch pieces
- 1/2 cup dry white wine
- 4 cups chicken stock or low-sodium chicken broth (32 fl oz)
- 1/2 cup heavy cream
- 1/2 teaspoon salt
- 1/4 teaspoon black pepper
- 6 (1/4-inch-thick) diagonal baguette slices
- 1/4 cup extra-virgin olive oil
- Kosher salt to taste
- Garnish: fresh Chinese parsley leaves or flat-leaf parsley leaves

Direction

- Prepare soup: thoroughly rinse leek in bowl with cold water, then take and drain thoroughly. Peel potato and chop. In a heavy,

3-quart saucepan, let shallot cook in oil and butter on medium heat for 2 minutes, mixing, till soft. Put in and cook leek for 5 minutes, mixing, till soft. Put in and cook potato and celery for 2 minutes, mixing. Pour in wine and let boil for a minute. Pour in broth and simmer for an hour, with cover, till celery is extremely soft.

- Use a blender to purée the soup in batches till extremely smooth, be careful once processing hot liquids, then pass through a big medium-mesh sieve right to bowl, forcing firmly on solids. Throw the solids. Turn soup onto a cleaned saucepan, then mix in salt, pepper and cream, and heat till hot on low heat. Add water to thin if wished.
- Meanwhile, prepare croutons: Preheat the oven to 350°F.
- Brush oil on slices of with and liberally season with pepper and kosher salt. Place on baking sheet in single layer, then bake for 12 to 15 minutes in center of the oven till crisp and golden brown.
- Put croutons on top of soup to serve.
- Notes: Soup may be done a day in advance and let cool with no cover, then refrigerate with cover.
- Croutons store at room temperature in airtight container for 2 days.

Nutrition Information

- Calories: 351
- Cholesterol: 42 mg(14%)
- Protein: 7 g(14%)
- Total Fat: 25 g(38%)
- Saturated Fat: 9 g(46%)
- Sodium: 779 mg(32%)
- Fiber: 3 g(10%)
- Total Carbohydrate: 24 g(8%)

72. Crispy Chicken Thighs With Kale, Apricots, And Olives

Serving: 4 servings | Prep: 30mins | Ready in:

Ingredients

- 8 small bone-in, skin-on chicken thighs (about 2 pounds total)
- 1 1/2 teaspoons kosher salt, divided
- 1/2 teaspoon freshly ground black pepper
- 2 tablespoons extra-virgin olive oil
- 1 cup dried apricots, halved lengthwise
- 1/4 cup white wine vinegar
- 4 garlic cloves, thinly sliced
- 2 bunches curly kale, stems removed, leaves torn into pieces
- 1 cup mild green olives, such as Castelvetrano, crushed, pitted, torn in half
- 1/4 teaspoon crushed red pepper flakes (optional)
- 1/2 cup dry white wine

Direction

- Set the rack on the top of the oven and preheat it to 400 degrees F. Season both sides of the chicken with 1/2 tsp. of pepper and 1 tsp. of salt. Put oil into a deep-sided skillet or a large braising pan. Place the chicken into the cold pan in an even layer, skin-side down. Set the pan over medium heat. Cook for 12-15 minutes until the skin is golden brown. Transfer the chicken into the plate, skin-side up. Take the pan away from the heat and reserve the fat.
- In the meantime, mix together 2 tbsp. of water, vinegar, and apricots into the small saucepan. Cook the liquid over high heat, stirring occasionally until boiling. Remove the mixture from the heat.
- Mix garlic into the pan with the remaining hot fat. Add the kale and coat them in batches for 3 minutes, tossing with tongs until well-coated and starts to wilt. (Take note that the kale must be dry or the fat will spatter.)

- Add the red pepper, apricot mixture, olives, and the remaining 1/2 tsp. of salt, if using, into the kale mixture. Toss the mixture well to combine. Nestle the chicken into the kale mixture, skin-side up. Make sure to fluff the kale up between the chicken pieces so that it would crisp inside the oven. Drizzle wine all around the chicken. Roast for 15 minutes until the chicken is cooked through.

Nutrition Information

- Calories: 912
- Total Fat: 62 g(95%)
- Saturated Fat: 15 g(76%)
- Sodium: 1173 mg(49%)
- Fiber: 7 g(28%)
- Total Carbohydrate: 33 g(11%)
- Cholesterol: 292 mg(97%)
- Protein: 55 g(110%)

73. Crispy Chicken Thighs With Spring Vegetables

Serving: 4 servings | Prep: 45mins | Ready in:

Ingredients

- 8 small bone-in, skin-on chicken thighs (about 3 pounds)
- 2 teaspoons kosher salt, divided
- 1 teaspoon freshly ground black pepper, divided
- 1 pound asparagus, trimmed
- 1 pound baby new potatoes, halved if larger than 1/2"
- 1 bunch radishes (about 1/2 pound), halved
- 2 tablespoons plus 2 teaspoons vegetable oil, divided
- 3 garlic cloves, finely chopped
- 1 tablespoon anchovy paste, or 6 fillets, finely chopped
- 1/2 cup (1 stick) cold butter, cut into 1-tablespoon pieces, divided
- 1/2 cup dry white wine
- 1 tablespoon fresh lemon juice
- 1 tablespoon finely chopped parsley, plus more for serving

Direction

- Preheat the oven to 450°F. Take bones off chicken thighs with kitchen shears, keep flesh and skin attach; throw the bones. Season the entire chicken with half teaspoon pepper and a teaspoon of salt.
- Toss in a big bowl with leftover 1/2 teaspoon pepper and 1 teaspoon salt, 2 tablespoons oil, radishes, potatoes and asparagus. Turn everything except asparagus onto one rimmed baking sheet and let roast for 15 minutes.
- Meantime, use a teaspoon of oil to grease a separate rimmed baking sheet. In big skillet, heat leftover 1 teaspoon of oil on moderately-high. Sear chicken for 5 to 7 minutes in batches, skin side facing down till skin is golden brown and crisp. Turn onto prepped sheet, skin side facing up. Once every chicken is seared, put fat in skillet aside, turn the baking sheet into oven and roast for 8 to 10 minutes, till chicken is cooked completely.
- Take the baking sheet of vegetables once you are about to open oven for roasting the chicken, place asparagus on top of radishes and potatoes, then keep roasting till asparagus is tender-crisp and radishes and potatoes are tender and nicely browned, for an additional of 8 to 10 minutes, it will be finish same amount of time as chicken.
- Meantime, cautiously drain extra fat off reserved skillet, keep the browned bits on base. Put to skillet with anchovy paste, 1 tablespoon butter and garlic, and cook on moderate heat for a minute, till garlic soften and aromatic. Pour in wine, scratching up browned bits using wooden spoon or spatula, and keep cooking for 2 minutes, mixing, till cooked down by 1/2. Take pan off heat and mix lemon juice in. Put in leftover butter one by one, tilting and mixing after every

increment to completely emulsify sauce. Mix in a tablespoon parsley.
- Turn the vegetables and chicken onto a platter, then top with sauce. Put additional parsley on top to serving.
- You may keep bones in the chicken thighs if you desire; roast for 12 to 14 minutes in the oven rather than 8 to 10.

Nutrition Information

- Calories: 959
- Saturated Fat: 26 g(131%)
- Sodium: 1280 mg(53%)
- Fiber: 6 g(24%)
- Total Carbohydrate: 29 g(10%)
- Cholesterol: 297 mg(99%)
- Protein: 46 g(92%)
- Total Fat: 73 g(112%)

74. Dried Fruit Compote With Vanilla And Orange

Serving: Makes 6 servings | Prep: | Ready in:

Ingredients

- 1 navel or juice orange
- 1 1/2 cups dry white wine
- 2/3 cup sugar
- 2 cups water
- 1 vanilla bean, halved lengthwise
- 1/2 lb dried figs (preferably Calimyrna; about 1 cup)
- 1/2 lb dried apricots (about 1 1/3 cups)
- 1/2 lb pitted prunes (about 1 1/4 cups)
- Accompaniment: lightly sweetened low-fat sour cream (optional)

Direction

- From half of orange and use a vegetable peeler to peel the zest in long strips. Remove any white pith and cut the zest in fine julienne strips. Slice the orange in half and squeeze out 1/3 cup of juice.
- In a 3-qt. heavy pot, mix 2 cups of water, wine, zest, sugar, and juice. Use a sharp knife to scrape the seeds out of vanilla bean in the wine mixture. Reserve its pod for another use. Boil and stir the mixture until the sugar dissolves completely. Continue to boil for 10 minutes until the mixture is reduced to 3 cups.
- Meanwhile, cut fig and discard its stems. Cut them in half lengthwise. Mix them in the syrup and simmer for 5 minutes, covered, until the figs are soft. Stir in prunes and apricot and cover the mixture. Simmer for 8-10 minutes until plump.
- Place the compote in a heatproof bowl. Allow it to cool for 1-2 hours to warm or room temperature.
- Note: The compote can be made a day ahead. Seal it with a cover and chill. You can reheat it on medium-low heat before serving.

Nutrition Information

75. Dried Fruit Compote With White Wine

Serving: Makes 6 dessert servings | Prep: 5mins | Ready in:

Ingredients

- 1 lb mixed dried fruit
- 1 cup water
- 1 cup dry white wine
- 2/3 cup sugar
- 2 (4- by 1-inch) strips fresh lemon or orange zest
- Accompaniment: plain yogurt

Direction

- In a heavy, 2-quart saucepan, mix every ingredient and simmer with covered for 15 minutes, on medium high heat till fruit soften.
- Turn onto bowl and cool down for 15 minutes.

Nutrition Information

- Calories: 287
- Total Fat: 1 g(1%)
- Saturated Fat: 0 g(0%)
- Sodium: 8 mg(0%)
- Fiber: 6 g(25%)
- Total Carbohydrate: 69 g(23%)
- Protein: 3 g(6%)

76. Duck Two Ways With Clementine Fig Relish

Serving: Serves 8 | Prep: | Ready in:

Ingredients

- 1 tablespoon black peppercorns, lightly crushed
- 1 tablespoon coriander seeds, lightly crushed
- 1 tablespoon fennel seeds, lightly crushed
- 8 duck legs (about 8 1/2 pounds), excess fat trimmed, frenched
- Kosher salt
- 4 duck breasts (about 3 1/2 pounds), fat trimmed
- 2 tablespoons vegetable oil
- 2 medium leeks, white and pale-green parts only, chopped
- 12 sprigs thyme
- 4 garlic cloves, crushed
- 2 bay leaves
- 2 cups dry white wine
- 2 clementines, very thinly sliced crosswise (with peel), seeds removed
- 1 cup dried black Mission figs, halved
- 1 1/2 cups cognac or brandy
- 1 cup sugar
- 2 tablespoons whole grain mustard
- 1/2 teaspoon crushed red pepper flakes
- 2 bay leaves
- 2 tablespoons sherry vinegar or red wine vinegar

Direction

- Duck: Mix fennel seeds, coriander seeds and peppercorns in small bowl. Use a paring knife to prick duck leg's skins all over; generously season with salt. Sprinkle spice mixture on duck legs, pressing to adhere. In a crosshatch pattern, score fat of every duck breast, 1/2-in. apart. Use salt to season all over. Divide breasts and legs to 2 big rimmed baking sheets; chill for 3 days, uncovered/sit for 1 hour in room temperature.
- 1 hour before braising, sit duck legs in room temperature if chilled.
- In lower oven third, put rack; preheat it to 300°F. Heat oil in a big wide Dutch oven/other heavy pot on medium heat; cook leeks for 8-10 minutes till browned around edges and soft, occasionally mixing. Add bay leaves, garlic and thyme sprigs; cook for 2 minutes till garlic is slightly soft and fragrant, occasionally mixing. Add wine; boil. Simmer for 5 minutes till reduced by half.
- Take off heat; slip duck legs into liquid, skin side down. It might overlap a lot, depending on pan's size; that is fine. To reach 3/4 of way up legs, add water. Cover pot; braise duck legs for 1 1/2-2 hours in oven till submerged in the duck's fat.
- Flip duck legs to skin side up; braise for 1 1/2-2 hours till bones easily wiggle in joints and tender, covered. Cool in braising liquid. Chill for 2 hours till fat solidifies and rises to surface.
- Relish and assembly: Cook bay leaves, red pepper flakes, mustard, sugar, cognac, figs and clementines in medium saucepan on medium heat for 10-15 minutes till it is syrupy and figs absorb some liquid, mixing occasionally to dissolve sugar. Cool; discard bay leaves. Mix in vinegar. Through fine mesh

sieve, strain 1/3 cup syrup into small bowl. To glaze duck, put aside. Put aside leftover relish for serving.
- Sit duck breasts for 1 hour till they're room temperature.
- Put 2 duck breasts in a big skillet, skin side down, on medium low heat; cook duck for 12-15 minutes till skin is crisp and golden brown. Occasionally pour extra fat from skillet into bowl; put aside. Flip duck; put heat on medium. Cook for 2 minutes on other side. Put onto cutting board. Wipe skillet out; let it cool. Repeat with leftover 2 breasts. You can cook all 4 breasts at the same time if you have 2 big skillets. 10 minutes before slicing, rest.
- Meanwhile, put rack in upper oven third; preheat it to 425°F. From braising liquid, remove duck legs; brush off fat/seeds clinging to surface. Put on wire rack, skin side up, inside foil-lined and rimmed baking sheet; brush reserved glaze lightly. Roast for 10-15 minutes till skin is crisp and golden brown.
- Serve the duck legs with reserved relish and sliced breasts.
- You can braise duck legs 2 days ahead, kept chilled.
- You can make relish 2 days ahead; separately cover relish and strained glaze and chill. Before using, bring to room temperature.

Nutrition Information

- Calories: 2393
- Total Carbohydrate: 40 g(13%)
- Cholesterol: 449 mg(150%)
- Protein: 78 g(156%)
- Total Fat: 198 g(305%)
- Saturated Fat: 65 g(327%)
- Sodium: 2021 mg(84%)
- Fiber: 3 g(12%)

77. Escargot With Garlic Parsley Butter

Serving: Serves 4 | Prep: | Ready in:

Ingredients

- 1 cup (2 sticks) European-style butter, room temperature
- 1 tablespoon dry white wine
- 1 1/2 teaspoons kosher salt
- 1/2 teaspoon freshly ground black pepper
- Pinch of ground nutmeg
- 12 garlic cloves, very finely chopped
- 1 large shallot, finely chopped
- 3/4 cup finely chopped parsley
- 24 large empty escargots shells
- 24 extra-large canned escargots, preferably from Burgundy

Direction

- Preheat an oven to 450°F. Beat butter with an electric mixer on medium in a medium bowl until the resulting mix is smooth. Switch off the motor and add nutmeg, pepper, salt and wine. Beat on medium until all contents are incorporated. Decease the speed to low and add parsley, shallot and garlic. Combine until incorporated. Place the butter into a resealable plastic bag or a disposable pastry bag and then snip off the end (or one corner in case of using plastic bag).
- Transfer the shells in a shallow 2-quart baking dish in a single layer and then pipe approximately two teaspoons of garlic-parsley butter into each. Then tuck a snail into every shell, and pipe in extra garlic-parsley butter to fill the shell and mound all over the top. Bake for 10 to 15 minutes until the garlic in butter no longer tastes raw and the snails are sizzling.
- Shells may be filled a day in advance. Put cover and refrigerate. Let come to room temperature prior to baking.

Nutrition Information

- Calories: 1206
- Fiber: 1 g(5%)
- Total Carbohydrate: 40 g(13%)
- Cholesterol: 122 mg(41%)
- Protein: 3 g(5%)
- Total Fat: 46 g(71%)
- Saturated Fat: 29 g(146%)
- Sodium: 722 mg(30%)

78. Farfalle With Forest Mushrooms, Peas, And Parsley

Serving: Makes 12 servings | Prep: | Ready in:

Ingredients

- 1/4 cup (1/2 stick) butter
- 4 large garlic cloves, minced
- 3 shallots, chopped
- 12 ounces shiitake mushrooms, stemmed, quartered
- 12 ounces crimini mushrooms, quartered
- 12 ounces chanterelle or crimini mushrooms, quartered
- 1 1/4 cups dry white wine
- 1 1/2 cups whipping cream
- 2 cups frozen peas
- 2/3 cup chopped fresh parsley
- 1 1/4 pounds farfalle (bow-tie pasta)

Direction

- Melt butter on medium-high heat in a big, deep skillet. Add shallots and garlic and sauté for a minute. Add cremini and shiitake mushrooms then sauté for 5 minutes. Place in chanterelles then sauté for about 5 minutes more until all the mushrooms become tender. Add wine then boil for about 5 minutes until it reduces to half. Add cream then simmer until liquid reduces to a consistency of sauce for about 5 minutes, occasionally stirring. Mix in parsley and peas. Take off from heat. Season with pepper and salt. Cover to retain warmth.
- In the meantime, cook pasta in a big pot of salted boiling water until tender yet firm to chew, occasionally stirring. Drain, keep a cup of pasta cooking liquid. Put pasta back in the pot.
- Add mushroom sauce on pasta then toss until coated. Moisten using leftover pasta cooking liquid if needed.

Nutrition Information

- Calories: 363
- Total Carbohydrate: 47 g(16%)
- Cholesterol: 43 mg(14%)
- Protein: 11 g(21%)
- Total Fat: 14 g(22%)
- Saturated Fat: 8 g(42%)
- Sodium: 48 mg(2%)
- Fiber: 4 g(17%)

79. Fish Fillets With Grapefruit Tarragon Beurre Blanc

Serving: Serves 4 | Prep: | Ready in:

Ingredients

- 1/4 cup minced shallot
- four 6- to 8-ounce white fish fillets such as red snapper or scrod
- 1/4 cup plus 2 tablespoons dry white wine
- 1/4 cup plus 2 tablespoons bottled clam juice
- 2/3 cup fresh grapefruit juice
- 1/4 cup heavy cream
- 3/4 stick (6 tablespoons) cold unsalted butter, cut into bits
- 2 teaspoons minced fresh tarragon leaves or 1/4 teaspoon crumbled dried, or to taste
- fresh grapefruit sections as an accompaniment

Direction

- Scatter shallot in a shallow baking dish that's greased with butter, just big enough to accommodate fish fillets in single pile, place fillets, skin sides facing down, on shallot, and add clam juice and wine on top. Scatter pepper and salt to taste on fillets and bake for 10 to 12 minutes, buttered wax paper piece as cover, in the center of prepped 425°F. oven, or till they are barely cooked completely. Turn fillets onto platter using slotted spatula and cover to retain their warmth.
- Use a fine sieve to drain the cooking liquid right into small saucepan, pour in grapefruit juice, and boil mixture till cooked down to roughly 2/3 cup. Put in cream and let mixture boil till cooled down by 1/2. Lower heat to low and mix butter in, a bit at one time, lift pan from heat from time to time to cool mixture and put in another bit of butter before the prior one has iquefied fully. Sauce must not get hot enough to iquefied. It should have the consistency of thin hollandaise. Mix in pepper and salt to taste and tarragon. Turn every fillet onto plate, skin side facing down, using slotted spatula. Top every fillet with 1/4 of sauce and place some of sections of grapefruit around every plate.

Nutrition Information

- Calories: 4337
- Saturated Fat: 21 g(105%)
- Sodium: 2843 mg(118%)
- Fiber: 0 g(2%)
- Total Carbohydrate: 7 g(2%)
- Cholesterol: 2209 mg(736%)
- Protein: 890 g(1780%)
- Total Fat: 56 g(87%)

80. Fish Fillets With Olives And Oregano

Serving: Makes 4 main-course servings | Prep: 15mins | Ready in:

Ingredients

- 4 (1 1/4-inch-thick) pieces white-fleshed skinless fish fillets, such as halibut (6 oz each)
- 1 teaspoon salt
- 1/4 teaspoon black pepper
- 3 tablespoons extra-virgin olive oil
- 4 very thin lemon slices
- 1/2 cup dry white wine
- 1/3 cup pitted brine-cured green olives such as picholine, halved lengthwise (2 oz)
- 1 to 1 1/2 teaspoons fresh lemon juice
- 2 tablespoons finely chopped fresh oregano or 3/4 teaspoon dried oregano, crumbled
- a 2 1/2-qt shallow ceramic or glass baking dish

Direction

- Place rack of oven in top third of the oven and preheat to 450°F.
- Blot fish dry and scatter with pepper and salt. In a heavy, 12-inch skillet, heat a tablespoon of oil on medium high heat till hot yet not smoking, then let fillets sear for 3 to 4 minutes, skinned sides facing down, till browned thoroughly. Turn onto baking dish, seared sides facing up, put the skillet aside, then put a lemon slice on top of every fillet.
- Pour wine into skillet and boil, scratching up brown bits. Let boil for half a minute, then add around the fish. Spread olives around the fish and bake for 8 to 12 minutes, with no cover, till fish is just cooked completely.
- Turn the fish onto platter, then mix into the cooking liquid in the baking dish with oregano, leftover 2 tablespoons of oil and lemon juice. Add pepper and salt to season sauce and scoop on top of fish.

Nutrition Information

- Calories: 297
- Cholesterol: 83 mg(28%)
- Protein: 32 g(65%)
- Total Fat: 15 g(23%)
- Saturated Fat: 2 g(11%)
- Sodium: 573 mg(24%)
- Fiber: 3 g(10%)
- Total Carbohydrate: 6 g(2%)

81. Fish Soup With Aïoli Croutons

Serving: Makes 6 to 8 servings | Prep: | Ready in:

Ingredients

- 3/4 cup mayonnaise
- 2 teaspoons Dijon mustard
- 2 teaspoons red wine vinegar
- 2 garlic cloves, minced
- 3/4 teaspoon hot pepper sauce
- 6 tablespoons olive oil
- 4 leeks (white and pale green parts only), sliced
- 2 carrots, cut into 1/2-inch pieces
- 1 fennel bulb, cut into 1/2-inch pieces
- 2 shallots, chopped
- 6 large garlic cloves, chopped
- 2 plum tomatoes, coarsely chopped
- 2 tablespoons tomato paste
- 1/2 teaspoon dried thyme
- 1/4 teaspoon saffron threads
- 1 1/2 cups dry white wine
- 5 cups (or more) chicken stock or canned low-salt chicken broth
- 3 pounds assorted fish fillets (such as sea bass, snapper, and orange roughy), cut into 2-inch pieces
- 1 French bread baguette, cut into 1/3-inch-thick slices, toasted
- Chopped fresh parsley

Direction

- In small bowl, mix the 3 tablespoons of oil and initial 5 ingredients to incorporate. Season with pepper and salt to taste. Aioli may be done a day in advance. Refrigerate with cover.
- In big, heavy pot, heat leftover 3 tablespoons of oil on moderate heat. Put in shallots, fennel, carrots and leeks; sauté for 15 minutes, till golden brown. Put in and sauté garlic for 2 minutes. Stir in saffron, thyme, tomato paste and tomatoes. Pour in wine and let boil for 5 minutes. Put in 5 cups of stock and boil. Lower the heat and let simmer to meld flavors for 15 minutes. Put in fish and simmer for 5 minutes, till fish is cooked completely. Cool partially.
- Use blender to puree soup in batches. Filter soup in batches using a coarse sieve place above a big bowl, forcing hard to pass as much solids as can be through the sieve. Put soup back to pot. Season with pepper and salt to taste. May be done a day in advance. Refrigerate with cover.
- Smear sufficient aioli on top of every toast to cover. Simmer soup, thin with additional stock, if wished. Scoop soup to bowls. Put 2 toasts on top of each. Scatter parsley over to serve.

Nutrition Information

- Calories: 865
- Saturated Fat: 8 g(38%)
- Sodium: 1001 mg(42%)
- Fiber: 5 g(21%)
- Total Carbohydrate: 54 g(18%)
- Cholesterol: 131 mg(44%)
- Protein: 59 g(118%)
- Total Fat: 44 g(67%)

82. Fish Stock

Serving: 12 | Prep: | Ready in:

Ingredients

- 3 pounds white fish heads and bones
- 2 cups dry white wine
- 2 onions, chopped
- 2 leeks, white parts only, cleaned and chopped
- 2 stalks celery, chopped
- 2 cloves garlic, crushed
- 4 sprigs fresh parsley
- 3 sprigs fresh thyme, or ½ teaspoon dried
- 1 bay leaf

Direction

- With cold water, wash fish bones. Put in non-aluminum stockpot along with bay leaf, thyme, parsley, garlic, celery, leeks, onions and wine. Put in sufficient cold water, approximately 3 1/2 quarts, to soak. Let come barely to boil. Lower heat to low, scoop off any froth and let simmer for 30 to 35 minutes with no cover, scooping off from time to time.
- Strain stock through a fine sieve.

Nutrition Information

83. Fish In Foil With Sweet Onions, Tomatoes, And Mojo Verde

Serving: Makes 4 servings | Prep: | Ready in:

Ingredients

- 3 tablespoons pure olive oil
- 2 tablespoons unsalted butter
- 2 medium red onions, sliced
- Kosher salt and freshly ground black pepper to taste
- 1 pound medium red potatoes, scrubbed and cut into 1/4-inch-thick slices
- One 4-pound snapper, gutted, scaled, and pectoral gill cut out (but tail left on; ask your fishmonger to do this)
- 1/4 cup Mojo Verde, plus extra for serving if desired
- 1 pound ripe tomatoes, sliced
- 1/4 cup dry white wine
- Lemon wedges for garnish

Direction

- Preheat oven to 400 degrees.
- Heat 1 tbsp. olive oil and butter in a big sauté pan on medium high heat. When butter foams, add onions, mixing to coat, then season with pepper and salt. Cook, occasionally stirring, for 8-12 minutes, until golden. Cool.
- Stack two aluminum foil pieces big enough to wrap fish on top of each other. Fold foil sides up to resemble a small boat. Pour in remaining 2 tbsp. olive oil in boat. Spread it on the bottom. Lay potatoes in one layer in the boat. Season with pepper and salt.
- Make slashes with a sharp knife on a fish side, 1 1/2-in. apart, going near the bone. Season with pepper and salt. Repeat process to other fish side. Lay it on potatoes. Spoon mojo verde on fish. Lay tomatoes on it. Spoon remaining mojo on them. Spoon caramelized onions on them. Pour wine around fish.
- Enclose fish by folding the foil over. Crimp the edges to seal it. Put on a baking sheet.
- Roast fish until cooked through for 1 hour. Open foil carefully to check, it should easily flake when tested using a fork. Depending on the thickness and kind of fish you use, cooking times vary significantly. You can keep baked fish warm for up to 30 minutes and retain moisture if it's still wrapped.
- Serve along with lemon wedges and extra mojo verse on the side if you want.
- A wine with soft acidity and sweetness such as Vouvray or American Pinot Blanc is recommended.
- Grilling: Burn a big amount of coals until they become white. "Bank" them to a side for indirect heat. Put foil-wrapped fish onto the other side. Add the fish as soon as the coals become white or they'll burn out before you finish cooking the fish. Cover the grill but leave bottom and top air vents open. While coats burn down, you can spread coals out to

offer even heat then replace cover quickly. The time it takes to cook vary a lot, so an instant-read thermometer is good. Cook fish until internal temperature is 130 degrees F.

Nutrition Information

- Calories: 729
- Sodium: 1777 mg(74%)
- Fiber: 5 g(19%)
- Total Carbohydrate: 29 g(10%)
- Cholesterol: 183 mg(61%)
- Protein: 97 g(194%)
- Total Fat: 22 g(35%)
- Saturated Fat: 6 g(32%)

84. Fontina Risotto Cakes With Fresh Chives

Serving: Makes 10 servings | Prep: | Ready in:

Ingredients

- 3 cups (about) low-salt chicken broth
- 2 tablespoons olive oil
- 1/2 cup finely chopped onion
- 1 cup plus 2 tablespoons arborio rice
- 1/4 cup dry white wine
- 6 tablespoons grated Parmesan cheese
- 2 tablespoons (1/4 stick) butter
- 1 1/2 cups panko (Japanese breadcrumbs), divided
- 1/2 cup (packed) coarsely grated Fontina cheese (about 2 ounces)
- 1/4 cup chopped fresh parsley
- 3 tablespoons chopped fresh chives
- 1 large egg yolk
- 2 large eggs
- Canola oil (for frying)
- Additional grated Parmesan cheese
- Fresh chives

Direction

- In small saucepan, simmer 3 cups of broth. Lower the heat to extremely low; cover to retain warmth. In medium, heavy saucepan, heat the olive oil on moderate heat. Put in onion; sauté for 5 minutes, till clear. Put in rice; mix for a minute. Pour in wine; mix for 30 seconds, till soaked in. Pour in broth, a third of a cup at one time, and simmer for 18 minutes, till risotto becomes creamy and rice is barely tender, letting the broth be soaked in before putting in additional, and mixing frequently. Take off heat. Stir in butter and 6 tablespoons of Parmesan. Season liberally with pepper and salt. Scatter risotto in a pan, 13x9x2-inch in size and cool fully.
- Stir into risotto with an egg yolk, chopped chives, parsley, Fontina cheese and half cup of panko. Form to balls, 1 1/4-inch in size; flatten to make 2-inches rounds. Place on a rimmed baking sheet. May be done 2 days in advance. Chill with cover.
- Preheat the oven to 250°F. Place one more rimmed baking sheet in the oven. Whip in shallow bowl with 2 eggs to incorporate. Put a cup of panko in a separate shallow bowl. Dunk risotto cakes in beaten egg, then dip in panko till coated. Into a big skillet, add sufficient canola oil to cover the base; heat the oil on moderately-high heat. Sauté risotto cakes in batches for 2 1/2 minutes on each side till brown and crisp. Turn onto baking sheet in oven.
- Sprinkle risotto cakes with cheese and garnish using chives to serve.

Nutrition Information

85. Franks And Beans

Serving: Makes 4 servings | Prep: | Ready in:

Ingredients

- 3 tablespoons olive oil, divided
- 1 medium onion, chopped
- 6 garlic cloves, smashed
- 1 1/2 pounds sweet Italian sausage links (about 6), divided
- 2 15-ounce cans cannellini (white kidney) beans, rinsed
- 1 cup dry white wine
- 10 flat-leaf parsley stems
- 10 sprigs thyme
- 2 bay leaves
- 2 cups low-sodium chicken broth
- 1 tablespoon unsalted butter
- 3 tablespoons chopped fresh herbs (such as oregano, flat-leaf parsley, and tarragon), divided
- Kosher salt, freshly ground pepper

Direction

- Heat 2 tbsp. oil on medium heat in a big heavy pot. Add garlic and onion; cook for 5-8 minutes till soft, occasionally mixing. Remove casings from 2 sausages; discard. Put sausages in pot; cook for 5 minutes till onions and sausages are lightly browned, breaking up using a spoon.
- Put wine and beans in pot; cook for 8-10 minutes till wine reduces by half. Tie thyme and parsley into bundle using kitchen twine; put into pot with broth and bay leaves. Cook for 40-50 minutes on medium low heat, mixing often, partially covered. Discard bay leaves and bundle. Mix in 2 tbsp. chopped herbs and butter; season with pepper and salt.
- Meanwhile, heat leftover 1 tbsp. oil in a big skillet on medium heat after beans cook for 25 minutes; cook leftover sausages for 15-20 minutes till cooked through and browned, occasionally turning. Cut.
- Divide bean mixture to bowls; put leftover 1 tbsp. chopped herbs and sausage slices over.

Nutrition Information

- Calories: 625
- Saturated Fat: 9 g(47%)
- Sodium: 1644 mg(69%)
- Fiber: 11 g(44%)
- Total Carbohydrate: 43 g(14%)
- Cholesterol: 59 mg(20%)
- Protein: 42 g(85%)
- Total Fat: 30 g(46%)

86. French Potato Salad

Serving: 5 | Prep: 15mins | Ready in:

Ingredients

- 9 potatoes
- 1/2 cup vegetable oil
- 1/4 cup tarragon vinegar
- 1/4 cup beef consomme
- 1/4 cup chopped green onions
- 2 tablespoons chopped fresh parsley
- 1 teaspoon salt
- 1 teaspoon ground black pepper

Direction

- Boil salted water in a big pot; put in potatoes. Cook for about 15mins until the potatoes are tender but still firm; drain. Place potatoes in a big bowl and allow them to cool for a bit. Skin and cut potatoes onto a big bowl.
- Mix pepper, oil, salt, vinegar, parsley, green onion, and consommé together in a small bowl.
- Toss dressing and warm potatoes together; cover. Chill for a few hours to overnight.

Nutrition Information

- Calories: 500 calories;
- Cholesterol: 1
- Protein: 9.3
- Total Fat: 22.4
- Sodium: 1474
- Total Carbohydrate: 68

87. Garlic Cheese Fondue

Serving: Serves 8 to 10 | Prep: | Ready in:

Ingredients

- 1 pound Swiss cheese, grated
- 1/2 Gruyère cheese, grated
- 3 tablespoons all purpose flour
- 1 teaspoon ground nutmeg
- 1/2 teaspoon ground white pepper
- 1 1/4 cups (about) dry white wine
- 3 large garlic cloves, minced
- 1 1-pound crusty French bread or sourdough bread, cut into 1 1/2-inch cubes

Direction

- Mix in big bowl white pepper, nutmeg, flour and both cheeses; toss till coated. In a big, heavy saucepan, simmer garlic and a cup of wine on low heat. Put in mixture of cheese by handfuls, mixing till smooth and melted after every increment. Stir in additional tablespoonfuls of wine in order to attain the preferred consistency. Turn onto pot of fondue.
- Place fondue above canned heat or candle. Serve fondue along with bread.

Nutrition Information

- Calories: 411
- Saturated Fat: 11 g(54%)
- Sodium: 395 mg(16%)
- Fiber: 1 g(6%)
- Total Carbohydrate: 36 g(12%)
- Cholesterol: 54 mg(18%)
- Protein: 22 g(45%)
- Total Fat: 18 g(27%)

88. Garlic Orange Pork Chops

Serving: Serves 2 | Prep: | Ready in:

Ingredients

- four 1/2-inch-thick pork chops
- 1 tablespoon vegetable oil
- 1 large garlic clove, minced
- 1/2 cup fresh orange juice
- 1/4 cup dry white wine
- 1 to 2 tablespoons fresh lemon juice

Direction

- Pat the pork dry. Add salt and pepper over pork to season. Place a skillet over moderately high heat. Heat the oil until hot but not smoking. Place the chops in the hot oil and brown until golden. Add lemon juice, wine, orange juice, and garlic. Simmer for 10 to 15 minutes, partially covered, until the pork is tender.

Nutrition Information

- Calories: 787
- Saturated Fat: 12 g(62%)
- Sodium: 221 mg(9%)
- Fiber: 0 g(1%)
- Total Carbohydrate: 8 g(3%)
- Cholesterol: 275 mg(92%)
- Protein: 83 g(166%)
- Total Fat: 43 g(66%)

89. Garlic Roasted Chicken Breasts

Serving: Makes 4 (main course) servings | Prep: 15mins | Ready in:

Ingredients

- 3 large garlic cloves
- 1 teaspoon dried oregano

- Scant 1/2 teaspoon dried hot red-pepper flakes
- 2 tablespoons extra-virgin olive oil
- 4 chicken breast halves with skin and bone (2 to 2 1/4 lb total)

Direction

- Preheat an oven with rack on upper third to 500°F.
- Mince and mash 1/2 tsp. salt and garlic to a paste; put into bowl. Mix in 1/2 tsp. pepper, 1/2 tsp. salt, oil, red-pepper flakes and oregano.
- Horizontally cut a 2-in. long, 1 1/2-in. deep pocket on side of every breast half; in each pocket, spread 1/2 tsp. garlic mixture. Coat chicken in leftover garlic mixture.
- Roast chicken in foil-lined big shallow baking pan, skin sides up, for 20-25 minutes till just cooked through.

Nutrition Information

- Calories: 216
- Total Carbohydrate: 2 g(1%)
- Cholesterol: 56 mg(19%)
- Protein: 18 g(37%)
- Total Fat: 15 g(23%)
- Saturated Fat: 3 g(16%)
- Sodium: 56 mg(2%)
- Fiber: 0 g(1%)

90. Garlic And Herb Braised Squid

Serving: Makes 6 servings | Prep: 15mins | Ready in:

Ingredients

- 1 1/2 pounds cleaned squid
- 2 cups flat-leaf parsley sprigs, divided
- 5 garlic cloves
- 3 tablespoons olive oil
- 1/4 teaspoon hot red-pepper flakes
- 3/4 cup Chardonnay
- 1 (28-ounce) can whole tomatoes in juice, coarsely chopped
- 1/4 cup water
- Accompaniment: crusty bread

Direction

- Rinse squid in cold water. Pat dry. Cut big tentacles to half, lengthwise. Cut bodies and flaps, if they're there, to 1/2-inch- wide rings, crosswise.
- Chop parsley to get 2 tbsp. Put aside. Chop leftover garlic and parsley together. In a 4-quart heavy pot, heat oil over low heat until hot. Cook red pepper flakes and garlic-parsley mixture for about 2 minutes, mixing, until garlic starts to sizzle. Bring heat up to medium-high, add the squid, for about 1 minute, cook and stir occasionally until it is barely opaque. Put the wine, simmering briskly and occasionally stirring, uncovered, for about 10 minutes until it reduces slightly. With their juice add tomatoes, 1/2 tsp. pepper, 1 1/4 teaspoons salt, and water. Simmer, occasionally stirring, covered, for 30-40 minutes until squid is very tender.
- Season with extra pepper and salt. Stir in leftover parsley.

Nutrition Information

- Calories: 221
- Sodium: 216 mg(9%)
- Fiber: 3 g(13%)
- Total Carbohydrate: 11 g(4%)
- Cholesterol: 264 mg(88%)
- Protein: 19 g(39%)
- Total Fat: 9 g(14%)
- Saturated Fat: 1 g(7%)

91. Garlicky Black Pepper Shrimp And Black Eyed Peas

Serving: Makes 6 servings | Prep: 25mins | Ready in:

Ingredients

- 4 bacon slices
- 4 scallions, chopped
- 1 medium carrot, finely chopped
- 1 celery rib, finely chopped
- 1/2 medium green bell pepper, chopped
- 2 large garlic cloves, finely chopped
- 2 Turkish bay leaves or 1 California
- 1 or 1 California
- 1 teaspoon dried thyme
- 1/8 teaspoon hot red-pepper flakes
- 2 (15-ounces) cans black-eyed peas, rinsed and drained
- 1 3/4 cups reduced-sodium chicken broth
- 3 tablespoons extra-virgin olive oil
- 1 pound large shrimp, peeled and deveined
- 3 large garlic cloves, finely chopped
- 1/2 cup dry white wine

Direction

- Prepare black-eyed peas: in a heavy 12-inch skillet, on moderate heat, let bacon cook till browned yet not crisp. Turn the bacon onto plate, then pull apart into small portions.
- In fat in the skillet, cook quarter teaspoon of pepper, 1/8 teaspoon of salt, red-pepper flakes, thyme, bay leaves, garlic, bell pepper, celery, carrot and scallions on moderate heat for 10 minutes, mixing from time to time, till vegetables turn light golden. Put in broth and black-eyed peas and let simmer for 5 minutes. Turn onto a bowl.
- Prepare shrimp: In skillet, heat the oil on moderately-high heat till it shimmers. Season the shrimp with half teaspoon of black pepper and quarter teaspoon of salt. Let shrimp cook along with garlic for 3 minutes, mixing from time to time, till barely opaque, shrimp will not cook completely. Put in wine and boil, then simmer briskly for 2 minutes. Put in mixture of black-eyed-pea and bacon and let simmer till barely heated completely, mixture will become juicy. Throw bay leaves.

Nutrition Information

- Calories: 333
- Sodium: 1144 mg(48%)
- Fiber: 6 g(23%)
- Total Carbohydrate: 25 g(8%)
- Cholesterol: 108 mg(36%)
- Protein: 21 g(42%)
- Total Fat: 16 g(24%)
- Saturated Fat: 4 g(19%)

92. Gemelli With Cheese And Quick Arrabbiata Sauce

Serving: Makes 4 servings | Prep: | Ready in:

Ingredients

- 1 pound gemelli or fusilli
- 3 tablespoons extra-virgin olive oil
- 2 large garlic cloves, finely chopped
- 1/4 teaspoon dried crushed red pepper
- 2 14 1/2-ounce cans petite diced tomatoes in juice
- 1/2 cup dry white wine
- 1 cup thinly sliced fresh basil
- 1 cup grated pecorino Romano cheese

Direction

- In big pot with salted boiling water, cook the pasta till tender yet remain firm to bite. Strain, put a third cup of cooking water aside.
- Meantime, in big skillet, heat the oil on moderately-high heat. Put in crushed red pepper and garlic and sauté for a minute. Put in tomatoes including juices and wine; boil. Boil for 8 minutes, till sauce is thick. Mix basil in. Season sauce with pepper and salt to taste.

- Put into sauce with half cup of cheese and pasta and toss for 3 minutes, till pasta is coated in sauce and cheese melts, putting in tablespoonfuls of reserved water to moisten if need be. Season pasta with pepper and salt to taste. Serve, separately passing the leftover half cup of cheese.

Nutrition Information

- Calories: 704
- Saturated Fat: 7 g(37%)
- Sodium: 808 mg(34%)
- Fiber: 6 g(22%)
- Total Carbohydrate: 95 g(32%)
- Cholesterol: 34 mg(11%)
- Protein: 27 g(55%)
- Total Fat: 21 g(32%)

93. Gemelli With Zucchini, Tomatoes, And Bacon

Serving: Makes 6 servings | Prep: | Ready in:

Ingredients

- 12 bacon slices, cut crosswise into 1-inch pieces
- 1 large red onion, chopped (about 2 cups)
- 1 1/2 cups dry white wine
- 12 ounces gemelli or rotini (about 3 cups)
- 3 slender zucchini, halved lengthwise and sliced crosswise into 1/2-inch-wide pieces
- 3 large plum tomatoes, seeded, coarsely chopped (about 1 1/2 cups)
- 1/3 cup chopped fresh oregano
- 1 cup crumbled soft fresh goat cheese (about 4 ounces)

Direction

- In big, heavy skillet, cook the bacon on moderately-high heat till crisp and brown. Turn onto paper towels with slotted spoon to let drain. Drain all except 3 tablespoons of skillet drippings. Put in and sauté onion for 3 minutes, till soft. Pour in wine; boil for 3 minutes, till cooked down by 1/3.
- Meantime, in big pot with salted boiling water, cook pasta till partially underdone. Put in zucchini and boil till zucchini is tender-crisp and pasta is tender yet firm to bite, mixing from time to time, for an additional of 2 minutes. Strain.
- Put to onion in skillet with oregano, tomatoes, bacon, zucchini and pasta. Toss on moderately-high heat for 3 minutes, till pasta is coated in sauce. Put in cheese and toss for 2 minutes, till starting to melt. Season with pepper and salt to taste and serve.
- Tip: halve tomato horizontally and slowly press out seeds to seed a plum tomato, you may use a spoon if need be.

Nutrition Information

- Calories: 571
- Sodium: 476 mg(20%)
- Fiber: 7 g(26%)
- Total Carbohydrate: 55 g(18%)
- Cholesterol: 46 mg(15%)
- Protein: 20 g(40%)
- Total Fat: 28 g(43%)
- Saturated Fat: 11 g(53%)

94. Gingered Beet Risotto

Serving: Serves 4 | Prep: | Ready in:

Ingredients

- 2 pounds beets with greens, beets scrubbed and trimmed, leaving about 1 inch of stems attached and reserving greens
- 3 cups water
- 1 small onion, chopped (about 1/2 cup)
- 1 tablespoon minced peeled fresh gingerroot
- 3 large garlic cloves, minced

- 3 tablespoons unsalted butter
- 1 cup Arborio* or long-grain rice
- 1/2 cup dry white wine
- 1/2 cup freshly grated Parmesan (about 2 ounces), or to taste
- *available at specialty foods shops

Direction

- Preheat the oven to 450°F.
- Use foil to tightly encase beets and roast for 1 1/2 hours in the center of the oven till tender. Cautiously remove beets wrap and rest till cool enough to hold. Throw the stems and remove the beets peel. Purée a cup of water and 1/2 of beets in blender and turn onto saucepan, mixing in leftover 2 cups of water to create beet broth.
- Thoroughly rinse beet greens and strain. Take and get rid of stems from leaves. Chop sufficient leaves to have 2 1/2 cups and chop the rest of the beets.
- Simmer beet broth and retain warmth.
- Cook gingerroot, garlic and onion in butter in a heavy, big saucepan on medium heat, mixing, till onion softens. Mix rice in and cook for a minute, mixing continuously. Pour in wine and cook, mixing, till soaked in. Keep simmering and putting in beet broth, approximately half cup at one time, mixing continuously and allowing every increment to be soaked in before putting in the next, till roughly 1/2 of broth has already been put in. Mix in chopped beet leaves and beets and keep simmering and putting in broth in exactly the same manner for 18 minutes, till rice is tender yet remain al dente. Mix in pepper and salt to taste and quarter cup of Parmesan.
- Sprinkle leftover Parmesan on risotto to serve.

Nutrition Information

- Calories: 426
- Cholesterol: 33 mg(11%)
- Protein: 13 g(25%)
- Total Fat: 13 g(20%)
- Saturated Fat: 8 g(40%)
- Sodium: 385 mg(16%)
- Fiber: 7 g(29%)
- Total Carbohydrate: 62 g(21%)

95. Glazed Sea Bass With Ginger Butter Sauce

Serving: Serves 4 | Prep: | Ready in:

Ingredients

- 1 cup dry white wine
- 1/3 cup chopped shallots
- 1/3 cup thinly sliced fresh ginger
- 1/2 cup whipping cream
- 6 tablespoons soy sauce
- 3 tablespoons honey
- 3 teaspoons rice vinegar
- 1 1/2 tablespoons cold water
- 1 1/2 teaspoons cornstarch
- 4 6- to 7-ounce sea bass fillets
- 4 tablespoons chilled butter, cut into small pieces

Direction

- Preparing the sauce: In a heavy small saucepan, mix together the ginger, shallots and wine on high heat. Let it boil for about 5 minutes, until the liquid reduces to 1/4 cup. Put in cream and let it boil for about 3 minutes, until the liquid has been reduced to half. Take it out of the heat.
- Preparing the fish: In a separate heavy small saucepan, combine the rice vinegar, honey, and soy sauce. In a small bowl, combine the cornstarch and water until it becomes smooth, then add to the soy sauce mixture. Mix the mixture on medium heat for about 2 minutes, until the glaze becomes a bit thick and boils. Take it out of the heat. Allow the glaze to cool to room temperature. The glaze and sauce can be made a day in advance with separate cover and chilled in the fridge.

- Set an oven to preheat to 350 degrees F. On a small baking tray, lay out the fish, then brush it using some of the glaze. Let it bake for about 15 minutes, until it becomes opaque in the middle, then take it out of the oven. Boil the leftover glaze. Scoop the glaze on top of the fish.
- In the meantime, simmer the sauce. Take it out of the heat and slowly add butter into the sauce and whisk just until it melts. Strain. Sprinkle with pepper and salt to season.
- Scoop the sauce on 4 plates and split it evenly. Put the fish on top, then serve.

Nutrition Information

- Calories: 479
- Sodium: 1461 mg(61%)
- Fiber: 1 g(3%)
- Total Carbohydrate: 21 g(7%)
- Cholesterol: 139 mg(46%)
- Protein: 37 g(74%)
- Total Fat: 25 g(38%)
- Saturated Fat: 14 g(70%)

96. Gratin Of Potatoes With White Cheddar And Tarragon

Serving: Makes 8 servings | Prep: | Ready in:

Ingredients

- 3 pounds Yukon Gold potatoes, peeled, cut into 1/8-inch-thick rounds
- 2 teaspoons salt
- 1 teaspoon ground black pepper
- 2 1/2 teaspoons dried tarragon
- 1 1/2 cups (packed) grated sharp white cheddar cheese (about 6 ounces)
- 1 cup whipping cream
- 1 cup dry white wine

Direction

- Preheat an oven to 400°F then butter a 13x9x2-in. glass baking dish. In a prepped dish, layer 1/3 potatoes, slightly overlapping; sprinkle with 1/3 pepper and 1/3 salt. Sprinkle with 1/3 cheese then 1/3 tarragon; repeat the layers twice more with leftover cheese, tarragon, pepper, salt and potatoes.
- Whisk wine and cream to blend in a medium bowl; put on potatoes. Bake for 1 hour till potatoes are tender when knife pierced it and top is golden, uncovered; stand gratin for 5 minutes. Serve.

Nutrition Information

- Calories: 321
- Total Fat: 17 g(26%)
- Saturated Fat: 10 g(50%)
- Sodium: 558 mg(23%)
- Fiber: 4 g(15%)
- Total Carbohydrate: 32 g(11%)
- Cholesterol: 55 mg(18%)
- Protein: 9 g(19%)

97. Greek Style Shrimp

Serving: 2 servings; can be doubled or tripled | Prep: | Ready in:

Ingredients

- 3 tablespoons olive oil
- 1 small onion, chopped
- 1 28-ounce can Italian plum tomatoes, drained, chopped
- 1/3 cup dry white wine
- 1 teaspoon dried oregano, crumbled
- 3/4 pound uncooked medium shrimp, peeled, deveined
- Salt and freshly ground pepper
- Feta and Mint Rice

Direction

- In big, heavy skillet, heat the oil on moderate heat. Put in and sauté onion for 8 minutes, till clear. Put in wine, oregano and tomatoes. Simmer for 5 minutes, till thick, mixing from time to time. Put in shrimp and mix for 3 minutes, till opaque. Add pepper and salt to season. Serve along with rice.

Nutrition Information

98. Green Grape Sangria

Serving: Makes 2 quarts | Prep: 15mins | Ready in:

Ingredients

- 1 pound green grapes
- 2 small Granny Smith apples, coarsely chopped
- 1/4 cup packed mint leaves
- 3/4 to 1 cup sugar (to taste)
- 1 (500-mg) vitamin C tablet, crushed to a powder with back of
- a spoon (see cooks' note, below)
- 2 bottles dry white wine (preferably Albariño or Pinot Grigio)

Direction

- Use a blender to puree two batches of 2 cups of wine, vitamin C, sugar, mint, apples and grapes until smooth. In a bowl, strain mixture with a fine-mesh sieve while pushing down on solids. Pour puree in a pitcher and add in left wine. Chill for 2 hours while covered. Serve with ice.

Nutrition Information

99. Greens And Beans With Fried Bread

Serving: 2 servings | Prep: | Ready in:

Ingredients

- 1/2 cup dry white wine
- 2 garlic cloves, thinly sliced
- 2 tsp. finely chopped oregano
- 3/4 tsp. kosher salt
- 1/4 tsp. crushed red pepper flakes
- 1 bunch Tuscan kale, ribs and stems removed
- 1 (15.5-oz.) can white beans (such as butter or cannellini), rinsed
- 1/2 cup plus 2 Tbsp. extra-virgin olive oil; plus more for serving
- 2 (1"-thick) slices crusty bread
- White wine vinegar (for serving)

Direction

- In a big skillet, boil quarter cup water, red pepper flakes, salt, oregano, garlic and wine. Put in kale, place pan cover, in case a large lid isn't available, use a baking sheet, and cook for 4 minutes, mixing from time to time, till greens wilt. Stir in half cup of oil and beans and cook for 2 minutes, with no cover, till beans are warmed completely.
- Meantime, in a separate big skillet, heat 2 tablespoons of oil on moderate. Let bread fry for 2 minutes on each side in skillet till golden brown. Turn onto paper towels to let drain. You may cook bread first and retain its warmth in oven at low while you use same skillet to prepare beans and kale in case you do not have 2 big skillets.
- To serve, put on plates with fried bread and top with scoop mixture of kale and sauce, distributing equally. Sprinkle with vinegar and a bit of oil.

Nutrition Information

- Calories: 1012
- Total Fat: 70 g(108%)

- Saturated Fat: 10 g(49%)
- Sodium: 906 mg(38%)
- Fiber: 16 g(63%)
- Total Carbohydrate: 72 g(24%)
- Protein: 24 g(47%)

100. Grilled Cheese With Sauteed Mushrooms

Serving: Makes 32 hors d'oeuvres | Prep: 45mins | Ready in:

Ingredients

- 1 1/4 sticks (10 tablespoons) unsalted butter
- 1 pound cremini mushrooms, trimmed and chopped
- 1/2 teaspoon salt
- 1/4 teaspoon black pepper
- 1/3 cup dry white wine
- 1/2 pound chilled Italian Fontina, rind discarded and cheese coarsely grated (2 cups)
- 2 tablespoons finely chopped fresh flat-leaf parsley
- 16 very thin slices firm white sandwich bread
- About 1/2 teaspoon white-truffle oil (optional)

Direction

- Over moderately high heat, heat two tablespoons of butter in 12-inch heavy nonstick skillet until the foam subsides. Cook the mushrooms along with pepper and salt while stirring often for about 8 minutes until the liquid from mushrooms has evaporated. Pour in wine and let boil while stirring often for about 5 minutes until the liquid has evaporated. Then cool the mushrooms for about 10 minutes to room temperature.
- In a bowl, mix the mushrooms with parsley and cheese.
- Separate the cheese mixture between eight slices of bread (scant half cup for each slice) and spread evenly. Add the remaining 8 slices on top.
- Over moderate heat, heat one tablespoon of butter in a clean skillet until the foam subsides. Cook two sandwiches for about 3 minutes without flipping over until the undersides turn brown. Place the sandwiches onto a cutting board. Then heat one tablespoon of butter in the skillet until the foam subsides. Place back the sandwiches into the skillet with the browned sides up. Let cook for about 3 more minutes until the undersides turn browned. Place back onto the cutting board when cooked. Create three more batches in the same way.
- Cut off the crusts and then slice each sandwich into four triangles. Add a drop of truffle oil (if using) on top of each triangle.

Nutrition Information

- Calories: 88
- Fiber: 0 g(2%)
- Total Carbohydrate: 4 g(1%)
- Cholesterol: 19 mg(6%)
- Protein: 3 g(7%)
- Total Fat: 6 g(10%)
- Saturated Fat: 4 g(20%)
- Sodium: 104 mg(4%)

101. Halibut With Capers, Olives, And Tomatoes

Serving: Makes 4 servings | Prep: | Ready in:

Ingredients

- 4 6- to 7-ounce halibut fillets
- All purpose flour
- 4 tablespoons olive oil, divided
- 2 large shallots, chopped
- 1/4 teaspoon dried crushed red pepper
- 4 plum tomatoes, seeded, chopped
- 1/2 cup chopped pitted Kalamata olives
- 1/2 cup chopped fresh basil, divided
- 1 tablespoon drained capers

- 1/3 cup bottled clam juice
- 1/4 cup dry white wine

Direction

- Scatter pepper and salt on fish. Dip in flour. In big, heavy skillet, heat 2 tablespoons of oil on moderately-high heat. Put in and sauté fish for 4 minutes on each side, till barely opaque in the middle and slightly browned. Turn the fish onto platter. In the same skillet, heat leftover 2 tablespoons of oil. Put in crushed red pepper and shallots; sauté for a minute. Stir in capers, quarter cup of basil, olives and tomatoes. Pour in wine and clam juice. Boil for 4 minutes, till sauce partially thickens. Stir quarter cup of basil in. Add pepper and salt to season the sauce. Scoop sauce on top of fish.

Nutrition Information

- Calories: 370
- Total Carbohydrate: 13 g(4%)
- Cholesterol: 90 mg(30%)
- Protein: 38 g(75%)
- Total Fat: 18 g(27%)
- Saturated Fat: 3 g(13%)
- Sodium: 421 mg(18%)
- Fiber: 3 g(11%)

102. Halibut With Spicy Sausage, Tomatoes, And Rosemary

Serving: 8 servings | Prep: | Ready in:

Ingredients

- 16 cherry and/or Sun Gold tomatoes, divided
- 6 garlic cloves, smashed, divided
- 2 sprigs rosemary, divided
- 8 ounces nduja, casing removed, crumbled, or Spanish-style chorizo, casings removed, thinly sliced, divided
- 3 pounds skinless halibut fillet, cut into 8 pieces, divided
- Kosher salt, freshly ground pepper
- 4 tablespoons dry white wine, divided
- 4 tablespoons olive oil, divided

Direction

- Preheat oven to 375°F/prep grill to medium heat. Tear 4 heavy-duty foil sheets to make 16x12-in. Put 2 sheets onto work surface. Put leftover foil sheet over each to make 2 double-layer packets. Divide nduja, rosemary, garlic and tomatoes to sheets, putting in middle. Generously season halibut with pepper and salt; put over. Drizzle oil and wine. Bring opposing foil edges together in middle; tightly crimp, pressing air out, to shut.
- Put foil packets directly onto grill grates/rimmed baking sheet for oven; cook for 14-16 minutes till halibut is opaque throughout and tomatoes start to burst. Rest for a few minutes at room temperature. Open carefully; put fish onto platter. Put cooking juices from packets and tomatoes over.
- You can assembly packets 1 day ahead, chilled.

Nutrition Information

- Calories: 446
- Sodium: 1147 mg(48%)
- Fiber: 1 g(2%)
- Total Carbohydrate: 33 g(11%)
- Cholesterol: 53 mg(18%)
- Protein: 27 g(54%)
- Total Fat: 38 g(58%)
- Saturated Fat: 10 g(50%)

103. Hazelnut, Sage, And Mushroom Stuffing

Serving: Makes 8 servings | Prep: 45mins | Ready in:

Ingredients

- 8 cups 1/2-inch cubes of firm white bread such as a Pullman loaf (1 pound)
- 1 1/2 cups finely chopped shallots (about 8 medium; 10 ounces)
- 1 1/2 sticks unsalted butter, divided
- 1 1/2 pounds cremini mushrooms, sliced 1/4 inch thick
- 1 1/2 cups finely chopped celery (from 3 ribs)
- 2 teaspoons chopped thyme
- 2 teaspoons finely chopped sage
- 1/2 cup dry white wine
- 2 cups hazelnuts (1/2 pound), toasted , any loose skins rubbed off in a kitchen towel, and coarsely chopped
- 1/2 cup finely chopped flat-leaf parsley
- 4 cups turkey stock , heated to liquefy if gelled, or reduced-sodium chicken broth
- 3 large eggs, lightly beaten
- Equipment: a 3-quart shallow ovenproof baking dish (2 to 3 inches deep)

Direction

- Preheat an oven with racks in lower and upper thirds to 400°F. Butter baking dish generously.
- In 1 layer, put bread in 2 big shallow baking pans; toast for 15 minutes till dry and golden, switching pan positions halfway through. Put in a big bowl. Leave the oven on.
- Meanwhile, cook shallots in a 12-in. heavy skillet with 1 stick butter on medium heat for 6 minutes till golden and soft, occasionally mixing. Add 1/2 tsp. salt, sage, thyme, celery and mushrooms; cook for 20-30 minutes till mushrooms are browned and mushroom's given off liquid evaporates, occasionally mixing.
- Add wine; deglaze skillet by boiling, mixing, and scraping brown bits for 2 minutes till wine reduces by half. Put bread in a bowl. Add parsley and hazelnuts; toss.
- Whisk 1/2 tsp. pepper, 1 tsp. salt, eggs and stock; mix into bread mixture. Put in a baking dish; dot stuffing's top using leftover 1/2 stick butter.
- Bake for 30 minutes in lower third of oven, covered loosely with a buttered foil sheet (buttered side down); remove foil, bake for 15 minutes more till top is browned.
- You can toast hazelnuts and bread cubes 2 days ahead, kept at room temperature in sealed bags. Stuffing, without stock and egg mixture and hazelnuts, can be assembled (but not baked) a day ahead; chilled, covered. Mix in stock mixture and nuts; continue with the recipe. You can bake stuffing 6 hours ahead, uncovered and chilled, till cool, then covered loosely. Reheat for 30 minutes till hot in a 400°F oven, covered.

Nutrition Information

- Calories: 713
- Saturated Fat: 16 g(81%)
- Sodium: 392 mg(16%)
- Fiber: 7 g(29%)
- Total Carbohydrate: 43 g(14%)
- Cholesterol: 168 mg(56%)
- Protein: 29 g(58%)
- Total Fat: 49 g(75%)

104. Herb Braised Ham

Serving: Makes 8 servings | Prep: 1.5hours | Ready in:

Ingredients

- 1 (11- to 13-pound) bone-in smoked pork shoulder (sometimes called picnic ham)
- 2 medium leeks (white and pale green parts only), chopped
- 1 large onion, chopped
- 3 medium carrots, cut into 1/2-inch cubes
- 2 celery ribs, cut into 1/2-inch cubes
- 2 garlic cloves, finely chopped
- 6 (5-inch) fresh thyme sprigs plus 2 tablespoons finely chopped leaves
- 6 fresh flat-leaf parsley stems plus 1/4 cup finely chopped leaves

- 1/4 whole nutmeg, smashed with side of a large heavy knife
- 1 teaspoon whole black peppercorns
- 4 whole cloves
- 5 tablespoons unsalted butter, softened
- 2 cups dry white wine
- 4 cups water
- 1/3 cup all-purpose flour
- a deep 10- to 20-quart pot (such as a stockpot, lobster pot, or canning pot); a wide 7-quart heavy ovenproof pot (if you have an 11-pound ham) or a wide 9- to 10-quart heavy ovenproof pot (if you have a 13-pound ham); an instant-read thermometer (preferably remote digital with probe)

Direction

- Place the ham in a deep 10-20-qt pot. Cover the ham with cold water (don't worry if the bone is sticking out). Bring the water to a boil; drain the ham.
- Place the oven rack in the lower third of the oven, removing the other racks. Set the oven to 350°F for preheating.
- In a bowl with cold water, rinse the leeks and drain them well. In a wide 7-10-qt heavy pot, cook the leeks, garlic, parsley stems, onion, peppercorns, cloves, carrots, thyme sprigs, nutmeg, and celery with 2 tbsp. of butter over moderately high heat for 10 minutes, stirring occasionally until the vegetables start to brown and softened. Add the wine and bring the mixture to a boil. Add the ham, skin-side down, and water (it shouldn't cover the ham). Bring the mixture back into a boil.
- Cover the pot with its lid tightly. Cover it with a heavy-duty foil if the ham sticks up over the top of the pot. Braise the ham inside the oven for 1 hour.
- Flip the ham, skin-side up. Braise the ham, covered, for another 1 hour (if the ham's label reads fully cooked) until the inserted thermometer into the center of the ham reads 120°F or for 2 hours (if the label reads partially cooked) until the thermometer registers 160°F.
- In the meantime, mash the remaining 3 tbsp. of butter and flour using the fork to make a beurre manié.
- Place the ham in a platter. Cover it loosely with a foil and allow it to stand for 45 minutes.
- While the ham stands, strain the braising liquid through a fine-mesh sieve into a 3-qt saucepan. Make sure to press and discard all the solids and to skim off any fat. Simmer the braising liquid. Mix in beurre manié, 1/2 tbsp. at a time until the sauce is lumpy. Simmer for 5 more minutes, stirring often until the sauce is slightly thickened and smooth. Remove the mixture from the heat. Mix in parsley and chopped thyme.
- Take the skin off the ham. Slice the meat and serve it together with the sauce.
- Note: The ham can be braised 2 days ahead. Just allow it to cool in braising liquid, uncovered, and then keep it chilled while covered. Before reheating the ham, skim off any fat from the braising liquid and heat it on top of the stove.

Nutrition Information

- Calories: 1354
- Saturated Fat: 36 g(182%)
- Sodium: 370 mg(15%)
- Fiber: 2 g(9%)
- Total Carbohydrate: 14 g(5%)
- Cholesterol: 381 mg(127%)
- Protein: 89 g(179%)
- Total Fat: 99 g(153%)

105. Herb Roasted Leg Of Lamb With Vegetables And Jus

Serving: Makes 8 to 10 servings | Prep: | Ready in:

Ingredients

- 4 medium onions, peeled (roots trimmed but still attached) and quartered

- 1 large stalk celery, quartered
- 6 large garlic cloves, lightly crushed and peeled
- 4 tablespoons extra-virgin olive oil
- 1 (7-pound) boneless leg of lamb, trimmed, rolled, and tied
- 1 teaspoon herbes de Provence
- 1 1/2 teaspoons kosher salt
- 1/2 teaspoon freshly ground black pepper
- 6 medium carrots, peeled and cut into 3-inch-long pieces
- 2 medium or 1 large celery root, peeled and cut into 1 1/2-inch chunks
- 1 1/2 cups dry white wine
- 1 1/2 cups low-sodium beef broth or chicken broth

Direction

- Preheat the oven to 400 °F.
- Mix celery, garlic cloves and onions in roasting pan. Sprinkle with a tablespoon of oil, toss thoroughly till coated, and pile in middle of the pan. Place lamb on top of mixture. Sprinkle with a tablespoon of oil and scatter salt, pepper and herbes de Provence over. Surround meat with celery root and carrots and sprinkle leftover 2 tablespoons of oil over. Add broth and wine to pan and use a heavy-duty foil to tightly cover the pan.
- Roast for an hour. Uncover and raise the heat to 425°F. Roast till inserted thermometer into chunkiest portion of lamb reads 130°F to get a medium-rare, for an additional of 15 minutes.
- Turn the lamb onto the carving board and tent using foil. Turn celery root, half of onions and carrots to medium size bowl and retain warmth. Use a medium-mesh strainer to press leftover contents of pan right into a medium size saucepan, forcing thoroughly on solids. Scoop off fat and throw. Or pass the juices from pan through strainer directly into a fat separator and rest till fat floats to surface, for a minute to two. Cautiously transfer the pan juices from separator to pan, throwing fat.
- Place the saucepan on medium heat and simmer. Cook for 10 minutes, with no cover, till cooked down by half. Season with pepper and salt to taste.
- Get rid of kitchen string from lamb and thinly slice meat crosswise to make pieces. Place on platter along with roasted vegetables. Serve while warm, along with jus on the side.

Nutrition Information

- Calories: 831
- Saturated Fat: 20 g(102%)
- Sodium: 775 mg(32%)
- Fiber: 5 g(18%)
- Total Carbohydrate: 23 g(8%)
- Cholesterol: 211 mg(70%)
- Protein: 61 g(122%)
- Total Fat: 52 g(80%)

106. Herb Rubbed Steaks With Olives Provencal

Serving: Makes 4 servings | Prep: | Ready in:

Ingredients

- 4 6-ounce beef tenderloin steaks (each about 1 inch thick)
- 2 tablespoons extra-virgin olive oil
- 3 bay leaves (2 finely crushed, 1 whole)
- 1/2 cup brine-cured olives (such as Kalamata)
- 1 cup dry white wine
- 3 tablespoons canned tomato puree

Direction

- Rub 1 tbsp. olive oil on tenderloin steaks; sprinkle crushed bay leaves. Put steaks in 1 layer in glass small baking dish; stand for 1-2 hours at room temperature. You can make it 1 day ahead. Cover; refrigerate.
- Boil a small saucepan of water on medium high heat. Add the olives; boil. Drain the olives.

- Scrape most bay leaves off the steaks; sprinkle pepper and salt on steaks. Heat leftover 1 tbsp. olive oil on medium high heat in big heavy skillet. Add steaks; sauté for 4 minutes each side for medium rare or to desired doneness. Put steaks onto plate. Put white wine in skillet; boil, scraping browned bits up. Put drained olives, whole bay leaf and tomato puree in skillet; cook for 5 minutes till sauce slightly thickens, frequently mixing. Put accumulated juices and steaks in skillet; to coat, turn. Cook steaks for 2 minutes till just heated through, flipping once. Put steaks on platter; throw bay leaf away. Put olives and sauce on steaks; serve.

Nutrition Information

- Calories: 519
- Protein: 33 g(66%)
- Total Fat: 38 g(58%)
- Saturated Fat: 13 g(65%)
- Sodium: 198 mg(8%)
- Fiber: 1 g(3%)
- Total Carbohydrate: 3 g(1%)
- Cholesterol: 140 mg(47%)

107. Herbed Fish Rolls In White Wine With Grapes

Serving: Serves 4 | Prep: | Ready in:

Ingredients

- 2/3 cup seedless green grapes
- 3/4 cup dry white wine
- four 6- to 8-ounce skinless flounder or orange roughy fillets
- 1/3 cup minced fresh parsley leaves
- 1 tablespoon minced fresh thyme leaves or 3/4 teaspoon crumbled dried
- 1/4 cup minced onion
- 2 tablespoons unsalted butter
- 1 tablespoon all-purpose flour
- 1/4 cup heavy cream
- 1 teaspoon fresh lemon juice

Direction

- Put 8 of grapes aside, slice the rest of the grapes in half, and allow halves of grape to macerate in wine for an hour in small saucepan. Slice the fillets in half lengthwise, add pepper and salt to season them, and scatter thyme and parsley on skinned sides. Roll every half of fillet up including a reserved grape in the center and seal it using wooden pick. Stand rolls up of fish in saucepan just big enough to accommodate them in single layer, do not crowd. Use slotted spoon to turn macerated grapes onto small bowl, boil wine, and add it on top of fish rolls. Let fish rolls cook with cover, for 10 to 15 minutes at bare simmer, or till they barely flake. Transfer the fish rolls with a slotted spoon to a plate, reserving the cooking liquid, and keep them warm, covered.
- Let onion cook in butter in small saucepan on medium heat for 5 minutes, mixing, mix flour in, and let roux cook on medium-low heat for 3 minutes, mixing. Take pan off heat and use a fine sieve to drain the reserved cooking liquid right into pan. Put in pepper and salt to taste, lemon juice, macerated grapes and cream and let sauce boil for 3 minutes, mixing. Drain any liquid that has gathered on plate, distribute fish rolls between 4 heated plates, and top with scoop of sauce.

Nutrition Information

- Calories: 308
- Protein: 34 g(67%)
- Total Fat: 13 g(20%)
- Saturated Fat: 7 g(36%)
- Sodium: 155 mg(6%)
- Fiber: 1 g(4%)
- Total Carbohydrate: 9 g(3%)
- Cholesterol: 155 mg(52%)

108. Holiday Ham With Riesling And Mustard

Serving: Makes 16 servings (with leftovers) | Prep: | Ready in:

Ingredients

- 1 14-16-pound whole cured, smoked bone-in ham
- 2 cups sweet (Auslese) Riesling, divided
- 2 tablespoons (1/4 stick) unsalted butter
- 1/4 cup finely chopped shallots
- 3 sprigs thyme plus 2 teaspoons fresh thyme leaves
- 1/2 cup whole grain mustard
- 1 tablespoon honey
- 1/2 teaspoon freshly ground black pepper
- Small pinch of kosher salt

Direction

- Place a rack in bottom of the oven; preheat the oven to 300°F. Keeping the fat attach, take the outer rind from majority of the ham, keeping a band on shank bone end surrounding. Cut slits in fat crosswise, avoid cutting into the meat, on ham top making parallel slits about half-inch apart. In a big roasting pan, put the ham. Boil in a saucepan with 7 cups water and a cup of Riesling for five minutes. Add to roasting pan bottom. Let ham bake for 2 1/2-3 hours, baste using pan juices from time to time, till an inserted instant-read thermometer into middle of ham reads 110°F.
- Meantime, in medium skillet, liquify the butter on moderate heat. Put in thyme sprigs and shallots; cook for 10 minutes, mixing frequently, till shallots are extremely soft. Take pan off heat; mix in the leftover one cup of Riesling. Put back to stove. Raise the heat to moderately-high, simmer, and cook for 8 minutes, till cooked down to quarter-cup. Take thyme sprigs and turn the mixture into food processor. Put in salt, pepper, honey, mustard and thyme leaves. Process till thoroughly incorporated.
- Take pan out of oven and raise the heat to 350°F. Smear Riesling mixture on ham with pastry brush. Put pan back to oven and let ham bake, with foil to tent in case browning very fast, till inner heat reads 135°F and crust turn golden brown in color, for 15 minutes to half an hour.
- Turn the ham onto a big platter. Sit for half an hour prior to carving. Scoop fat off juices from pan, rewarm, and put the juices to a medium size pitcher; serve on the side.

Nutrition Information

- Calories: 816
- Total Carbohydrate: 22 g(7%)
- Cholesterol: 255 mg(85%)
- Protein: 70 g(141%)
- Total Fat: 45 g(70%)
- Saturated Fat: 15 g(77%)
- Sodium: 4546 mg(189%)
- Fiber: 0 g(1%)

109. Holiday Punch

Serving: Makes about 8 cups | Prep: | Ready in:

Ingredients

- 3 3/4 cups chilled lemon-lime soda (about 30 ounces)
- 3 cups chilled cranberry-apple juice drink
- 1 cup chilled dry white wine
- 2 tablespoons brandy

Direction

- Mix every ingredient in big bowl. Mix till thoroughly incorporated. Serve cold.

Nutrition Information

- Calories: 167
- Total Fat: 0 g(0%)
- Saturated Fat: 0 g(0%)
- Sodium: 23 mg(1%)
- Fiber: 4 g(15%)
- Total Carbohydrate: 33 g(11%)
- Protein: 0 g(1%)

110. Honey Poached Pears With Mascarpone

Serving: Serves 4 | Prep: | Ready in:

Ingredients

- 2 firm but ripe large Bosc pears, peeled, halved, cored
- 2 tablespoons fresh lemon juice
- 1 cup water
- 1/2 cup dry white wine
- 6 tablespoons honey
- 1/2 vanilla bean, split lengthwise
- 1/2 cup mascarpone cheese*
- 2 teaspoons sugar
- 2 teaspoons brandy or dark rum

Direction

- Toss in big bowl with lemon juice and pears. Put aside. In medium size saucepan, mix wine, honey and a cup of water. Scoop in vanilla bean seeds; put in bean. Mix on moderate heat till honey dissolves. Put pears in. Use a round parchment paper piece to cover the mixture. Lower the heat to moderately-low. Simmer for 15 minutes, till pears are just soft one pricked, flipping mid-way through.
- Turn the pears onto big bowl with slotted spoon. Let poaching liquid boil for 2 minutes, till cooked down to 3/4 cup. Let syrup cool. Add the syrup on top of pears. Refrigerate with cover till cold, for not less than 8 hours to overnight. Take the vanilla bean.
- In big bowl, mix sugar, brandy and mascarpone cheese till smooth. Put in quarter cup of chilled poaching syrup and mix to soft peak.
- Slice every half of pear thinly lengthwise, keeping slices connected at stem end. Turn the pears onto plates with metal spatula. Slowly push on pears to slightly fan. Scoop some of the syrup on top of pears. Scoop mascarpone cream on the side of every half of pear to serve.

Nutrition Information

- Calories: 304
- Cholesterol: 31 mg(10%)
- Protein: 2 g(4%)
- Total Fat: 10 g(15%)
- Saturated Fat: 6 g(28%)
- Sodium: 110 mg(5%)
- Fiber: 4 g(15%)
- Total Carbohydrate: 49 g(16%)

111. Horseradish Crusted Salmon With Beet Sauce

Serving: Makes 6 servings | Prep: | Ready in:

Ingredients

- 3 medium beets, trimmed
- 1 1-inch piece fresh ginger
- 3 garlic cloves, unpeeled
- 2 tablespoons olive oil
- 1 shallot, finely chopped
- 1 tablespoon chopped fresh thyme
- 2 cups fish stock or bottled clam juice
- 1/2 cup dry white wine
- 2 tablespoons balsamic vinegar
- 4 tablespoons (about) water
- 1 1/2 cups finely grated peeled fresh horseradish root (about 5 ounces)
- 1/4 cup whipping cream
- 6 6-to-8 ounce salmon fillets
- 3 tablespoons sour cream

Direction

- Preheat the oven to 425°F. Put in glass, small baking dish with garlic, ginger and beets. Use foil to cover and bake for an hour, till beets are soft. Let cool. Peel garlic, beets and ginger; put into a blender.
- In big, heavy skillet, heat a tablespoon of oil on moderate heat. Put in thyme and shallot; sauté for four minutes. Put in wine and fish stock; simmer for 10 minutes, till cooked down to 1 1/4 cups. Put into mixture of beet in blender with vinegar and fish stock mixture. Process till smooth, incase very thick, use water to thin it to consistency of a sauce.
- Stir in small bowl with cream and horseradish. Add pepper and salt to season. Horseradish mixture and beet sauce may be done a day in advance. Separately cover; refrigerate.
- Preheat the oven to 425°F. Scatter pepper and salt on salmon. In big, heavy skillet, heat the leftover 1 tablespoon of oil on moderately-high heat. Put into skillet with 3 salmon fillets; cook for 2 minutes on each side, barely till golden. Place salmon on big baking sheet, skin side facing down. Redo with the rest of the salmon. Slather horseradish mixture on top of salmon. Bake for 12 minutes, till salmon is cooked completely.
- Simmer beet sauce in pan, mixing. Take off heat. Stir sour cream in. Add pepper and salt to season. Put on plates with salmon. Surround salmon with scoop of sauce.

Nutrition Information

- Calories: 570
- Cholesterol: 123 mg(41%)
- Protein: 47 g(95%)
- Total Fat: 36 g(55%)
- Saturated Fat: 9 g(47%)
- Sodium: 761 mg(32%)
- Fiber: 2 g(10%)
- Total Carbohydrate: 11 g(4%)

112. If It Ain't Broke, Don't Fix It Stuffing

Serving: 8 servings | Prep: | Ready in:

Ingredients

- 1 cup (2 sticks) unsalted butter, plus more
- 1 1/2 pound loaf sourdough bread, sliced 1" thick, torn into 1/2"–3/4" pieces
- 1 tablespoon extra-virgin olive oil
- 1 pound breakfast sausage, casings removed if needed
- 1 large onion, finely chopped
- 1 fennel bulb, finely chopped
- 4 celery stalks, finely chopped
- 2 teaspoon Diamond Crystal or 1 1/4 tsp. Morton kosher salt, plus more
- 1 tsp. freshly ground black pepper, plus more
- 1/2 cup dry white wine
- 1/4 cup finely chopped parsley
- 1 tablespoon finely chopped sage
- 1 tablespoon finely chopped thyme
- 3 large eggs
- 4 cups Thanksgiving Stock or low-sodium chicken broth, divided

Direction

- In center and upper of oven, put the racks; preheat the oven to 300°F. With butter, grease a 3-quart baking dish. Distribute bread among 2 rimmed baking sheets and on center rack, bake for 25 to 35 minutes, tossing from time to time, till dried out, prevent from browning more than just a little on the edges. Allow to cool.
- Meantime, in big skillet, heat oil over moderately-high. Set sausage in 1 layer and cook for 3 minutes, without mixing, till browned beneath. Using 2 spoons or spatulas, crumble into bite-size portions and keep cooking, tossing from time to time, till cooked completely for 5 minutes more. To a plate, put the sausage.
- Lower heat to moderate and in same skillet, liquify a cup of butter. Put in celery, fennel

and onion; slightly season with pepper and salt. Cook for 12 to 15 minutes, mixing from time to time, till vegetables are extremely soft yet not browned. Pour in wine and scratch base of skillet to loosen any browned bits. Boil and cook for 3 minutes till wine is vaporized. Toss in thyme, sage and parsley, and cool mixture in the skillet.

- Raise oven heat to 350 °F. In a huge bowl, beat 2 cups stock and eggs. Put in onion mixture, sausage and bread, and toss thoroughly to incorporate. Put in 2 teaspoon or 1 1/4 teaspoon salt and 1 teaspoon pepper. Sprinkle leftover 2 cups of stock on top and toss once more to incorporate. Allow to rest for 10 minutes, tossing from time to time, till bread soaks in all liquid.
- To prepped dish, put the stuffing; butter a foil sheet and cover on dish, butter side facing down. On center rack, bake till extremely hot entirely, it must sense very hot to comfortably touch in the middle; an inserted instant-read thermometer into the middle should read 160 °F, for 35 to 40 minutes.
- Raise oven heat to 425 °F. Take off foil and move baking dish onto upper rack. Keep baking the stuffing till golden brown for 25 minutes to half an hour more.
- Do Ahead: Stuffing may be assembled a day in advance. Place cover and refrigerate.

Nutrition Information

- Calories: 715
- Cholesterol: 174 mg(58%)
- Protein: 24 g(49%)
- Total Fat: 44 g(68%)
- Saturated Fat: 21 g(103%)
- Sodium: 1167 mg(49%)
- Fiber: 4 g(16%)
- Total Carbohydrate: 55 g(18%)

113. Instant Pot Shrimp Scampi

Serving: 4 main course or 8 appetizer servings | Prep: 10mins | Ready in:

Ingredients

- 1 1/2 lb. jumbo shrimp, peeled, deveined
- 1/4 cup dry white wine
- 4 garlic cloves, finely chopped
- 2 tsp. kosher salt
- 1/4 tsp. freshly ground black pepper
- 6 Tbsp. unsalted butter
- 1/4 cup finely chopped parsley
- 2 tsp. fresh lemon juice
- An Instant Pot

Direction

- Preparation: In cooker insert, toss the garlic, wine and the shrimp in. Use pepper and salt to season it. Lock its lid and make sure that the steam-release valve is in the proper sealed position. Program for 1 minute, select "Manual" at high pressure.
- Turn the cooker off as soon as the time has elapsed. "Quick Release" the steam once done. Unlock the lid and the shrimp should be opaque all the way through. Put it in a medium bowl using a slotted spoon. Leave the juices behind.
- Select "Sauté" and for 6 minutes, simmer the liquid until reduced by half. Put the butter in. Mix it well until incorporated and melted and until the sauce becomes thick. Put the shrimp back to the pot. Put the lemon juice and the parsley. To mix, toss it and put it in a platter once done. Serve.

Nutrition Information

114. Italian Chicken With Mushroom And Wine Sauce

Serving: Makes 6 servings | Prep: | Ready in:

Ingredients

- 6 large chicken breast halves with skin and bones
- 4 tablespoons olive oil
- 1 pound mushrooms, thickly sliced
- 2 cups chopped onions
- 1 large red bell pepper, cut into 1-inch pieces
- 1 cup dry white wine
- 1 cup canned low-salt chicken broth
- 1 1.42-ounce package spaghetti sauce seasoning mix

Direction

- Preheat the oven to 350°F. Scatter pepper and salt on chicken. In big, heavy skillet, heat 2 tablespoons of oil on moderately-high heat. Put in three chicken breasts, skin side facing down; sauté for 3 minutes, till skin becomes brown. Turn the chicken into glass, 15x10x2-inch baking dish, skin side facing up. Redo with the rest of the chicken.
- In the same skillet, heat leftover 2 tablespoons of oil on moderately-high heat. Put in onions, bell pepper and mushrooms. Sauté for 12 minutes, till mushrooms start to brown and vegetables turn tender. Pour in wine; boil for two minutes. Put in seasoning mix and broth and boil. Top chicken with sauce.
- Use foil to cover the dish. Let chicken bake for 25 minutes. Remove cover and bake till sauce thickens and chicken is cooked completely, for an additional of 15 minutes.

Nutrition Information

- Calories: 360
- Fiber: 3 g(12%)
- Total Carbohydrate: 15 g(5%)
- Cholesterol: 70 mg(23%)
- Protein: 27 g(55%)
- Total Fat: 20 g(31%)
- Saturated Fat: 4 g(22%)
- Sodium: 91 mg(4%)

115. Italian Fish Soup

Serving: Makes 6 to 8 main-course servings | Prep: 1hours | Ready in:

Ingredients

- 1 lb cleaned squid, bodies and tentacles separated but kept intact
- 1/2 lb large shrimp in shell (21 to 25 per lb), peeled, leaving tail and first segment of shell intact, and deveined
- 1/8 teaspoon black pepper
- 3/4 teaspoon salt
- 1/4 cup olive oil
- 3 garlic cloves, finely chopped
- 1/2 teaspoon dried hot red pepper flakes
- 1/4 teaspoon dried oregano, crumbled
- 1 cup dry white wine
- 4 1/2 cups water
- 12 small hard-shelled clams such as littlenecks (less than 2 inches in diameter), scrubbed
- 12 mussels (preferably cultivated), scrubbed and beards removed
- 4 cups fish stock or bottled clam juice (32 fl oz)
- 2 (14-oz) cans diced tomatoes in juice
- 1 teaspoon sugar
- 1 lb skinless halibut fillet, cut into 1-inch pieces
- 1/4 cup chopped fresh basil
- 1/4 cup chopped fresh flat-leaf parsley
- 1 (12-inch) Italian loaf, cut into 1/2-inch-thick slices
- 2 tablespoons olive oil
- 1 garlic clove, halved crosswise
- 2 tablespoons finely chopped fresh flat-leaf parsley
- Accompaniment: extra-virgin olive oil for drizzling

Direction

- Soup: rinse squid with cold running water. Pat dry. Halve ring tentacles and cut longer tentacles to 2-inch pieces, crosswise, if squid is big. Pull flaps off squid bodies. Cut to 1/4-inch thick slices. Slice bodies to 1/4-inch thick rings, crosswise.
- Pat dry shrimp. Sprinkle 1/4 teaspoon salt and pepper. In a wide 6-8-quart heavy pot, heat oil on medium high heat until hot yet not smoking. In 2 batches, sear shrimp for 2 minutes per batch, flipping once, until golden yet not cooked through. Place shrimp in a bowl using a slotted spoon.
- Sauté oregano, red pepper flakes, and garlic in a pot for about 30 seconds until golden, stirring. Add 1/2 cup water and wine then boil. Mix in clams. Cook on medium heat, covered, until shells open wide. Frequently check after 6 minutes then use a slotted spoon as they open to the bowl with the shrimp. Throw out any clams that didn't open after 8 minutes. Mix in mussels and cook on medium high heat, covered, until shells open, frequently checking after 3 minutes, moving opened ones using a slotted spoon to the bowl with shrimp. Throw out mussels that didn't open after 6 minutes.
- Preheat oven to 425 degrees F with the oven rack in the center.
- In a pot, add stock, 1/2 teaspoon salt, sugar, tomatoes with juice, and 4 cups water. Simmer for 15 minutes, uncovered.
- Make toast as stock simmers. Place 1 layer of bread slices on a baking sheet. Drizzle with oil and season using salt. Bake for about 10 minutes in total, flipping once, until golden. Place toast on a rack to slightly cool. Lightly rub with cut side of garlic. Sprinkle on parsley.
- Completely soup: Add the halibut to stock. On a bare simmer, cook for about 2 minutes, covered, until cooked through. Mix in leftover shellfish and squid. Take off heat and let stand for a minute, covered. Mix in parsley and basil. Immediately serve with toast for a dip.

Nutrition Information

- Calories: 580
- Total Carbohydrate: 52 g(17%)
- Cholesterol: 254 mg(85%)
- Protein: 43 g(86%)
- Total Fat: 27 g(41%)
- Saturated Fat: 5 g(26%)
- Sodium: 1639 mg(68%)
- Fiber: 4 g(17%)

116. John Dory With Fried Fennel And Anchovy Butter Sauce

Serving: Serves 4 | Prep: | Ready in:

Ingredients

- 4 7-ounce John Dory or sea bass fillets
- 1 tablespoon olive oil
- 2 cups dry white wine
- 7 canned anchovies, drained, finely chopped
- 1/4 cup (1/2 stick) chilled butter, cut into pieces
- Fried Fennel
- 1/4 cup chopped fresh Italian parsley

Direction

- Brush oil on John Dory. Scatter pepper and salt over. On moderately-high heat, heat big, heavy skillet till hot. Put in fish and cook for 3 minutes on each side, till barely opaque in the middle. Turn the fish onto platter; tent using foil to retain warmth. Drain any oil off skillet. Put in anchovies and wine and boil for 12 minutes, till cooked down to 1/3 cup. Put in butter and mix till smooth and melted. Season sauce with pepper to taste.
- Place Fried Fennel in the middle of the plates. Put fish on top. Top with sauce. Scatter parsley over to serve.

Nutrition Information

117. Kir

Serving: 1 | Prep: 5mins | Ready in:

Ingredients

- 3/4 cup white wine
- 4 teaspoons creme de cassis liqueur

Direction

- In a wine glass, add creme de cassis and wine. Stir to serve.

Nutrition Information

118. Kir II

Serving: Serves 1 | Prep: | Ready in:

Ingredients

- 1/2 cup chilled dry white wine
- 1 tablespoon crème de cassis
- Chilled sparkling water (optional)

Direction

- In a wine glass, pour chilled dry white wine and crème de cassis. Add chilled sparkling water if desired. Mix and serve.

Nutrition Information

119. Kris Kringle

Serving: Makes 1 drink. | Prep: | Ready in:

Ingredients

- 4 1/2 ounces medium-dry white wine (such as Liebfraumilch or a Gewürztraminer), well chilled
- 1/2 ounce kirsch, well chilled

Direction

- Put white wine into a cold glass of white-wine. Mix kirsch in. Serve.

Nutrition Information

- Calories: 137
- Total Carbohydrate: 3 g(1%)
- Sodium: 7 mg(0%)
- Protein: 0 g(0%)

120. Lamb Shanks With Tomatoes And Fresh Herbs

Serving: Makes 4 servings | Prep: | Ready in:

Ingredients

- 2 teaspoons salt
- 2 teaspoons chopped fresh rosemary
- 2 teaspoons chopped fresh thyme
- 1 teaspoon fennel seeds
- 1 teaspoon freshly ground black pepper
- 1/2 teaspoon ground coriander
- 4 large lamb shanks
- 3 tablespoons olive oil
- 2 ounces thinly sliced capocollo or pancetta, cut into thin strips
- 1 1/2 cups chopped onion
- 1 cup chopped carrots
- 1/2 cup chopped celery
- 6 garlic cloves, chopped
- 3 3 x 1/2-inch strips lemon peel
- 2 small bay leaves
- 2 teaspoons chopped fresh thyme
- 2 cups dry white wine

- 2 cups drained canned diced tomatoes in juice
- 1 1/2 cups low-salt chicken broth
- 3 tablespoons chopped fresh parsley
- 1 tablespoon grated lemon peel
- 1/2 teaspoon freshly ground black pepper

Direction

- Combine the first 6 ingredients in a small bowl. Rub the mixture all over the lamb. Allow it to stand for 30 minutes.
- Set the oven to 350°F for preheating. Put oil in a large ovenproof pot and heat it over medium-high heat. Cook the lamb for 12 minutes, flipping it with tongs until browned. Transfer it onto a plate. Adjust the heat to medium and stir in capocollo for 1 minute. Add the celery, onion, and carrots. Cover the pot and cook the vegetables for 10 minutes, stirring occasionally until softened. Stir in garlic and cook for 1 minute. Stir in bay leaves, lemon peel strips, and thyme. Add the wine and bring the mixture to a boil while scraping up any browned bits. Add the broth and tomatoes. Place the lamb back into the pot. Bring the mixture to a boil. Cover the pot and place it inside the oven.
- Cook the lamb for 1 1/2 hours, flipping occasionally until just tender. Get the pot from the oven and tilt it to remove any fat that is visible on the top of the sauce. Set the pot over medium heat. Boil the uncovered mixture for 30 minutes until the lamb is very tender and the sauce is reduced enough to coat the spoon. Season the mixture with salt and pepper to taste. Discard the bay leaves and lemon peel. (This can be prepared a day ahead. Let the mixture cool for 30 minutes. Let it chilled uncovered until cold, and then cover and keep it chilled. Rewarm the mixture over low heat before proceeding.)
- In a small bowl, mix the grated lemon peel, 1/2 tsp. of pepper, and parsley for the gremolata. Place the lamb in a shallow bowl and sprinkle with the gremolata to serve.

Nutrition Information

- Calories: 1437
- Saturated Fat: 40 g(199%)
- Sodium: 1888 mg(79%)
- Fiber: 6 g(24%)
- Total Carbohydrate: 20 g(7%)
- Cholesterol: 383 mg(128%)
- Protein: 112 g(223%)
- Total Fat: 93 g(144%)

121. Lamb Shoulder With Citrus Fennel Salad

Serving: 8 servings | Prep: | Ready in:

Ingredients

- 1 (5 1/2–6-lb.) lamb shoulder (not tied)
- Kosher salt, freshly ground black pepper
- 6 garlic cloves, finely grated, plus 2 heads, halved crosswise
- 2 Tbsp. extra-virgin olive oil
- 1 tsp. crushed red pepper flakes
- 1 tsp. finely grated orange zest, plus one (3x1") strip zest
- 2 Tbsp. finely chopped rosemary, plus more for serving
- 1 cup dry white wine
- 6–8 mixed small oranges (such as blood, mandarin, and navel), peeled, halved, sliced or torn into small sections
- 1 large fennel bulb with fronds, thinly sliced
- 2 Tbsp. fresh lemon juice

Direction

- Prepare the oven by preheating to 300 degrees F. Score fat across the top of the lamb shoulder with a sharp knife to make a crosshatch form, slicing about 1/4-inch deep and spacing cuts about 3/4-inch apart. Generously dust with pepper and salt all over.
- In a small bowl, mix 2 tablespoons rosemary, grated zest, red pepper flakes, oil, and grated

garlic. Knead all over the lamb, working into score marks and anywhere there is an opening. Transfer the lamb to a baking dish or a large cast-iron skillet. (You can cover and chill the lamb up to 1 day if you want to break up the prep at this point.)

- Surround lamb with garlic heads with the cut side down and put in a strip of zest. Add wine and use foil to cover it tightly. Roast for 5 to 5 1/2 hours until meat is fork-tender and falling off the bone. Keep it covered and allow it to rest for 30 minutes.
- In a medium bowl, carefully toss fennel and orange pieces with lemon juice; add salt lightly to taste.
- Pull the meat off the bones in large pieces and mound on a platter. Arrange fennel salad and citrus next to the meat. Put additional rosemary on top of the meat and dot with pan juices all over.
- DO AHEAD: You can roast the lamb 1 day in advance. Allow it to cool; chill it covered. Cautiously reheat in the oven at 300 degrees F, covered, for at least 1 hour until warmed all the way through, before serving.

Nutrition Information

- Calories: 782
- Total Fat: 59 g(91%)
- Saturated Fat: 24 g(122%)
- Sodium: 1110 mg(46%)
- Fiber: 3 g(14%)
- Total Carbohydrate: 15 g(5%)
- Cholesterol: 185 mg(62%)
- Protein: 44 g(88%)

122. Lavender And Thyme Roasted Poussins

Serving: Makes 4 Servings | Prep: | Ready in:

Ingredients

- 2 teaspoons dried untreated lavender flowers
- 3/4 stick (6 tablespoons) unsalted butter, softened
- 1 teaspoon fresh thyme leaves, minced
- 1/4 teaspoon finely grated fresh lemon zest
- 4 poussins (young chickens; about 1 pound each) or 4 small Cornish hens (about 1 1/4 pounds each)
- 1 small lemon, halved
- 1/4 cup Sauternes
- Garnish: lavender and thyme leaves

Direction

- Crush lavender coarsely using a mortar and pestle and mix with pepper and salt to taste, zest, thyme and butter in small bowl till blended thoroughly. Scoop the mixture to a plastic wrap sheet and shape to make a 4-inches long log. Refrigerate compound butter for not less than 30 minutes to no longer than 3 days, encased thoroughly in plastic wrap, till firm.
- Preheat the oven to 475° F.
- Throw the birds gizzards and cut off necks flush with bodies if need be. Wash in and out of birds and blot dry. Beginning at each bird neck end, slip the fingers among skin and meat to detach the skin, ensure not to poke holes in skin. Slice the butter to make 16 quarter-inch-thick pieces and softly press 4 pieces beneath the skin of every bird, placing a piece on every thigh and breast half. Use kitchen string to bind together the legs of every bird and use bamboo skewers or wooden picks to fixed wings to sides.
- In flame-safe roasting pan, big enough to accommodate them, place the birds, do not crowd. Softly rub lemon halves on birds, press juice on them, and add pepper and salt to season. Let birds roast in the center of the of oven for half an hour, for poussins; and for Cornish hens, 45 minutes, or till an inserted instant-read thermometer in chunkiest portion of a thigh, without touching the bone, reads 170° F.

- Turn the birds onto platter and use foil to loosely cover and retain warmth. To roasting pan, put the Sauternes and deglaze on medium heat, scratching brown bits up. Turn the jus into a small saucepan. Scoop fat off jus and simmer till cooked down to roughly half cup.
- Jazz birds up using herbs and serve along with jus.

Nutrition Information

123. Leg Of Lamb Poached In White Wine Court Bouillon

Serving: Makes 6 to 8 servings | Prep: | Ready in:

Ingredients

- 1 small leg of lamb, boned and tied
- Garlic cloves, dried rosemary
- 1 bottle white wine (Pouilly Fuissé)
- 2 onions, stuck with cloves
- 1 carrot
- 1 stalk celery
- 1 tablespoon salt
- 1 teaspoon freshly ground black pepper
- Sauce Soubise

Direction

- Use garlic slivers to pique tied and boned lamb leg, cut small slashes and put in the garlic, and massage with dried rosemary. In a big kettle, add the wine, and equal amount of vegetables, seasonings and water, boil and let simmer for twenty-five minutes. Put in the lamb and boil liquid once more. Place pan cover, lower the heat and simmer, letting 15 minutes in every pound of meat. Serve along with Sauce Soubise.

Nutrition Information

124. Lemon Chicken

Serving: Serves 2 | Prep: | Ready in:

Ingredients

- 1 tablespoon butter
- 1 tablespoon olive oil
- 2 boneless chicken breast halves
- 1/2 pound mushrooms, thinly sliced
- 4 garlic cloves, chopped
- 8 paper-thin slices lemon
- 1/2 cup dry white wine
- 2 tablespoons fresh lemon juice
- Chopped fresh parsley

Direction

- In medium, heavy skillet, liquify butter together with olive oil on high heat. Add pepper and salt to chicken to season. Place the chicken to skillet and sauté for 2 minutes each side, till brown. Turn the chicken onto plate with tongs. Put to skillet with the garlic and mushrooms. Sauté for 4 minutes, till mushrooms becomes tender. Put chicken back to skillet. On every chicken piece, overlap 4 slices of lemon. Add lemon juice and white wine around the chicken. Lower the heat to low. Put skillet cover and simmer for 5 minutes, till chicken is cooked completely. Add pepper and salt to season.
- Turn the chicken onto plates. Surround chicken with scoop of sauce. Jazz up using parsley to serve.

Nutrition Information

- Calories: 396
- Fiber: 8 g(32%)
- Total Carbohydrate: 30 g(10%)
- Cholesterol: 71 mg(24%)

- Protein: 25 g(50%)
- Total Fat: 22 g(33%)
- Saturated Fat: 7 g(35%)
- Sodium: 72 mg(3%)

125. Lemon Risotto

Serving: Makes 6 first-course or 4 main-course servings | Prep: | Ready in:

Ingredients

- 6 cups canned low-salt chicken broth
- 3 1/2 tablespoons butter
- 1 1/2 tablespoons olive oil
- 2 large shallots, chopped
- 2 cups arborio rice or medium-grain white rice
- 1/4 cup dry white wine
- 1 cup freshly grated Parmesan cheese (about 3 ounces)
- 2 tablespoons chopped fresh parsley
- 2 tablespoons fresh lemon juice
- 4 teaspoons grated lemon peel

Direction

- In big saucepan, simmer broth on moderate heat. Lower heat to low; retain warmth with cover. In big, heavy saucepan, liquify 1 1/2 tablespoons of butter along with oil on moderate heat. Put in and sauté shallots for 6 minutes, till tender. Put in rice; mix for a minute. Pour in wine and mix till vaporized, for half a minute. Pour in 1 1/2 cups of the hot broth; simmer till soaked in, mixing often. Put in leftover broth, half cup at one time, letting broth be soaked in prior to putting in additional and mixing often for 35 minutes, till rice is tender and creamy. Mix in leftover 2 tablespoons of butter and cheese. Mix in lemon juice, lemon peel and parsley. Use pepper and salt to season risotto. Turn onto bowl to serve.

Nutrition Information

- Calories: 444
- Sodium: 273 mg(11%)
- Fiber: 1 g(4%)
- Total Carbohydrate: 60 g(20%)
- Cholesterol: 27 mg(9%)
- Protein: 15 g(30%)
- Total Fat: 16 g(24%)
- Saturated Fat: 8 g(38%)

126. Lemon Dill Sauce

Serving: Makes about 3/4 cup | Prep: | Ready in:

Ingredients

- 3/4 cup dry white wine
- 3 tablespoons chopped shallot
- 2 tablespoons fresh lemon juice
- 1/2 cup (1 stick) chilled unsalted butter, cut into 8 pieces
- 1 1/2 tablespoons chopped fresh dill

Direction

- In medium size saucepan, boil shallot, lemon juice and wine on high heat for 6 minutes, till cooked down to quarter cup. Lower heat to low; put in butter, 1 bit by 1 time, mixing till liquified prior to putting in additional. Take pan off heat. Mix dill in. Season with pepper and salt to taste.

Nutrition Information

- Calories: 622
- Total Carbohydrate: 7 g(2%)
- Cholesterol: 163 mg(54%)
- Protein: 1 g(3%)
- Total Fat: 61 g(95%)
- Saturated Fat: 39 g(194%)
- Sodium: 16 mg(1%)
- Fiber: 1 g(3%)

127. Lemony Mushroom Risotto

Serving: Serves 4 (main course) or 6 to 8 (side dish) | Prep: | Ready in:

Ingredients

- 2 2/3 cups boiling-hot water
- 1/2 oz dried porcini mushrooms
- 3 cups chicken broth
- 1/2 stick (1/4 cup) unsalted butter
- 1/2 lb small cremini mushrooms, quartered
- 1 small onion, finely chopped
- 1 cup plus 2 tablespoons Arborio rice (8 oz)
- 1/4 cup dry white wine
- 1 teaspoon finely grated fresh lemon zest
- 1/4 cup finely grated parmesan
- 2 tablespoons chopped fresh flat-leaf parsley

Direction

- Put 2/3 cup of hot water over porcini in a cup that's heatproof and let it sit until tender, for about 10 minutes. Take porcini out of the water and squeeze out the excess liquid back into the cup. Wash well to take out any grit. Coarsely chop the porcini. Put the soaking liquid through a sieve lined with paper towel into a measuring glass and set aside.
- Simmer remaining 2 cups of hot water and broth. Keep on a bare simmer, cover it with lid.
- Heat 1 tbsp. butter in a heavy skillet over moderately high heat until foam subsides, then sauté cremini, stirring until browned, for about 7 minutes. Put the reserved soaking liquid and porcini to skillet and let it boil, stirring for a minute. Take out from the heat.
- Cook onion in 1 1/2 tbsp. butter in a 3-qt heavy saucepan over moderate heat, stirring from time to time until tender for 3 to 4 minutes.
- Cook rice and stir frequently for a minute. Put the wine and let it simmer, stirring frequently until absorbed.
- Add in half cup simmering broth mixture and cook at a strong simmer, stirring frequently until the broth is absorbed. Let it simmer and then add the broth, half cup at a time, stirring frequently and let each addition become absorbed before adding the next, until the rice is soft but still al dente and creamy (it should be like thick soup), for 18 minutes. (There will be leftover broth.)
- Add in mushrooms, remaining 1 1/2 tbsp. butter, parmesan, parsley, pepper and zest. (Thin risotto with the remaining broth if needed.) Serve right away.

Nutrition Information

- Calories: 436
- Saturated Fat: 9 g(46%)
- Sodium: 369 mg(15%)
- Fiber: 3 g(11%)
- Total Carbohydrate: 59 g(20%)
- Cholesterol: 41 mg(14%)
- Protein: 13 g(26%)
- Total Fat: 16 g(24%)

128. Lima Beans With Clams

Serving: Serves 6 | Prep: | Ready in:

Ingredients

- 1 tablespoon extra-virgin olive oil
- 1 large onion, quartered, cut crosswise into 1/4-inch-thick slices
- 1 bay leaf
- 1/3 cup dry white wine
- 2 10-ounce packages frozen baby lima beans, thawed
- 2 large garlic cloves, minced
- 24 small clams, scrubbed
- 3 large tomatoes, seeded, diced
- 1/4 cup finely chopped fresh parsley

Direction

- Heat oil in heavy big deep skillet over medium low heat. Add bay leaf and onion; sauté for 10 minutes till onion is golden. Add wine; simmer for a minute. Season with pepper and salt. Put clams on top of beans. Bring heat to medium high; cover. Cook for 8 minutes till clams open. Discard unopened clams. Put clams in dish. Remove 1/2 clams from shells; mix into beans. Mix parsley and tomatoes into beans. In big shallow bowl, mound lima bean mixture. Put leftover clams in shells on top; serve.

Nutrition Information

129. Linguine With Mussels And Arugula Cream Sauce

Serving: Serves 4 to 6 | Prep: | Ready in:

Ingredients

- 1 onion, chopped
- 2 tablespoons olive oil
- 1/2 cup dry white wine
- 1/2 cup bottled clam juice
- 1/2 cup water
- 36 mussels (preferably cultivated), scrubbed and the beards pulled off
- 1/2 cup heavy cream
- 2 small bunches of arugula, coarse stems discarded and the leaves washed well, spun dry, and chopped coarse (about 3 cups)
- 1 pound linguine

Direction

- Cook the onion in oil over moderately-low heat in a kettle, mixing, till tender, put water, clam juice and wine, and boil the mixture. Put the mussels, allow to steam for 2 minutes with cover, or till they opened, using tongs, putting them once open to a bowl, and throw any remain closed. Allow the mussels to cool till easily be handled and take them off from shells, throwing the shell.
- In the kettle, Boil the leftover liquid till reduced to approximately a cup, put cream, and allow the sauce to simmer for 3 minutes, mixing from time to time, or till thickened. With any gathered liquid in bowl, mix in arugula, mussels, and season with pepper and salt to taste. Boil linguine in a kettle of boiling salted water till tender yet firm to the bite, drain thoroughly, and put to a big bowl. Put mussel mixture and toss mixture thoroughly.

Nutrition Information

130. Linguine With Salmon And Arugula

Serving: Makes 4 Servings | Prep: | Ready in:

Ingredients

- 2 tablespoons butter
- 2 tablespoons olive oil
- 2 shallots, minced (about 3/4 cup)
- 3 garlic cloves, minced
- 3 plum tomatoes, chopped
- 1 1/3 cups dry white wine
- 1/2 cup bottled clam juice
- 2 tablespoons fresh lemon juice
- 1 teaspoon dried marjoram
- 1 3/4 pounds skinless salmon fillets, cut into 1/2- to 3/4-inch pieces
- 3 cups loosely packed fresh arugula
- 2 tablespoons drained capers
- 1 tablespoon chopped fresh basil
- 1 tablespoon chopped fresh parsley
- 12 ounces linguine

Direction

- In big, heavy skillet, liquify butter along with olive oil on moderate heat. Put in and sauté garlic and shallots for 3 minutes. Put in tomatoes and cook for 5 minutes, barely till soft. Raise the heat to moderately-high. Put in marjoram, lemon juice, clam juice and wine; let simmer for five minutes. Put in salmon and simmer for 5 minutes, till nearly cooked completely, mixing from time to time. Put to mixture of salmon with the capers, fresh herbs and arugula. Simmer for 2 minutes till arugula is barely wilted and salmon is barely cooked completely. Season with pepper and salt to taste.
- Meantime, in big pot with salted boiling water, let linguine cook till tender yet remain firm to bite, mixing from time to time.
- Thoroughly strain pasta and put back to pot. Put to pasta with the mixture of salmon-arugula and toss till coated. Serve while warm.

Nutrition Information

- Calories: 925
- Fiber: 5 g(19%)
- Total Carbohydrate: 73 g(24%)
- Cholesterol: 124 mg(41%)
- Protein: 55 g(111%)
- Total Fat: 41 g(63%)
- Saturated Fat: 11 g(55%)
- Sodium: 426 mg(18%)

131. Lobster Pasta With Herbed Cream Sauce

Serving: Makes 10 servings | Prep: | Ready in:

Ingredients

- 3 1 3/4-pound live lobsters
- 3 tablespoons olive oil
- 1/4 cup tomato paste
- 2 large plum tomatoes, chopped
- 1/3 cup dry white wine
- 2 tablespoons white wine vinegar
- 2 garlic cloves, sliced
- 2 fresh tarragon sprigs
- 2 fresh thyme sprigs
- 2 fresh Italian parsley sprigs
- 6 cups whipping cream
- 1 1/2 pounds fettuccine or linguine

Direction

- Boil huge pot with salted water. Put in lobsters. Boil for 12 minutes, till cooked completely, or if need be, cook in batches. Turn the lobsters into a big rimmed baking sheet with tongs. Take the meat from claws and tail; put the meat in a medium size bowl. Take any roe from the bodies and put in a small bowl. Refrigerate roe if there is any and meat with cover. Take and throw tomalley, the green thing from bodies. Put shells and bodies aside.
- In big, heavy pot, heat the oil on high heat. Put in the reserved lobster shells and bodies. Sauté for three minutes. Lower the heat to low. Put in tomato paste; mix for 3 minutes. Mix in parsley, thyme, tarragon, garlic, vinegar, wine and tomatoes. Put in cream; let boil for two minutes. Lower the heat to moderately-low. Simmer for 20 minutes, barely till cream is infused with flavor of lobster, mixing from time to time. Filter the sauce to big bowl, forcing on solids to release as much liquid as there is. Throw the strainer contents. Sauce and lobster may be prepped a day in advance. Separately cover and refrigerate.
- Turn the sauce onto a big, heavy saucepan. Slice meat of lobster to make bite-size portions; break roe up coarsely, in case using. Put into sauce. Slowly reheat on low heat, mixing from time to time.
- Meantime, let pasta cook in big pot with salted boiling water till barely tender yet remain firm to bite, mixing from time to time. Strain; put pasta back to pot. Put in sauce; toss for 4 minutes on moderately-high heat till pasta is coated with sauce. Add pepper and salt to season. Turn onto big shallow bowl to serve.

Nutrition Information

- Calories: 906
- Fiber: 3 g(11%)
- Total Carbohydrate: 58 g(19%)
- Cholesterol: 462 mg(154%)
- Protein: 52 g(104%)
- Total Fat: 51 g(79%)
- Saturated Fat: 29 g(145%)
- Sodium: 1114 mg(46%)

132. Lobster Shepherd's Pie

Serving: 4 Servings | Prep: | Ready in:

Ingredients

- 2 lb. russet potatoes, scrubbed, pricked all over with a fork
- 8 Tbsp. (1 stick) unsalted butter, divided
- 1 1/2 lb. lobster tails, meat removed from shells and cut into 2" pieces, shells broken into 2" pieces
- 2 Tbsp. tomato paste
- 1/2 cup dry white wine
- 1 medium yellow onion, peeled, halved through root end
- 1 head of garlic, halved crosswise
- 2 celery stalks, halved crosswise
- 2 bay leaves
- 1 tsp. black peppercorns
- Kosher salt
- 4 medium carrots, peeled, cut on a diagonal into 2" pieces, divided
- 1 1/2 cups half-and-half, divided
- Freshly ground black pepper
- 2 large egg yolks
- ¼ cup chopped dill
- 2 Tbsp. prepared horseradish
- 8 oz. pearl onions, peeled
- 1/4 cup all-purpose flour
- Flaky sea salt

Direction

- Put rack in the top-most position of the oven then preheat it to 400°F. Directly roast potatoes on rack for 60-70 minutes till tender. Let sit till cool enough to the touch.
- Meanwhile, heat 2 tablespoons butter in big saucepan on medium high heat till foaming and melted. Add lobster shells; cook, mixing often, for 5 minutes till bright red. Add tomato paste; cook, mixing, for 1 minute till it sticks to pot and begins to brown. Add wine; cook, scraping browned bits up, for 3 minutes till nearly completely evaporated. Add 4 cups water, 1 carrot, peppercorns, bay leaves, celery, garlic and yellow onion. Toss a big pinch of kosher salt in; boil on medium high heat. Lower heat. Briskly simmer for 50-60 minutes till the liquid is reduced by 2/3. Through a fine-mesh sieve, strain stock into heatproof measuring glass then discard solids. You will have about 1 1/2 cups.
- As potatoes cool, warm 2 tbsp. butter and 1 cup half and half in medium saucepan on low heat to melt butter.
- Lengthwise, split potatoes. Scoop flesh into the half-and-half mixture. Use a potato masher to smash till mixture is lump-free and smooth. Generously season with pepper and kosher salt. Take off heat. Mix horseradish, dill and egg yolks in. Use plastic wrap to cover. Put aside.
- Melt leftover 4 tablespoons butter in big clean saucepan on medium heat. Add leftover carrots and pearl onions. Cook, mixing, for 5-8 minutes till onions begin to be translucent. Sprinkle on flour; mix to combine. Cook, mixing, till flour leaves film on pot's bottom for 4 minutes. Constantly mixing, stream stock in slowly; simmer. Take off heat. Mix leftover 1/2 cup half-and-half in. Season sauce with pepper and kosher salt. Slightly cool.
- Put lobster pieces into 1 1/2-qt. shallow baking dish. Ladle sauce on. Top with dollops of mashed potatoes. Use back of spoon to spread across the surface, making decorative swirls. Sprinkle with sea salt. On foil-lined

baking sheet, bake for 20-25 minutes till filling is bubbling around edges and lobster is cooked through. Turn broiler on; broil pie for 1 minute till topping browns in spots. Before serving, let rest for 5-10 minutes.
- You can assemble pie 1 day ahead, covered and chilled. Before baking, bring to room temperature; uncover.

Nutrition Information

- Calories: 802
- Protein: 41 g(83%)
- Total Fat: 38 g(58%)
- Saturated Fat: 22 g(112%)
- Sodium: 1739 mg(72%)
- Fiber: 8 g(33%)
- Total Carbohydrate: 75 g(25%)
- Cholesterol: 403 mg(134%)

133. Lobster Stock

Serving: Makes about 2 1/2 cups | Prep: | Ready in:

Ingredients

- 3 tablespoons corn oil
- 1 pound cleaned, uncooked lobster shells (from about three 1 3/4-pound lobsters), coarsely chopped
- 1/4 cup brandy
- 2 medium cloves garlic, peeled and cut across into very thin slices
- 3 large shallots, peeled and cut across into very thin slices
- 1/4 small fennel bulb, cut across into very thin slices
- 2 tablespoons tomato paste
- 4 cups water

Direction

- In a wide, big pot, heat oil over high heat until just smoking. Put lobster shells and sear for 1 minute, do not tossing (the shell may glue to the pot). Tossing gently and keeping cooking, tossing occasionally for 5 minutes until the shells are well-browned but not burnt.
- Add fennel, shallots, garlic, and brandy. Scrub up any pieces glued to the bottom of the pot using a wooden spoon. Mix in tomato paste. Set the heat to medium-low and cook for 3 minutes until the vegetables are tender.
- Mix in water and boil it. Let boil for 15 minutes. Take away from heat and let sit for 10 minutes. Use a fine-mesh sieve to drain through. Push down hard on the solids to squeeze out as much flavorful liquid as possible (see the tips below). Save, put a cover on tightly, refrigerate for a maximum of 3 days or 2 months in the freezer.
- Tips: in a saucepan, add the lobster stock and boil it. Reduce the heat slightly and simmer until there is 1 scant cup left. Reserve as above. To reuse your shells, make a quick lobster stock (remouillage). Add the drained solids back to the pot, barely fill with water and boil for 12 minutes. Let sit for 10 minutes and drain again. Dispose of the solids. Reserve as above.

Nutrition Information

- Calories: 21
- Saturated Fat: 0 g(1%)
- Sodium: 61 mg(3%)
- Fiber: 0 g(1%)
- Total Carbohydrate: 1 g(0%)
- Cholesterol: 12 mg(4%)
- Protein: 2 g(3%)
- Total Fat: 1 g(1%)

134. Lobster And Shrimp Cioppino

Serving: Makes 8 servings | Prep: | Ready in:

Ingredients

- 2 1 1/3- to 1 1/2-pound live lobsters
- 2 pounds uncooked large shrimp with shells
- 1 1/4 cups olive oil
- 2 medium onions, chopped
- 1 cup chopped celery
- 1 cup chopped fresh fennel bulb
- 12 garlic cloves, peeled, flattened
- 1/4 cup tomato paste
- 1 28-ounce can plus 2 cups diced tomatoes in juice
- 1 bunch fresh basil
- 4 large fresh thyme sprigs
- 4 large fresh parsley sprigs
- 2 large fresh oregano sprigs
- 2 bay leaves
- 1 teaspoon dried crushed red pepper
- 4 8-ounce bottles clam juice
- 2 cups dry white wine
- 3 pounds red snapper fillets
- 16 large sea scallops
- 1 pound large lump crabmeat (optional)
- 1/2 cup all purpose flour
- 6 tablespoons olive oil
- 3 tablespoons unsalted butter
- 6 tablespoons chopped fresh parsley
- 2 large garlic cloves, minced
- 1 large shallot, minced
- 1/2 cup dry white wine

Direction

- Preparing the stew base: Fill a big pot with water and boil. Put in 1 lobster starting with its head. Put the lid onto the pot and let the lobster cook for 5 minutes. In a bowl with ice, put in the cooked lobster. Let the rest of the lobster cook and cool down after. Twist the big claws and tail of each of the lobsters over a rimmed baking sheet until they came off the lobsters. Crack the claws with a nutcracker or a lobster cracker and carefully remove the piece of lobster meat inside. Remove the meat from the shell of each of the lobster tails as well and cut each tail meat crosswise to form 6 medallions. In a small bowl, put in the lobster meat then cover the bowl and keep it in the fridge. In a heavy ziplock plastic bag, put in the juices and shells of the lobsters and use a kitchen mallet to crush the shells to small pieces; put the cracked shells aside.
- Peel the shell off the shrimp and devein it keeping the tails attached to the shrimp; put the shells aside. In a medium-sized bowl, put in the peeled shrimp then cover the bowl and keep it in the fridge.
- In a big pot that can hold at least 8 quarts of ingredients, put in the oil and heat up over medium-high heat setting. Put in the fennel, onions, garlic and celery and cook in hot oil for 5 minutes. Add in the tomato paste and let the mixture cook for another 5 minutes. Mix in the herbs, crushed pepper and tomatoes with juices and cook for 5 minutes. Put in the snapper, clam juice, shrimp shells, wine, lobster shells and its juices; allow the mixture to boil. Lower the heat setting and let the mixture simmer for 1 hour without cover.
- Use a big sieve to strain the cooked stew, by batch, into another big pot; reserve the filtered solids. Place a food mill on top of the second pot. Use the food mill to grind the reserved filtered solids, 2 cups per batch, so that any remaining broth and some of the vegetables and fish are extracted from the solids until you get 13 cups of stew base. Throw away any leftover filtered solids.
- Let the stew base mixture boil for about 15 minutes while stirring it from time to time until the mixture has reduced in volume to 10 cups. (You can prepare the stew base a day in advance. Put the stew base in the fridge without cover first until it is cold, then put on the cover and store it in the fridge. Keep the shrimp and lobster in the fridge as well.)
- Finishing up the stew: Allow the stew base to simmer then stay warm. In a big bowl, mix the shrimp, scallops, lobster meat and crabmeat (optional) together. Put in the flour and lightly mix everything together until well-coated. In a sieve, put in the coated seafood and give it a shake to remove any excess flour. In a big and heavy skillet, put in 3 tablespoons of oil and heat up over medium-high heat setting. Put in half of the coated seafood and cook for 1

minute. Put in 1/2 of the butter followed by 1/2 of the garlic, 1/2 of the shallot and 2 tablespoons of parsley. Let the mixture cook for about 4 minutes until all the seafood turn brown in color and the shrimp and scallops are opaque inside. Place the cooked seafood mixture in a big bowl. Do the same process for the remaining seafood, garlic, butter, 2 tablespoons of parsley, shallot and oil; place it into the same bowl where the first batch of seafood mixture is. Pour wine into the skillet and boil for about 3 minutes until the wine has reduced in volume to form a glaze, scrape any browned bits of food off the skillet. Add the prepared glaze into the seafood mixture and mix well.
- Serving: In separate shallow bowls, put in the stew base. Place the seafood mixture in the middle of each of the bowls. Top it off with 2 tablespoons of parsley.

Nutrition Information

- Calories: 863
- Protein: 65 g(130%)
- Total Fat: 52 g(80%)
- Saturated Fat: 10 g(48%)
- Sodium: 2670 mg(111%)
- Fiber: 6 g(24%)
- Total Carbohydrate: 27 g(9%)
- Cholesterol: 380 mg(127%)

135. Make Ahead Gravy

Serving: 8 | Prep: 5mins | Ready in:

Ingredients

- 1/2 cup butter
- 1/4 cup diced onion
- 1/4 cup thinly sliced celery
- 1 1/2 teaspoons chopped fresh thyme
- 1/2 cup all-purpose flour
- 1 (32 ounce) carton College Inn® Chicken Broth, divided

Direction

- Over medium-high heat, melt butter in a big saucepan. Cook thyme, celery and onion for about 5 minutes until vegetables are golden brown and very soft.
- Stir flour in and let it cook for about 3 minutes just until it's beginning to turn brown, stirring constantly.
- Stir 2 cups of broth in gradually. Cook for about 3 minutes, using a whisk to stir frequently until smooth and thickened. Let it cool. Keep remaining 2 cups of broth and gravy base in the refrigerator for up to 2 days before serving.
- When turkey is roasted, take it out from the pan to let it rest. From pan drippings, skim fat. In a medium saucepan, put turkey pan drippings to refrigerated gravy base, then, heat, stirring frequently over medium heat. Put 1/4 cup of reserved broth at a time until desired thickness and simmer until heated through. Serve.

Nutrition Information

- Calories: 140 calories;
- Sodium: 525
- Total Carbohydrate: 6.6
- Cholesterol: 31
- Protein: 1.5
- Total Fat: 12.1

136. Mango Wine Cooler

Serving: Serves 1 | Prep: | Ready in:

Ingredients

- 1/2 cup chilled dry white wine
- 1 pony(1 ounce) Mohala (mango liqueur)
- 1/4 pitted and peeled mango, cut into strips

- Garnish: 1 strip of mango

Direction

- Mix Mohala, mango and wine in one tall glass packed with ice cubes. Jazz cooler up using reserved strip of mango.

Nutrition Information

- Calories: 285
- Protein: 1 g(2%)
- Total Fat: 0 g(1%)
- Saturated Fat: 0 g(1%)
- Sodium: 9 mg(0%)
- Fiber: 1 g(5%)
- Total Carbohydrate: 39 g(13%)

137. Manhattan Seafood Chowder

Serving: Makes about 16 cups, serving 6 generously as a main course | Prep: | Ready in:

Ingredients

- 6 dozen small hard-shelled clams such as littlenecks (less than 2 inches in diameter)
- cheesecloth for lining sieve
- 1/2 cup water
- 1/2 pound bacon (about 8 slices)
- 2 medium onions
- 4 garlic cloves
- 3 large Yukon Gold or other boiling potatoes (about 1 1/2 pounds)
- 2 large turnips (about 1 pound total)
- 2 medium fennel bulbs (sometimes called anise; about 1 pound total)
- a 28- to 32-ounce can whole tomatoes
- 1 cup dry white wine
- 2 tablespoons tomato paste (optional)
- 1 1/2 pounds skinless halibut fillets
- 1 cup packed fresh flat-leafed parsley or cilantro leaves

Direction

- Scour the clams thoroughly and line a double layer of cheesecloth on big sieve. Let clams steam in water with cover in a heavy, 8-quart kettle that has lid, for 8 to 10 minutes, mixing from time to time, to just open. Throw any clams that remain closed and strain the rest in sieve that was lined place on top of a bowl. Put clam juice aside. Take 2/3 clams out of shells, keep the rest in shells. Turn all clams onto a separate bowl and use foil to slightly cover. Clams can be prepped up to this part 4 hours in advance and refrigerate with cover. Use paper towels to wipe clean the kettle and throw the cheesecloth.
- Slice bacon crosswise to make half-inch-wide pieces. Slice onions to cubes, half-inch in size and mince the garlic. Peel turnips and potatoes and slice to make half-inch cubes. Cut fennel stalks flush with the bulbs, throwing stalks, and remove core from bulbs. Slice bulbs in half lengthwise and slice crosswise to make half-inch-thick pieces. Let bacon cook in kettle on medium heat till crisp, mixing from time to time. Using a slotted spoon, turn bacon onto paper towels to let drain.
- Cook onion and garlic in fat retaining in kettle for 2 minutes, on medium heat, mixing. Mix in reserved clam juice, fennel, turnips and potatoes and simmer with cover for 20 minutes, mixing from time to time, till potatoes become tender.
- Use a sieve place on top of a bowl to strain tomatoes and reserve juice. Chop the tomatoes and put to vegetables including pepper and salt to taste, tomato paste, wine and juice, and simmer for 15 minutes with cover. Chowder can be done up to this portion 4 hours in advance and refrigerate with cover. Bring chowder back to simmer prior to continuing.
- Slice halibut to make 2-inches cubes and take any bones. Chop cilantro or parsley. Put to chowder with clams and halibut, mixing slowly to thoroughly incorporate, and cook for 3-4 minutes, till halibut is barely cooked

completely. Mix in cilantro or parsley and sprinkle bacon over chowder to serve.

Nutrition Information

- Calories: 576
- Total Fat: 19 g(29%)
- Saturated Fat: 6 g(29%)
- Sodium: 1625 mg(68%)
- Fiber: 9 g(35%)
- Total Carbohydrate: 41 g(14%)
- Cholesterol: 132 mg(44%)
- Protein: 56 g(112%)

138. Melon And Blueberry Coupe With White Wine, Vanilla And Mint

Serving: Serves 6 | Prep: | Ready in:

Ingredients

- 1 1/2 cups dry white wine
- 1/2 cup sugar
- 1 vanilla bean, split lengthwise
- 2 1/3 cups cantaloupe cubes (about 1/2 melon)
- 2 1/3 cups honeydew cubes (about 1/2 small melon)
- 2 1/3 cups watermelon cubes (about 1/4 small melon)
- 3 cups fresh blueberries (about 1/12 half-pint baskets)
- 1/2 cup chopped fresh mint

Direction

- In a small saucepan, mix sugar and 1/2 cup of wine. Scrape in seeds from vanilla bean, then put in bean. Stir on low heat for 2 minutes, until syrup is hot and sugar has dissolved. Take away from the heat and allow to soak about half an hour. Take the vanilla bean out of syrup.
- In a big bowl, mix all fruit together. Put into the sugar syrup with leftover 1 cup wine and mint, then drizzle over fruit. Chill, covered, for a minimum of 2 hours. You can make it 6 hours in advance and keep chilled.
- Scoop into big stemmed goblets with a small amount of syrup and fruit.

Nutrition Information

- Calories: 222
- Saturated Fat: 0 g(0%)
- Sodium: 24 mg(1%)
- Fiber: 3 g(14%)
- Total Carbohydrate: 49 g(16%)
- Protein: 2 g(5%)
- Total Fat: 1 g(1%)

139. Mexican Chicken Sauté

Serving: Serves 4 | Prep: | Ready in:

Ingredients

- 3 1/2 to 4 pound chicken, quartered
- 4-6 tablespoon butter
- 2 tablespoons finely chopped onion
- 1 finely chopped garlic clove
- 3 peeled hot green chilis
- Salt
- 2/3 cup white wine (Pouilly Fuissé or White Pinot)
- Garnish: chopped toasted almonds

Direction

- Brown chicken pieces in butter, flipping each piece to evenly color; add 2 tablespoons chopped onion when nearly brow. Gently cook till chicken and onion are blended and brown. Add chilis, garlic and salt to taste. Put 2/3 cup white wine on the mixture; gently simmer till chicken is tender. Put chicken onto hot platter; put pan juices over. Garnish using chopped toasted almonds and serve with polenta.

Nutrition Information

- Calories: 1078
- Fiber: 1 g(2%)
- Total Carbohydrate: 5 g(2%)
- Cholesterol: 357 mg(119%)
- Protein: 80 g(160%)
- Total Fat: 79 g(121%)
- Saturated Fat: 27 g(137%)
- Sodium: 1179 mg(49%)

140. Michael Lewis's Cassoulet De Canard

Serving: Makes 10 servings | Prep: 2hours | Ready in:

Ingredients

- 2 1/2 pounds dried white beans such as Great Northern
- 1/2 pound fresh pork rind
- 2 1/2 pounds confit duck legs
- 6 fresh parsley stems (without leaves)
- 4 fresh thyme sprigs
- 5 whole cloves
- 12 garlic cloves
- 1 (1-pound) piece smoked salted slab bacon, halved crosswise
- 3 cups chopped onion (1 pound)
- 1 teaspoon salt
- 1 pound meaty mutton or lamb bones, cracked by butcher
- 1 cup rendered goose fat
- 6 large tomatoes (3 pounds)
- 5 bay leaves (not California)
- 1 quart beef stock (not canned broth)
- 1 (750-ml) bottle dry white wine
- 2 teaspoons black pepper
- 2 1/2 pounds fresh garlic-pork sausage (not sweet or very spicy) such as saucisson à l'ail au vin rouge, saucisse de canard à l'armagnac, or a mixture of the two
- 1 1/2 cups plain dry bread crumbs
- 1 cup chopped fresh flat-leaf parsley
- a small square of cheesecloth and a wide 10-quart enameled cast-iron pot

Direction

- In a heavy, 8-quart pot, boil 5 quarts of water. Let beans boil for 1 1/2 minutes, with no cover, then switch heat off and immerse them for 50 minutes.
- Meanwhile, in 3-quart saucepan with cold water, 3/4 full, add the pork rind and boil. Let pork rind boil for a minute. Strain and wash in running cold water, then redo. You will know if it's ready when it grows nipples sometimes. Once drained, cut the boiled pork rind into 2-inch pieces, so you can take them out prior to serving.
- Scrape fat off confit duck legs and throw then pull meat apart, better if it's is shredded even more.
- Place in cheesecloth with 8 garlic cloves, whole cloves, thyme and parsley stems and bind to make bundle for bouquet garni.
- Initial seasoning of beans: put to beans with the salt, bouquet garni, 1 cup onion, bacon halves and rind pieces. Simmer for 1 1/4 hours, with cover, scooping off fat periodically. Cool with no cover.
- Meanwhile, let mutton bones brown. To do this, in cast-iron, enameled pot, let goose fat heat on medium heat till it smokes, then let mutton bones cook for 5 minutes, mixing from time to time, till browned. Put aside on plate. Add to pot with leftover 2 cups of onion and brown. This takes 15 minutes. Mix periodically.
- Peel tomatoes, remove the seed and chop.
- Flavoring the meat: put shredded duck and browned bones into onion. Put in pepper, white wine, leftover 4 garlic cloves, tomatoes, beef stock and bay leaves. Simmer for 1 1/2 hours, with cover. Let come to room temperature, with no cover.

- Refrigerate both pot of meat and of beans with cover, overnight.
- Use fork to prick the sausage and slowly grill it in ridged grill pan that is well-seasoned for 20 minutes, on medium low heat, till fat is rendered out. Sausage will remain a bit undercooked on inside one you are done. Turn onto a chopping board and cool a bit. Cut thinly to make quarter-inch rounds.
- Take bay leaves and bones from pot of meat and throw. Use a slotted spoon to take duck and place on plate. Put aside the cooking liquid left in pot.
- Take bacon from the beans and slice to make fat-free, tiny portions. Place the pieces on plate and throw the rest of the bacon fat. Throw bouquet garni and pork rind from beans.
- You may drain the beans and combine with meat cooking juices. Usually there is no liquid left to drain. Instead look for a fairly solid beans wall, with some gluey goop in between. So, add the reserved meat cooking juices to pot of bean. Simmer on medium high heat, mixing from time to time, and let simmer for five minutes, scooping off any scum. Then switch off heat and rest for 5 minutes longer.
- Last Assembly: Preheat the oven to 375° F.
- Scatter beans on bottom of cast-iron, enameled pot in one layer. Top with layer of 1/2 the sausage and bacon, then one more beans layer, then 1/2 of the duck including any mutton, then one more beans layer, and so on, finishing with a layer of the beans. Then pour in sufficient leftover liquid from pot of bean till beans are soaked. Scatter parsley and bread crumbs over.
- Simmer the whole thing, with no cover, on medium low heat. Place in oven for 20 minutes. Use a spoon to break through the bread crumbs in a few areas, letting liquid flow everywhere. Then lower the heat to 350°F and keep it in for 40 minutes longer. Serve while extremely hot.

Nutrition Information

- Calories: 1645
- Protein: 73 g(146%)
- Total Fat: 103 g(158%)
- Saturated Fat: 33 g(163%)
- Sodium: 1583 mg(66%)
- Fiber: 21 g(84%)
- Total Carbohydrate: 96 g(32%)
- Cholesterol: 217 mg(72%)

141. Minestrone With Cabbage And Spinach

Serving: Serves 6 | Prep: | Ready in:

Ingredients

- 2 cups finely chopped celery
- 1 cup finely chopped onion
- 3/4 cup finely chopped leek (white and pale green parts only)
- 1/2 cup dry white wine
- 9 cups canned low-salt chicken broth
- 4 cups diced green cabbage (about 10 ounces)
- 2 cups diced zucchini (from about 2 medium)
- 6 ounces (about 3/4 cup) acini di pepe or other small pasta
- 3 cups (packed) coarsely chopped fresh spinach
- 1/3 cup thinly sliced fresh basil
- Freshly grated Parmesan cheese

Direction

- In big, heavy pot, mix wine, leek, onion and celery on moderate heat. Simmer for 12 minutes, till vegetables turn soft yet not brown, mixing often. Pour in broth and boil. Put in zucchini and cabbage and simmer for 10 minutes. Put in pasta; simmer with cover for 10 minutes, till pasta is barely tender. Put in and cook spinach for 5 minutes. Mix sliced basil in. Season with pepper and salt to taste. Scoop soup to bowls and serve, separately passing the grated Parmesan cheese.

Nutrition Information

- Calories: 218
- Sodium: 164 mg(7%)
- Fiber: 4 g(16%)
- Total Carbohydrate: 35 g(12%)
- Protein: 13 g(26%)
- Total Fat: 3 g(5%)
- Saturated Fat: 1 g(4%)

142. Mini Meatballs In Saffron Sauce

Serving: Makes about 32 | Prep: | Ready in:

Ingredients

- 8 ounces ground pork
- 8 ounces ground veal
- 4 tablespoons chopped fresh Italian parsley
- 2 garlic cloves, minced
- 1 large egg, beaten to blend
- 1 1/2-inch-thick slice French bread, crust removed, soaked in water 3 minutes and squeezed dry
- 1 1/2 teaspoons salt
- 1/2 teaspoon ground black pepper
- All purpose flour
- 1/4 cup extra-virgin olive oil
- 1/4 cup chopped onion
- 1/2 teaspoon Hungarian sweet paprika
- 1 cup (or more) low-salt chicken broth
- 1/4 cup dry white wine
- 1/4 teaspoon crumbled saffron threads

Direction

- Mix 1/2 teaspoon pepper, 1 1/4 teaspoon salt, bread, egg, 1/2 garlic, 1 tablespoon parsley, veal and pork to blend in medium bowl; form meat mixture to 1-in. balls. Use flour to dust meatballs; put aside.
- Heat oil in heavy big skillet on medium high heat then add meatballs; sauté for 10 minutes till browned on all sides. Put meatballs on plate with slotted spoon. Put onion in skillet; lower heat to medium. Sauté for 2 minutes till tender; mix paprika in then wine and 1 cup broth. Put meatballs and any gathered juices back in skillet; simmer then cover. Cook for 25 minutes till meatballs are tender then uncover. Add saffron, leftover garlic and 2 tablespoon parsley; simmer for 10 minutes till sauce thickens, occasionally turning meatballs. Season sauce with pepper and salt to taste; you can make this 1 day ahead, slightly cool then cover and refrigerate. Simmer, thinning using broth if needed.
- Put meatballs and sauce on platter; put 1 tablespoon parsley over.

Nutrition Information

- Calories: 55
- Total Fat: 4 g(7%)
- Saturated Fat: 1 g(6%)
- Sodium: 67 mg(3%)
- Fiber: 0 g(0%)
- Total Carbohydrate: 1 g(0%)
- Cholesterol: 14 mg(5%)
- Protein: 3 g(6%)

143. Mixed Mushroom Risotto

Serving: Makes 8 first-course or 4 main-course servings | Prep: | Ready in:

Ingredients

- 2 tablespoons olive oil
- 1 onion, finely chopped
- 4 garlic cloves, minced
- 6 ounces shiitake mushrooms, stemmed, caps sliced
- 6 ounces crimini mushrooms, sliced
- 2 cups arborio rice or medium-grain rice
- 1 1/2 cups dry white wine
- 5 1/2 cups vegetable stock or canned vegetable broth

- 2 bay leaves
- 1 cup grated Parmesan cheese (about 3 ounces)
- 2 tablespoons chopped fresh basil
- 1 tablespoon chopped fresh thyme
- 2 tablespoons (1/4 stick) butter
- White truffle oil* (optional)
- Additional grated Parmesan cheese

Direction

- Heat oil on medium heat in a big heavy skillet. Add garlic and onion; sauté for 10 minutes till tender. Add all mushrooms; sauté for 3 minutes till brown. Add rice; mix for 3 minutes. Add wine; mix till nearly absorbed.
- Add bay leaves and stock; simmer for 20 minutes till rice is just cooked, it is creamy and liquid is nearly absorbed, occasionally mixing, uncovered. Discard bay leaves. Mix in butter, herbs and 1 cup parmesan cheese; season with pepper and salt to taste. Lightly drizzle truffle oil (optional). Serve, separately passing extra parmesan.

Nutrition Information

- Calories: 319
- Saturated Fat: 4 g(21%)
- Sodium: 178 mg(7%)
- Fiber: 1 g(5%)
- Total Carbohydrate: 45 g(15%)
- Cholesterol: 15 mg(5%)
- Protein: 8 g(17%)
- Total Fat: 10 g(15%)

144. Monkfish Saganaki

Serving: Makes 4 servings | Prep: | Ready in:

Ingredients

- 1 small fennel bulb (sometimes called anise) with fronds
- 1 (4- to 5-inch-long) fresh red chile, chopped, including seeds
- 2 scallions, finely chopped
- 1/3 cup extra-virgin olive oil
- 2/3 cup Chardonnay or other dry white wine
- 8 (1/4-lb) pieces monkfish fillet (about 1 1/2 inches thick), trimmed of all membranes
- 1/4 lb feta (preferably Greek), crumbled

Direction

- Cut stalks off fennel bulb and put 4 fronds aside to use for garnish, then throw the stalks. Slice bulb in half lengthwise, remove core, and slice thinly crosswise.
- In a heavy, 12-inch skillet, sauté chile, scallions and fennel in oil on medium-high heat for 4 to 5 minutes, mixing from time to time, till fennel starts to soften. Pour in wine and boil.
- Add pepper and salt to season fish and put to mixture of fennel. Cook for 5 to 6 minutes with cover, on high heat till fish is barely cooked completely. Uncover and scatter fish and cooking liquid with feta, then cook, tilting the skillet often, barely till cheese melts and sauce turns creamy, for a minute to two, prevent it from boiling. Scoop sauce over the fish and serve right away. Jazz up using fennel fronds.

Nutrition Information

- Calories: 281
- Sodium: 288 mg(12%)
- Fiber: 2 g(7%)
- Total Carbohydrate: 7 g(2%)
- Cholesterol: 27 mg(9%)
- Protein: 6 g(12%)
- Total Fat: 24 g(37%)
- Saturated Fat: 7 g(34%)

145. Monkfish And Clam Bourride

Serving: Makes 4 servings | Prep: | Ready in:

Ingredients

- 6 small (1 1/2- to 2-inch) red potatoes (3/4 pound)
- 2 large leeks (white parts only), cut crosswise into 1/4-inch-thick slices
- 1 (1-pound) piece monkfish fillet, cut into 2-inch chunks
- 3 tablespoons extra-virgin olive oil
- Slow-braised tomatoes
- 1 large fennel bulb (sometimes called anise), stalks discarded and bulb halved lengthwise, cored, and thinly sliced lengthwise
- 1 cup thinly sliced shallots (4 medium)
- 4 garlic cloves, 3 thinly sliced and 1 halved crosswise
- 24 small hard-shelled clams (2 pounds) such as littlenecks (less than 2 inches wide), scrubbed well
- 1/2 cup dry white wine
- 1/2 cup water
- 1 teaspoon dried hot red pepper flakes
- 1 teaspoon finely grated fresh lemon zest
- 8 fresh basil leaves, chopped
- 2 tablespoons chopped fresh parsley
- 4 (3/4-inch-thick) slices crusty bread (about 4 inches wide), toasted
- Accompaniments: aïoli and green olive tapenade
- Garnish: 8 whole fresh basil leaves

Direction

- Slice potatoes into 4, then soak in 3-quart saucepan in 1-inch of cold salted water and simmer for 7 to 10 minutes, with cover, till barely soft. Use a colander to drain, then cool down.
- Rinse the leeks in bowl with cold water, moving the water to remove any grit, and take leeks out of water into sieve to let drain. Blot dry.
- Blot dry the monkfish and add pepper and salt to season. In a 12-inch, heavy, deep skillet, heat the oil on medium high heat till hot yet not smoking, then lightly sear monkfish on every side for a total of 2 minutes till golden, fish won't be cooked fully. Use tongs to turn the fish onto plate.
- In skillet, heat 2 tablespoons of oil from tomatoes that was braised slowly on medium high heat till hot yet not smoking, then sauté fennel, shallots and leeks for 4 to 6 minutes, mixing, till soft and edges start to become brown. Put in and sauté sliced garlic for 2 minutes, mixing, till aromatic.
- Put in the tomato halves, zest, red pepper flakes, water, wine and clams and cook with cover for 6 to 10 minutes, to completely open the clams, monitoring each minute, 6 minutes after and taking out the clams once completely open. Throw any clams remain closed 10 minutes after. Turn the clams onto a soup tureen or big bowl with tongs.
- Put to skillet the potatoes and monkfish and simmer for 4 to 6 minutes, with cover, till fish is barely cooked completely. Take off heat and mix in parsley and basil. Add salt to season and put on top of clams.
- Meanwhile, rub the cut part of garlic clove halved on a side of every toast. Distribute bourride between 4 shallow bowls. Put in 1 garlic toast and place a spoonful of aïoli and a spoonful of tapenade on top.

Nutrition Information

- Calories: 480
- Saturated Fat: 2 g(12%)
- Sodium: 760 mg(32%)
- Fiber: 7 g(28%)
- Total Carbohydrate: 49 g(16%)
- Cholesterol: 54 mg(18%)
- Protein: 37 g(73%)
- Total Fat: 14 g(22%)

146. Moules Marinière

Serving: Makes 4 servings | Prep: | Ready in:

Ingredients

- 3 pounds mussels, rinsed and bearded
- 1/2 cup dry white wine, such as Sancerre
- 2 cloves garlic, minced
- Freshly ground black pepper
- 1 handful flat-leaf parsley

Direction

- Boil garlic, white wine and mussels in big stockpot on medium high heat, covered; cook for 1 minute more, occasionally shaking pan till mussels open. Take off heat; shower mussels using black pepper. Mince parsley; shower over mussels. Divide mussels evenly to 4 shallot soup bowls; put cooking juices on all. Immediately serve.

Nutrition Information

- Calories: 314
- Sodium: 976 mg(41%)
- Fiber: 0 g(2%)
- Total Carbohydrate: 14 g(5%)
- Cholesterol: 95 mg(32%)
- Protein: 41 g(82%)
- Total Fat: 8 g(12%)
- Saturated Fat: 1 g(7%)

147. Muscovy Duck Breasts With Pomegranate Wine Sauce

Serving: Makes 8 servings | Prep: | Ready in:

Ingredients

- 3 tablespoons olive oil, divided
- 1 1/2 cups minced shallots (about 8 large)
- 6 garlic cloves, minced
- 1 1/4 cups dry white wine, divided
- 3/4 cup dry red wine
- 2 14-ounce cans low-salt chicken broth
- 1 14-ounce can low-salt beef broth
- 3/4 cup fresh orange juice
- 2 tablespoons pomegranate molasses*
- 3 teaspoons minced fresh marjoram, divided
- 1 fresh bay leaf
- 4 pounds boneless Muscovy duck breasts (4 to 8 breast halves, depending on size)
- 1 1/2 tablespoons all purpose flour

Direction

- Put 2 tbsp. of oil in a heavy medium saucepan and heat it over medium heat. Add and sauté the shallots for about 18 minutes until golden brown. Add the garlic and sauté for 3 minutes. Add a 3/4 cup of red wine and a cup of white wine. Let the mixture boil for about 10 minutes until most of the liquid is evaporated. Add the orange juice, both broths, 1 tsp. of marjoram, bay leaf, and pomegranate molasses. Bring the mixture to a boil for about 20 minutes until it is reduced to 2 cups. Discard the bay leaf. Take note that the sauce can be prepared 3 days ahead. Keep it covered and chilled.
- Place the rack at the lowest position of the oven and preheat it to 450°F. Rub the duck breast's meat side with 2 tsp. of marjoram and 1 tbsp. of olive oil. Sprinkle the meat with salt and pepper. Working in batches, sear the breasts in a heavy large skillet over high heat, skin-side down, for about 8 minutes until the fat is rendered and the skin is browned.
- Arrange the duck breasts on a rimmed baking sheet, skin-side down. Drain all the fat from the skillet except for 1 1/2 tbsp.; reserve the skillet. Roast the duck for about 20 minutes until the inserted thermometer in its thickest part registers 145°F (medium-rare).
- In the meantime, simmer the sauce. Reheat the reserved duck fat in the skillet over medium heat. Stir in the flour for 1 minute. Whisk in sauce gradually.
- Place the duck breasts on a cutting board. Pour off all the fat from the baking sheet. Add a 1/4 cup of white wine into the baking sheet. Scrape any browned bits and add them into the sauce. Simmer the sauce for 3 minutes until the flavors are well-blended. Season the sauce with salt and pepper. Slice the duck

breasts thinly. Distribute the slices among 8 plates. Drizzle slices with the sauce.

Nutrition Information

- Calories: 433
- Saturated Fat: 4 g(20%)
- Sodium: 265 mg(11%)
- Fiber: 1 g(5%)
- Total Carbohydrate: 16 g(5%)
- Cholesterol: 175 mg(58%)
- Protein: 49 g(98%)
- Total Fat: 15 g(24%)

148. Mushroom And Leek Soup

Serving: 6 | Prep: 15mins | Ready in:

Ingredients

- 4 ounces fresh mushrooms, sliced
- 1 cup sliced leeks
- 2 tablespoons margarine
- 2 tablespoons olive oil
- 1/2 cup dry sherry
- 3 (10.5 ounce) cans condensed beef broth
- 3 3/4 cups water
- 1/2 teaspoon ground black pepper
- 1/2 cup uncooked orzo pasta

Direction

- Sauté the leeks and mushrooms in olive oil and margarine or butter in a big pot on medium high heat, until tender. Pour in sherry and let the liquid reduce by 1/2.
- Add ground black pepper, water and beef broth; boil. Add the pasta and gently boil for 10 minutes or until the pasta becomes tender. If desired, add sliced mushrooms on top to garnish.

Nutrition Information

- Calories: 182 calories;
- Total Fat: 8.4
- Sodium: 1233
- Total Carbohydrate: 19.6
- Cholesterol: 6
- Protein: 6.7

149. Mussel Chowder

Serving: Makes 8 first-course servings | Prep: 1hours | Ready in:

Ingredients

- 4 1/2 lb mussels (preferably cultivated), cleaned and steamed, using half white wine and half water and reserving cooking liquid
- 2 medium leeks (white and pale green parts only), finely chopped
- 2 medium carrots, finely chopped
- 2 large orange bell peppers, finely chopped
- 1 large shallot, finely chopped
- 1/2 teaspoon salt
- 1/4 teaspoon black pepper
- 1/2 stick (1/4 cup) unsalted butter
- 2 tablespoons olive oil
- 2 large garlic cloves, minced
- 1/2 cup dry white wine
- 1/4 cup heavy cream
- Accompaniment: crusty bread

Direction

- In a dampened paper towel-lined-fine sieve, pass the reserved mussel cooking liquid right into bowl. Put aside 2 dozen of mussels in shells, then shuck the rest and slice them in half crosswise.
- Rinse in bowl with cold water with the chopped leeks, then remove and drain thoroughly.
- In a heavy, 5-quart pot, cook shallot, bell peppers, carrots and leeks along with pepper

and salt in oil and butter on medium heat for 7 minutes, with cover, mixing from time to time, till soft. Mix garlic in and cook, with no cover, mixing, for a minute. Put in wine and the strained mussel cooking liquid and let simmer for 10 minutes.
- Mix cream and halved mussels in and simmer for 5 minutes, mixing. Put in reserved mussels in shells and simmer for a minute, till barely heated completely. Add pepper and salt to season.

Nutrition Information

- Calories: 375
- Saturated Fat: 7 g(35%)
- Sodium: 865 mg(36%)
- Fiber: 2 g(8%)
- Total Carbohydrate: 19 g(6%)
- Cholesterol: 97 mg(32%)
- Protein: 32 g(64%)
- Total Fat: 18 g(27%)

150. Mussels And Fries With Mustard Mayonnaise

Serving: Makes 2 servings | Prep: 10mins | Ready in:

Ingredients

- 1 (15- to 16-ounce) package frozen french fries
- 1 small onion
- 2 garlic cloves, forced through a press
- 3 tablespoons unsalted butter
- 2 teaspoons dry mustard
- 2 teaspoons water
- 1/2 cup mayonnaise
- 1 cup dry white wine
- 2 pounds cultivated mussels, rinsed
- 2 tablespoons chopped flat-leaf parsley
- Equipment: an adjustable-blade slicer
- Accompaniment: crusty bread (preferably a baguette)

Direction

- Cook the french fries depending on the package directions and keep warm in the oven if needed.
- At the same time, use a slicer to cut very thin slices of onion, then cook along with garlic and a pinch of salt in butter using a heavy wide medium pot on medium-high heat, keeping it covered and occasionally stirring, until it becomes pale golden.
- While the onions cook, whisk water and mustard together until smoothened and then whisk in 1/4 teaspoon pepper and mayonnaise.
- Add the wine into the onions and simmer briskly while covered, occasionally stirring, for 5 minutes until the onions turn almost tender. Add the mussels and cook while covered, stirring often, for 4 - 6 minutes, until the mussels are wide open. Check the mussels frequently after 4 minutes and move them onto a bowl as they cook. Discard any that didn't open. Stir the parsley into the cooking liquid and season with some salt. Pour over the mussels and serve with mustard mayonnaise and fries.
- You can double this recipe using a heavy 8-quart pot.

Nutrition Information

- Calories: 1362
- Saturated Fat: 22 g(112%)
- Sodium: 2408 mg(100%)
- Fiber: 5 g(22%)
- Total Carbohydrate: 76 g(25%)
- Cholesterol: 195 mg(65%)
- Protein: 61 g(121%)
- Total Fat: 84 g(129%)

151. Mussels And Zucchini Marinière

Serving: Serves 2 | Prep: | Ready in:

Ingredients

- 2 cups chopped onion
- 2 tablespoons unsalted butter
- 2 garlic cloves, minced
- 3/4 cup dry white wine or vermouth
- 1/3 cup heavy cream
- 3 tablespoons fresh fine bread crumbs
- 2 zucchini, scrubbed, halved lengthwise, and cut into 1/8-inch-thick slices
- 2 pounds mussels, scrubbed and the beards pulled off
- 1/3 cup minced fresh parsley leaves
- crusty bread as an accompaniment

Direction

- Over moderate heat, cook onion with butter in a kettle, mixing from time to time, till softened, put garlic, and allow the mixture to cook for a minute. Mix in wine, let the mixture simmer for 2 minutes, and mix in bread crumbs and cream. Simmer the cream mixture, put mussels and zucchini, and allow the mixture to steam for 3 minutes with cover or till mussels are opened and zucchini is crisp-tender. Throw any mussels that remain closed. Mix in parsley and season to taste with salt, among 2 soup plates, distribute mussel mixture, and serve together with bread.

Nutrition Information

- Calories: 819
- Total Fat: 38 g(58%)
- Saturated Fat: 19 g(94%)
- Sodium: 1419 mg(59%)
- Fiber: 6 g(22%)
- Total Carbohydrate: 49 g(16%)
- Cholesterol: 212 mg(71%)
- Protein: 61 g(122%)

152. Mussels In Green Peppercorn Sauce

Serving: Makes 4 servings | Prep: 25mins | Ready in:

Ingredients

- 2 large shallots, chopped (1/2 cup)
- 2 tablespoons unsalted butter
- 1 1/2 teaspoons dried green peppercorns, crushed
- 1 cup dry white wine
- 4 pounds cultivated mussels, scrubbed
- 1/2 cup heavy cream
- 2 tablespoons chopped flat-leaf parsley

Direction

- To prepare: In a 5 to 6-qt. heavy pot, cook the shallots in butter with 1/4 tsp salt for 3-4 minutes on medium heat, stirring from time to time, until they become soft. Add peppercorns and cook for 2 minutes, mixing, and add the wine, then simmer. Add the mussels and let it cook for 5-7 minutes on high heat with a cover, mixing once, until the mussels just open wide. After 7 minutes, get rid of any mussels remaining closed.
- Use a slotted spoon to move the mussels to serving bowls. Mix the cream into the cooking liquid, then boil. Mix in the salt to taste and parsley, then scoop the sauce on top of the mussels.

Nutrition Information

- Calories: 593
- Fiber: 1 g(4%)
- Total Carbohydrate: 23 g(8%)
- Cholesterol: 183 mg(61%)
- Protein: 55 g(111%)
- Total Fat: 27 g(42%)
- Saturated Fat: 12 g(62%)
- Sodium: 1315 mg(55%)

153. Mussels In Romesco Sauce

Serving: Serves 8 to 10 as part of a tapas buffet | Prep: | Ready in:

Ingredients

- 2 dried mild red chilies such as New Mexico*, seeded and torn into large pieces (wear rubber gloves)
- 1/3 cup red-wine vinegar
- 1/4 cup whole blanched almonds
- 2/3 cup olive oil
- 2 slices firm white sandwich bread
- 1 medium onion, chopped
- 3 large garlic cloves, chopped coarse
- 4 plum tomatoes (about 1/2 pound), peeled, seeded, and chopped
- 1 teaspoon sweet paprika
- 1/2 cup dry white wine
- 1/2 cup water
- 2 pounds mussels (preferably cultivated), scrubbed well and beards pulled off
- 2 tablespoons finely chopped, washed-well, and spun-dry fresh coriander sprigs
- *available at Hispanic markets and some specialty foods shops

Direction

- Prep sauce: immerse chilies in vinegar in small bowl, flesh sides facing down for half an hour. Take chilies, save vinegar in bowl, and scoop flesh off chilies skins, throw the skins. Put chili flesh back to the reserved vinegar.
- Let almonds cook in 2 tablespoons of oil in heavy skillet on medium-low heat, mixing, till golden and use slotted spoon to turn onto paper towels and let drain. Heat the oil left in skillet on medium heat till hot yet not smoking and let bread fry till golden, flipping it. Turn the bread onto a chopping board and slice to make cubes.
- Heat leftover oil in skillet on medium heat till hot yet not smoking and let onion cook till edges are barely golden, mixing. Put in and cook garlic, mixing, till garlic turn light golden. Put in paprika, tomatoes, bread cubes, almonds and chili mixture and cook for 2 minutes, mixing from time to time. Coarsely purée the mixture in food processor and add salt to season. Sauce can be done a week in advance and refrigerate with cover.
- Mix water, a cup of sauce and wine in heavy kettle, putting the rest of the sauce aside for other use, and boil. Put in mussels and gently boil for 4 minutes with cover, or till most of them opened.
- Turn the mussels onto serving dish, throw any that remain closed. Let sauce simmer, mixing, till cooked down and thickened partially and scoop on top of mussels. Scatter coriander on mussels.

Nutrition Information

- Calories: 322
- Sodium: 366 mg(15%)
- Fiber: 2 g(6%)
- Total Carbohydrate: 12 g(4%)
- Cholesterol: 32 mg(11%)
- Protein: 16 g(31%)
- Total Fat: 23 g(35%)
- Saturated Fat: 3 g(16%)

154. Mussels In Saffron And White Wine Broth

Serving: Makes 8 servings | Prep: 25mins | Ready in:

Ingredients

- 2 teaspoons butter
- 3 garlic cloves, chopped
- 1 cup dry white wine
- 2 tablespoons half and half
- 2 1/2 teaspoons saffron threads
- 1 cup clam juice
- 4 scallions, thinly sliced

- 3 tomatoes, seeded, and chopped
- 3 tablespoons lemon juice
- 8 pounds mussels, scrubbed and debearded
- 2 1/2 tablespoons chives, chopped

Direction

- Melt butter in big pot and add garlic. Sauté for 1 minute till garlic is fragrant. Add saffron, half and half and wine; simmer for 5 minutes. Add clam juice, scallions, tomato, and lemon juice, scallions, tomato, and lemon juice; simmer for 5 minutes.
- Add mussels, then cover; steam for 5-7 minutes till they open. Shake pot to redistribute mussels, holding lid down with kitchen towel. Discard unopened mussels. Divide mussels to 8 bowls; evenly distribute broth to bowls; put fresh chives over each.
- Cleaning mussels: Under cold running water, hold mussel. Use brush with stiff bristles to scrub mussel thoroughly to remove mud, sand and grit from shell's exterior. From each mussel, especially non-farmed ones, they usually have dark, shaggy beard extending from each shell. Remove them for cleaner appearance in final dish. Pull beard away from shell till taut after scrubbing a mussel; sharply pull beard down toward dark hinge. It will easily snap away. Do this before cooking because it kills the mussel.

Nutrition Information

- Calories: 441
- Saturated Fat: 3 g(14%)
- Sodium: 1492 mg(62%)
- Fiber: 1 g(3%)
- Total Carbohydrate: 21 g(7%)
- Cholesterol: 131 mg(44%)
- Protein: 57 g(113%)
- Total Fat: 12 g(18%)

155. Mussels On The Half Shell With Pesto

Serving: Makes 40 | Prep: | Ready in:

Ingredients

- 1 cup dry white wine
- 1 cup water
- 1/4 cup chopped shallots
- 2 tablespoons white wine vinegar
- 4 garlic cloves, crushed with side of knife
- 40 fresh mussels, scrubbed, debearded
- 4 cups fresh basil leaves
- 4 garlic cloves, chopped
- 3 tablespoons olive oil
- 6 tablespoons freshly grated Parmesan cheese
- 2 tablespoons low-fat mayonnaise

Direction

- Boil initial 5 ingredients in a big pot. Put mussels in pot in batches; cover. Cook for 4 minutes till mussels open. Put mussels in big bowl using slotted spoon; discard unopened ones. Cool mussels and strain cooking liquid; keep 1 cup.
- From shells, remove mussels; keep half of every shell. Put mussels in medium bowl; refrigerate.
- In processor, finely chop garlic and basil. Add oil and reserved 1 cup of cooking liquid slowly as processor runs; process till blended well. Blend in mayonnaise and cheese. Put pesto in big bowl; season with pepper and salt. Add mussels; toss to coat. Chill for minimum of 1 hour. You can make it 1 day ahead and refrigerate kept shells.
- Put pesto and mussels in reserved shells; put on platter.

Nutrition Information

156. Mussels With Fennel And Roasted Red Pepper Butter

Serving: Serves 8 as a first course | Prep: | Ready in:

Ingredients

- 1 stick (1/2 cup) unsalted butter, softened
- 2 red bell peppers, roasted (procedure follows)
- 1 garlic clove, chopped, if desired
- 1/4 teaspoon dried hot red pepper flakes
- 3 1/2 pounds mussels
- 1 1/2 cups dry white wine
- 1/4 cup medium-dry Sherry
- 2 cups thinly sliced fennel bulb
- 1 1/2 cups thinly sliced shallot
- 1/4 teaspoon dried hot red pepper flakes
- 1 teaspoon fennel seeds
- 2 fresh thyme sprigs or 1/4 teaspoon dried
- 1/2 teaspoon salt

Direction

- Red pepper butter: Blend salt to taste, red pepper flakes, garlic and roasted peppers with butter in blender/food processor till smooth; you can make it 2 days ahead, chilled, covered.
- In few changes of cold water, scrub mussels well, scrape beards off then rinse mussels. Boil salt, thyme, fennel seeds, red pepper flakes, shallot, fennel bulb, sherry, white wine and 4 cups water in big kettle for 3 minutes, covered. Add mussels; boil for 4-6 minutes till shells open, occasionally shaking kettle, covered; discard unopened mussels. Put shallot, fennel bulb and mussels in shallow bowls; put hot broth on top. Put 1 tbsp. red pepper butter in middle of every serving; separate serve leftover red pepper butter.
- Roast peppers: Char peppers above open flame with long-handled fork for 2-3 minutes till skins blacken, turning them; or, broil peppers on rack of broiler pan under preheated broiler 2-in. from heat for 15-25 minutes till skins are charred and blistered, turning every 5 minutes. Put peppers in bowl; steam till cool enough to handle, covered. Peel, starting at blossom end, keeping peppers whole; discard ribs and seeds. When handling chiles, wear rubber gloves.

Nutrition Information

- Calories: 340
- Sodium: 733 mg(31%)
- Fiber: 3 g(10%)
- Total Carbohydrate: 17 g(6%)
- Cholesterol: 86 mg(29%)
- Protein: 25 g(50%)
- Total Fat: 16 g(25%)
- Saturated Fat: 8 g(41%)

157. Mussels With Garlic And Fines Herbes

Serving: Serves 4 | Prep: | Ready in:

Ingredients

- Special Equipment: Coffee filter or cheesecloth
- 3 pounds mussels
- 1 1/2 cups white wine
- 4 shallot lobes, sliced thin
- 1 bay leaf
- 2 tablespoons olive oil
- 2 cloves garlic, sliced thin
- 1 tablespoon chopped flat-leaf parsley leaves (about 3 sprigs)
- 1/2 tablespoon chopped chervil leaves (about 4 sprigs)
- 2 teaspoons chopped tarragon leaves (about 2 branches)
- 1 teaspoon thinly sliced chive blades (about 3 blades)

Direction

- Clean mussels: Scrub well in cold running water. If needed, debeard them, pulling any wiry fronds out coming through the shell's seams.

- Mix bay leaf, 1/2 shallot and white wine in a big pot/deep sauté pan. Put mussels over the top; cover with a lid. Boil on high heat for 3-4 minutes to steam open mussels. After 2 minutes, mix to evenly disperse the heat among the mussels. Put opened mussels to 4 shallows bowl; discard unopened mussels as this is an indication that they are dead or bad.
- Through either several of cheesecloth layer/coffee filter, strain the cooking liquid into a clean pan. Add garlic, leftover shallot and olive oil; boil on high heat. Slightly reduce the mixture to condense to an opaque liquid. Taste; add a little water if too salty. Sprinkle herbs; put sauce on mussels. Immediately serve with a tangy baguette torn into big pieces which you can use to soak up the broth when you are finished with the mussels.

Nutrition Information

- Calories: 443
- Cholesterol: 95 mg(32%)
- Protein: 42 g(84%)
- Total Fat: 14 g(22%)
- Saturated Fat: 2 g(12%)
- Sodium: 984 mg(41%)
- Fiber: 2 g(8%)
- Total Carbohydrate: 25 g(8%)

158. Mussels With Roasted Potatoes

Serving: Makes 4 first-course or light-lunch servings | Prep: | Ready in:

Ingredients

- 4 large Yukon Gold or russet (baking) potatoes (2 pounds total)
- 6 tablespoons extra-virgin olive oil
- 1/2 tablespoon kosher salt
- 1/3 cup finely chopped shallot
- 3 garlic cloves, minced
- Rounded 1/4 teaspoon dried hot red pepper flakes
- 1 cup dry white wine
- 3/4 cup water
- 2 pounds mussels (preferably cultivated), scrubbed well and beards removed
- 3 tablespoons chopped fresh parsley

Direction

- Preheat an oven to 450°F.
- Slice potatoes in half lengthwise and from side opposite of the cut side of every potato half, cut a quarter-inch-thick portion to create 8 flat slabs with 1/2 to 3/4-inch thick. Throw clippings, then with 2 tablespoons of oil, coat the potato slabs and scatter all of salt over. In a big shallow 1-inch deep baking pan, lay in single layer and let roast in center oven for 25 minutes to half an hour in all, flipping over one time midway through roasting, till soft and golden brown.
- Just prior potatoes are finish, in a deep 12-inch heavy skillet over moderate heat, cook red pepper flakes, garlic and shallot in 2 tablespoons of oil for 3 minutes, mixing, till tender. Put water and wine and simmer. Put the mussels and allow to cook with cover over moderate -high heat till they open wide, monitoring often after 3 minutes and to a bowl, putting opened mussels. Throw any mussels still closed after 6 minutes.
- Into mussel broth, mix leftover 2 tablespoons oil and parsley and put pepper and salt to season.
- Between 4 shallow bowls, distribute the potatoes and put broth and mussels on top.

Nutrition Information

- Calories: 583
- Protein: 32 g(64%)
- Total Fat: 26 g(39%)
- Saturated Fat: 4 g(19%)
- Sodium: 1302 mg(54%)
- Fiber: 5 g(21%)
- Total Carbohydrate: 50 g(17%)

- Cholesterol: 64 mg(21%)

159. Mussels À La Marinière

Serving: Makes 6 servings | Prep: | Ready in:

Ingredients

- 2 liters (8 cups) of mussels cooked as above [see note from Gourmet's food editors, below]
- 3 deciliters (1 1/4 cups) of cooking liquid
- 1 1/2 deciliters (5 fluid ounces, 2/3 cup) of white wine
- 20 grams (2/3 ounce) of shallot finely minced
- 2 good pinches of minced parsley
- 75 grams (2 2/3 ounces, 1/3 cup) of butter
- 2 good soup spoons of bread crumbs ground into a fine semolina

Direction

- Carefully pour liquid that mussels have rendered into a separate container to get rid of sand to enable to use the same casserole that was used to cook the mussels.
- Wash casserole. Put in shallot and white wine. Cook it down vigorously till leftover is roughly 3 tablespoons. Then put in carefully measured 1 1/4 cups or 3 deciliters mussels cooking water. Ensure it is not very salty, otherwise you will need to put in additional water, to dilute cooking liquid. Boil for several seconds without cooking it down. Switch heat off.
- Put pepper to sauce, in case it has not been included as peppercorns, turn off fire always; and butter, cut into extremely small portions, same as the size of very small hazelnuts. Scatter on top of bread crumbs, stirring thoroughly and shaking casserole till butter is liquified; and some of the minced parsley; and in case using, some of the lemon juice.
- Return mussels to casserole. Shake in sauce for several seconds just without placing them right on heat. For the mussels are heated well and covered in sauce fully, prevent form boiling or even overheating, otherwise butter would lose its creaminess and become oil.
- Into a heated plate or a heated timbale, put everything in pile, pell-mell.
- Cook mussels with a cup water, a pinch white pepper, 1/3 Turkish bay leaf, 5 thyme sprigs and one sliced medium onion for 6 to 8 minutes, with cover, on high heat till mussels barely open wide, throw the mussels that remain closed 8 minutes after.

Nutrition Information

160. Mustard Seed Crusted Salmon With Mustard Cream Sauce

Serving: Makes 4 servings | Prep: | Ready in:

Ingredients

- 1/2 cup dry white wine
- 1/4 cup (packed) chopped shallots
- 3 tablespoons yellow mustard seeds
- 3/4 cup whipping cream
- 5 tablespoons whole grain Dijon mustard
- 1 tablespoon chopped fresh tarragon
- 4 6-ounce skinless salmon fillets
- 2 tablespoons butter

Direction

- In small, heavy saucepan, boil shallots, a tablespoon of mustard seeds and wine for 2 minutes, till mixture is cooked done to half cup. Mix in 2 1/2 tablespoons Dijon mustard, tarragon and cream. Boil for 3 minutes, till thickened into consistency of a sauce. Add pepper and salt to season. Take off heat; put in cover.
- Brush leftover 2 1/2 tablespoons of Dijon mustard on each side of salmon. Scatter salt,

pepper and leftover 2 tablespoons mustard seeds on each side of salmon. In nonstick, big skillet, liquify butter on moderate heat. Put in and cook salmon for 4 minutes on each side, barely till opaque in the middle. Turn onto platter. Top salmon with scoop of mustard sauce.

Nutrition Information

- Calories: 594
- Sodium: 326 mg(14%)
- Fiber: 2 g(7%)
- Total Carbohydrate: 6 g(2%)
- Cholesterol: 159 mg(53%)
- Protein: 38 g(76%)
- Total Fat: 45 g(69%)
- Saturated Fat: 18 g(88%)

161. Mustard Watercress Sauce

Serving: Makes about 2 cups | Prep: | Ready in:

Ingredients

- 1/4 cup minced shallots
- 2 tablespoons unsalted butter
- 1/4 cup dry white wine
- 1 cup sour cream
- 3 tablespoons coarse-grained mustard
- 2 tablespoons Dijon-style mustard
- 1 cup finely chopped watercress
- 1/3 cup hot water

Direction

- Let shallot cook in butter in saucepan on medium low heat, mixing, till soft, pour in wine, and let the mixture boil till wine is nearly vaporized. Take pan off heat and mix in pepper and salt to taste, water, watercress, mustards and sour cream. Let sauce come to room temperature and serve along with grilled or steamed vegetables or poached fish.

Nutrition Information

- Calories: 189
- Sodium: 241 mg(10%)
- Fiber: 1 g(4%)
- Total Carbohydrate: 5 g(2%)
- Cholesterol: 45 mg(15%)
- Protein: 2 g(5%)
- Total Fat: 18 g(27%)
- Saturated Fat: 10 g(52%)

162. Mykonos Fillet Of Sole

Serving: Makes 4 servings | Prep: 30mins | Ready in:

Ingredients

- 2 lemon sole fillets (2 lb total), each cut in half crosswise
- 1 lemon, thinly sliced
- 1/4 cup dry white wine
- 3/4 teaspoon salt
- 1 large egg, lightly beaten
- 1/4 cup whole milk
- 3/4 cup fine dry bread crumbs
- 1 large garlic clove, minced
- 2 tablespoons chopped fresh parsley
- 1/4 teaspoon black pepper
- 4 tablespoons olive oil
- 1 tablespoon unsalted butter

Direction

- Position rack of oven in center place and preheat the oven to 200°F.
- In shallow dish, mix quarter teaspoon of salt, wine, half the slices of lemon and fish. Marinate for half an hour at room temperature with cover.
- In a separate shallow dish, mix milk, quarter teaspoon of salt and egg. Mix in shallow bowl

the leftover quarter teaspoon of salt, pepper, parsley, garlic and bread crumbs.
- Dunk pieces of fish in egg mixture, 1 by 1, allowing excess to drip off, then dip in mixture of bread-crumb, shake excess off. Turn onto a wax paper sheet, placing fish in single layer.
- Heat in a nonstick, 12-inch skillet half tablespoon of butter and 2 tablespoons of oil on medium high heat till hot yet not smoking, then fry 2 fish pieces for a total of 4 to 5 minutes, flipping over one time, till just cooked completely and golden. Turn onto a baking sheet and put in oven to retain warmth, then cook leftover 2 fish pieces in leftover half tablespoon of butter and 2 tablespoons of oil in the exact same manner. Serve the fish including leftover slices of lemon.

Nutrition Information

- Calories: 324
- Saturated Fat: 5 g(25%)
- Sodium: 417 mg(17%)
- Fiber: 1 g(6%)
- Total Carbohydrate: 18 g(6%)
- Cholesterol: 92 mg(31%)
- Protein: 15 g(30%)
- Total Fat: 21 g(32%)

163. Nectarine And Blueberry Clafouti

Serving: Serves 6 to 8 | Prep: | Ready in:

Ingredients

- 2 nectarines (about 1/2 pound)
- 1 cup blueberries (about 5 ounces)
- 1 cup fruity white wine such as Riesling
- 5 tablespoons unsalted butter
- 4 large eggs
- 1/2 cup granulated sugar
- 1/8 teaspoon salt
- 1/2 cup all-purpose flour
- 1 cup whole milk
- 1 tablespoon vanilla
- confectioners'sugar for dusting

Direction

- Preheat the oven to 325°F. and use butter to grease a shallow, 2-quart baking dish.
- Slice nectarines to make wedges about quarter-inch-thick and macerate in wine in bowl along with blueberries for 15 minutes.
- Liquify butter and partially cool. Beat granulated sugar, salt and eggs in a big bowl. Mix in flour till blended thoroughly and mix in quarter cup wine from mixture of fruit, vanilla, butter and milk till smooth. Turn the fruit onto a baking dish using slotted spoon, saving wine for other use, like sangría, and place in base. Cautiously put the batter on top of fruit, fruit will float to surface and bake in oven's top third till set in the middle and puffed, for 55 minutes to an hour. Turn clafouti onto rack to cool down.
- Barely prior to serving, sprinkle confectioners' sugar on clafouti. Serve clafouti at room temperature or while warm.

Nutrition Information

- Calories: 336
- Sodium: 115 mg(5%)
- Fiber: 1 g(6%)
- Total Carbohydrate: 38 g(13%)
- Cholesterol: 154 mg(51%)
- Protein: 7 g(14%)
- Total Fat: 14 g(22%)
- Saturated Fat: 8 g(40%)

164. New Coq Au Vin

Serving: Makes 4 to 6 servings | Prep: 25mins | Ready in:

Ingredients

- 6 chicken thighs with skin and bone
- 2 tablespoons olive oil
- 10 garlic cloves, halved
- 3 celery ribs, cut crosswise into 1-inch pieces
- 1 cup dry white wine
- 1 cup water
- 1/4 cup finely chopped flat-leaf parsley
- Olive-oil Mashed Potatoes

Direction

- Blot chicken dry and put in half teaspoon of pepper and a teaspoon of salt to season. In a heavy 12-inch skillet, heat the oil on moderately-high heat till it shimmers. Working in 2 batches, sear the chicken for 3 to 5 minutes, skin side facing down, till golden brown, without flipping, then turn onto plate.
- Drain all except 2 tablespoons of fat from the skillet. In skillet, cook celery and garlic on moderate heat for 5 minutes, mixing often, till golden and barely starting to soften. Put in wine and boil with no cover for 3 to 5 minutes, till cooked down by roughly 1/2. Put in water and simmer.
- Put chicken back to skillet, skin side facing up, slightly cover and simmer for 20 to 25 minutes till cooked completely. Scatter with parsley.

Nutrition Information

- Calories: 645
- Total Carbohydrate: 5 g(2%)
- Cholesterol: 219 mg(73%)
- Protein: 38 g(75%)
- Total Fat: 49 g(75%)
- Saturated Fat: 12 g(59%)
- Sodium: 213 mg(9%)
- Fiber: 1 g(3%)

165. Oka Cheese Fondue

Serving: Makes 8 to 10 servings | Prep: 30mins | Ready in:

Ingredients

- 1 1/4 cups heavy cream
- 1/2 cup dry white wine (preferably Riesling)
- 1/2 cup ice wine (preferably Canadian)
- 3 tablespoons all-purpose flour
- 1 lb Oka cheese or Port-Salut, rind removed and cheese coarsely grated (4 cups)
- Accompaniments: cubed baguette; apple and pear wedges
- apple wedges
- pear wedges
- a fondue pot with long-handled forks

Direction

- In a heavy, 2-quart saucepan, mix wines, flour and cream till smooth, then boil on medium heat for 5 minutes, mixing continuously, till silky and thick. Put in 1/2 of cheese and slowly mix till nearly melted, then put in the rest of the cheese and cook for 3 minutes, mixing, till cheese melts and fondue becomes smooth. Serve in pot of fondue.
- Note: Fondue may be done a day in advance. Place a wax paper piece on top and cool fully, then refrigerate. Rewarm on medium low heat, mixing continuously, till smooth.

Nutrition Information

166. Orange Spice Fruit Compote

Serving: Makes 6 servings | Prep: | Ready in:

Ingredients

- Spiced bouquet garni (leaves from 1 fresh rosemary branch; two 5-inch-long strips orange peel; 1 teaspoon whole black peppercorns)
- 3 cups orange juice

- 2 cups dried apricots (preferably whole Mediterranean; about 12 ounces)
- 3/4 cup dried tart cherries
- 3/4 cup golden raisins
- 3/4 cup dry white wine
- 3/4 cup sugar

Direction

- On 3 layers of big dampened cheesecloth square, place the orange peel, peppercorns and rosemary. Collect cheesecloth and firmly bind. Mix in big saucepan the bouquet garni and the rest of the ingredients. Boil on high heat, mixing till sugar is dissolved. Lower the heat to moderately-low and simmer for 35 minutes, with no cover, till liquid is syrupy and thick and fruit becomes tender, mixing from time to time. Turn the compote including bouquet garni into bowl; refrigerate till cold, for not less than 6 hours to no more than 2 days. Take bouquet garni with tongs to serve.

Nutrition Information

- Calories: 400
- Fiber: 6 g(22%)
- Total Carbohydrate: 98 g(33%)
- Protein: 3 g(7%)
- Total Fat: 1 g(1%)
- Saturated Fat: 0 g(1%)
- Sodium: 13 mg(1%)

167. Oranges Poached In Riesling And Rosemary Syrup

Serving: Makes 4 servings | Prep: | Ready in:

Ingredients

- 1 750-ml bottle Johannisberg Riesling
- 2/3 cup sugar
- 4 navel oranges, peel and white pith removed, oranges cut crosswise in half
- 2 3x1/2-inch strips orange peel (orange part only), cut into slivers
- 1 teaspoon fresh whole rosemary leaves (stripped from stems)

Direction

- In heavy big saucepan, boil sugar and wine on medium high heat, mixing till sugar melts. Lower heat to medium low then simmer for 10 minutes. Add rosemary, peel and oranges. Simmer to blend flavors for 8 minutes. Transfer oranges with a slotted spoon into medium bowl. In saucepan, boil liquid for 8 minutes till reduced to 1 1/3 cups. Put syrup on oranges. Refrigerate for 4 hours to chill well. You can make this 1 day in advanced, chilled and covered.

Nutrition Information

- Calories: 349
- Saturated Fat: 0 g(0%)
- Sodium: 2 mg(0%)
- Fiber: 3 g(13%)
- Total Carbohydrate: 58 g(19%)
- Protein: 1 g(3%)
- Total Fat: 0 g(0%)

168. Orecchiette With Rabbit, Tomato, And Basil Sauce

Serving: Makes 4 to 6 servings | Prep: | Ready in:

Ingredients

- 5 tablespoons extra-virgin olive oil
- 1 large onion, chopped
- 2 garlic cloves, minced
- 1 2 3/4- to 3-pound rabbit, cut into pieces, meat finely chopped, or 1 pound finely chopped skinless boneless chicken thigh meat
- 1 cup dry white wine
- 1 pound plum tomatoes, chopped

- 1 28-ounce can crushed tomatoes with added puree
- 1 1/2 cups chopped fresh basil (from about 3 large bunches)
- 1/4 teaspoon dried crushed red pepper
- 1 pound orecchiette (little ear-shaped pasta)
- Freshly grated Parmesan cheese

Direction

- In big, heavy skillet, heat 3 tablespoons of oil on moderately-high heat. Put in garlic and onion and sauté for 5 minutes, till golden and tender. Put in the chopped rabbit; sauté for 4 minutes, till pale brown. Pour in wine and boil for 3 minutes, till cooked down a bit. Mix in leftover 2 tablespoons of oil, crushed red pepper, a cup of basil, crushed tomatoes, and chopped tomatoes. Boil. Lower the heat to moderately-low. Simmer till sauce partially thickens, mixing from time to time, for half an hour. Liberally season sauce using pepper and salt.
- Meantime, in big pot with salted boiling water, let pasta cook till barely tender yet remain firm to bite. Strain. Put pasta back to pot. Put in sauce; toss till coated. Turn onto bowl. Scatter Parmesan cheese and leftover half cup of basil on top.

Nutrition Information

- Calories: 1147
- Saturated Fat: 8 g(41%)
- Sodium: 520 mg(22%)
- Fiber: 10 g(38%)
- Total Carbohydrate: 109 g(36%)
- Cholesterol: 186 mg(62%)
- Protein: 85 g(170%)
- Total Fat: 38 g(58%)

169. Paccheri With Shellfish, Squid, And Tomatoes

Serving: 8 servings | Prep: | Ready in:

Ingredients

- 3 medium tomatoes, halved, seeds and cores removed
- 12 oz. cleaned squid, bodies and tentacles separated
- 6 Tbsp. extra-virgin olive oil, divided, plus more for drizzling
- 1 1/2 lb. small shrimp, preferably head-on, peeled, deveined, shells and heads reserved
- 2 cups dry white wine, divided
- 6 garlic cloves, thinly sliced
- 1 lb. cockles or Manila clams, scrubbed
- 1 lb. mussels, scrubbed, debearded
- 1/2 tsp. crushed red pepper flakes
- 2 lb. paccheri or other large tube pasta
- Kosher salt
- 1 Tbsp. fish sauce (optional)
- 1 cup torn basil

Direction

- Grate tomatoes on the biggest holes of a box grater, cut sides down, into a medium bowl until skin remains. Chop skin finely and add to the bowl.
- Cut squid bodies, lengthwise, in half. Cut every half to 1/2 inch pieces, crosswise. Put in a small bowl. Cut tentacles crosswise in half. Add to the bowl.
- In a heavy pot or big Dutch oven, heat 3 tbsp. oil on medium-high. Add leftover shrimp heads (if using) and shells. Cook for 10-12 minutes, until shells start to brown, smashing down on heads and shells. Add 1 cup of wine. Cook for about 5 minutes until alcohol smell is gone and until it reduces to half. Add 2 cups water and boil. Lower heat to a bare simmer. Cook for 15-20 minutes until reduces to 1/3. Cool stock for 20 minutes. Strain using a fine-mesh sieve into a heatproof measuring glass,

pressing on solids. You should have 1 1/2 cups. Put aside.
- Wipe pot out. Pour in leftover 3 tbsp. oil. And heat on medium heat. Add garlic and cook, occasionally stirring, for about 5 minutes until golden. Add grated tomatoes and cook for 6-8 minutes, until tomatoes slightly thicken and start to stick to the bottom of the pot, occasionally stirring. Add leftover 1 cup of wine, red pepper flakes, mussels, and cockles. Cover pot and cook, occasionally shaking, for about 5 minutes until mussels and cockles open. Place mussels and cockles in a medium bowl using a slotted spoon, leaving any that didn't open. Cover pot and cook unopened mussels and cockles for a minute or so. Put in bowl with others. At this point, throw out any that didn't open. Retain the warmth of shellfish sauce.
- In a big pot of boiling salted water, cook pasta for 6-8 minutes until just slightly under al dente.
- Scoop 1 cup of pasta water with a heatproof measuring cup. Place pasta in pot with sauce using a mesh spider or slotted spoon. Add leftover stock; boil. Lower heat to simmer. Add squid and shrimp to sauce. Cook for about 5 minutes, constantly tossing and adding a splash of pasta water at a time as necessary, until sauce is glossy and thick enough to cling to noodles and pasta is al dente. Add fish sauce, optional, and fold in steamed mussels and cockles. Taste. Season with salt if needed.
- Place pasta on a platter. Drizzle oil and top with basil.

Nutrition Information

- Calories: 746
- Fiber: 4 g(17%)
- Total Carbohydrate: 95 g(32%)
- Cholesterol: 222 mg(74%)
- Protein: 48 g(96%)
- Total Fat: 15 g(23%)
- Saturated Fat: 2 g(12%)

- Sodium: 1053 mg(44%)

170. Pan Fried Trout With Green Onions

Serving: Serves 2 can be doubled | Prep: | Ready in:

Ingredients

- 2 whole 11- to 12-ounce trout, boned
- All purpose flour
- 1 tablespoon olive oil
- 3 green onions, chopped
- 1/2 cup dry white wine
- 1 tablespoon butter

Direction

- Open every trout flat to resemble a book. Generously sprinkle pepper and salt. Dust flour on trout. Shake excess off. In a heavy big skillet, heat 1/2 tbsp. olive oil on medium high heat. Put 1 trout. Sauté for 2 minutes per side until trout is just opaque at the middle and coating is crisp. Put trout on a plate. Use foil to tent to retain warmth. Repeat process with leftover 1/2 tbsp. oil and trout.
- Use paper towels to wipe out skillet. Put aside 2 tbsp. green onions. Add butter, wine and leftover green onions to the same skillet. Simmer on medium heat for 3 minutes, occasionally stirring, until mixture nearly reduces to a glaze. Spoon sauce on trout. Sprinkle reserved 2 tbsp. green onions on trout. Serve.

Nutrition Information

- Calories: 804
- Total Carbohydrate: 6 g(2%)
- Cholesterol: 283 mg(94%)
- Protein: 91 g(183%)
- Total Fat: 41 g(62%)
- Saturated Fat: 11 g(54%)

- Sodium: 237 mg(10%)
- Fiber: 1 g(3%)

- Total Fat: 21 g(32%)
- Saturated Fat: 7 g(34%)
- Sodium: 251 mg(10%)
- Fiber: 2 g(6%)

171. Pan Seared Swordfish Steaks With Shallot, Caper, And Balsamic Sauce

Serving: Serves 2 | Prep: | Ready in:

Ingredients

- two 1-inch-thick swordfish steaks, each about 6 ounces
- 1 tablespoon unsalted butter
- 1/2 tablespoon olive oil
- 3 shallots, sliced thin
- 1/4 cup dry white wine
- 2 tablespoons balsamic vinegar
- 1 tablespoon drained capers, chopped
- 1 tablespoon water
- 1 tablespoon chopped fresh parsley leaves (wash and dry before chopping)

Direction

- Blot the swordfish dry and add pepper and salt to season. Heat oil and butter in heavy skillet on medium high heat till froth settles and sauté shallots for a minute with salt to taste, mixing. Move shallots to skillet side. Put in swordfish and sauté for 3 minutes, till golden. Flip the fish over and put in water, capers, vinegar and wine. Let mixture simmer for 3 minutes, or till fish is barely cooked completely.
- Turn the fish onto 2 plates and mix into sauce with parsley. Top fish with scoop of sauce.

Nutrition Information

- Calories: 388
- Total Carbohydrate: 11 g(4%)
- Cholesterol: 128 mg(43%)
- Protein: 35 g(70%)

172. Pappardelle With Chicken Ragù, Fennel, And Peas

Serving: 4 servings | Prep: | Ready in:

Ingredients

- 2 tablespoons olive oil
- 6 ounces bacon, thinly sliced
- 1 1/2 pounds skin-on, bone-in chicken thighs (about 6 total)
- Kosher salt
- 2 medium onions, finely chopped
- 1 fennel bulb, finely chopped, plus 1/4 cup coarsely chopped fronds
- 6 sprigs thyme
- 1/2 cup dry white wine
- 1/2 cup whole milk
- 1 cup shelled fresh peas (from about 1 pound pods) or frozen peas, thawed
- Freshly ground black pepper
- 12 ounces fresh (or dried) pappardelle
- 2 tablespoons unsalted butter, cut into pieces
- 1/2 cup finely grated Parmesan, plus shaved for serving
- 2 tablespoons finely chopped parsley

Direction

- In a big, wide saucepan or a Dutch oven, heat the oil on moderate. Let bacon cook for 5 minutes, mixing frequently, till crisp and browned. Use a slotted spoon to turn onto small bowl.
- Raise the heat to moderately-high. Season the entire chicken using salt, then place, skin side facing down, in pan. Cook, flipping midway

- through, till golden brown on each side, for a total of 6 minutes. Turn onto plate.
- Drain all except 2 tablespoons of fat from pan. Put in chopped fennel and onions and cook for 6 to 8 minutes, mixing from time to time, till golden and soft. Put in thyme and cook for 30 seconds, till aromatic. Add in wine and simmer for 5 minutes, mixing and scratching up brown bits, till cooked down by 1/2. Put chicken and bacon back to pan, chicken should suit snugly in one layer; pour in water to just submerge the chicken. Simmer. Lower the heat to moderately-low and put lid askew. Cook for 45 minutes to an hour, till chicken become tender.
- Turn the chicken onto one clean plate; cool. Pull apart the meat of chicken finely; throw the skin and bones.
- Pour milk into pan and place on moderately-high. Cook for 8 to 12 minutes, mixing from time to time to avoid sticking, till sauce is almost cooked down by 1/2 and thickened partially.
- Combine chicken and peas to sauce and cook till peas are barely soft, for fresh peas, 4 minutes and for frozen, 2 minutes. Add a lot of pepper and salt to season ragù. Retain warmth while pasta is cooking.
- In a big pot with boiling salted water, cook the pasta, mixing from time to time, till extremely al dente. Strain, setting aside a cup of pasta cooking liquid.
- Put to ragù with half cup of pasta water, half cup of grated Parmesan, butter and pasta and stir till sauce coats the pasta. Raise the heat to moderate, sauce must slightly bubble, and keep cooking, mixing and putting in additional cooking liquid as necessary in case sauce is very thick, till cheese and butter melt and blends into ragù and sauce thoroughly coats the pasta. Put in parsley and toss to equally scattered through pasta.
- Distribute the pasta between bowls. Put shaved Parmesan and fennel fronds on top.
- Ragù may be done 2 days in advance. Cool; refrigerate with cover. Rewarm slowly prior to using.

Nutrition Information

- Calories: 1088
- Sodium: 1198 mg(50%)
- Fiber: 8 g(32%)
- Total Carbohydrate: 83 g(28%)
- Cholesterol: 213 mg(71%)
- Protein: 49 g(98%)
- Total Fat: 60 g(93%)
- Saturated Fat: 19 g(94%)

173. Parmesan Monkfish With Pastina Pasta And White Clam Sauce

Serving: Makes 4 servings | Prep: | Ready in:

Ingredients

- 4 (1-inch-thick) monkfish fillets (about 1 pound total), any membrane and dark meat discarded, cut crosswise into 8 medallions
- 2 teaspoons kosher salt
- 1 teaspoon freshly ground black pepper
- 1/2 cup panko (Japanese bread crumbs)
- 1/2 cup Parmigiano-Reggiano, grated
- 2 tablespoons fresh Italian flat-leaf parsley, coarsely chopped
- 6 tablespoons all-purpose flour
- 2 large eggs, lightly beaten
- 4 tablespoons olive oil
- 2 tablespoons kosher salt (for salting water)
- 3/4 cup dried pastina pasta
- 1 tablespoon extra-virgin olive oil
- 5 tablespoons Parmigiano-Reggiano, grated
- 2 teaspoons freshly ground black pepper
- 2 pounds small (less than 2 inches wide; about 24 total) hard-shelled clams such as littlenecks or cockles, scrubbed
- 1 cup white wine
- 1 lemon, cut into 2 halves
- 3 teaspoons garlic, chopped

- 2 teaspoons freshly ground black pepper
- 2 teaspoons shallot, chopped
- 1/4 teaspoon red pepper flakes
- 6 tablespoons butter, cut into 16 pieces
- 1 tablespoon fresh Italian flat-leaf parsley, coarsely chopped
- 4 tablespoons Parmigiano-Reggiano, grated
- Freshly ground black pepper, to taste
- 4 sprigs fresh Italian flat-leaf parsley

Direction

- To cook fish: Preheat the oven to 200°F. Blot dry monkfish with paper towels. Put every medallion among 2 pieces of plastic wrap and use rolling pin or mallet to gently pound to make quarter-inch-thick. Add pepper and salt to season.
- Put in food processor with Parmigiano-Reggiano, parsley and panko, and pulse till ground finely, then put into a shallow bowl. Put egg and flour in another shallow bowls. Dip a medallion in the flour, shake excess off, then dunk in the egg, allowing excess to drip off, then dredge in mixture of panko till coated evenly. Put onto a big plate. Redo with the rest of medallions, then refrigerate for not less than 45 minutes to 2 hours.
- Heat 2 tablespoons of oil in nonstick, big skillet on medium-high heat till hot yet not smoking. Wipe clean the pan, fry monkfish in 2 batches, adding 2 tablespoons of oil in each batch, flipping one time, till cooked completely, for a total of 6 minutes. Transfer to ovenproof platter, loosely cover with foil, and keep warm in oven.
- Prepare pastina: cook pasta in 4-quarts pot with salted boiling water approximately 6 minutes, till al dente. Strain, then put in medium size bowl and toss along with Parmigiano-Reggiano, pepper and olive oil. Use foil to cover the bowl to retain warmth and put aside.
- Prepare Clam sauce: mix a teaspoon of pepper, a teaspoon of garlic, 1 half of lemon, wine and clams in 6-quart pot. Boil, then put cover on, reduce the heat, and simmer for 4 to 5 minutes till clams open. Throw any that remain closed. Drain, save both clams and broth. Drain broth once more with cheesecloth-lined-fine-mesh strainer, bring back to pot. Take meat from clams, chop coarsely, and put to broth in the pot. Put in juice from leftover half of lemon, red pepper flakes, shallots, leftover teaspoon of pepper and the leftover 2 teaspoons of garlic and boil. Lower the heat to low and mix butter in. Take off heat and mix parsley in.
- Put quarter cup of pastina on every of the 4 soup plates, to serve. Top each with 2 monkfish medallions, and add quarter cup of clam sauce into every bowl surrounding the pastina. Scatter pepper and Parmigiano-Reggiano and jazz up with parsley sprigs.

Nutrition Information

- Calories: 1351
- Saturated Fat: 29 g(145%)
- Sodium: 2321 mg(97%)
- Fiber: 3 g(13%)
- Total Carbohydrate: 46 g(15%)
- Cholesterol: 452 mg(151%)
- Protein: 132 g(264%)
- Total Fat: 68 g(104%)

174. Parsley Soup

Serving: Makes 2 to 4 servings (about 3 cups) | Prep: | Ready in:

Ingredients

- 1 medium leek (white and pale green parts only)
- 1 large bunch fresh flat-leaf parsley (1/4 pound), leaves separated from stems and stems coarsely chopped
- 2 tablespoons olive oil
- 1 medium zucchini (1/2 pound), peeled and cut into 1/2-inch cubes
- 1 teaspoon salt

- 1/4 cup dry white wine
- 2 cups water

Direction

- Chop the leek and rinse it in a bowl filled with cold water, making sure to agitate it. Lift out the leek and pat it until dry.
- Cook the leek and parsley stems in a 2-3-qt heavy saucepan with oil over moderately low heat for 5 minutes, stirring occasionally until softened. Add the salt and zucchini. Cook and stir for 1 minute. Add water and wine. Cover the pan and simmer for 10 minutes until the zucchini is very tender.
- In a blender, puree the mixture with parsley leaves until smooth. (Be careful in blending the hot liquids.) Season the mixture with salt and pepper. If you want, you can pour the mixture into the clean saucepan through the fine-mesh sieve, pressing the solids thoroughly before discarding them. Reheat if needed.

Nutrition Information

- Calories: 200
- Total Fat: 14 g(22%)
- Saturated Fat: 2 g(10%)
- Sodium: 1124 mg(47%)
- Fiber: 4 g(15%)
- Total Carbohydrate: 14 g(5%)
- Protein: 4 g(7%)

175. Pasta With Roasted Romanesco And Capers

Serving: 4 servings | Prep: | Ready in:

Ingredients

- 1/4 cup chopped almonds
- 1/4 cup plus 3 tablespoons olive oil; plus more for drizzling
- 2 tablespoons drained capers, patted dry, divided
- Kosher salt
- 1/2 medium romanesco or cauliflower, cored, cut into small florets
- 8 garlic cloves, very thinly sliced
- 1/2 teaspoon crushed red pepper flakes, plus more for serving
- 1/2 cup dry white wine
- 12 ounces lumaconi (snail shells) or other medium shell pasta
- 2 ounces aged Asiago cheese or Pecorino, finely grated
- 2 tablespoons unsalted butter

Direction

- Preheat the oven to 425°F. In small saucepan, cook quarter cup of oil, 1 tablespoon of capers and almonds on moderately-low heat for 5 minutes, tilting pan from time to time, till capers pop and almonds turn golden brown in color and has a toasty scent. Use slotted spoon to turn capers and almonds onto small bowl; add salt to season. Cool. On rimmed baking sheet, toss romanesco and pan oil; add salt to season. Roast for 20 to 25 minutes, tossing midway through, till tender and golden brown.
- Meantime, in a big Dutch oven or a different heavy pot, heat 3 tablespoons oil on moderately-high. Put in half teaspoon red pepper flakes, leftover 1 tablespoon capers and garlic and cook for 3 minutes, mixing frequently, till garlic turn golden. Pour in wine and cook for 2 minutes, till liquid is nearly fully vaporized.
- Let pasta cook in a big pot with salted boiling water, mixing from time to time, till extremely al dente, approximately 3 minutes less compared to packaging instructions.
- Turn the pasta onto pot with garlic with a slotted spoon or a spider; pour in a cup of pasta cooking liquid. Lower the heat to moderate and cook for 3 minutes, tossing frequently, till liquid thickens partially and pasta becomes al dente. Put in quarter cup of

pasta cooking liquid, then slowly put in the cheese, tossing till liquified and dissolved into a glossy, rich sauce. Take off heat; put in butter and toss till blended. Toss romanesco in.
- Distribute the pasta between bowls. Put capers and fried almonds on top and additional red pepper flakes and sprinkle with oil.

Nutrition Information

- Calories: 727
- Fiber: 6 g(23%)
- Total Carbohydrate: 72 g(24%)
- Cholesterol: 25 mg(8%)
- Protein: 20 g(40%)
- Total Fat: 39 g(60%)
- Saturated Fat: 10 g(50%)
- Sodium: 561 mg(23%)

176. Pastry Twists With Spiced Sugar Honey Glaze

Serving: Makes about 20 | Prep: | Ready in:

Ingredients

- 1 1/2 cups all purpose flour
- 1/4 teaspoon (generous) salt
- 1/8 teaspoon (generous) active dry yeast
- 1/4 cup lard, cut into 1/2-inch cubes, room temperature
- 1/2 cup dry white wine, room temperature
- Extra-virgin olive oil (for frying)
- 1 cup honey
- 1 cup powdered sugar
- 1 tablespoon ground cinnamon
- 1/2 teaspoon ground nutmeg
- Fluted pastry wheel

Direction

- For the pastries: mix yeast, salt, and flour until blended in a medium bowl. Add the lard then rub in using fingertips until it looks like coarse meal. Create a well in the middle of the mixture then pour wine in the well. Mix with a fork until you form a shaggy dough. Bring dough together then place on a work surface that's lightly floured. Knead the dough until elastic and smooth, add teaspoonfuls of warm water if it's dry, for about 10 minutes.
- Line parchment paper on a big baking sheet. Roll dough on surface that's lightly floured to get a 1/8-inch thickness. Use a fluted pastry wheel to cut the dough to 1 1/4-inch wide by 4-inch long strips. Carefully twist every strip in the middle, creating bow. Put pastry twist on the prepared baking sheet. Roll dough scraps again to a thickness of 1/8-inch then cut out additional strips. Twist the strips then put on the prepared baking sheet.
- Place enough olive oil in a big saucepan until it reaches 1 1/2 inches deep. Put a deep-fry thermometer on the pan's side, making sure the bulb is submerged in the oil. Heat the oil to 360 degrees F. Cooking in batches, fry the dough twists in oil, occasionally turning, for 2-3 minutes until all sides turn golden. Use a slotted spoon to move the fried pastries to a paper towel to drain. Completely cool. Do ahead: you can make this a day in advance. Store it in an airtight container in room temperature.
- Spiced honey-sugar glaze: line parchment paper in a separate big baking sheet. Simmer honey in a medium saucepan. Take off heat. Cool until warm. Mix nutmeg, cinnamon, and sugar powder in a medium sized bowl until combined.
- Working one fried pastry at one time, dip the pastry in the warm honey. Lift the pastry and gently shake, letting extra honey drip back in the pan. Roll the pastry in the powdered sugar mixture until coated. Place on prepared baking sheet. Place pastries on a platter. For better results, dip the pastry twists in mild-flavored honey like orange blossom. A strongly flavored honey will overwhelm the spiced powdered sugar and pastry.

Nutrition Information

177. Peach White Wine Sangria

Serving: Makes 8 to 10 drinks | Prep: 15mins | Ready in:

Ingredients

- 1 cup loosely packed fresh basil leaves plus 8 to 10 sprigs
- 3/4 cup sugar
- 1/4 cup fresh lemon juice
- 2 cans peach nectar (23 fluid ounces total)
- 1 (750-ml) bottle chilled dry white wine
- 1 large peach (peeled if desired), diced

Direction

- In a small pot, put lemon juice, sugar, and basil leaves; use a wooden spoon to mash and bruise leaves. Pour in one can of nectar and let it simmer, stir until the sugar dissolves. Take off heat and set aside for 5mins. Strain the mixture using a medium-mesh sieve into a heatproof pitcher to remove the basil leaves. Mix in basil sprigs, wine, leftover can of nectar, and peach. Refrigerate for an hour to a whole day while covered. Serve with ice.

Nutrition Information

- Calories: 223
- Saturated Fat: 0 g(0%)
- Sodium: 13 mg(1%)
- Fiber: 1 g(5%)
- Total Carbohydrate: 40 g(13%)
- Protein: 1 g(2%)
- Total Fat: 0 g(0%)

178. Peaches And Raspberries In Spiced White Wine

Serving: Serves 8 | Prep: | Ready in:

Ingredients

- 1 bottle (750ml) Italian dry white wine, such as Pinot Bianco or Pinot Grigio
- 1/2 cup sugar
- 4 3/4 x 2-inch orange peel strips (orange part only)
- 3 cinnamon sticks
- 6 peaches
- 2 1/2-pint baskets raspberries
- Biscotti

Direction

- In a small saucepan, combine cinnamon, orange peel, sugar and 1 cup of wine. Over low heat, stir until the sugar dissolves then turn the heat up. Let it simmer for 15 minutes before moving it away from the heat and adding the remainder of the wine. In a big pot of boiling water, blanch the peaches for 20 seconds. Use a slotted spoon to transfer the peaches into a bowl of cold water then drain it. Use a little sharp knife to peel the skin off. Cut the peaches up into slices and put them in a big bowl then add the wine mixture and raspberries. Cover and keep it in the fridge for a minimum of 1 hour. (This can be prepped 6 hours in advance. Stir it from time to time.) Among the glass goblets, distribute the fruit and wine. Serve together with biscotti.

Nutrition Information

179. Pear Butter With Cardamom And Cinnamon

Serving: Makes about 3 2/3 cups | Prep: | Ready in:

Ingredients

- 5 pounds ripe pears, peeled, cored, cut into 1-inch pieces
- 1 1/3 cups Johannisberg Riesling wine
- 1/3 cup fresh lemon juice
- 1 1/4 cups sugar
- 1 1/4 teaspoons ground cinnamon
- 1 teaspoon ground cardamom

Direction

- In big, heavy Dutch oven, mix wine, lemon juice and pears. Boil. Lower the heat to moderately-low; simmer with cover for 20 minutes, till pears are soft, mixing from time to time and pressing the pears to liquid to soak.
- Turn mixture onto processor in batches; puree. Put back to the same pot. Put in cinnamon, cardamom and sugar. Simmer on low heat for 2 hours till mixture mounds a bit on spoon and thickens, mixing frequently and covering slightly in case mixture splatters. Turn hot pear butter onto jars that are clean. Cool down with cover. Chill. May be done 2 weeks in advance. Store in refrigerator.

Nutrition Information

- Calories: 319
- Total Carbohydrate: 77 g(26%)
- Protein: 1 g(2%)
- Total Fat: 0 g(1%)
- Saturated Fat: 0 g(0%)
- Sodium: 5 mg(0%)
- Fiber: 9 g(36%)

180. Pear Ice Cream With Spiced Pear Compote

Serving: Serves 8 | Prep: | Ready in:

Ingredients

- 2 1/4 pounds ripe Anjou or Comice pears, peeled, halved, cored, thinly sliced (about 4 cups)
- 1 cup pear nectar
- 1 tablespoon fresh lemon juice
- 6 large egg yolks
- 3/4 cup sugar
- 2 cups whipping cream
- 1 2-inch piece vanilla bean, split lengthwise
- 1/2 cup light corn syrup
- 2 cups GewÜrztraminer wine
- 1/2 cup sugar
- 2 whole cloves
- 1 4 1/2-inch piece vanilla bean, split lengthwise
- 2 1/2 pounds firm but ripe Anjou or Comice pears (about 6), peeled, halved, cored, cut into 1/3-inch-thick slices

Direction

- Ice cream: in medium, heavy saucepan mix pear nectar, lemon juice and pears. Boil on moderately-high heat. Turn onto processor; puree to make smooth consistency. Refrigerate till cold.
- In medium size bowl, whip sugar and yolks to incorporate. Use a medium, heavy saucepan to simmer a cup of cream. Slowly whip hot cream into mixture of yolk. Put back to the same saucepan. Scrape into mixture with vanilla bean seeds; put in bean. Mix on low heat for 7 minutes, till custard is thick and leaves trace on back of spoon once finger is run across, prevent boiling. Pass through a strainer right into bowl. Stir a cup of cream in. Cool down for 15 minutes.
- Put to custard with 3 cups pear puree and corn syrup and whip till incorporated, put aside any leftover pear puree for other use. Refrigerate custard for not less than 4 hours to overnight, till cold.
- Turn custard onto an ice cream maker. Process following manufacturer's directions. Turn onto container with cover and place in freezer. May be done 2 days in advance.

- For compote: in big, heavy saucepan, mix sugar, cloves and wine. Scoop vanilla bean seeds into the saucepan; put in bean. Mix on moderate heat till sugar is dissolved. Boil. Put in the pears; simmer for 5 minutes, till tender. Turn the pears into medium size bowl using slotted spoon. Let liquid boil in saucepan for 12 minutes, till syrupy and thickened partially, putting in any juices from pears bowl. Add on top of pears. Refrigerate for not less than 4 hours to overnight, or till cold. Throw cloves and vanilla bean. May be done a day in advance. Keep refrigerated with cover.
- Scoop the ice cream and put in goblets. Top with scoop of syrup and pears to serve.

Nutrition Information

- Calories: 589
- Fiber: 7 g(27%)
- Total Carbohydrate: 89 g(30%)
- Cholesterol: 205 mg(68%)
- Protein: 4 g(8%)
- Total Fat: 22 g(34%)
- Saturated Fat: 13 g(64%)
- Sodium: 47 mg(2%)

181. Penne With Shrimp, Asparagus, And Sun Dried Tomatoes

Serving: Makes 4 servings | Prep: | Ready in:

Ingredients

- 1/2 cup drained oil-packed sun-dried tomatoes
- 1 pound asparagus, trimmed, cut on diagonal into 1/2-inch pieces
- 1 1/4 pounds uncooked shrimp, peeled, deveined
- 1/2 cup chopped fresh basil
- 2 large garlic cloves, chopped
- 1/2 teaspoon dried oregano
- 1/4 teaspoon dried crushed red pepper
- 1 3/4 cups canned low-salt chicken broth
- 1/2 cup dry white wine
- 2 tablespoons tomato paste
- 12 ounces penne pasta
- 3/4 cup grated Parmesan cheese

Direction

- In big, heavy skillet, heat the oil reserved from tomatoes on moderately-high heat. Put in asparagus and sauté for 5 minutes, till tender-crisp. Turn the asparagus onto bowl with slotted spoon. Put crushed red pepper, oregano, garlic, quarter cup basil, shrimp and sun-dried tomatoes to the same skillet and sauté for 3 minutes, till shrimp are barely opaque in the middle. Turn the mixture of shrimp onto bowl of asparagus. Put to same skillet with wine, tomato paste and broth. Boil for 6 minutes, till sauce partially thickens, mixing from time to time.
- In big pot with salted boiling water, let pasta cook till soft yet remain firm to bite. Strain; put the pasta back to the same pot. Put to pasta with cheese, leftover quarter cup basil, sauce and shrimp mixture. Toss on moderate heat till warmed completely and sauce covers the pasta. Add pepper and salt to season to serve.

Nutrition Information

- Calories: 595
- Cholesterol: 193 mg(64%)
- Protein: 44 g(88%)
- Total Fat: 11 g(17%)
- Saturated Fat: 5 g(23%)
- Sodium: 1234 mg(51%)
- Fiber: 6 g(26%)
- Total Carbohydrate: 77 g(26%)

182. Pineapple Sangria

Serving: 8 | Prep: 25mins | Ready in:

Ingredients

- 2 (750 milliliter) bottles Sauvignon Blanc
- 2 cups pineapple juice
- 1 cup triple sec
- 1/2 cup brandy (optional)
- 1/2 cup chopped fresh pineapple
- 1/2 cup chopped orange
- 1 lemon, seeded and chopped
- 1/4 cup chopped lime
- 2 cups lemon-lime flavored carbonated beverage (such as 7-Up®)

Direction

- Combine together triple sec, pineapple juice, brandy, and Sauvignon Blanc into a big pitcher. Put in lemon, orange, lime, and sliced pineapple. Keep in the refrigerator with cover for 8 hours to overnight.
- Mix in lemon-lime soda. Serve.

Nutrition Information

- Calories: 383 calories;
- Total Fat: 0.3
- Sodium: 26
- Total Carbohydrate: 38.5
- Cholesterol: 0
- Protein: 0.8

183. Pink Gooseberry, Peach, And Elderflower Soup With Vanilla Ice Cream

Serving: Serves 6 | Prep: | Ready in:

Ingredients

- 1 cup pink gooseberries (about 6 ounces)
- 1 1/4 cups dry white wine
- 1/2 cup water
- 1/3 cup elderflower concentrate*
- 1/2 cup sugar
- 2 small firm-ripe peaches (preferably white)
- 6 large fresh basil leaves
- 1 pint super premium vanilla ice cream
- *available at some specialty foods shops and by mail order from Dean DeLuca, tel. (212) 226-6800, ext. 268

Direction

- Preparation: Pull off the tails and tops of gooseberries; halve lengthwise. Transfer the berries to a heatproof bowl or 1-qt. heatproof jar. In a small saucepan, boil sugar, elderflower concentrate, water and wine, stirring till the sugar is dissolved; transfer the hot syrup on top of the berries. Let the mixture cool. Cover and chill the mixture for at least 2 hours and up to 6 hours, till cold.
- Peel peaches; cut into very thin wedges. Mix the peaches gently into the berry mixture; distribute among 6 soup plates. Slice basil thinly; sprinkle on top of the soup. Scoop ice cream into the soup.

Nutrition Information

184. Poached Artichokes

Serving: Serves 4 | Prep: | Ready in:

Ingredients

- 4 medium artichokes
- 2 to 3 teaspoons crushed rosemary
- 3 cloves garlic, minced
- 1 medium sliced onion
- 1 lemon, sliced in rounds
- 1 cup white wine
- 1/2 cup water
- 2 bay leaves
- 1 tablespoon olive oil
- Freshly ground pepper

Direction

- Trim the stem off at the base of each artichoke. Snip off the point of each leaf using scissors. Trim about 1/2-inch off the top of every artichoke. Combine minced garlic gloves and rosemary then split up between the 4 artichokes, putting the mixture between layers of leaves. In a deep, wide saucepan, place the rest of ingredients then put in artichokes. Bring to a simmer and cook for 45-50 minutes, covered, or until leaves are very tender.

Nutrition Information

185. Poached Asian Pears With Star Anise And Tropical Fruit

Serving: Serves 4 | Prep: | Ready in:

Ingredients

- 2 cups water
- 1 cup dry white wine
- 3/4 cup sugar
- 2 tablespoons fresh lemon juice
- 2 star anise*
- 1 2-inch piece cinnamon stick
- 1 2-inch piece fresh ginger, sliced
- 4 large (10 ounces each) Asian pears
- 1 1 3/4-pound papaya, diced
- 1 14-to 16-ounce mango, diced
- *A brown star-shaped seed pod; available at Asian markets and specialty food stores and some supermarkets.

Direction

- In a big and heavy pot, boil and stir the first seven ingredients together until the sugar dissolves; cover. Let it simmer for 5mins.
- Skin and remove the core from pears; place in the pot with syrup. Cover the pears with enough water; put the lid of the pot. Let it simmer for about 40mins until tender. Move the pears onto a bowl using a slotted spoon. Turn the heat up and boil for about 25mins until the liquid reduces to 3/4 cup. Strain and pour syrup over the pears. Place in the refrigerator until cold. It can be prepared two days in advance. Chill.
- Place one pear in the middle of every plate. Spoon mango and papaya all around the pear. Pour in syrup. Serve.

Nutrition Information

- Calories: 300
- Total Carbohydrate: 70 g(23%)
- Protein: 2 g(3%)
- Total Fat: 1 g(1%)
- Saturated Fat: 0 g(1%)
- Sodium: 18 mg(1%)
- Fiber: 5 g(20%)

186. Poached Oranges With Candied Zest And Ginger

Serving: Makes 10 to 12 servings | Prep: 45mins | Ready in:

Ingredients

- 1 (2-oz) piece fresh ginger (2 to 3 inches long)
- 12 navel oranges (preferably small)
- 1 1/2 cups water
- 2 cups sugar
- 1/4 teaspoon salt
- 1 1/2 cups dry white wine
- 1 cup fresh orange juice
- 1/2 cup plus 2 tablespoons Grand Marnier

Direction

- Peel ginger; halve crosswise. Lengthwise, cut pieces to 1/16-in. thick slices. Cut slices to 1/8-in. wide julienne strips. Put into a 2-qt. heavy saucepan.

- In long wide strips, use a vegetable peeler to remove zest from 3 oranges. Use a paring knife to remove white pith from zest. Put ginger into pan. Use cold water to fill pan to 3/4 full; boil for 1 minute. Drain through a sieve. Put ginger and zest into pan. Refill using cold water; boil. Lower heat and simmer for 10 minutes, uncovered. Drain ginger and zest. Repeat simmering for 10 more minutes with extra cold water; drain.
- Boil salt, 1 cup sugar and 1 1/2 cups water in saucepan, mixing till sugar melts. Add ginger and zest; simmer gently, occasionally mixing, uncovered, for 15-20 minutes till syrup is thick and ginger and zest are completely translucent. In a sieve, drain candied ginger and zest; throw syrup.
- Meanwhile, use a sharp knife to cut 1/2-in. from bottom and top of all oranges, exposing both ends of fruit. Cut pith and peel from sides, don't leave white parts, using a paring knife. If big but keeping orange shape, trim fruit to 2 1/2 - 2 3/4-in. wide in the middle then throw trimmings.
- Boil leftover cup sugar, 1/2 cup grand marnier, orange juice and wine in a 12-in. deep heavy skillet, mixing till sugar melts. Boil for 3 minutes. In 1 layer, add oranges; simmer for 10 minutes, covered using a tight fitting lid. With a slotted spoon, put oranges into serving dish, inverting to coat oranges in syrup. Add candied ginger and zest into syrup; boil on medium heat for 10-15 minutes, uncovered, till mixture reduces to 1 1/4 cups and syrup is thick. Take off heat. Mix leftover 2 tbsp. grand marnier in.
- When oranges are cool to touch, crosswise cut each to thirds on cutting board. Assemble again "whole" in the serving dish. Spoon zest mixture and syrup on oranges, decoratively putting ginger and zest on them. In serving dish, chill oranges for 1 hour minimum till cold.
- Prior to serving, spoon syrup on oranges in dish to coat. Serve at room temperature/chilled.

- You can chill oranges for up to a day, loosely covered, preferably with invested big bowl after an hour. Put syrup on oranges again before serving.

Nutrition Information

- Calories: 302
- Fiber: 4 g(15%)
- Total Carbohydrate: 65 g(22%)
- Protein: 2 g(4%)
- Total Fat: 0 g(1%)
- Saturated Fat: 0 g(0%)
- Sodium: 64 mg(3%)

187. Poached Pears In Phyllo Overcoat With Madeira Zabaglione `21' Club

Serving: Serves 4 | Prep: | Ready in:

Ingredients

- 4 small firm-ripe pears (preferably Bosc) with stems intact
- 3 cups water
- 1/2 cup dry white wine
- 1/3 cup sugar
- 1 cinnamon stick
- 2 whole cloves
- 1 small dried chili such as habanero or 1/4 teaspoon dried hot red pepper flakes
- 12 sheets phyllo, thawed if frozen, stacked between 2 sheets wax paper and covered with a dampened kitchen towel
- 1 stick (1/2 cup) unsalted butter, melted
- 1/4 cup sugar
- 3 large egg yolks
- 1/4 cup Portuguese Madeira (preferably sweet, such as Malmsey)
- Garnish: 1/4 cup dried cranberries or dried sour cherries, soaked in hot water 20 minutes and drained

Direction

- Simmer chili, cloves, cinnamon stick, wine, sugar and water in saucepan barely big enough to accommodate pears in single layer upright for 10 minutes to incorporate the flavors. Remove pears peel, keep the stems attach, and slice off a thin piece from base of every pear to make them stand upright. Put pears into poaching liquid and simmer for 10 to 12 minutes, till tender once pricked with sharp knife. Turn the pears onto plate and cool fully. Core the pears from base, keeping the stem ends attach, and blot dry.
- Set the oven to 400 degrees F for preheating.
- Brush some liquified butter on a phyllo sheet on work counter and put 2 additional layers of phyllo and butter on top in exactly the same manner. Place 1 pear in the middle of phyllo and hold phyllo up surrounding pear top, letting excess fold back and keeping the stem bare. Clip extra phyllo to approximately 3-inch if need be and brush more butter on the outside of phyllo. Create additional wrapped pears with leftover phyllo, butter and pears in exactly the same manner. Let pears bake on baking sheet for 20 minutes, or till phyllo turn golden, and cool partially. Pears in phyllo can be done 4 hours in advance and store at room temperature.
- Meanwhile, prep zabaglione: whip yolks, Madeira and sugar in metal bowl till blended. Place the bowl on saucepan with simmering water and let mixture heat, mixing, till foamy, light golden, and every whisk stroke leaves neat path. An instant-read thermometer must read 140°F. for 3 minutes to guarantee eggs are safely cooked.
- Distribute pears and zabaglione between 4 dessert plates and jazz up using dried fruit.

Nutrition Information

- Calories: 500
- Total Carbohydrate: 62 g(21%)
- Cholesterol: 199 mg(66%)
- Protein: 3 g(7%)
- Total Fat: 27 g(41%)
- Saturated Fat: 16 g(79%)
- Sodium: 21 mg(1%)
- Fiber: 7 g(27%)

188. Poached Pears With Chocolate Pear Sauce

Serving: Makes 8 servings | Prep: | Ready in:

Ingredients

- 1 cup pear nectar
- 1 cup dry white wine
- 1/2 cup sugar
- 4 slightly under-ripe pears, peeled, halved, cored
- 4 ounces bittersweet (not unsweetened) or semisweet chocolate, chopped
- Vanilla ice cream

Direction

- In big, heavy saucepan, mix sugar, white wine and pear nectar on moderately-high heat till sugar melts and syrup boils. Put to syrup in saucepan with pears. Put pan cover, lower heat to moderately-low and simmer for 8 minutes, till pears are soft. Turn pears onto plate with slotted spoon. Raise heat to moderately-high and let poaching liquid boil for 8 minutes, till cooked down to 3/4 cup. Take pan off heat. Put in chocolate; beat till sauce turn smooth and chocolate liquifies.
- Put a warm half of pear on every plate, cut side facing up. Place vanilla ice cream on top and top with warm chocolate sauce. Alternatively, separately cover chocolate sauce and pears and chill for maximum of 2 days; then serve the cold pears along with sauce and ice cream, reheat sauce, if wished.

Nutrition Information

189. Poached Salmon In Aspic

Serving: Makes 8 main-course servings | Prep: | Ready in:

Ingredients

- 1 (6-lb) whole salmon (with skin), cleaned and backbone removed, head and tail left intact
- 1 teaspoon salt
- 6 qt cold water
- 1/2 cup fresh lemon juice
- 1 large onion, coarsely chopped
- 2 carrots, coarsely chopped
- 2 celery ribs with leaves, cut into 4-inch pieces
- 2 bay leaves (not California)
- 6 fresh parsley stems (without leaves)
- 2 fresh thyme sprigs
- 1/4 teaspoon whole black peppercorns
- 1 cup dry white wine
- 2 tablespoons Sercial Madeira
- 1 fresh thyme sprig
- 1 teaspoon salt
- 1 large leek, white and pale green parts chopped and 2 outer leaves reserved
- 1 carrot, coarsely chopped
- 1 celery rib, coarsely chopped
- 3 large eggs, whites lightly beaten and shells crushed (reserve yolks for another use)
- 1 tablespoon unflavored gelatin (from two 1/4-oz envelopes)
- 1/4 cup cold water
- Accompaniment: green mayonnaise
- 2 (35-inch-long) pieces of cheesecloth; kitchen string; a 24-inch fish poacher*; a long (25-inch) platter

Direction

- Poaching salmon: wash the salmon inside and out. Sprinkle salt inside. Unfold 1 cheesecloth piece on top of other to create a double layer. Snugly wrap fish in it then tie ends close to the fish using kitchen string. Put onto poacher rack in the poacher. Across 2 burners on the stovetop, straddle poacher. Add peppercorns, herbs, veggies, lemon juice and 6-qt. cold water to cover fish by 1-in.
- Boil on high heat, partially covered for 25 minutes. An inserted instant-read thermometer in thickest area of fish should register 145°F. Put poacher into metal rack. Cool fish in broth for 30 minutes, uncovered. Chill fish in the poaches without pouring broth off for 8 hours minimum, uncovered.
- Reduce broth for the aspic: Lift the fish on the poacher rack out of the broth; drain well. Put onto rack into a big shallow baking pan; chill. Through a sieve, pour broth into a big bowl. In a 4-qt. heavy pot, put 8 cups broth. Keep remainder for another time. Add salt, thyme sprig, madeira and white wine; boil for 30-40 minutes till reduced to 5 cups then cool for 20 minutes.
- Salmon glaze: in a bowl with cold water, wash chopped leeks and reserved leek leaves. Lift out; drain well. Slice leaves to decorative strips. In saucepan with boiling water, blanch strips for 1 minute. Put into bowl with cold water and ice; drain. Pat dry.
- Take strings out of cheesecloth. Open cheesecloth; don't remove. Remove small bones (they resemble combs) from fish spine from tail to head and fatty strips. Trim any fat off belly's edges. Remove bony section carefully under grills. Remove dark flesh and skin from top/visible side of fish by scraping gently using a sharp, small knife. Roll fish over on a platter with a cheesecloth. Remove bony section under the gills. Remove dark flesh and skin from opposite fish side. Wipe the platter clean. Use dampened paper towels to cover fish. Chill till aspic is ready.
- Clarify broth with egg shells and white and create aspic: In a 4-6-qt. heavy pot, whisk egg shells and whites, celery, carrot, chopped leek and reduced broth. Boil, constantly whisking. Lower heat. Cook on low heat at a bare simmer for 30 minutes, undisturbed. Through a sieve that is lined using a double thickness of

dampened paper towels, ladle broth into a 1-qt. glass measure. Firmly press onto solids.
- In a 1-qt. saucepan, soften gelatin in cold water for a minute. Put 3 cups broth; simmer for 2 minutes, mixing, till gelatin melts.
- Aspic and glaze salmon: In a metal bowl set inside a bigger bowl with cold water and ice, ladle 2/3 cup aspic. Let stand till aspic has the consistency of a raw egg white, occasionally mixing. Take bowl out of ice water. In a thin layer, spoon aspic on fish. Chill fish for 10 minutes till aspic is set. On fish, put leek garnish. Glaze fish with extra aspic. Chill fish till serving time, uncovered.
- In a 13x9-in. baking dish, put leftover aspic in. Chill for 1 hour till firm. Slice to 1/2-in. cubes. Put cubes around the salmon.
- You can poach and chill salmon in broth for up to 2 days. You can keep aspic-glazed salmon for 1 day chilled and uncovered.

Nutrition Information

- Calories: 830
- Total Fat: 48 g(74%)
- Saturated Fat: 11 g(56%)
- Sodium: 894 mg(37%)
- Fiber: 2 g(7%)
- Total Carbohydrate: 9 g(3%)
- Cholesterol: 277 mg(92%)
- Protein: 82 g(163%)

190. Poached Salmon With Tarragon Sauce And Fingerling Potatoes

Serving: Serves 6 | Prep: | Ready in:

Ingredients

- 2 large bunches fresh tarragon (about 1 ounce total)
- 1 large bunch fresh chives (about 2/3 ounce)
- 1 large shallot
- 3/4 cup fresh flat-leafed parsley leaves
- 1 cup mayonnaise
- 1/3 cup rice vinegar (not seasoned)
- 2 teaspoons Dijon mustard
- 2 1/2 cups dry white wine
- 2 1/2 cups water
- a 2 1/2- to 3-pound salmon fillet with skin
- 1 1/2 pounds pink fingerling or other new potatoes
- Garnish: 1/2 pound cooked sugar snap peas, diagonally cut into thirds

Direction

- Sauce: Pick sufficient tarragon leaves to get 1/2 cup; don't pack. Chop sufficient chives to get 1/3 cup. Chop shallot coarsely. Puree leftover sauce ingredients, shallot, chives and tarragon till smooth in a food processor; season with pepper and salt. You can make sauce 1 day ahead, covered, chilled; before serving, bring sauce down to cool to room temperature.
- Create fish: Simmer water and wine in a 10-in. deep skillet, covered. Cut salmon to 6 pieces; season with pepper and salt. Submerge 3 salmon pieces in simmering liquid, skin sides down; if needed, add hot water just to cover salmon. Poach at bare simmer for 8 minutes or till just cooked through, covered. Use a slotted spatula to put cooked salmon on a platter; cool. The same way, poach leftover salmon. Peel skin off when salmon is cool to handle; scrape dark meat off with a sharp knife, if desired. You can cook salmon 1 day ahead, covered, chilled. Before serving, bring it to cool down to room temperature.
- Assemble: Lengthwise cut potatoes to 1/8-in. thick slices. Steam potatoes in a steamer set above boiling water for 4-5 minutes till just tender. Ladle sauce on 6 plates; in a circle, put some potatoes over sauce, slightly overlapping. Season potatoes using salt; put salmon over potatoes. Use peas to garnish salmon.

Nutrition Information

- Calories: 819
- Sodium: 385 mg(16%)
- Fiber: 2 g(9%)
- Total Carbohydrate: 15 g(5%)
- Cholesterol: 129 mg(43%)
- Protein: 46 g(93%)
- Total Fat: 59 g(90%)
- Saturated Fat: 11 g(55%)

191. Poached Wild Salmon With Peas And Morels

Serving: 2 servings | Prep: | Ready in:

Ingredients

- 2 (6–8-ounce) center-cut wild salmon fillets (each about 1 1/2" thick)
- 1 cup dry white wine
- 2 tablespoons kosher salt plus more for seasoning
- 4 tablespoons (1/2 stick) unsalted butter
- 4 ounces fresh morels; sliced, stemmed shiitake; or other mushrooms
- 1/2 cup shelled fresh (or frozen, thawed) peas
- 1/2 cup heavy cream
- Freshly ground black pepper
- 2 tablespoons minced fresh chives or 2 pea tendrils

Direction

- In a big frying pan with a high side, put salmon with the skin-side turning down. Add cold water, 2 tablespoons salt, and wine until covering the salmon 1/2-inch. Put a cover on the pan; simmer the liquid over medium heat. Lower the heat to medium-low, remove the cover, and lightly poach salmon for 6 minutes according to the thickness, until the salmon is slightly opaque in the middle. Remove 2 tablespoons poaching liquid and the salmon onto a dish, use foil to loosely tent.
- In the meantime, in a medium-sized frying pan, heat butter over medium heat to melt. Add mushrooms and cook for 3 minutes until they start to get tender, tossing sometimes. Add peas and 1/2 cup salmon poaching liquid and simmer for 2-3 minutes until the peas start to get tender. Add cream and simmer the sauce. Cook for 5 minutes until partially thickened. Use pepper and salt to season.
- Remove the salmon onto paper towels with a spatula, the skin-side should be up. Carefully remove the skin and dispose. Turn onto serving dishes and add the sauce over. Use chives to garnish.

Nutrition Information

- Calories: 805
- Fiber: 3 g(11%)
- Total Carbohydrate: 12 g(4%)
- Cholesterol: 232 mg(77%)
- Protein: 48 g(97%)
- Total Fat: 57 g(88%)
- Saturated Fat: 31 g(154%)
- Sodium: 1061 mg(44%)

192. Pomegranate Aperitif

Serving: 6 Servings | Prep: | Ready in:

Ingredients

- 1 cup pomegranate juice
- 2 tablespoons saba
- 2 cups Lillet Blanc
- 4 dashes celery bitters
- Club soda

Direction

- In a big pitcher, whisk together saba and pomegranate juice, then stir in bitter and Lillet. Transfer into rocks glasses filled with ice, then splash with club soda on top.

Nutrition Information

---
193. Porcini Mushroom Risotto

Serving: Makes 6 first-course or 4 main-course servings | Prep: | Ready in:

Ingredients

- 2 cups water
- 1 ounce dried porcini mushrooms*
- 1 tablespoon butter
- 1 tablespoon olive oil
- 1 1/2 cups arborio rice or medium-grain white rice (about 9 1/2 ounces)
- 3 large shallots, chopped
- 1 teaspoon fennel seeds
- 1/2 cup dry white wine
- 2 cups (or more) low-salt chicken broth
- 1/2 teaspoon salt
- 1 cup freshly grated Parmesan cheese (about 3 ounces)
- 2 tablespoons chopped fresh parsley
- pressure cooker

Direction

- In a small heavy saucepan, boil 2 cups water. Add mushrooms; cover. Stand for 10 minutes till mushrooms soften. Put mushrooms on a work surface using slotted spoon; keep soaking liquid. Coarsely chop mushrooms.
- Melt oil and butter on medium high heat in pressure cooker. Add fennel seeds, shallots and rice; mix for 1 minute. Add wine; cook for 1 minute till nearly evaporated, frequently mixing. Mix in salt, 2 cups broth then mushrooms with reserved mushroom soaking liquid; leave sediment in pan behind. In place, lock lid; bring to high pressure on high heat. Cook rice, adjusting heat as needed to maintain high pressure, for 4 minutes. Quick-release the pressure.
- Release lid slowly, standing back, letting steam escape. Cook rice for 2 minutes on medium high heat till tender yet firm to chew and creamy, mixing often, adding extra broth by 1/4 cupfuls if you want thinner consistency. Mix in parsley and cheese; season risotto with pepper to taste.

Nutrition Information

- Calories: 320
- Fiber: 3 g(13%)
- Total Carbohydrate: 48 g(16%)
- Cholesterol: 15 mg(5%)
- Protein: 11 g(22%)
- Total Fat: 9 g(13%)
- Saturated Fat: 4 g(20%)
- Sodium: 424 mg(18%)

---
194. Pork Chops Scarpariello

Serving: Serves 4 | Prep: 30mins | Ready in:

Ingredients

- 2 red bell peppers
- 5 garlic cloves, finely chopped, divided
- 1 teaspoon finely chopped rosemary
- 3 tablespoons extra-virgin olive oil, divided
- 4 (1-inch-thick) bone-in pork chops (2 pounds total)
- 1 medium onion, chopped
- 4 fresh red or green cherry peppers or 2 fresh red jalapeños (1/4 pounds total), finely chopped
- 1/2 cup dry white wine
- 1/2 cup reduced-sodium chicken broth
- 2 tablespoons unsalted butter
- 1 teaspoon fresh lemon juice
- 1/4 cup coarsely chopped flat-leaf parsley

Direction

- On gas burners racks, roast the bell peppers on high heat for 10 to 12 minutes, or on broiler pan rack, approximately 2-inch away from heat, flipping using tongs, till skins are charred. Turn onto a big bowl and use plastic wrap to cover tightly. Rest for 20 minutes with cover. Remove the peel, then slice in half lengthwise, throwing seeds and stems. Slice peppers to make an-inch pieces.
- Meanwhile, mince 1/2 of garlic and crush with 3/4 teaspoon of salt till paste form. Mix with a tablespoon of oil, half teaspoon of pepper and rosemary. Massage on chops.
- In a nonstick, heavy, big skillet, heat leftover 2 tablespoons of oil on moderately-high heat till it shimmers. Sauté pork for 4 to 6 minutes, flipping one time, till light golden in patches and just cooked completely. Turn onto plate and use foil to loosely cover to retain warmth.
- Put roasted peppers into skillet along with quarter teaspoon of salt, cherry peppers, leftover garlic and onion. Cook for 5 to 6 minutes, mixing from time to time, till onion softens. Pour in broth and wine and boil for 5 minutes till liquid is cooked down into a glaze. Put in meat juices from the plate and take skillet off heat. Put in butter, mixing till blended. Mix in parsley, salt to taste and lemon juice, and scoop on top of chops.

Nutrition Information

- Calories: 534
- Total Fat: 34 g(53%)
- Saturated Fat: 11 g(55%)
- Sodium: 187 mg(8%)
- Fiber: 2 g(8%)
- Total Carbohydrate: 9 g(3%)
- Cholesterol: 153 mg(51%)
- Protein: 43 g(86%)

195. Pork Loin Roast With Fennel Garlic Rub

Serving: Makes 8 servings | Prep: 30mins | Ready in:

Ingredients

- 2 tablespoons chopped garlic (4 to 5 cloves)
- 1 tablespoon kosher salt
- 1 tablespoon chopped fresh thyme
- 2 teaspoons fennel seeds
- 1 teaspoon black peppercorns
- 1 6 pound bone-in pork loin roast
- 1 cup dry white wine
- 1 cup water
- 2 tablespoons cold unsalted butter, cut into pieces
- a coffee/spice grinder; an instant read thermometer

Direction

- Make rub: use a heavy, big knife to mince and crush salt, thyme and garlic till a paste form and turn onto small bowl.
- Grind in spice grinder with peppercorns and fennel seeds until finely ground and mix to garlic paste.
- Massage the entire meat and fat side of roast with paste, forcing to cling. Put in a baking pan, 13- by 9-inch in size or small roasting pan, fat side facing up, and refrigerate to marinate, with loose cover, for not less than 2 hours to no longer than 6 hours. Rest for an hour at room temperature prior to roasting.
- Roast pork loin: Preheat the oven to 350°F.
- Place in small roasting pan with roast, fat side facing up, add water and wine to the pan bottom in case it is not in the roasting pan yet.
- Let pork roast in center of the oven, or bottom third in case preparing whole menu, till an inserted instant read thermometer into middle of meat, without touching the bone, reads 140°F, for approximately 1 1/2 to 1 3/4 hours.
- Take roast out of oven, use foil to cover loosely and sit for 25 minutes to half an hour in

roasting pan, inner heat will rise 10 ° while meat rests.
- Turn roast onto a chopping board, and slice meat off bone in a piece with a lengthy knife. Cut to make half-inch thick slices, keep the pieces together.
- Turn bones onto a big serving platter and place the meat on bone.
- In roasting pan, heat the juices till bubbling, then put in butter and mix to pan till blended.
- Serve sauce on the side of meat.

Nutrition Information

- Calories: 76
- Total Fat: 5 g(7%)
- Saturated Fat: 2 g(12%)
- Sodium: 162 mg(7%)
- Fiber: 0 g(2%)
- Total Carbohydrate: 2 g(1%)
- Cholesterol: 17 mg(6%)
- Protein: 3 g(6%)

196. Pork Medallions With Mustard Chive Sauce

Serving: Makes 6 servings | Prep: | Ready in:

Ingredients

- 2 tablespoons (1/4 stick) butter, divided
- 2 tablespoons olive oil, divided
- 2 cups chopped leeks (white and pale green parts only; about 2 medium)
- 1 cup low-salt chicken broth
- 1/2 cup dry white wine
- 2 garlic cloves, minced
- 1/2 cup crème fraîche or sour cream
- 3 tablespoons whole grain Dijon mustard
- 2 1-pound pork tenderloins, each cut crosswise into 6 slices
- 2 tablespoons chopped fresh chives
- 1 tablespoon chopped fresh tarragon
- 2 tablespoons chopped fresh parsley

Direction

- In big skillet, liquify a tablespoon of butter along with a tablespoon of oil on moderately-high heat. Put in and cook leeks for 5 minutes, till starting to become golden, mixing often. Mix in wine, garlic and broth. Boil for 4 minutes, till mixture is cooked down to 1 2/3 cups. Mix in mustard and crème fraîche; put aside. Sauce may be done 2 hours in advance. Rest at room temperature. In a separate big skillet, liquify a tablespoon of butter along with a tablespoon of oil on moderately-high heat. Scatter pepper and salt on pork. Sauté for 5 minutes on each side, till cooked and browned. Turn the pork onto platter. Put the sauce into skillet; let sauce simmer on moderate heat for 2 minutes, till partially thickened, scratching up browned bits. Mix in tarragon and chopped chives. Add pepper and salt to season.
- Put pork back to skillet. Cook on moderate heat for a minute, barely till reheated, mixing often. Turn onto platter, scatter parsley over to serve.

Nutrition Information

- Calories: 324
- Total Fat: 18 g(27%)
- Saturated Fat: 7 g(35%)
- Sodium: 187 mg(8%)
- Fiber: 1 g(4%)
- Total Carbohydrate: 7 g(2%)
- Cholesterol: 113 mg(38%)
- Protein: 32 g(64%)

197. Pork With Gorgonzola Sauce

Serving: Makes 6 servings | Prep: | Ready in:

Ingredients

- 1/4 cup Dijon mustard
- 1 tablespoon olive oil
- 1 tablespoon dried thyme
- 2 3/4-pound pork tenderloins
- 1 tablespoon butter
- 1 tablespoon all purpose flour
- 1 cup whipping cream
- 1/4 cup dry white wine
- 1/4 cup canned low-salt chicken broth
- 1 cup crumbled Gorgonzola cheese (about 4 ounces)

Direction

- Preparation for pork: Oil a large rimmed baking sheet. In a small bowl, whisk thyme, olive oil, and Dijon mustard to combine. Sprinkle pepper and salt over the pork tenderloins. Heat the heavy large non-stick skillet on high. Put in pork and sear, turning from time to time, for about 10 minutes until they are browned all over. Place the seared pork into the oiled baking sheet. Spread the Dijon mustard mixture on all sides of pork. (This can be made up to 2 hours ahead. Uncover and put the pork in the fridge).
- Set an oven to 425°F and start preheating. Roast the pork for about half an hour until a thermometer inserted into the thickest part of the meat reads 150°F. Take away from the oven and allow to stand for 5 minutes.
- At the same time, prepare the sauce: In a heavy small saucepan, melt a tablespoon butter on medium heat. Put in a tablespoon of flour and whisk for a minute. Slowly whisk in chicken broth, white wine, and whipping cream. Boil, regularly whisking, for about a minute until the mixture thickens enough to coat the spoon. Put in the crumbled Gorgonzola, then whisk for about 5 minutes until the sauce reduces to the desired degree of consistency and the cheese melts and becomes smooth.
- Cut the pork and place into the plates. Ladle some sauce over the pork. Serve and pass additional sauce separately.

Nutrition Information

- Calories: 488
- Sodium: 457 mg(19%)
- Fiber: 1 g(2%)
- Total Carbohydrate: 4 g(1%)
- Cholesterol: 199 mg(66%)
- Protein: 49 g(97%)
- Total Fat: 30 g(46%)
- Saturated Fat: 15 g(76%)

198. Potato Gnocchi With Pork And Wild Mushroom Ragù

Serving: Makes 6 to 8 servings | Prep: | Ready in:

Ingredients

- 1 ounce dried porcini mushrooms*
- 1 1/2 cups boiling water
- 3 tablespoons olive oil, divided
- 8 ounces sliced crimini (baby bella) mushrooms
- 2 garlic cloves, minced
- Coarse kosher salt
- 2 1/2 cups dry white wine, divided
- 1 pound boneless country-style pork ribs, cut into 1/2-inch cubes
- 2 ounces 1/4-inch-thick slices coppa or prosciutto, chopped
- 6 ounces fresh mild Italian sausages, casings removed (about 2 links)
- 1 medium onion, finely chopped
- 1 carrot, peeled, finely chopped
- 1 celery stalk, finely chopped
- 2 cups crushed tomatoes or crushed tomatoes with added puree (from one 28-ounce can; preferably San Marzano or Muir Glen)
- 1 cup (or more) low-salt chicken broth

- 2 bay leaves
- 1 tablespoon chopped fresh basil
- Potato Gnocchi
- 1 cup grated Parmesan cheese

Direction

- Put in medium size bowl with the dried porcini mushrooms; add 1 1/2 cups of boiling water on top. Rest for 45 minutes, till mushrooms soften. Turn the mushrooms onto chopping board using slotted spoon and coarsely chop. Set the soaking water aside.
- Meantime, in big, heavy skillet, heat a tablespoon of oil on moderately-high heat. Put in garlic and crimini mushrooms; scatter with pepper and coarse salt and sauté for 2 to 3 minutes, till starting to soften. Put in half cup of wine and simmer for 4 minutes, till crimini mushrooms softens. Put aside, there might remaining liquid in skillet.
- In big, heavy pot, heat leftover 2 tablespoons of oil on moderately-high heat. Scatter pepper and coarse salt on pork. Put the pork to pot and sauté for 6 minutes, till browned in patches. Turn pork onto medium size bowl with slotted spoon. Drain all except a tablespoon of pot fat. Lower the heat to moderate. Put in coppa and mix for a minute. Put in sausages and cook till brown for 3 minutes, crumbling to make small pieces using back of the spoon. Put in carrot, celery and onion. Put pot cover and let vegetables cook for 8 minutes till soft, mixing from time to time. Put in leftover 2 cups of wine; boil, scratching up browned bits. Simmer till nearly all liquid is soaked in. Put in porcini mushrooms, reserved pork, bay leaves, a cup of broth and tomatoes. Add in the reserved porcini soaking water, keeping any sediment in bowl. Boil; lower heat to moderately-low and simmer with no cover for an hour, till pork is soft, putting in additional broth by quarter-cupfuls in case dry.
- Mix mixture of crimini mushroom into ragù in skillet. Add pepper and salt to season. May be done a day in advance. Cool partially. Refrigerate with no cover till cool. Place cover; keep in refrigerator. Reheat prior to proceeding.
- Skim fat off ragù top and mix basil in. Put in Potato Gnocchi; toss softly till coated. Simmer on moderate heat for 3 to 5 minutes, till gnocchi are heated completely.
- Distribute ragù and gnocchi between bowls. Scatter some of cheese over and serve, passing the rest of the cheese on the side.

Nutrition Information

199. Pots De Crème With Riesling Poached Grapes

Serving: Makes 8 servings | Prep: 40mins | Ready in:

Ingredients

- 1 750 milliliter bottle off-dry Riesling
- 4 cups black seedless grapes or red seedless grapes
- 10 tablespoons sugar, divided
- 11 large egg yolks
- Pinch of sea salt
- 2 1/4 cups heavy cream
- 3/4 cup whole milk
- 3/4 cup sour cream
- Eight 3/4-cup ramekins

Direction

- In a big saucepan, boil 4 tablespoons of sugar, grapes and wine on medium high heat. Stir so that the sugar dissolves. Lower the heat and let it simmer for an hour while occasionally stirring until the liquid measures two cups. Let it chill.
- Set oven to 325 degrees F. Use an electric mixer to beat salt, 6 tablespoons of sugar and yolks in a big bowl for 2 minutes until light yellow.

- Let the cream simmer on medium heat in a pot. Slowly whisk cream in the yolk mixture. Mix in sour cream and milk. Strain through a fine-mesh sieve on top of a pitcher. Split between ramekins then use foil to cover and place in a big roasting pan. Pour hot water in the pan so it is halfway up the sides of the ramekins.
- Let the pots of de crème bake for an hour until set in the middle. Take the covers off and refrigerate for 3 hours. Garnish with grapes.

Nutrition Information

200. Provencal Fish Soup With Saffron Rouille

Serving: Makes 8 (first course) servings | Prep: 1.25hours | Ready in:

Ingredients

- 4 medium leeks (white and pale green parts only), chopped
- 1 large fennel bulb, stalks discarded, reserving fronds for garnish, and bulb chopped
- 3 medium carrots, chopped
- 2 large celery ribs, chopped
- 4 large garlic cloves, finely chopped
- 1/3 cup extra-virgin olive oil
- 1 tablespoon herbes de Provence
- 2 California or 4 Turkish bay leaves
- 1/4 teaspoon cayenne
- 1/8 teaspoon crumbled saffron threads
- 5 pounds whole whiting, perch, or cod (preferably with heads), cleaned and rinsed well
- 5 medium tomatoes, chopped (4 cups)
- 2 cups dry white wine
- 4 (3- by 1-inch) strips fresh orange zest
- 6 cups water
- 3 tablespoons tomato paste
- 1 baguette, cut into 3/4-inch-thick slices
- Equipment: a food mill fitted with medium disk
- Accompaniment: saffron rouille

Direction

- Wash leeks.
- Cook garlic, celery, carrots, fennel bulb, leeks, 1/2 tsp. pepper, 1 tbsp. salt, saffron, cayenne, bay leaves and herbes de Provence in oil in 8-qt. heavy pot on medium heat for 10 minutes till soft, occasionally mixing.
- As veggie mixture cooks, cut fish crosswise into 2- to 3-in. lengths.
- Add zest, wine and tomatoes to veggie mixture; boil for 30 seconds. Add tomato paste, water and fish; simmer for 30 minutes till fish fully falls apart, uncovered, occasionally mixing.
- Preheat an oven with rack in center to 350°F.
- Put baguette slices on baking sheet in 1 layer; bake for 20 minutes till thoroughly dried and golden brown.
- Through food mill, force soup into big heavy pot; discard solids. Reheat soup on medium heat, occasionally mixing.
- On croutons, mound rouille; put 1 on bottom of every soup bowl. Put soup around croutons.
- You can make soup without croutons and rouille 2 days ahead, uncovered and chilled, till fully cooled, then covered. Before serving, reheat.

Nutrition Information

- Calories: 529
- Saturated Fat: 2 g(11%)
- Sodium: 525 mg(22%)
- Fiber: 4 g(15%)
- Total Carbohydrate: 34 g(11%)
- Cholesterol: 190 mg(63%)
- Protein: 58 g(116%)
- Total Fat: 14 g(22%)

201. Provençal Braised Lamb Chops

Serving: Makes 4 servings | Prep: 30mins | Ready in:

Ingredients

- 4 (1/2-inch-thick) lamb shoulder chops (1 3/4 pounds total)
- 1/4 cup extra-virgin olive oil
- 6 garlic cloves, thinly sliced lengthwise (1/4 cup)
- 2 medium onions, sliced (4 cups)
- 1 Turkish or 1/2 California bay leaf
- 1 1/2 cups dry white wine
- 1 1/2 pounds boiling potatoes
- 3 large thyme sprigs
- 1/3 cup oil-cured black olives
- 1 (14 1/2-ounce) can reduced-sodium chicken broth

Direction

- Set the rack in the middle of the oven and preheat it to 375°F.
- Pat dry the chops. Season the chops with 1/2 tsp. of salt and 1/2 tsp. of pepper. Put oil in a 12-inches heavy skillet and heat it over medium-high heat until it shimmers. Cook the garlic for 1 minute, stirring often until golden. Use a slotted spoon to transfer it onto a plate. Working in batches, brown each batch of the chops for 4 minutes, flipping only once. Transfer them onto a plate.
- Add 1/8 tsp. of pepper, 1/4 tsp. of salt, onions, and bay leaf into the skillet. Cook them over medium-high heat for 10-12 minutes, stirring often until lightly browned. Add the wine. Bring the mixture to a boil, scraping up any browned bits. Remove the mixture from the heat.
- Peel the potatoes and cut them into 1/8-inch thick. Scatter half of the potatoes into the bottom of the shallow 3-qt baking dish. Top the tomatoes with half of the onions. Scatter the olives, garlic, and thyme all over the onions. Place the lamb chops on top of the ingredients. Repeat the layers with the remaining potatoes and onions. Pour the meat juices, wine, and broth all over the top of the layers.
- Let them bake for 1 1/2 hours, uncovered and basting the top with juices at least once or twice until the top of the potatoes are browned and tender and the meat is tender when pierced with the knife's tip.

Nutrition Information

- Calories: 689
- Total Fat: 39 g(61%)
- Saturated Fat: 13 g(64%)
- Sodium: 401 mg(17%)
- Fiber: 7 g(29%)
- Total Carbohydrate: 49 g(16%)
- Cholesterol: 82 mg(27%)
- Protein: 26 g(52%)

202. Puerto Rican Crab

Serving: Makes 4 to 6 first-course servings | Prep: | Ready in:

Ingredients

- 1 tablespoon olive oil
- 1 1/2 cups chopped onion
- 1/4 cup chopped green bell pepper
- 2 garlic cloves, minced
- 1/2 teaspoon dried oregano
- 1/2 cup tomato sauce
- 1/2 cup dry white wine
- 1 pound lump crabmeat, picked over
- 4 pimiento-stuffed olives, chopped
- 1 tablespoon chopped fresh cilantro
- 1 teaspoon hot pepper sauce
- 4 to 6 small crab shells (optional) or scalloped dishes
- 1 lime, cut into wedges

Direction

- In nonstick, big skillet, heat the oil on moderately-high heat. Put in oregano, garlic, bell pepper and onion; sauté for 6 minutes, till soft. Put in wine and tomato sauce and boil for a minute, till nearly vaporized. Put in crabmeat; reduce heat to moderate, and cook with cover for 5 minutes. Mix in cilantro, hot sauce and olives. Season with pepper and salt to taste. Take off heat. Rest for 5 minutes. Scoop the mixture in shells of crabs, if wished. Juice lime wedges on top to serve.

Nutrition Information

- Calories: 201
- Saturated Fat: 1 g(4%)
- Sodium: 900 mg(38%)
- Fiber: 2 g(9%)
- Total Carbohydrate: 11 g(4%)
- Cholesterol: 125 mg(42%)
- Protein: 25 g(50%)
- Total Fat: 5 g(8%)

203. Pumpkin Cannelloni With Clams And Sage Brown Butter

Serving: Makes 4 first-course servings | Prep: | Ready in:

Ingredients

- 2 tablespoons unsalted butter
- 1 pound sugar pumpkin or other sweet winter squash such as butternut, peeled, seeded, and cut into 1-inch cubes (3 cups)
- 3/4 cup diced (1/4 inch) fennel bulb (sometimes called anise)
- 1/2 teaspoon salt
- 1/4 teaspoon black pepper
- 2 tablespoons chopped shallot
- 1/4 cup water
- 4 (6- by 4-inch) fresh pasta rectangles
- 1 tablespoon olive oil
- 2 bacon slices, cut crosswise into 1/4-inch-wide strips
- 1/3 cup thinly sliced shallot
- 1 garlic clove, minced
- 20 small hard-shelled clams (2 pounds) such as littlenecks (less than 2 inches wide), scrubbed well
- 1/2 cup dry white wine
- 1/4 teaspoon fennel seeds
- 1 tablespoon chopped fresh sage
- 1/2 stick (1/4 cup) unsalted butter
- 8 fresh sage leaves
- 2 tablespoons minced shallot
- 1 teaspoon fresh lemon juice
- 1/4 cup chopped fresh parsley

Direction

- Make filling and make cannelloni: In a 12-in. heavy skillet, heat butter till foam subsides on medium high heat; sauté fennel, pepper, salt and squash for 4 minutes till golden, occasionally mixing. Add water and shallot; simmer for 10 minutes till veggies are tender, covered. Cool veggies; puree till smooth in a food processor. Season with pepper and salt.
- Preheat an oven to 400°F.
- Cook pasta sheets for 1-2 minutes till al dente in a 4-6-qt. pot with boiling salted water; use a slotted spoon to transfer in a bowl with cold water and ice to cool immediately. Drain well; on paper towels, pat dry sheets. Put into a well-oiled big shallow baking pan in 1 layer. Along 1 rectangle's short end, put 1/4 cup filling; roll filling up in pasta. In same manner, create 3 more rolls; put in baking pan, seam side down. Drizzle oil on cannelloni.
- Bake cannelloni and make clam sauce: Cook bacon for 5 minutes till fat renders yet bacon isn't crisp in a 12-in. heavy skillet on medium heat, mixing. Add shallot; cook for 4 minutes till soft, mixing. Add garlic; cook for 1 minute till fragrant, mixing. Add sage, fennel seeds, wine and clams; cook for 6-10 minutes till clams fully open, checking every minute after about 6 minutes then removing clams when they fully open. Throw unopened clams after 10 minutes.

- Bake cannelloni in center of oven for 6-8 minutes till heated through as clams cook.
- Create sage brown butter: In a 1 1/2-qt. heavy saucepan, heat butter till foam subsides on medium high heat; fry sage leaves for 3 minutes till crisp. Put leaves on paper towels with a slotted spoon; drain. Season using salt. Put shallot in butter; cook for 1-2 minutes till butter is deep golden and shallot is golden, mixing. Add lemon juice; the butter will foam. Take off heat. Mix in parsley; season brown butter using pepper and salt.
- Serving: In middle of each of the 4 warm big plates, put a cannelloni; divide clams with juices to plates. Drizzle brown butter; put fried sage leaves over.

Nutrition Information

- Calories: 470
- Fiber: 6 g(24%)
- Total Carbohydrate: 37 g(12%)
- Cholesterol: 77 mg(26%)
- Protein: 17 g(35%)
- Total Fat: 28 g(43%)
- Saturated Fat: 14 g(69%)
- Sodium: 754 mg(31%)

204. Pumpkin And Shrimp Bisque

Serving: Makes 8 servings | Prep: | Ready in:

Ingredients

- 1 pound large shrimp (16 to 20)
- 2 tablespoons extra-virgin olive oil
- 3/4 cup dry white wine
- 3 cups homemade or canned low-sodium chicken stock
- Pinch saffron threads (about 24)
- 2 ribs celery, coarsely chopped
- 1 medium onion (about 8 ounces), coarsely chopped
- 4 fresh bay laurel leaves, torn, or 2 dried
- 3 3-inch springs fresh sage
- 2 cups pumpkin purée, fresh (see Note) or canned
- 1/2 cup heavy cream
- About 3/4 teaspoon salt, less if using canned stock
- Scant 1/8 teaspoon cayenne pepper
- 1 tablespoon freshly squeezed lemon juice
- Freshly ground black pepper
- 1 tablespoon extra-virgin olive oil
- 2 teaspoons finely chopped fresh sage

Direction

- Shrimp stock: Peel the shrimp and devein, put the shells aside. Refrigerate the shrimp with cover. In 3-quart, medium, heavy-based saucepan, heat olive oil on high heat till it starts to smoke. Put shrimp shells to pan and cook for 3 to 4 minutes, mixing continuously, till they become deep orange and are barely starting to brown. Take the time to pan roast the shells cautiously for it gives the stock much flavor. Roasted shells must give off toasty, concentrated, shrimp fragrant that fills the kitchen. Pour wine to pan, turn the gas flames off first to avoid igniting the alcohol, then let it boil on medium heat till all liquid is vaporized. Put in sage, bay leaves, onion, celery, saffron and chicken stock. Boil, then lower heat to as low setting as possible. Slightly cover pan and gently simmer for half an hour. Drain stock in fine sieve, forcing on solids using back of spoon to release all liquid. Wash the saucepan and return the stock into it.
- Soup: mix into shrimp stock with cayenne, salt (omit in case using canned stock), cream and pumpkin. Simmer soup, then cook extremely slowly for 10 minutes with no cover on low heat. Mix lemon juice in, check for taste, and add additional salt if necessary and black pepper to season. Soup may be done up to this part a day in advance, keep in refrigerator with cover. Keep peeled shrimp in a sealable bag place under ice in bowl inside the fridge.

- Finishing the soup: add to a big sauté pan with olive oil on moderate heat. Put in sage and reserved shrimp once hot and cook for 2 to 3 minutes, tossing frequently, till shrimp is barely cooked completely, not clear anymore, and pink, however not bended into circle. They must remain tender once you bite into them. Place shrimp in heated a tureen or serving bowls. Return soup to simmer and then scoop it on top of shrimp. Serve immediately.

Nutrition Information

- Calories: 209
- Saturated Fat: 5 g(24%)
- Sodium: 368 mg(15%)
- Fiber: 4 g(16%)
- Total Carbohydrate: 13 g(4%)
- Cholesterol: 92 mg(31%)
- Protein: 11 g(23%)
- Total Fat: 12 g(19%)

205. Pumpkin Seed Crusted Trout

Serving: Serves 4 | Prep: | Ready in:

Ingredients

- 1 cup loosely packed fresh cilantro sprigs
- 3/4 cup hulled green pumpkin seeds* (about 1/4 pound)
- 2 large eggs
- 1/2 cup all-purpose flour
- four 3- to 4-ounce trout fillets with skin
- 2 tablespoons olive oil
- 2 tablespoons fresh lime juice
- 1/2 cup dry white wine
- 3/4 stick (6 tablespoons) cold unsalted butter
- *available at natural foods stores

Direction

- Chop cilantro finely. Lightly crush pumpkin seeds in a sealable plastic bag using a rolling pin. Lightly beat eggs in a shallow dish. Have pumpkin seeds and flour ready in 2 separate shallow dishes. Use tweezers to remove the fine bones from the fillets. Season trout with pepper and salt. Dredge 1 fillet, flesh side, in flour. Shake excess off. Dip the flesh side into eggs, let excess drip off. Coat the fillet in pumpkin seeds. Put on a plate, seed side up. Coat leftover fillets the same way.
- Heat oil in a 12-in. nonstick skillet on medium heat until hot yet not smoking. Cook fillets for 3 minutes, seed sides down, until they're golden. Use a spatula to carefully flip. Cook for 3 more minutes on low heat until they're just cooked through. Put on a heated platter with a spatula. Retain warm while creating sauce.
- Boil wine and lime juice in a small heavy saucepan for 2 minutes until reduced by half. Cut butter to pieces. Add, one by one, whisking until sauce it smooth and incorporated. It shouldn't be so hot that it separates. Take pan off heat. Add cilantro. Season with salt.
- Spoon the sauce on trout fillets.

Nutrition Information

- Calories: 621
- Total Carbohydrate: 16 g(5%)
- Cholesterol: 197 mg(66%)
- Protein: 33 g(67%)
- Total Fat: 47 g(72%)
- Saturated Fat: 17 g(83%)
- Sodium: 94 mg(4%)
- Fiber: 2 g(9%)

206. Quick Cioppino

Serving: Makes 4 servings | Prep: | Ready in:

Ingredients

- 3 tablespoons olive oil
- 2 cups finely chopped onions
- 2 large garlic cloves, minced
- 2 teaspoons chopped fresh rosemary
- 1/4 teaspoon dried crushed red pepper
- 1 2/3 cups canned crushed tomatoes in puree (from one 28-ounce can)
- 2 8-ounce bottles clam juice
- 3/4 cup dry white wine
- 12 ounces halibut fillets, cut into 1-inch pieces
- 1/2 pound uncooked peeled deveined medium shrimp
- 1/2 pound bay scallops
- 1/3 cup chopped fresh parsley, divided

Direction

- In big pot, heat the oil on moderately-high heat. Put in the following 4 ingredients; sauté for six minutes. Put in clam juice, wine and tomatoes; boil. Lower the heat to moderate; simmer, mixing from time to time, for 18 minutes. Put in 2 tablespoons of parsley and all seafood. Simmer for 3 minutes, till seafood turn opaque in the middle. Season with pepper and salt to taste, scoop to bowls, and scatter parsley over.

Nutrition Information

- Calories: 370
- Total Fat: 13 g(19%)
- Saturated Fat: 2 g(10%)
- Sodium: 1553 mg(65%)
- Fiber: 4 g(14%)
- Total Carbohydrate: 19 g(6%)
- Cholesterol: 127 mg(42%)
- Protein: 41 g(82%)

207. Quince Compote

Serving: Makes about 3 cups | Prep: | Ready in:

Ingredients

- 4 pounds quinces, peeled, quartered, cored, cut into 1/2-inch cubes
- 2 cups water
- 2 cups sugar
- 2 cups dry white wine
- 1 vanilla bean, split lengthwise

Direction

- In big, heavy saucepan, boil the initial 4 ingredients, mixing frequently. Scoop in vanilla bean seeds; put in the bean. Lower the heat, place cover, and simmer for 40 minutes, till fruit soften, mixing from time to time. Turn the fruit onto bowl with slotted spoon. Let juices boil with no cover till cooked down to 3 cups, roughly half an hour. Top fruit with syrup. Refrigerate overnight with cover.
- Tip: quince hard core should be taken off using paring knife once every fruit is sliced into 4. In case core is very hard to safely remove using knife, clip fruit pieces from surrounding then slice the pieces to make smaller cubes.

Nutrition Information

- Calories: 355
- Saturated Fat: 0 g(0%)
- Sodium: 14 mg(1%)
- Fiber: 4 g(17%)
- Total Carbohydrate: 86 g(29%)
- Protein: 1 g(2%)
- Total Fat: 0 g(0%)

208. Rabbit, Carrot, Leek, And Green Bean Ragoût

Serving: Makes 4 servings. | Prep: 1.25hours | Ready in:

Ingredients

- 1 (3-pound) rabbit (thawed if frozen), cut into 8 serving pieces

- 1 tablespoon unsalted butter
- 1/4 cup dry white wine
- 2 cups fat-free chicken broth
- 2 tablespoons chopped garlic
- 1/2 tablespoon fresh thyme
- 1 teaspoon kosher salt
- 1 bay leaf (not California)
- 4 small (2-inch) red onions (1/2 pound total)
- 3 large leeks, white and pale green parts only, cut into 1/2-inch-thick rounds
- 3 large carrots, cut diagonally into 1/2-inch-thick slices
- 1/2 pound small (1-inch) boiling potatoes (about 8)
- 1/2 pound haricots verts or regular green beans, cut diagonally into 2-inch pieces

Direction

- Take liver, kidneys and fat off rabbit if needed. Blot rabbit dry and add pepper and salt to season. In a heavy 6-quart wide pot, on medium high heat, heat 1/2 tablespoon of butter and oil till froth settles, then in 2 batches, let rabbit brown for 2 to 3 minutes on each side. Turn onto plate as browned. To pot, put wine and boil for half a minute. Put in broth and boil to deglaze the pot, scratching up brown bits. Mince and crush the garlic along with salt and thyme and mix into broth together with rabbit and bay leaf. Simmer for 40 minutes with cover.
- Meanwhile, slice onions into 4 lengthwise, keeping sufficient of the core attached to maintain layers together. In big bowl with water, submerge leeks for 10 minutes, mixing from time to time to remove any sand and allowing sand sink to base of bowl. Pull leeks out of water.
- Spread potatoes, carrots, leeks and onions on top and on rabbit surrounding and keep simmering with cover for 40 to 50 minutes, till vegetables and rabbit are soft.
- Once rabbit is nearly done, in big pot with boiling salted water, let beans cook for 3 to 5 minutes till barely soft, and allow to drain in colander.
- Into ragout, mix beans, then using a slotted spoon, turn the vegetables and rabbit onto deep platter and retain warmth. Let cooking liquid boil till cooked down to approximately 3/4 cup and mix in leftover half tablespoon of butter. Add some sauce on top of vegetables and rabbit and serve the remaining alongside.

Nutrition Information

209. Rack Of Lamb With Red Currant Wine Sauce

Serving: Makes 4 servings | Prep: | Ready in:

Ingredients

- 3 tablespoons olive oil
- 2 pounds lamb neck bones
- 1 shallot, minced
- 4 cups chicken stock or canned low-salt chicken broth
- 3 tablespoons red wine vinegar
- 1 1/2 tablespoons dry white wine
- 3 tablespoons red currant jelly
- 1 tablespoon butter, room temperature
- 1 tablespoon all purpose flour
- 2 1 1/2-pound lamb racks
- 2 teaspoons minced fresh thyme

Direction

- Heat 1 tbsp. oil on high heat in big heavy pot. Add lamb bones; brown well for 8 minutes, occasionally turning. Add shallot; sauté for 1 minute. Add wine, vinegar and stock; boil. Lower heat to medium; simmer for 1 hour till liquid reduces to 1 cup. Into medium heavy saucepan, strain broth; whisk in jelly. Blend flour and butter till smooth in small bowl. Boil sauce on medium heat; whisk in the butter mixture. Simmer for 1 minute till sauce is smooth and thickens, constantly whisking.

Season with pepper and salt to taste. You can make it 1 day ahead. Cover; refrigerate. Before serving, rewarm, frequently whisking.
- Preheat an oven to 425°F. Heat leftover 2 tbsp. oil on high heat in big heavy skillet. Sprinkle pepper, salt and thyme on lamb. Put 1 lamb rack in skillet; brown all sides for 6 minutes. Put browned lamb rack on rimmed baking sheet, meat side up; repeat using 2nd lamb rack. Roast lamb for 12 minutes till inserted thermometer in middle reads 125°F for medium-rare. Stand lamb for 5 minutes. Between bones, cut lamb to individual chops. On 4 plates, put chops. Put sauce over; serve.

Nutrition Information

- Calories: 1716
- Sodium: 656 mg(27%)
- Fiber: 1 g(3%)
- Total Carbohydrate: 23 g(8%)
- Cholesterol: 367 mg(122%)
- Protein: 82 g(165%)
- Total Fat: 142 g(218%)
- Saturated Fat: 59 g(293%)

210. Raspberry Syllabub

Serving: Makes 8 servings | Prep: | Ready in:

Ingredients

- 3/4 cup sugar
- 2/3 cup dry white wine
- 1/2 cup fresh lemon juice
- 1/3 cup dry Sherry
- 2 tablespoons grated lemon peel
- 2 cups chilled whipping cream
- 2 1/2-pint baskets raspberries

Direction

- Mix in medium size bowl with the initial 5 ingredients till sugar is dissolved. In big bowl, whip cream till stiff peaks form. Fold into mixture of wine with whipped cream. Distribute mixture between 8 wineglasses. Chill with cover overnight, mixture of syllabub will separate. Scatter berries over to serve.

Nutrition Information

- Calories: 313
- Saturated Fat: 12 g(58%)
- Sodium: 58 mg(2%)
- Fiber: 7 g(26%)
- Total Carbohydrate: 34 g(11%)
- Cholesterol: 66 mg(22%)
- Protein: 3 g(5%)
- Total Fat: 19 g(29%)

211. Rhubarb Sabayon With Strawberries

Serving: Makes 6 servings | Prep: | Ready in:

Ingredients

- 1 cup chopped fresh rhubarb stalks (2 large ribs)
- 1/2 cup sugar
- 1 cup orange Muscat wine such as Essensia
- 1 qt fresh strawberries, trimmed and quartered
- 2 large eggs
- an instant-read thermometer

Direction

- In a heavy, small saucepan simmer sugar, wine and rhubarb, mixing till sugar dissolves, then simmer for 5 minutes, with no cover, till rhubarb becomes tender and starts to crumble apart. Use a blender to purée till smooth, be careful once processing hot liquids.
- Distribute strawberries between 6 stemmed glasses.

- In a deep, big metal bowl, whip eggs at moderately-high speed using handheld electric mixer for a minute, then put hot rhubarb purée in stream, whipping continuously. Place the bowl on top of a saucepan with simmering water and whip for 6 minutes, till mixture is tripled in bulk, extremely thick, and thermometer reads 160°F. Take off heat and scoop sabayon on top of strawberries. Serve right away.
- Note: Rhubarb purée may be done 2 hours in advance and store at room temperature. Rewarm prior to putting into eggs.

Nutrition Information

212. Riesling Poached Trout With Thyme

Serving: Makes 4 servings | Prep: | Ready in:

Ingredients

- 6 tablespoons (3/4 stick) chilled butter
- 1 very large leek (white and pale green parts only), thinly sliced
- 1 carrot, peeled, cut into matchstick-size strips
- 4 trout, boned, butterflied
- 2 teaspoons minced fresh thyme
- 2 bay leaves, broken in half
- 1 cup Johannisberg Riesling

Direction

- Prepare the oven by preheating to 450 degrees F. In a heavy large skillet over medium heat, put 1 tablespoon butter to melt. Put in carrot strips and sliced leek; stir-fry for about 5 minutes until crisp-tender. Open fish flat and arrange in a large roasting pan with skin side down. Dust 1 1/2 teaspoons minced fresh thyme, pepper, and salt over the fish. Place bay leaves and carrot and leek mixture on top.

Drizzle with 2 tablespoons butter. Put Riesling over the fish.
- Bake the fish for about 15 minutes until the center is just opaque. Place vegetables and fish onto plates. Use foil to tent them to keep warm. In a heavy medium saucepan, put pan juices. Boil for about 6 minutes, until reduced to 3/4 cup. Get rid of bay leaves. Add 1/2 teaspoon thyme and the rest 3 tablespoons butter and stir just until butter melts. Add pepper and salt to taste. Shower sauce over the fish then serve.

Nutrition Information

- Calories: 863
- Total Fat: 45 g(70%)
- Saturated Fat: 17 g(86%)
- Sodium: 250 mg(10%)
- Fiber: 1 g(4%)
- Total Carbohydrate: 8 g(3%)
- Cholesterol: 313 mg(104%)
- Protein: 91 g(182%)

213. Rigatoni With Braised Lamb Ragù

Serving: Serves 6 | Prep: | Ready in:

Ingredients

- 2 tablespoons olive oil
- 6 lamb shanks (each about 3/4 pound)
- 2 cups chopped onions
- 1 pound small button mushrooms, halved
- 4 garlic cloves, chopped
- 1/3 cup chopped fresh basil
- 1 teaspoon chopped fresh rosemary
- 1/2 teaspoon dried crushed red pepper
- 1/2cup dry white wine
- 3 cups beef stock or canned beef broth
- 1 1/2 cups canned crushed tomatoes in purée
- 1 1/4 pounds rigatoni pasta
- Freshly grated Parmesan cheese

Direction

- Preheat your oven to 325°F. In a large ovenproof pot, heat the oil over high heat. Sprinkle salt and pepper over the lamb shanks. Transfer to the pot and brown the lamb on all sides in the pot for 12 minutes. Transfer to a platter. In the pot, add and sauté crush red pepper, rosemary, basil, garlic, mushrooms, and onions for 8 minutes, until the vegetables are tender. Place the lamb back into the pot. Pour wine into the pot and boil for 6 minutes, until the liquid has evaporated. Add tomatoes and 3 cups of beef stock and return to a boil.
- Cover and transfer the pot to the oven. Bake for 1 1/2 hours, until the lamb is tender. Transfer the lamb to a bowl using tongs and allow to cool for 10 minutes. Cut the meat into 1/2-inch pieces after slicing off the bones; discard the bones. Place the cut meat back into the sauce and season with salt and pepper to taste. If making a day ahead, refrigerate until cold, uncovered. Then cover and keep in refrigerator. Before continue cooking, rewarm over medium-low.
- Meanwhile, in a large pot with boiling salted water, cook the pasta until al dente but still firm to bite. Drain thoroughly. Place the cooked pasta in a large serving bowl. Spoon the sauce over the pasta and serve. Place Parmesan cheese on the side separately for anyone to add to their serving.

Nutrition Information

- Calories: 1388
- Cholesterol: 299 mg(100%)
- Protein: 103 g(206%)
- Total Fat: 68 g(104%)
- Saturated Fat: 30 g(150%)
- Sodium: 703 mg(29%)
- Fiber: 6 g(24%)
- Total Carbohydrate: 85 g(28%)

214. Risotto Milanese Style (Risotta Alla Milanese)

Serving: Makes 6 servings | Prep: | Ready in:

Ingredients

- 6 cups chicken stock or low-sodium broth
- 1/4 cup olive oil
- 1 small onion, minced (about 1/2 cup)
- 2 1/2 cups Carnaroli or Vialone Nano rice
- 3/4 tablespoon saffron threads, crumbled
- 3/4 cup dry white wine
- 5 tablespoons unsalted butter
- 3 ounces freshly grated Parmigiano-Reggiano (about 3/4 cup)
- Salt and freshly ground black pepper
- Beef marrow for garnish (optional)

Direction

- Heat chicken stock in small saucepan. Retain warmth.
- Heat olive oil on medium low heat in big saucepan. Put in and sauté onion for 5 minutes, mixing from time to time, just till soft but before it takes on color. Put in saffron and rice, and lightly toast for a minute without allowing onion or rice to take on any color. Pour in wine and cook till nearly fully soaked in.
- Put in most of chicken stock, it must reach approximately half-inch over rice and simmer. Let risotto cook for 14 minutes, mixing from time to time, till rice is al dente and liquid has been soaked in. Pour in additional liquid as necessary as rice starts to soak in liquid.
- When rice has soaked in nearly all broth, take off heat, put in Parmigiano-Reggiano and butter, and mix firmly for a minute till surface starches developed. Season with pepper and salt to taste.
- Serve risotto right away, jazz up with a meat marrow piece, if wished.

Nutrition Information

- Calories: 537
- Total Fat: 23 g(35%)
- Saturated Fat: 10 g(49%)
- Sodium: 867 mg(36%)
- Fiber: 1 g(2%)
- Total Carbohydrate: 67 g(22%)
- Cholesterol: 35 mg(12%)
- Protein: 11 g(22%)

215. Roast Chicken Provençale

Serving: Serves 4 | Prep: | Ready in:

Ingredients

- a 3-pound chicken
- 1 small onion
- 1 garlic clove
- 2 plum tomatoes
- 1/4 cup Kalamata olives
- 1/2 cup packed fresh basil leaves
- 1/2 cup dry white wine
- 3/4 cup veal stock

Direction

- Preheat an oven to 450°F. Season the chicken with pepper and salt. Roast the chicken for 20 minutes in an 8- to 10-inch ovenproof skillet in the center of the oven.
- Lower the temperature to 350°F.
- Roast the chicken for about 40 minutes or until juices run clear and a thermometer inserted into the fleshy part of inner thigh reaches 170°F. Place the chicken onto a cutting board and cover loosely to keep it warm.
- As the chicken roasts, finely chop garlic and onion separately. Seed the tomatoes and slice into 1/4-inch dice. Then pit the olives and chop finely. Slice plenty of basil to measure two tablespoons and then chop the remaining leaves into thin strips.
- Drain all except two teaspoons of fat from the skillet and then sauté onion on moderately high heat while stirring for 30 seconds. Place in garlic and then sauté while stirring for 30 seconds. Pour in wine and deglaze the skillet while scraping up the brown bits. Simmer the mixture until decreased by about half. Pour in stock and heat the mixture to simmer. Add olives and tomato and let to simmer for about 3 minutes until the sauce is thickened slightly. Mix in basil strips and transfer the pan from the heat source. Slice the chicken into four serving pieces.
- Spread the sauce on the chicken and drizzle with chopped basil.

Nutrition Information

- Calories: 552
- Sodium: 285 mg(12%)
- Fiber: 1 g(4%)
- Total Carbohydrate: 6 g(2%)
- Cholesterol: 175 mg(58%)
- Protein: 45 g(90%)
- Total Fat: 36 g(56%)
- Saturated Fat: 10 g(51%)

216. Roast Chicken Stuffed With Fennel And Garlic

Serving: Makes 6 servings | Prep: | Ready in:

Ingredients

- 3 large fresh fennel bulbs, trimmed, each cut into 8 wedges
- 2 tablespoons plus 1/4 cup extra-virgin olive oil
- 10 garlic cloves, peeled
- 2 tablespoons fennel seeds, coarsely crushed in resealable plastic bag
- 2 tablespoons chopped fresh thyme
- 2 tablespoons chopped fresh rosemary
- 2 tablespoons chopped fresh tarragon
- 2 tablespoons chopped fresh marjoram
- 3/4 teaspoon salt

- 1/2 teaspoon ground black pepper
- 2 3-pound whole chickens
- 2 lemons, halved
- 1 cup Vernaccia di San Gimignano wine or other dry white wine
- 1/3 cup low-salt chicken broth

Direction

- In big pot with salted boiling water, cook fennel for 8 minutes, till soft once pricked with knife. Strain. Turn onto bowl. Stir in 2 tablespoons of oil, garlic, a tablespoon fennel seeds, a tablespoon thyme, a tablespoon rosemary, a tablespoon tarragon, and a tablespoon marjoram; then half teaspoon of pepper and 3/4 teaspoon of salt.
- Preheat the oven to 450°F. Stir in small bowl with leftover 1 tablespoon fennel seeds and 1 tablespoon herbs. Wash in and out of chickens; blot dry. Rub halves of lemon on in and out of chickens, squeeze some juice inside the cavities. Massage quarter cup of oil, then the mixture of fennel seed on the outer part of chickens. Liberally scatter pepper and salt on chickens. Use some of fresh mixture of fennel to loosely stuff the chickens. Bind the legs together. Put the chickens in big roasting pan, breast side facing down. Surround the chickens with the rest of the fresh fennel mixture.
- Let chickens roast for half an hour, basting from time to time using pan juices. Mix broth and wine and add on top of chickens. Let roast for 15 minutes. Flip the chickens, breast side facing up. Let chickens roast till juices run clear once pricked using fork in chunkiest portion of thigh, for an additional of 40 minutes. Turn the fennel mixture and chickens onto platter. Add juices from pan to bowl; scoop off fat. Add the juices on top of chickens to serve.

Nutrition Information

- Calories: 877
- Fiber: 7 g(27%)
- Total Carbohydrate: 17 g(6%)
- Cholesterol: 231 mg(77%)
- Protein: 61 g(121%)
- Total Fat: 61 g(94%)
- Saturated Fat: 15 g(77%)
- Sodium: 592 mg(25%)

217. Roast Chicken With Lemon And Fresh Herbs

Serving: Serves 4 | Prep: | Ready in:

Ingredients

- 1 4-pound chicken
- 3 large fresh tarragon sprigs plus 2 teaspoons chopped
- 3 large fresh thyme sprigs plus 2 teaspoons chopped
- 4 3x1-inch lemon peel strips plus 2 teaspoons grated lemon peel
- 2 tablespoons olive oil
- 1/2 cup dry white wine
- 1/2 cup canned low-salt chicken broth

Direction

- Preheat an oven to 375°F. Rinse the chicken; pat dry. Inside and out, sprinkle chicken with pepper and salt. Inside the main cavity, put lemon strips and herb sprigs; rub oil outside then grated lemon peel and chopped herbs. Put chicken into the pan.
- Roast the chicken for 45 minutes; put broth and wine over. Cook for 30 minutes till juices are clear when you pierce the thigh, basting with pan juices often; serve pan juices with chicken.

Nutrition Information

- Calories: 752
- Fiber: 1 g(3%)
- Total Carbohydrate: 3 g(1%)

- Cholesterol: 231 mg(77%)
- Protein: 59 g(117%)
- Total Fat: 54 g(82%)
- Saturated Fat: 14 g(72%)
- Sodium: 227 mg(9%)

218. Roast Chicken With White Bean Stew And Pancetta

Serving: Makes 6 servings | Prep: | Ready in:

Ingredients

- 2 cups dried cannellini (white kidney beans; about 1 pound)
- 2 tablespoons olive oil
- 6 whole chicken leg-thigh pieces
- 6 ounces pancetta (Italian bacon), chopped
- 1 leek (white part only), cut into 1/2-inch cubes
- 1 small onion, cut into 1/2-inch cubes
- 1 celery stalk, cut into 1/2-inch cubes
- 1 small carrot, peeled, cut into 1/2-inch cubes
- 1 small fennel bulb, trimmed, cut into 1/2-inch cubes
- 1 bay leaf
- 6 garlic cloves, chopped
- 2 tablespoons tomato paste
- 3 tablespoons all purpose flour
- 1 cup dry white wine
- 6 cups low-salt chicken broth
- 1 6-inch-long fresh rosemary sprig plus 2 tablespoons finely chopped rosemary
- 2 tablespoons chopped fresh parsley
- 1 tablespoon finely grated lemon peel

Direction

- In big saucepan, put the beans. Pour in sufficient water to soak by 4-inch. Rest overnight.
- Preheat the oven to 350°F. In an ovenproof, big, heavy pot, heat the oil on moderately-high heat. Scatter pepper and salt on chicken. Cook chicken in batches for 7 minutes on each side, till golden brown. Turn chicken onto a big plate. Put to same pot with pancetta and the following 6 ingredients. Cook for 10 minutes, till vegetables soften and start to brown, mixing often. Put in garlic; mix for a minute. Put in tomato paste; mx for 2 minutes. Put in flour; mix for a minute. Pour in wine and let simmer for a minute. Strain the beans. Put the beans into pot; mix to incorporate. Pour in broth; add pepper and salt to season. Put the chicken and rosemary sprig over mixture of bean.
- Place pot cover; turn into the oven. Braise for an hour, till beans and chicken are extremely tender. Turn the chicken onto plate. Season the beans using pepper and salt.
- In small bowl, combine parsley, lemon peel and 2 tablespoons of finely chopped rosemary. Distribute beans between 6 shallow bowls. Put chicken on top of each. Scatter parsley mixture over each to serve.

Nutrition Information

- Calories: 1210
- Protein: 81 g(162%)
- Total Fat: 73 g(112%)
- Saturated Fat: 20 g(100%)
- Sodium: 638 mg(27%)
- Fiber: 18 g(71%)
- Total Carbohydrate: 53 g(18%)
- Cholesterol: 339 mg(113%)

219. Roast Fillet Of Beef With Cornichon Tarragon Sauce

Serving: Serves 18 | Prep: | Ready in:

Ingredients

- 3 trimmed 3-to-3 1/2-pound fillets of beef, tied at room temperature
- 1/3 cup vegetable oil

- 2 sticks (1 cup) unsalted butter, softened
- 2/3 cup Dijon-style mustard
- 1 1/4 cups minced shallot
- 5 cups dry white wine
- 1/2 cup minced fresh tarragon leaves or 2 tablespoons dried
- 1/3 cup heavy cream
- 40 cornichons (French sour gherkins, available at specialty foods shops and some supermarkets), cut into julienne strips (about 1 cup)

Direction

- Rub oil on fillets; season with pepper and salt. Put in a big roasting pan; leave space between fillets. In the preheated 550°F oven, roast till meat thermometer reads 130°F to get medium-rare meat for 23 minutes. Put fillets on a platter; stand for 15 minutes, loosely covered with foil. Cream together mustard and butter with electric mixer in a bowl. Cook tarragon, wine and shallot in a big saucepan on medium high heat till wine reduces to 1 cup. You can make shallot mixture and mustard mixture 1 day ahead, kept chilled, covered. Before continuing, reheat the shallot mixture. Add cornichons and cream; lower the heat to low. Little at a time, whisk mustard butter in and any meat juices that have accumulated on the platter; season the sauce with pepper and salt. Keep warm; don't boil. Slice the fillets; nap the meat with sauce.

Nutrition Information

- Calories: 283
- Cholesterol: 58 mg(19%)
- Protein: 7 g(15%)
- Total Fat: 22 g(34%)
- Saturated Fat: 10 g(50%)
- Sodium: 2113 mg(88%)
- Fiber: 3 g(11%)
- Total Carbohydrate: 8 g(3%)

220. Roast Pork With Fruit Stuffing And Mustard Sauce

Serving: Makes 4 servings | Prep: | Ready in:

Ingredients

- 1 4-bone center-cut pork rib roast, bones frenched, roast well trimmed (about 2 pounds)
- 8 whole dried apricots
- 8 whole pitted prunes
- 2 tablespoons corn oil
- 1 1/2 teaspoons dried marjoram
- 1 onion, coarsely chopped
- 2 large carrots, coarsely chopped
- 6 garlic cloves, peeled
- 1 1/2 tablespoons butter, room temperature
- 1 1/2 tablespoons all purpose flour
- 1 tablespoon Dijon mustard
- 1 tablespoon coarse-grained Dijon mustard
- 1 1/2 cups low-salt chicken broth
- 1/2 cup dry white wine

Direction

- Set the oven and preheat at 350°F. Carve the center of the pork out using a long slender knife to make 3/4-inch in diameter horizontal tunnel. Get the carved out meat and slice; set aside for later use. Fill the tunnel with prunes and apricots using the handle of your wooden spoon. Transfer it to a rack in a roasting pan and massage it with 1 tablespoon of oil. Flavor the roast with salt, pepper, and a half teaspoon of marjoram. Arrange carrots, garlic cloves, onion, and the sliced meat around the rack in the roasting pan. Drizzle 1 tbsp. of oil and sprinkle 1 tsp. of marjoram on veggies. Roast the pork for 85 minutes while occasionally stirring the vegetables. You know it's done when an inserted instant-read thermometer in the thickest part of the meat (not the stuffed part) reads 150°F. Transfer the roasted pork to a clean cutting board and cover it with foil to keep warm.
- In a small bowl, mix both mustards, butter, and flour until incorporated. Place the roasting

pan over 2 burners with medium heat. Pour broth and wine in pan and simmer the mixture for 3 minutes until the liquid is reduced to 1 1/2 cups. Scrape bottom of the pan to stir up browned bits. Drain and place the liquid in a small pot. Remove fat from the liquid's surface. Boil the liquid and stir mustard mixture in. Simmer sauce for 3 minutes while stirring it constantly until the sauce is slightly thick. Spice it up with pepper and salt.
- Slice the pork between its ribs making chops. Serve the roasted pork together with its delicious sauce.

Nutrition Information

- Calories: 864
- Cholesterol: 145 mg(48%)
- Protein: 35 g(70%)
- Total Fat: 65 g(100%)
- Saturated Fat: 26 g(128%)
- Sodium: 242 mg(10%)
- Fiber: 4 g(18%)
- Total Carbohydrate: 33 g(11%)

221. Roasted Asparagus And Wild Mushroom Fricassée

Serving: Makes 4 (first-course) servings | Prep: | Ready in:

Ingredients

- 1 pound medium asparagus, tough ends trimmed
- 2 teaspoons olive oil
- 3 tablespoons butter
- 1 large shallot, minced
- 12 ounces assorted wild mushrooms (such as crimini, oyster, chanterelle, and stemmed shiitake), sliced
- 1/2 cup dry white wine
- 1 tablespoon minced fresh Italian parsley
- 1 teaspoon minced fresh tarragon

Direction

- Preheat an oven to 475°F. On a rimmed baking sheet, put asparagus; drizzle oil. Flip to coat; generously sprinkle pepper and salt. Roast for 10 minutes till just tender.
- Meanwhile, melt butter in a big skillet on medium high heat then add shallot; sauté for a minute. Add mushrooms; sauté for 5 minutes till starting to brown. Cover; cook for 3 minutes till mushrooms are tender. Add wine; cook for 2 minutes till wine is absorbed, uncovered. Mix tarragon and parsley in; season with pepper and salt to taste.
- Divide asparagus to 4 plates; put mushrooms over the top of each serving.

Nutrition Information

- Calories: 182
- Fiber: 6 g(25%)
- Total Carbohydrate: 14 g(5%)
- Cholesterol: 23 mg(8%)
- Protein: 4 g(9%)
- Total Fat: 12 g(18%)
- Saturated Fat: 6 g(29%)
- Sodium: 15 mg(1%)

222. Roasted Asparagus With Brazil Nuts

Serving: Makes 8 servings | Prep: | Ready in:

Ingredients

- 2 pounds asparagus, trimmed
- 3 tablespoons extra-virgin olive oil, divided
- 1 cup Brazil nuts (about 5 ounces), toasted, chopped
- 3 tablespoons dry white wine

Direction

- Preheat the oven to 350 °F. Line foil on a big rimmed baking sheet. Toss on prepped baking

sheet 2 tablespoons of olive oil and asparagus. Scatter with pepper and salt. Roast for 15 minutes, till asparagus is barely tender. May be prepped 3 hours in advance. Rest at room temperature.
- In big skillet, heat leftover one tablespoon of oil on moderately-high heat. Put in nuts, wine and asparagus. Toss for 3 minutes, till asparagus is heated completely. Add pepper and more salt to season, if wished. Place on a platter.

Nutrition Information

- Calories: 189
- Total Fat: 17 g(26%)
- Saturated Fat: 4 g(18%)
- Sodium: 3 mg(0%)
- Fiber: 4 g(15%)
- Total Carbohydrate: 7 g(2%)
- Protein: 5 g(10%)

223. Roasted Chicken, Ramps, And Potatoes

Serving: Serves 4 | Prep: 20mins | Ready in:

Ingredients

- 3/4 pound ramps
- 1 (3- to 3,-pound) chicken, cut into 8 pieces
- 1 pound small red potatoes, halved
- 2 1/2 tablespoons olive oil
- 1/2 cup dry white wine
- 1 cup chicken broth

Direction

- Preparation Preheat oven to 500°F.
- Clip ramps roots and remove bulbs outer skin in case detach. Slice leaves off and put aside, keeping white bulbs and slender pink stems intact.
- Place the bulbs and leaves in individual bowls.
- Blot dry the chicken. Place in a shallow, big, flameproof roasting pan, do not crowd, and put potatoes around. Sprinkle with 2 tablespoons of oil and massage entirely to evenly coat. Place the chicken, skin sides facing up and add pepper and salt to season. Roast for 20 minutes in top third of the oven.
- Toss leftover half tablespoon of oil and bulbs, and add salt to season. Spread the bulbs on chicken surrounding and let mixture roast for 10 to 15 minutes till pieces of breast are just cooked completely. Turn the pieces of breast onto platter and retain warmth. Roast the vegetables and the rest of the chicken for an additional of 5 minutes, or till cooked completely. Turn onto platter and use foil to loosely cover to retain warmth. Broil the chicken only for 2 minutes, skin sides facing up if you want a crisper skin.
- Drain pan fat and span the pan across two burners. Pour in wine and cook on high heat to deglaze the pan, scratching brown bits up.
- Let wine boil till cooked down to roughly quarter cup and pour in broth. Put ramp leaves once broth boils and mix for 1 to 2 minutes, till tender and wilted. Use tongs to transfer to chicken. Let pan juices boil till cooked down to approximately half cup and add on surrounding of chicken.

Nutrition Information

- Calories: 712
- Total Carbohydrate: 27 g(9%)
- Cholesterol: 174 mg(58%)
- Protein: 48 g(96%)
- Total Fat: 44 g(68%)
- Saturated Fat: 11 g(57%)
- Sodium: 282 mg(12%)
- Fiber: 4 g(17%)

224. Roasted Double Veal Chops

Serving: Serves 6 | Prep: 20mins | Ready in:

Ingredients

- 1 1/2 ounces sliced pancetta, cut into 1/4-inch-thick strips
- 1 to 2 tablespoons olive oil
- 2 (2-rib) veal chops (4 pounds total)
- 1 garlic clove, minced
- 1/2 cup dry white wine
- 1 cup veal stock or chicken broth
- 2 teaspoons unsalted butter
- 1 tablespoon finely chopped fresh parsley
- 1 teaspoon finely chopped fresh thyme

Direction

- Cook chops and pancetta: Preheat an oven to 400°F.
- In 1 tbsp. oil, cook pancetta in big heavy skillet on medium low heat till fat is rendered and browned, occasionally mixing. Put pancetta on paper towels; drain. Keep fat in skillet.
- Pat dry chops; season with pepper and salt. Put skillet heat on medium high; brown chops on all sides in fat. If needed, add more oil. Put chops, bone sides down, in small flameproof roasting pan; put aside.
- Roast chops in center of oven for 1 hour till inserted instant-read thermometer 2-in. in middle of meat, not touching bone, reads 135°F for medium. Put chops on cutting board; stand for 15 minutes, loosely covered with foil. Internal temperature will raise to 140°F.
- As chops roast, start sauce: Discard all fat from skillet but 1 tbsp.; heat till hot yet not smoking on medium heat. Cook garlic for 30 seconds till fragrant, mixing. Add wine to skillet; deglaze by boiling on high heat, scraping brown bits up. Add stock; boil till it reduces to 3/4 cup.
- As chops stand, finish sauce:
- Use wine mixture to deglaze roasting pan; put into small saucepan. Skim fat off. Reheat; swirl in thyme, parsley and butter. Mix in accumulated juices on cutting board, pepper to taste and pancetta.
- Parallel to bones and chops on their sides, cut to thin slices; serve with sauce.

Nutrition Information

- Calories: 1310
- Cholesterol: 627 mg(209%)
- Protein: 144 g(288%)
- Total Fat: 76 g(116%)
- Saturated Fat: 30 g(151%)
- Sodium: 799 mg(33%)
- Fiber: 0 g(0%)
- Total Carbohydrate: 1 g(0%)

225. Roasted Farm Raised Barramundi With Fennel And Orange

Serving: Makes 4 servings | Prep: | Ready in:

Ingredients

- 2 teaspoons fennel seeds
- 1 1/2 teaspoons coarse kosher salt
- 5 Valencia oranges
- 4 1/2 tablespoons extra-virgin olive oil, divided, plus additional for brushing
- 2 medium fennel bulbs, trimmed, halved through core, sliced, plus a few fronds for garnish
- 2 garlic cloves, pressed
- 1 1 1/2-pound U.S. barramundi fillet with skin or four 6-ounce skinless fillets
- 1 shallot, minced
- 1/2 cup dry white wine

Direction

- In small, heavy skillet, let fennel seeds toast on moderately-high heat till aromatic and starting to brown. Grind fennel seeds coarsely along

with 1 1/2 teaspoons of coarse salt with spice grinder. Fennel salt may be done 2 days in advance. Keep at room temperature with cover.
- Finely grate sufficient orange peel from an orange to get 1 1/2 teaspoons; put aside. Slice peel off 3 oranges including the white pith with small sharp knife. Slice among membranes, do it on top of bowl, to loosen orange segments right into bowl. Squeeze sufficient juice from leftover 2 oranges to get half cup. Orange segments, juice and peel may be done 4 hours in advance. Separately cover; rest at room temperature.
- Place a rack in upper third and a rack in lower third of the oven; preheat the oven to 400°F. Brush oil on a big rimmed baking sheet. Toss big bowl with half teaspoon of orange peel, a teaspoon of fennel salt, 1 1/2 tablespoons of oil and sliced fennel. Turn onto prepped sheet, evenly scattering. Let fennel roast on lower rack for 8 minutes, till staring to soften.
- Meantime, brush oil on big shallow roasting pan. Combine in small bowl with a teaspoon of orange peel, garlic and 2 tablespoons of oil. Put fish fillet in pan, skin side facing down, in case using fillet with skin and brush orange-peel mixture on top. In case using four skinless fillets, brush orange-peel mixture on each side with and place in pan, space apart. Scatter a teaspoon of fennel salt on fish.
- Mix fennel; surround with sections of orange. Turn the fennel on upper oven rack and put the fish on lower rack. Roast till fish is barely opaque in the middle and fennel is soft, for an additional of 13 minutes.
- Turn the fish onto platter; use foil to tent. Put the same pan on top of 2 burners; heat on moderately-high heat. Put in shallot; mix for 2 minutes, till tender. Pour in orange juice and wine; boil for 4 minutes, scratching up browned bits on pan base, till cooked down to half cup. Mix in leftover 1 tablespoon of oil. Add half teaspoon of fennel salt to season sauce, putting in additional to taste if wished. Surround the fish on platter with oranges and fennel. Add sauce on top, scatter reserved fronds over to serve.

Nutrition Information

- Calories: 410
- Total Carbohydrate: 22 g(7%)
- Cholesterol: 63 mg(21%)
- Protein: 37 g(74%)
- Total Fat: 18 g(28%)
- Saturated Fat: 3 g(13%)
- Sodium: 819 mg(34%)
- Fiber: 5 g(19%)

226. Roasted Lamb Shoulder (Agnello De Latte Arrosto)

Serving: Makes 6 servings | Prep: | Ready in:

Ingredients

- 6-pound lamb shoulder, cut by butcher into 4 very thick chops, about 1 1/2 pounds each
- 2 celery ribs, cut in 1-inch chunks (about 2 cups)
- 2 medium carrots, cut in 1-inch chunks (about 2 cups)
- 2 medium onions, cut in large chunks (about 3 cups)
- 3-inch piece cinnamon stick
- 6 garlic cloves, crushed and peeled
- 4 small branches fresh rosemary
- 8 fresh sage leaves
- 1/2 teaspoon coarsely ground black pepper
- 1 teaspoon coarse sea salt or kosher salt, or more to taste
- 2 cups dry white wine
- 1/3 cup red wine vinegar
- cup extra-virgin olive oil
- 3 cups light stock (chicken, turkey, or vegetable broth), or more if needed
- A large, heavy-duty roasting pan, 17 by 20 inches preferred

- Aluminum foil

Direction

- Trim most of fat from chops; leave very thin layer on outside surfaces. Pull each chop apart with your fingers, roughly in half, with natural break lines between muscles.
- Put meat and all leftover ingredients but stock in a big bowl; toss well to distribute all seasonings. Submerge meat in marinade. Use plastic wrap to seal the bowl; refrigerate for 24 hours, occasionally turning meat.
- Heat an oven to 425°F. Put meat chunks in roasting pan; spread marinade all around meat chunks. Add stock; cover pan with tent of aluminum foil. Firmly press it against sides. In foil, pierce few slits as steam vents.
- Roast, basting then turning meat around every 30 minutes, for 2-2 1/2 hours. Remove foil after 1st hour; roast, uncovered. Flip and baste more frequently as meat begins to caramelize and pan liquid evaporates. Lower oven temperature if meat dries too quickly. Remove pan from oven when pan juices reduce by half and meat is nicely browned all over and very tender; put meat chunks on warm platter.
- Sauce: Mash all veggies with a big spoon/potato masher in the roasting pan; to deglaze all caramelized bits, mix pan juices around bottom and sides of pan. Put all of it into sturdy wire-mesh sieve above a big measuring cup/bowl. Press on veggies to release juices and force veggies through sieve, scraping puree into bowl to flavor and thicken the sauce. From surface, skim fat; to taste, adjust seasoning.
- Put 1/2 sauce, meat juices on platter and lamb pieces in a big skillet when it is serving time; slowly heat to simmer, turning meat over and over till it heats through. Put meat onto platter; drizzle thickened sauce from skillet over. Immediately serve with leftover sauce separately.

Nutrition Information

227. Roasted Pork Loin With Poached Plums

Serving: Makes 6 servings | Prep: | Ready in:

Ingredients

- 6 sweet firm red or black plums (such as Burgundies, Satsumas, or El Dorados; about 2 pounds), quartered, pitted
- 2 cups Pinot Gris or Viognier
- 1 cup dry red wine
- 2 whole star anise*
- cinnamon stick
- 1/4 cup plus 1 1/4 teaspoons sugar, divided
- 2 cups low-salt chicken broth
- 5 fresh thyme sprigs plus 1 teaspoon finely chopped thyme, divided
- 2 tablespoons chopped shallot
- 2 1 1/4-pound pork tenderloins
- 3 tablespoons olive oil, divided
- 2 teaspoons chopped fresh thyme
- 2 garlic cloves, minced
- Chopped fresh chives

Direction

- Boil 1/4 cup sugar and initial 5 ingredients in big heavy saucepan, mixing till sugar melts. Lower heat; simmer for 20 minutes till plums are tender. Put plums on platter; strain the wine mixture.
- Put strained liquid in same saucepan. Add shallot, thyme sprigs and broth; boil for 25 minutes till reduced to 1 cup. Strain sauce; mix chopped thyme and 1 1/4 teaspoons sugar in; season with pepper and salt.
- You can make it 1 day ahead; separately cover sauce and plums, refrigerate. Bring the plums to room temperature and rewarm sauce on medium heat.
- Pork: Preheat an oven to 400°F. Brush 1 tablespoon oil on pork; sprinkle pepper, salt, garlic and thyme. Heat leftover 2 tablespoons

oil in big ovenproof skillet on medium high heat then add pork; cook for 5 minutes till brown on all sides, flipping often. Put skillet in oven; roast pork for 20 minutes till inserted thermometer in middle reads 140°F. Take skillet from oven; stand pork for 10 minutes. Crosswise cut pork to 1/2-in. thick slices; serve with sauce and poached plums. Sprinkle chopped chives.

Nutrition Information

- Calories: 452
- Saturated Fat: 3 g(16%)
- Sodium: 120 mg(5%)
- Fiber: 2 g(9%)
- Total Carbohydrate: 23 g(8%)
- Cholesterol: 117 mg(39%)
- Protein: 40 g(79%)
- Total Fat: 14 g(21%)

228. Roasted Red Snapper With Olives

Serving: Serves 12 | Prep: | Ready in:

Ingredients

- 1/3 cup dry white wine
- 3 garlic cloves, sliced thin
- 1/4 cup fresh lemon juice
- 1/3 cup extra-virgin olive oil
- 1 1/2 tablespoons chopped fresh thyme leaves
- 1 1/2 cups mixed green and black brine-cured olives (preferably unpitted)
- six 6- to 7-ounce red snapper fillets with skin
- 6 tablespoons extra-virgin olive oil

Direction

- Prepare the oven by preheating to 425 degrees F.
- For the sauce: Place garlic and wine in a small skillet and boil until reduced to about 2 tablespoons. Add pepper and salt to taste and the rest of sauce ingredients then bring to a simmer. You can prepare the sauce 1 day in advance then cover and chill. Heat the sauce again to warm before continuing.
- Pat snapper fillets dry then dust with pepper and salt. Split up oil between 2 shallow baking pans big enough to hold fillets in a single layer without touching then evenly spread with oil. Heat the baking pans for 7 minutes in the lower and upper thirds of the oven. Place fillets, working rapidly, with skin sides down, in the hot baking pans and roast for 7-10 minutes on the lower and upper thirds of the oven, or until fish is just cooked through.
- Use a metal spatula to remove fillets into a large platter, flipping them with skin sides up, and pour sauce over top.

Nutrition Information

- Calories: 228
- Protein: 19 g(38%)
- Total Fat: 16 g(24%)
- Saturated Fat: 2 g(11%)
- Sodium: 170 mg(7%)
- Fiber: 1 g(3%)
- Total Carbohydrate: 2 g(1%)
- Cholesterol: 34 mg(11%)

229. Roasted Shellfish With Coriander, Fennel, And Meyer Lemon

Serving: Makes 4 servings | Prep: | Ready in:

Ingredients

- 1 tablespoon coriander seeds
- 1 tablespoon fennel seeds
- 2 tablespoons olive oil
- 2 pounds stone crab claws or Canadian snow crab legs, shells cracked with mallet or cut with scissors

- 8 farmed Manila clams or quahogs (about 1 1/2 pounds), scrubbed
- 16 farmed mussels, scrubbed, debearded
- 1/2 cup chopped shallots
- 1/2 cup dry white wine
- 1/3 cup fresh Meyer lemon juice or 1/4 cup fresh lemon juice and 1/4 cup fresh orange juice
- 2 tablespoons (1/4 stick) butter
- Chopped fresh chives

Direction

- Set oven to 500 degrees F. Using a spice grinder or coffee mill, process fennel seeds and coriander seeds until ground coarsely. Place a big heavy roasting pan onto 2 burners and heat on medium heat. Add the fennel seeds and ground coriander then stir for 1 minute. Add the mussels, Manila clams, cracked crab, and olive oil, stirring to coat, then place the pan in the oven. Roast, occasionally stirring, for 10 minutes until the crab is heated through and the mussels and clams open, transferring the shells onto a platter as they open.
- Use tongs to transfer the mussels, clams, and crab onto a platter, discarding unopened mussels and clams, then tent with foil to keep them warm. Heat the same pan on 2 burners on high heat. Add wine and shallots, boiling for 1 minute. Add in lemon juice and boil for 2 minutes until the sauce slightly thickens, then whisk in butter. Season with pepper and salt to taste, then pour the sauce over the shellfish. Sprinkle with chives to serve.

Nutrition Information

230. Roasted Spiced Pork Loin With Root Vegetables

Serving: Serves 8 | Prep: | Ready in:

Ingredients

- 6 bacon slices, cut in half
- 6 cups canned low-salt chicken broth
- 1 1/2 cups dry white wine
- 1/2 cup red currant jelly
- 1 1/4 teaspoons minced fresh rosemary
- 3 tablespoons unsalted butter
- A mortar and pestle or even a coffee grinder can be used to grind the spices.
- 2 teaspoons cumin seeds
- 2 teaspoons coarse salt
- 1 teaspoon black peppercorns
- 1 teaspoon black cardamom seeds (from about 30 whole green or white cardamom pods)
- 1 4- to 4 1/4-pound center-cut boneless pork loin (about
- 1 tablespoon olive oil
- 2 1/2 pounds large russet potatoes (about 5), peeled, halved lengthwise, cut into 2-inch pieces
- 1 1/2 pounds large parsnips (about 4), peeled, cut into 2-inch pieces, thick portions halved lengthwise
- 1 1/2 pounds large carrots (about 4), peeled, cut into 2-inch pieces, thick portions halved lengthwise
- 8 large shallots, peeled, halved
- 8 large garlic cloves, peeled
- 3 large fresh rosemary sprigs
- 6 tablespoons olive oil
- 8 medium beets, peeled, cut into 1-inch wedges

Direction

- Sauce: Cook bacon till crisp in big heavy saucepan on medium heat. Put bacon on paper towels using tongs; from pan, discard drippings. Put rosemary, jelly, wine and broth in pan; boil for 35 minutes till reduced to 2 1/2 cups. Put bacon in sauce; boil for 10 minutes till liquid reduces to 1 1/3 cups. Into small saucepan, strain sauce; add butter. Wisk on low heat for 2 minutes till sauce is smooth. Season with pepper and salt. You can make it 1 day ahead. Cover; refrigerate.

- Prep pork: Grind initial 4 ingredients finely. In 13x9x2-in. glass baking dish, put pork. Rub oil all over pork then spice mixture; cover. Refrigerate for 4 hours – 1 day.
- Roasting: Put racks in bottom and middle third of oven; preheat to 400°F. In big roasting pan, put garlic, rosemary, shallots, carrots, parsnips and potatoes. Drizzle 5 tbsp. oil; sprinkle pepper and salt. Roast on middle rack for 45 minutes, occasionally turning veggies.
- In small roasting pan, put beets. Drizzle 1 tbsp. oil; sprinkle pepper and salt. Take big roasting pan from oven. Push veggies to pan's sides, clearing space in middle for pork. Put pork in middle of pan. Put big roasting pan in middle rack; on bottom rack, put pan with beets.
- Roast pork with veggies for 1 hour till inserted thermometer in middle of pork reads 150°F and veggies are cooked through and brown, occasionally turning veggies; roast beets for 1 hour till tender, turning occasionally. Remove all veggies and pork from oven; stand for 10 minutes.
- Put pork roast in middle of big platter and surround with all veggies. Rewarm sauce on low heat, constantly whisking.

Nutrition Information

- Calories: 1110
- Sodium: 951 mg(40%)
- Fiber: 14 g(57%)
- Total Carbohydrate: 90 g(30%)
- Cholesterol: 201 mg(67%)
- Protein: 74 g(147%)
- Total Fat: 50 g(76%)
- Saturated Fat: 12 g(61%)

231. Roman Bortsch

Serving: Makes 6 servings | Prep: | Ready in:

Ingredients

- 500 milliliters (2 cups plus 4 teaspoons) white wine
- 500 milliliters (2 cups plus 4 teaspoons) water
- 100 g (3.6 ounces or about 1/4 cup) honey
- 1 leg and thigh of a large chicken
- 2 tablespoons olive oil
- 4 medium-sized raw beetroot
- salt and freshly ground pepper to taste

Direction

- In a medium saucepan, mix water, honey and wine. Put in chicken and slowly heat. Use whole chicken if making a bigger quantity. Peel the beetroot and grate while simmering the stock. Put to soup and pour over additional water or wine as it cooks down. Let cook for roughly 1 1/2 hours. Remove chicken, skin and pull meat off bone and put some or most of it back to serving bowl. Scoop fat from top of soup, add pepper and salt to season, put on top of meat to serve.

Nutrition Information

232. Roman Style Fish Soup (Zuppa Di Pesce Alla Romana)

Serving: Serves 4 | Prep: | Ready in:

Ingredients

- 2 cloves garlic, chopped
- pinch of red pepper flakes
- 1/3 cup olive oil
- 2 lb squid, cleaned and cut into 1/2-inch rings (about 1 lb when cleaned)
- 1 cup dry white wine
- 2 tomatoes, peeled, seeded, and chopped
- 2 tablespoons chopped fresh flat-leaf Italian parsley
- pinch of salt
- 2 cups water

- 1 lb small hard-shell clams or cockles, soaked in cool water for 30 minutes and well scrubbed
- 1 1/2 lb assorted firm-fleshed fish filets such as whiting, monkfish, turbot, porgy bream, red snapper, and sea bass, cut into chunks
- 4 slices coarse country bread, toasted and rubbed on one side with a garlic clove

Direction

- Sauté pepper flakes and garlic in olive oil in a big saucepan on moderate heat for 2 minutes, till garlic turn golden. Take garlic with slotted spoon and throw. Put in and cook squid for 2 minutes, mixing till opaque. Pour in wine and simmer for an additional of 1 minute. Put in parsley, salt and tomatoes, and cook for 10 minutes more, till juices vaporize.
- Pour in water and simmer. Put in clams, throw any that remain open when touched, and the fish, place cover, and cook for 5 minutes, till fish is opaque throughout and all clams open. Throw any clams that remain closed. Fix the seasonings.
- Put a slice of bread in every heated soup plate. Scoop soup on top of bread to serve.

Nutrition Information

- Calories: 684
- Fiber: 1 g(4%)
- Total Carbohydrate: 16 g(5%)
- Cholesterol: 625 mg(208%)
- Protein: 88 g(176%)
- Total Fat: 25 g(38%)
- Saturated Fat: 4 g(20%)
- Sodium: 975 mg(41%)

233. Romano Risotto With Radishes

Serving: Serves 8 (first course) or 6 (main course) | Prep: 35mins | Ready in:

Ingredients

- 6 cups reduced-sodium chicken broth (48 fl ounces)
- 2 cups hot water
- 3/4 stick unsalted butter, divided
- 1 medium onion, finely chopped (1 cup)
- 3 garlic cloves, finely chopped
- 1 pound Arborio rice (2 1/2 cups)
- 2/3 cup dry white wine
- 1/2 cup grated Pecorino Romano
- 1 tablespoon white-wine vinegar
- 1 tablespoon extra-virgin olive oil
- 1 pound trimmed radishes, julienned
- 1 tablespoon finely chopped chives
- Accompaniment: extra-virgin olive oil for drizzling

Direction

- Risotto: Simmer water and broth in a 3-4-qt. saucepan. Meanwhile, heat 3 tbsp. butter in a 4-5-qt. heavy pot on medium heat till foam subsides; cook onion for about 5 minutes till just soft, occasionally mixing. Add garlic; cook for 6-8 minutes till soft, occasionally mixing. Mix in rice; cook for 1 minute while mixing. Add wine; cook for about 1 minute till absorbed while mixing.
- Mix 1 cup of simmering broth into rice; cook till absorbed, keeping at a strong simmer, constantly mixing. Keep adding broth and cooking, 1 cup at a time, for 18-22 minutes till rice is creamy-looking but still al dente and just tender, frequently mixing and letting every addition get absorbed before adding in next. If needed, thin with some leftover broth; you might have some remaining. Take off the heat; mix in the leftover 3 tbsp. butter, 1/2 tsp. pepper, 1 tsp. salt and cheese.
- Radishes: Whisk 1/8 tsp. pepper, 1/4 tsp. salt, oil and vinegar; toss radishes with chives and dressing. Serve risotto with radishes on top.

Nutrition Information

- Calories: 388

- Saturated Fat: 7 g(36%)
- Sodium: 562 mg(23%)
- Fiber: 3 g(12%)
- Total Carbohydrate: 55 g(18%)
- Cholesterol: 31 mg(10%)
- Protein: 10 g(20%)
- Total Fat: 13 g(20%)

234. Rotini With Roasted Peppers, Spinach And Pine Nuts

Serving: Makes 4 (appetizer) or 2 (main-course) servings | Prep: | Ready in:

Ingredients

- 2 red bell peppers
- 1 tablespoon all purpose flour
- 1 tablespoon butter, room temperature
- 1 tablespoon olive oil
- 1 1/2 cups chopped onions
- 2 teaspoons minced garlic
- 1 1/4 cups canned low-salt chicken broth
- 3/4 cup dry white wine
- 1/2 teaspoon dried thyme
- 1/4 teaspoon dried crushed red pepper
- 1 10-ounce bag spinach leaves, stems removed, leaves chopped
- 1/2 pound rotini pasta
- 3/4 cup freshly grated Parmesan cheese (about 2 1/2 ounces)
- 1/2 cup pine nuts, toasted

Direction

- Char bell peppers above gas flame/in broiler till all sides blacken. Wrap in a paper bag; stand for 10 minutes. Peel then seed peppers; slice to 1/2-in. strips.
- Mix butter and flour to make a paste in a small bowl. Heat oil in a big skillet on medium heat then add onions; sauté for 5 minutes till tender. Add garlic; sauté for 1 minute. Add dried red pepper, thyme, wine and broth; simmer for 6 minutes till liquid reduces by half. Whisk flour paste in; simmer for 1 minute till sauce slightly thickens. Season with pepper and salt. Add spinach and roasted peppers; simmer for 2 minutes till spinach wilts.
- Meanwhile, cook pasta till just tender yet firm to chew in a big pot with boiling salted water, occasionally mixing; drain pasta well.
- Add pine nuts, parmesan cheese and pasta to sauce; toss to coat.

Nutrition Information

- Calories: 552
- Fiber: 6 g(26%)
- Total Carbohydrate: 61 g(20%)
- Cholesterol: 20 mg(7%)
- Protein: 21 g(42%)
- Total Fat: 24 g(37%)
- Saturated Fat: 6 g(32%)
- Sodium: 333 mg(14%)

235. Rustic Pear Tart With Late Harvest Riesling

Serving: Makes 6 to 8 servings | Prep: | Ready in:

Ingredients

- 1 1/2 cups all purpose flour
- 3 tablespoons sugar
- 1/2 teaspoon salt
- 10 tablespoons (1 1/4 sticks) chilled unsalted butter, cut into pieces
- 1 large egg yolk
- 1 tablespoon late-harvest Riesling or other sweet white dessert wine
- 3 large ripe Anjou pears, peeled, cored, thinly sliced
- 1 tablespoon plus 1/2 cup sugar
- 1 tablespoon all purpose flour
- 1 cup plus 2 tablespoons late-harvest Riesling or other sweet white dessert wine

- 1/2 cup water
- Vanilla ice cream

Direction

- Preparing the crust: Use a food processor to mix the sugar, salt and flour together until blended. Put in the butter and pulse the food processor to cut the butter into the mixture until the texture is like that of a coarse meal. Put in the wine and egg yolk and pulse the mixture until you see moist lumps in the mixture. Form the dough mixture in the shape of a ball and roll it out into a flat disk. Use a plastic wrap to cover the dough then keep it in the fridge for not less than 40 minutes and up to 2 days.
- Preparing the filling mixture: Put the oven rack in the middle layer of the oven and preheat the oven to 375°F. Put the chilled dough in between 2 sheets of parchment paper and flatten it out into a 12-inch round. Take the sheet of parchment paper on top of the dough and place the dough along with the bottom parchment paper onto a rimmed baking sheet. In a big bowl, mix 1 tablespoon of sugar, flour and pear slices together until combined. Scoop the prepared pear filling mixture in the center of the round-shaped dough, keep 1 1/2 inches off the edges of the dough uncoated with filling. Use the bottom parchment paper to help you fold the uncoated edges of the dough over the edges of the filling mixture. Let it bake for about 20 minutes until the pears have softened.
- While waiting for the pear tart to bake, let 1/2 cup of water, remaining 1/2 cup of sugar and 1 cup of wine boil in a medium-sized saucepan for about 10 minutes until the syrup mixture has reduced in volume to 1/2 cup.
- Lower the temperature of the oven to 325°F. Sprinkle 1/2 of the prepared syrup mixture on top of the filling. Keep baking the tart for about 20 minutes until the juices are thick and bubbly. Let the baked tart cool down.
- Add 2 tablespoons of wine into the remaining half of the syrup mixture and mix. Slice the baked tart into wedges. Top it off with the syrup mixture and serve it together with ice cream.

Nutrition Information

- Calories: 513
- Cholesterol: 82 mg(27%)
- Protein: 5 g(9%)
- Total Fat: 20 g(31%)
- Saturated Fat: 12 g(62%)
- Sodium: 203 mg(8%)
- Fiber: 5 g(19%)
- Total Carbohydrate: 72 g(24%)

236. Sage Roasted Chicken With Madeira Sauce

Serving: Makes 4 servings | Prep: | Ready in:

Ingredients

- 2 1/2 pounds chicken wings
- 1 large onion, chopped
- 2 carrots, chopped
- 5 cups chicken stock or canned low-salt chicken broth
- 1 cup dry white wine
- 16 large fresh sage leaves
- 4 chicken breast halves with skin and ribs
- 4 chicken thighs
- 1 tablespoon vegetable oil
- 5 tablespoons chilled butter
- 2 large shallots, chopped
- 1/4 cup Madeira
- 2 teaspoons chopped fresh thyme
- 2 teaspoons chopped fresh sage
- 2 large carrots, peeled, sliced diagonally (about 1 1/2 cups)
- 1 cup frozen peas

Direction

- Brown chicken stock: Over medium-high heat, heat heavy big pot. In pot, put chicken wings in batches and sauté for 10 minutes each batch, or till deep brown. Take chicken wings out of pot with a slotted spoon; turn out onto a big bowl. In the pot of drippings, put carrots and onion; sauté for 10 minutes, or till brown. Put chicken wings back to pot. Put in the wine and stock and let simmer for 1 1/2 hours with a cover. Drain the stock, dispose of solids. Stock may be done up to 2 days in advance. Cool lightly. Chill without a cover till cool, then put cover on and refrigerate.
- Chicken: Preheat an oven to 400 °F. Beneath the skin of every chicken thigh and breast, put 2 sage leaves. In a heavy big skillet, heat the oil on high heat. Put in the chicken thighs and breasts and sauté for 10 minutes, or till brown on every side. On big rimmed baking sheet, put the thighs of chicken. Let roast for 10 minutes. On baking sheet, put the breasts and keep roasting the chicken for 20 minutes, or till cooked completely.
- In the meantime, make the sauce: Get rid of grease from skillet. In the same skillet, liquefy a tablespoon of butter over medium-high heat. Put in shallots and sauté for 2 minutes. Put in Madeira and boil, scratching up browned bits. In a skillet, put sage, thyme and stock and boil. Put in carrots and cook on high heat for 8 minutes, or till crisp-tender. Put in the peas; let simmer for 10 minutes, or till sauce is lightly decreased. In the sauce, mix leftover 4 tablespoons of butter, a tablespoon at a time. Season sauce with pepper and salt to taste. Serve the chicken along with the sauce.

Nutrition Information

- Calories: 1450
- Cholesterol: 564 mg(188%)
- Protein: 105 g(210%)
- Total Fat: 93 g(143%)
- Saturated Fat: 31 g(157%)
- Sodium: 946 mg(39%)
- Fiber: 8 g(33%)

- Total Carbohydrate: 39 g(13%)

237. Salmon Burgers With Lemon And Capers

Serving: Makes 10 burgers | Prep: | Ready in:

Ingredients

- 5 tablespoons (or more) olive oil
- 1 cup chopped shallots (about 3 large)
- 1 cup dry white wine
- 1/2 cup fresh lemon juice
- 1 4-ounce jar capers, drained, chopped
- 2 pounds chilled skinless salmon fillets, cut into 1-inch pieces, any bones removed
- 3 cups fresh breadcrumbs made from French bread
- 2 large eggs, beaten to blend
- 3 tablespoons chopped fresh dill
- 1 1/2 teaspoons salt
- 3/4 teaspoon ground black pepper
- 10 hamburger buns, split, toasted
- Mayonnaise
- Lettuce leaves
- Tomato slices

Direction

- In medium, heavy skillet, heat 4 tablespoons of olive oil on moderate heat. Put in shallots and sauté for 4 minutes, till clear. Raise the heat to moderately-high. Put in lemon juice, drained capers and white wine, and cook for 12 minutes, till nearly all liquid vaporizes. Turn the mixture of shallot onto big bowl. Chill for an hour, till shallot mixture is thoroughly chilled.
- Use a processor to grind salmon fillets coarsely with on/off turns. Put to shallot mixture with ground salmon. Stir in 3/4 teaspoon of pepper, 1 1/2 teaspoons of salt, dill, beaten eggs and fresh breadcrumbs. Shape mixture of salmon to make 10 patties, distributing evenly. Salmon patties may be prepped 6 hours in

advance. Turn onto baking sheet, then use plastic wrap to cover and chill.
- In big, heavy skillet, heat a tablespoon of olive oil on moderately-high heat. Put the patties of salmon to skillet in batches and cook till patties turn golden brown and cooked completely, for 2 minutes on each side, putting in additional oil to skillet as necessary. Put salmon burgers on hamburger buns that is toasted along with lettuce leaves, tomato slices and mayonnaise, and serve.

Nutrition Information

- Calories: 538
- Total Carbohydrate: 49 g(16%)
- Cholesterol: 87 mg(29%)
- Protein: 29 g(58%)
- Total Fat: 23 g(36%)
- Saturated Fat: 5 g(24%)
- Sodium: 785 mg(33%)
- Fiber: 3 g(13%)

238. Salmon Chowder

Serving: 8 | Prep: 15mins | Ready in:

Ingredients

- 3 tablespoons butter
- 3/4 cup chopped onion
- 1/2 cup chopped celery
- 1 teaspoon garlic powder
- 2 cups diced potatoes
- 2 carrots, diced
- 2 cups chicken broth
- 1 teaspoon salt
- 1 teaspoon ground black pepper
- 1 teaspoon dried dill weed
- 2 (16 ounce) cans salmon
- 1 (12 fluid ounce) can evaporated milk
- 1 (15 ounce) can creamed corn
- 1/2 pound Cheddar cheese, shredded

Direction

- Set a large saucepan over medium heat and melt butter. Add in garlic powder, onions, and celery; cook until onions become tender and translucent. Mix in dill, salt and pepper, potatoes, broth, and carrots. Let mixture come to boil and lower the heat. Let the covered mixture simmer for 20 minutes.
- Add cheese, corn, salmon, and evaporated milk. Stir until the soup is well heated through.

Nutrition Information

- Calories: 490 calories;
- Total Fat: 25.9
- Sodium: 1140
- Total Carbohydrate: 26.5
- Cholesterol: 104
- Protein: 38.6

239. Salmon Fillets With Lemon Thyme Sauce

Serving: Serves 4 | Prep: | Ready in:

Ingredients

- 4 6-ounce salmon fillets
- 1/2 cup dry white wine
- 1/2 cup whipping cream
- 1/2 cup chopped shallots (about 6)
- 1 tablespoon white wine vinegar
- 1/2 teaspoon dried thyme
- 6 tablespoons (3/4 stick) chilled unsalted butter, cut into 6 pieces
- 1 1/2 teaspoons fresh lemon juice

Direction

- Set an oven to 375°F and start preheating. On a baking sheet, place the salmon and flavor with pepper and salt. Bake for 20 minutes just until cooked thoroughly.

- In the meantime, in a heavy medium saucepan, boil the next 5 ingredients on high heat, stirring from time to time, for 12 minutes until the mixture reduces to generous half a cup. Drain the sauce to the heavy small saucepan and press on the solids hard to remove as much liquid as you can. Heat the saucepan to very low heat, then beat in a piece of butter at a time. Beat in lemon juice; then season with pepper and salt to taste.
- Place the salmon into the plates. Scoop the sauce on and serve.

Nutrition Information

- Calories: 625
- Sodium: 116 mg(5%)
- Fiber: 1 g(3%)
- Total Carbohydrate: 5 g(2%)
- Cholesterol: 173 mg(58%)
- Protein: 36 g(72%)
- Total Fat: 49 g(76%)
- Saturated Fat: 22 g(110%)

240. Salmon Rillettes

Serving: Makes around 1 1/2 cups or around 8 servings | Prep: 15mins | Ready in:

Ingredients

- 1 celery stalk, sliced thin
- 1 onion, sliced thin
- 1 leek, sliced thin
- 1 teaspoon whole peppercorns
- 1 bay leaf
- 1 cup white wine
- 1 lemon, halved
- 6 ounces king salmon filet
- 2 ounces crème fraîche (budget partiers can substitute sour cream or a cream and sour cream combo)
- 2 tablespoons minced chives
- 3 tablespoons lemon extra virgin olive oil
- salt and freshly ground black pepper

Direction

- Simmer big pot of water. Add lemon, wine, bay leaf, peppercorns, leek, onion and celery; simmer for 25 minutes.
- Add salmon; cover pot. Take off heat; stand for 10 minutes.
- Take out salmon; chill in the fridge. Discard veggie water.
- Whip salmon with olive oil, chives and crème fraiche by hand/in food processor. To taste, add pepper and salt; keep spread chilled till serving.

Nutrition Information

- Calories: 129
- Protein: 5 g(10%)
- Total Fat: 9 g(14%)
- Saturated Fat: 2 g(11%)
- Sodium: 177 mg(7%)
- Fiber: 1 g(3%)
- Total Carbohydrate: 3 g(1%)
- Cholesterol: 15 mg(5%)

241. Salmon Trout Poached In White Wine

Serving: Serves 6 as a first course | Prep: | Ready in:

Ingredients

- 3 cups dry white wine
- 1 1/2 cups water
- 1 onion, cut into 1/2-inch-thick rounds
- 2 teaspoons black peppercorns
- 2 teaspoons salt
- 8 5- to 6-ounce salmon trout steaks or salmon steaks (3/4 to 1 inch thick)
- 1 12-ounce jar sweet gherkin pickles, coarsely chopped
- 1/2 cup chopped fresh parsley

Direction

- Divide first 5 ingredients to 2 heavy big skillets. Put 4 fish steaks in each skillet. Simmer liquid on medium low heat. Simmer gently for 6 minutes until the middle of the fish is opaque. Take off heat. Flip fish in skillet with a metal spatula. Cool fish for 1 hour in the poaching liquid. Put liquid and fish in a big glass baking dish. Chill, covered, for 1-2 days.
- Mix parsley and pickles in a bowl. Serve the fish with the pickle mixture.

Nutrition Information

- Calories: 553
- Sodium: 986 mg(41%)
- Fiber: 1 g(6%)
- Total Carbohydrate: 6 g(2%)
- Cholesterol: 129 mg(43%)
- Protein: 42 g(85%)
- Total Fat: 33 g(51%)
- Saturated Fat: 14 g(70%)

242. Salmon In Saffron Mussel Sauce

Serving: Makes 4 servings | Prep: | Ready in:

Ingredients

- 1 pound mussels, scrubbed, debearded
- 1/2 cup dry white wine
- 1/2 teaspoon saffron threads, crushed
- 3/4 cup (about) whipping cream
- 1/2 cup canned crushed tomatoes with added puree
- 1 garlic clove, minced
- 1 bay leaf
- 1/8 teaspoon cayenne pepper
- 1 tablespoon olive oil
- 4 8-ounce skinless salmon fillets
- 1/2 teaspoon fresh lemon juice

Direction

- Mix wine and mussels in big saucepan on medium high heat. Cover; cook for 4 minutes till mussels start to open, occasionally mixing. Put mussels in big bowl with slotted spoon; discard unopened mussels. Put liquid from saucepan in 2-cup measuring cup. Mix saffron in. Stand cooking liquid for 15 minutes.
- Add enough cream to cooking liquid to get 1 1/3 cups. Put in big saucepan. Mix in cayenne, bay leaf, garlic and tomatoes. Simmer on medium heat for 5 minutes till sauce slightly thickens. Season with pepper and salt. You can make this 4 hours ahead. Chill and cover sauce and mussels separately.
- Heat oil in big nonstick skillet on high heat. Add salmon, rounded side down. Cook for 3 minutes till bottom is golden. Flip. Lower heat to low, then cover; cook for 4 minutes till salmon is opaque in the middle. Put off heat. To keep warm, keep covered.
- Simmer sauce in big saucepan on low heat. Add mussels in shells; mix for 2 minutes till heated through. Mix in lemon juice.
- On each of 4 plates, put 1 salmon fillet. Divide mussels onto plates. Put sauce over mussels and salmon.

Nutrition Information

- Calories: 757
- Fiber: 1 g(3%)
- Total Carbohydrate: 9 g(3%)
- Cholesterol: 206 mg(69%)
- Protein: 61 g(123%)
- Total Fat: 50 g(77%)
- Saturated Fat: 17 g(83%)
- Sodium: 531 mg(22%)

243. Salmon With Sesame And Orange Ginger Relish

Serving: Makes 8 servings | Prep: | Ready in:

Ingredients

- 1/3 cup dry white wine
- 1/3 cup fresh orange juice
- 2 1/2 tablespoons soy sauce
- 1 2 1/2-pound salmon fillet
- 3 large navel oranges
- 1/2 cup matchstick-size strips red pepper
- 1/2 cup thinly sliced red onion
- 2 1/2 tablespoons chopped fresh cilantro
- 2 teaspoons minced peeled fresh ginger
- 2 teaspoons grated orange peel
- 1 teaspoon oriental sesame oil
- 1/2 teaspoon coarse kosher salt
- 1/4 teaspoon dried crushed red pepper
- Vegetable oil
- 1 tablespoon sesame seeds, toasted

Direction

- Mix in small bowl with the initial 3 ingredients to incorporate; turn onto a glass, 13x9x2-inch baking dish. Put the salmon in mixture of orange juice, skin side facing up; use plastic to cover and refrigerate for nor less than 2 hours to no more than 4 hours. Let come to room temperature for half an hour prior to cooking.
- Slice peel off oranges including white pith with small sharp knife. Slice between the membranes, doing it on top of bowl, to loosen segments right into bowl.
- In medium size bowl, combine the red pepper and the following 7 ingredients to incorporate. Fold in reserved the segments of orange including any gathered juices. May be prepped an hour in advance. Rest at room temperature.
- Preheat the oven to 450°F. Line foil on a rimmed baking sheet; liberally brush using vegetable oil. Put the fish on prepped baking sheet, skin side facing down. Scatter pepper and salt over. Bake for 20 minutes, till fish is barely opaque in middle. Slowly detach salmon from foil with big spatula. Cautiously lift salmon off sheet with the foil as help, and let salmon slip from foil to platter. Pile orange relish down the middle of the fish, scatter sesame seeds over to serve.

Nutrition Information

- Calories: 388
- Saturated Fat: 5 g(24%)
- Sodium: 478 mg(20%)
- Fiber: 2 g(8%)
- Total Carbohydrate: 11 g(4%)
- Cholesterol: 78 mg(26%)
- Protein: 30 g(61%)
- Total Fat: 24 g(37%)

244. Sauerkraut With Apples

Serving: Makes 8 servings | Prep: 15mins | Ready in:

Ingredients

- 1 large onion, thinly sliced
- 2 tablespoons unsalted butter
- 4 pounds sauerkraut, rinsed and drained
- 2 Gala, Fuji, or Red Delicious apples, thinly sliced
- 1 cup dry white wine
- 1 to 2 tablespoons packed dark brown sugar

Direction

- Cook onion in butter for 6 minutes till golden in a 4-5-qt. heavy pot on medium high heat, occasionally mixing. Mix in wine, apples and sauerkraut; simmer.
- Cover pot; lower heat. Simmer for 2 hours till sauerkraut is very tender, occasionally mixing.
- Mix in 1/2 tsp. each pepper and salt and 1 tbsp. brown sugar; add more pepper, salt and brown sugar to taste.
- You can make sauerkraut with apples 3 days ahead, chilled. Before serving, reheat.

Nutrition Information

- Calories: 132
- Saturated Fat: 2 g(10%)
- Sodium: 1502 mg(63%)
- Fiber: 8 g(32%)
- Total Carbohydrate: 22 g(7%)
- Cholesterol: 8 mg(3%)
- Protein: 2 g(5%)
- Total Fat: 3 g(5%)

245. Sauteed Baby Artichokes With Oven Dried Tomatoes And Green Olive Dressing

Serving: Makes 4 servings | Prep: | Ready in:

Ingredients

- 1 lemon
- 2 pounds baby artichokes (about 18)
- 6 tablespoons olive oil
- 4 garlic cloves, thinly sliced
- 1 teaspoon dried herbes de Provence*
- 1/2 cup canned vegetable broth
- 1/3 cup dry white wine
- 8 ounces fresh crimini mushrooms, quartered
- Oven-dried Tomatoes
- Green-Olive Dressing
- Lemon slices

Direction

- Fill cold water in a big bowl. Halve lemon; press the juice into the bowl of water, then put in the halves of lemon. Trim stem and top quarter of an artichoke. Lean back the outer, dark green leaves and break off at base of artichoke till just the light green and yellow leaves left. Halve artichoke lengthwise. Take any leaves with purple tip from the middle of artichoke with tip of knife. Put the halves of artichoke into lemon water. Redo with the rest of the artichokes.
- Thoroughly strain the artichokes. In big, heavy pot, heat 3 tablespoons of oil on moderate heat. Put in the artichokes, scatter pepper and salt over and sauté for three minutes. Put in herbes de Provence and garlic and sauté for 6 minutes, till artichokes start to partially brown. Pour in wine and broth and boil. Lower the heat; simmer with cover for 10 minutes, till artichokes are soft and most of the liquid is soaked in. Remove cover and simmer for 3 minutes, till all liquid is soaked in. Turn the artichokes onto platter; retain warmth with cover.
- Using the same pot, heat leftover 3 tablespoons of oil on moderately-high heat. Put in and sauté mushrooms for 8 minutes, till golden brown and tender; season with pepper and salt to taste. Turn the Oven-dried Tomatoes and mushrooms onto platter along with artichokes. Top with scoop of Green-Olive Dressing. Jazz up using slices of lemon to serve.
- You may substitute dried herb mixture with a mix of fennel seeds, savory, basil and dried thyme.

Nutrition Information

246. Sauteed Chicken With White Wine And Tomatoes

Serving: | Prep: | Ready in:

Ingredients

- 1 4-lb Chicken
- 1/4 cup olive oil
- 1 tablespoon onion, finely chopped
- 1/2 cup dry white wine
- 4 medium-sized tomatoes, peeled, seeded, chopped coarse
- 1 clove garlic, chopped adn mashed
- 1 tablespoon finely minced parsley
- 12 black Italian olives, pitted

Direction

- Slice 4-pounds of chicken to make serving pieces, pat dry, add pepper and salt to season, and lightly dredge in flour. Brown on every side in quarter cup hot olive oil using a broad frying or sauté pan. Put in a tablespoon finely chopped onion and gently cook till golden. Put in half cup dry white wine and cook till cooked down by 1/2. Then put in a small garlic clove, chopped and crushed, a tablespoon finely minced parsley and four medium-size tomatoes, peel removed, seeded, and coarsely chopped. Cover and gently cook the chicken for 15 minutes to 20 minutes. Put in 12 pitted black Italian olives 5 minutes prior it's done. Serve along with steamed potatoes.

Nutrition Information

- Calories: 278
- Total Fat: 20 g(31%)
- Saturated Fat: 5 g(26%)
- Sodium: 98 mg(4%)
- Fiber: 1 g(2%)
- Total Carbohydrate: 2 g(1%)
- Cholesterol: 77 mg(26%)
- Protein: 20 g(39%)

247. Sauteed Fresh Chanterelles

Serving: Serves 6 | Prep: | Ready in:

Ingredients

- 1 1/4 pounds fresh chanterelles or Portobellos
- 2 tablespoons unsalted butter
- 1 tablespoon olive oil
- 1/4 cup dry white wine
- 3 tablespoons coarsely chopped fresh flat-leafed parsley leaves
- fresh lemon juice to taste

Direction

- Slice chanterelles in half lengthwise or slice Portobellos to make half-inch-thick pieces. Liquify butter along with oil in a non-stick, big skillet on medium high heat till froth settles and sauté mushrooms along with pepper and salt to taste for 2 minutes, mixing, till just tender. Pour in wine and cook for 5 minutes, mixing, till mushrooms are soft and liquid is vaporized. Toss parsley, lemon juice and mushrooms in bowl.

Nutrition Information

248. Sauteed Langoustine With Chardonnay Reduction

Serving: Serves 4 | Prep: | Ready in:

Ingredients

- 20 langoustines (about 4 pounds) (You may substitute with king prawn, Australian Crayfish or large 2 to 3 oz.-shrimp with heads)
- 1 oz. shellfish butter (see below)
- pepper
- sea salt ("fleur de sel")
- 5 shellfish heads
- 6 oz. unsalted butter
- 12 oz. water
- 15 langoustine (shellfish) heads
- 2 cups chicken stock
- 1 1/2 oz. shellfish butter
- 3 oz. red onion (3 small pieces)
- 4 oz. quince
- 10 oz. Chardonnay
- 10 oz. langoustine broth
- 3 grapefruit peelings (use a vegetable peeler)
- 20 peppercorns (preferably Indonesian)
- 1/4 vanilla bean
- 3 oz. unsalted butter
- 1/4 dry chili

- 1 mint leaf
- pepper
- 1 lb. salsify
- 1/4 oz. olive oil
- 1/2 oz. duck fat
- 1 oz. butter
- 1 1/2 cup chicken stock
- sea salt (fleur de sel)
- black pepper
- 2 oz. olive oil
- 1/2 oz. truffle juice
- 1 oz. lemon juice
- salt
- white pepper
- 3 basil leaves
- 4 oz. broccoli sprouts

Direction

- Langoustines: Separate head from tail; keep heads. Carefully cut shell with kitchen shears on the underside of tail up to final section before fins. Leave this on because it protects the thinner part of tail meat to avoid overcooking. Discard shell fragments; wrap then refrigerate cleaned tails right away.
- Shellfish butter: Preheat an oven to 300°F. Place heads in a roasting pan. Roast slowly for 15 minutes at 300°F till dry. Add butter; let melt till it foams yet before milk solids begin to brown/noisette. Add water; cook at 200°F for 2 hours. Strain into bowl; let congeal in the fridge and separate butter from water. Throw leftover water; melt butter then strain through cheese cloth. Makes about 3 ounces.
- Langoustine broth; slowly sauté langoustine heads with shellfish butter in a sauté pan on medium heat. Put chicken stock in; slowly cook. Skim surface of broth. Cook for 1 hour; through cheesecloth, strain broth. Makes around 1 1/2 cups.
- Chardonnay reduction: Slice onions to quarters, dice quince; slowly simmer in pot with 1 tablespoon of unsalted butter. Vegetables shouldn't take on color. Add pepper, vanilla seed and grapefruit zest. Add langoustine broth and wine; quickly reduce on stove. Add leftover butter when liquid halves. Continue for 15 minutes till sauce reaches the desired consistency. Add mint and chili; allow to infuse for several minutes. Strain sauce. Set aside for final part of dish.
- Salsify: Peel salsify; cut to 2-inch pieces on bias. Season with olive oil and salt. Add 1/2 of the duck fat in a sauté pan; pan fry the salsify then add butter and chicken stock. Quickly cook on stove; completely reduce stock. Remove salsify. Heat clean frying pan till very warm; add leftover duck fat. Roast till salsify is golden in color. Season with fleur de sel and pepper. Put aside till you plate the dish.
- Truffle dressing: Stir together all ingredients: macerate the whole basil leaves in vinaigrette. Right before serving, season broccoli sprouts with truffle vinaigrette.
- Final assembly: All ingredients should be served warm except broccoli sprouts. Be sure all components for dish are ready to plate before cooking the shellfish. Sauce and salsify should be warm and broccoli sprouts should be dressed with vinaigrette. To serve: Heat sauté pan; add leftover shellfish butter. Put seasoned shellfish in pan; flip shellfish after 1 minute and finish cooking for 2-3 minutes.
- Presentation: Put salsify around plate. Put langoustine over, tail out then dressed broccoli sprouts in the middle of plate. Put Chardonnay reduction on langoustine tails. Immediately serve.

Nutrition Information

- Calories: 1267
- Saturated Fat: 50 g(250%)
- Sodium: 2310 mg(96%)
- Fiber: 17 g(66%)
- Total Carbohydrate: 74 g(25%)
- Cholesterol: 220 mg(73%)
- Protein: 22 g(45%)
- Total Fat: 96 g(148%)

249. Sauteed Pasta With Lobster

Serving: Makes 6 servings | Prep: | Ready in:

Ingredients

- 4 (1- to 1 1/4-pound) live lobsters
- 1/2 cup dry white wine
- 1/4 teaspoon crumbled saffron
- 6 tablespoons olive oil
- 1 large onion, sliced
- 1 bay leaf
- 1 1/2 pound vine-ripened tomatoes, peeled, seeded, and coarsely chopped
- 2 garlic cloves, chopped
- 1 pound angel's hair pasta nests or fideos (fideus in Catalan) coils, broken in half, or capellini, broken into 2-inch lengths
- 2 tablespoons chopped fresh flat-leaf parsley

Direction

- To cook the lobsters, fill an 8-quart pot three fourths with salted water and boil it. Put 2 lobsters into the water for 3 minutes with the heads in first and boil, put a cover on. To cool down, use tongs to move the lobsters to a strainer. Do the same with the other 2 lobsters.
- Once the lobsters are cool enough to touch, separate the shell from meat, collect the juice in another bowl. Put the shell in the bowl with the juice. Slice the meat into 1-inch chunks and refrigerate with a cover on.
- To make the stock, combine saffron and wine and let the mixture marinate for 10 minutes. In an 8-quart pot, boil the mixture of lobster shells with juices, 14 cups of water and wine mixture. Boil for 1 hour, until 8 cups left. Use cheesecloth to line a sieve and place on a bowl. Filter the stock through the sieve and dispose the solids.
- To make the sofregit: In a heavy frying pan, heat 2 tablespoons of oil on low heat until hot, then cook bay leaf and onion for 45 minutes until onion is browned and very tender. Add garlic and tomatoes and cook, tossing frequently for 15 minutes until the sofregit is very firm. Dispose the bay leaf.
- To cook pasta: Start preheating the oven to 400°F
- In an oven-safe 12-inch heavy frying pan or a cassola, heat 1 tablespoon of oil on moderately low heat until hot but not smoking. Then cook pasta in 4 batches, tossing until golden brown. Move the pasta to a bowl as browned and add 1 more tablespoon of oil for every batch.
- Once all pasta is browned, put back to the pan and toss in 4 cups of stock and sofregit (If you cook in a cassola, use 4Bõps stock, because the plate's side is straight, you'll need more liquid). Save the rest of the stock for later use. Simmer the pasta mixture, keep simmering for 4 minutes, and put a cover on. Mix in the stored lobster and use pepper and salt to season. Move the pan to the center of an oven, take away the cover, and bake until the pasta on top is crunchy and the liquid is soaked up, about 10 minutes. Mix in parsley.
- Tips:
- You can prepare stock and lobsters 1 day in advance, let them cool fully, put a cover on and refrigerate.
- Leftover stock can be used as a base for a sauce armoricaine or great for lobster bisque and can be stored frozen up to 3 months.
- Aïfregit can be prepared 1 day in advance, put a cover on and refrigerate.

Nutrition Information

- Calories: 705
- Saturated Fat: 3 g(14%)
- Sodium: 1452 mg(61%)
- Fiber: 4 g(17%)
- Total Carbohydrate: 64 g(21%)
- Cholesterol: 432 mg(144%)
- Protein: 67 g(135%)
- Total Fat: 17 g(27%)

250. Sautéed Pork Tenderloin With Prunes

Serving: Makes 4 main-course servings | Prep: | Ready in:

Ingredients

- 1 cup dry or semisweet white wine
- 1/2 pound pitted prunes
- 2 pork tenderloins, about 1 pound each
- Salt
- Pepper
- 3 tablespoons olive oil
- 2 tablespoons meat glaze (see below)
- 1/2 cup heavy cream

Direction

- For preparation: In a bowl put the prunes, soak in the wine for 1 hour or overnight.
- Cut fat off pork tenderloins and cut into 3/4 inch thick rounds seasoned with salt and pepper on both side.
- In a pan large enough to hold the pork rounds, add the olive oil and heat on high heat. When it smokes add the rounds. Turn once, 3 minutes per side or until tender and firm. Do not overcook or turn the heat down after they get too brown. Transfer the pork to the platter and separate the fat out.
- Drain the prunes. Reserve the wine. Add 1/2 cup of wine and prunes to the same pan over high heat. Use the wooden spoon to scrape any brown bits from the bottom of the pan. Stir in the meat glaze if using and bring to boil until it reduces to half. Stir continuously until thickens and turns into light syrup. Add cream and keep boiling until a reduced light sauce consistency is achieved. Then add salt and pepper to taste.
- Place the pork rounds on plates and spoon the glaze on the top.
- Meat glaze or glaze meat is a method of reducing the broth or simmering down to plump up the flavor. The more it reduces the more it thickens or the syrupier the sauce will be. From original volume that reduces to its 1/15 is called demi-glaze. You can reduce it again by half, to bring out the flavorful sauce made from its broth to get meat glaze or commercial meat glaze, specifically the excellent More-than-Gourmet brand.
- To make a glaze use a 5 quarts beef broth and put it on the stove and gently simmer. Put the pot slightly off the middle of the burner and change heat so the liquid only bubbles on one side of the pot. While simmering, skim the fat and froth frequently as they accumulate with ladle. Let it simmer and reduce the broth to half. Remove from heat then strain using a fine-mesh colander and transfer to a smaller pot and continue the procedure until it reduces to 2/3 cup. Transfer to a container and let it cool. Cover and keep it chilled or freeze, is good for 3 months. You can also make a demi glaze by reducing it to 1 1/3 cup where you get twice as much.

Nutrition Information

- Calories: 625
- Total Fat: 29 g(45%)
- Saturated Fat: 11 g(55%)
- Sodium: 850 mg(35%)
- Fiber: 4 g(17%)
- Total Carbohydrate: 39 g(13%)
- Cholesterol: 184 mg(61%)
- Protein: 47 g(95%)

251. Scallops Verde

Serving: Serves 4 to 6 | Prep: | Ready in:

Ingredients

- 3 ounces dried tomatoes (about 1 cup), not packed in oil
- 1 pound sea scallops
- 1 pound penne or bow-tie pasta
- 1 tablespoon olive oil

- 1 1/2 tablespoons minced shallots
- 1 cup dry white wine
- 1/2 cup pine nuts, toasted until golden
- 2 cups heavy cream
- 1/4 cup freshly grated Parmesan
- 1/2 cup prepared basil pesto

Direction

- Add sufficient boiling water in a heatproof, small bowl on top of tomatoes to soak and rest for 20 minutes to half an hour, or till tender. Strain tomatoes, throw the liquid, and thinly slice.
- Meanwhile, take hard muscle from side of every scallop if need be and slice scallops in half in case big. Boil 5 quarts of salted water in 6-quarts kettle for pasta.
- Heat the oil in a heavy, big skillet on medium high heat till hot yet not smoking and sauté scallops for 2 minutes per side, till cooked thoroughly and light golden on edges. Turn the scallops onto a heat-safe dish and cover to retain warmth.
- To oil left in skillet, put the shallots and cook on medium heat, with cover, mixing from time to time, till soften. Pour in wine and boil with no cover, mixing to scratch browned bits up, till cooked down to roughly 3 tablespoons. Put in tomatoes, cream and pine nuts, and let come to just a boil. Mix pesto and Parmesan in and take skillet off heat. Mix scallops in.
- In boiling water, let pasta cook till al dente and use a colander to strain. Put pasta back to kettle and put in mixture of scallop, softly tossing to incorporate.

Nutrition Information

- Calories: 1414
- Protein: 38 g(75%)
- Total Fat: 95 g(146%)
- Saturated Fat: 33 g(167%)
- Sodium: 936 mg(39%)
- Fiber: 5 g(20%)
- Total Carbohydrate: 98 g(33%)
- Cholesterol: 198 mg(66%)

252. Scallops With Mushrooms In White Wine Sauce

Serving: Makes 8 first-course servings | Prep: | Ready in:

Ingredients

- 1/4 cup coarse fresh bread crumbs from a baguette
- 1/4 cup finely grated Parmigiano-Reggiano (1/2 ounce)
- 1 1/4 cups dry white wine
- 1 cup water
- 1/2 small onion, sliced
- 1/2 Turkish or 1/4 California bay leaf
- 1/2 teaspoon salt
- 1/4 teaspoon black pepper
- 1 lb sea scallops, tough muscle removed from side of each if necessary and scallops cut into 3/4-inch pieces
- 1/2 lb small mushrooms, halved lengthwise, then thinly sliced lengthwise
- 3/4 stick (6 tablespoons) unsalted butter
- 1/2 cup heavy cream
- 1 large egg yolk
- 1 tablespoon all-purpose flour
- 8 cups kosher salt to stabilize scallop shells (if using)
- 1 1/2 tablespoons minced fresh flat-leaf parsley
- 16 (2 1/2-inch) scallop shells* or 8 (2-oz) ramekins

Direction

- Preheat the oven to 350°F.
- On baking sheet in the center of the oven, let bread crumbs toast for 6 to 8 minutes, till light golden, then toss along with the cheese.
- In heavy, 2 1/2- to 3-quart saucepan, simmer pepper, salt, bay leaf, onion, water and wine for 5 minutes, with no cover, then put in

scallops and simmer for 2 to 3 minutes, with no cover, mixing from time to time, till barely cooked completely. Use slotted spoon to turn scallops onto platter to cool down, putting any onions back to pan, then let cooking liquid boil for 8 to 10 minutes, till cooked down to roughly a cup. Use a sieve to pass cooking liquid through right into a bowl.

- In a heavy, 10- to 12-inch skillet, let mushrooms cook in 2 tablespoons of butter on medium heat for 5 minutes, mixing from time to time, till most of the liquid from mushrooms is vaporized. Add pepper and salt to season.
- In heatproof bowl, mix yolk and cream. In a 2 1/2- to 3-quart, cleaned saucepan, liquify 2 tablespoons butter on medium low heat, then put in flour and let roux cook for 2 minutes, mixing. Take pan off heat and put in the reduced cooking liquid in stream, mixing continuously. Bring pan back heat and simmer for a minute, mixing. Add sauce to cream mixture in gentle stream, mixing constantly, then return sauce in pan and simmer for a minute, mixing. Take off heat and add pepper and salt to season.
- Preheat the broiler.
- Mix into sauce the mushrooms and scallops, then distribute between ramekins or scallop shells and scatter mixture of bread crumb over. Evenly scatter kosher salt in big shallow baking pan in case using shells, then put shells snugly in salt. Scatter leftover 2 tablespoons of bits butter on scallops, then broil for 2 minutes, approximately 4-inch away from heat till golden.
- Scatter parsley over.

Nutrition Information

- Calories: 247
- Saturated Fat: 10 g(48%)
- Sodium: 485 mg(20%)
- Fiber: 1 g(2%)
- Total Carbohydrate: 9 g(3%)
- Cholesterol: 89 mg(30%)

- Protein: 14 g(27%)
- Total Fat: 16 g(24%)

253. Sea Bass Amandine On Watercress

Serving: Makes 2 servings; can be doubled | Prep: | Ready in:

Ingredients

- 1 small bunch watercress, trimmed
- 6 tablespoons sliced almonds
- 1/4 cup all purpose flour
- 8 ounces sea bass fillets, cut into 1/2-inch-wide strips
- 3 tablespoons butter
- 1/3 cup dry white wine
- Lemon wedges

Direction

- Divide the watercress among 2 plates and set aside. In a processor, blend together flour and 4 tablespoons of almonds until the almonds are ground finely, then transfer onto a shallow bowl. Sprinkle the fish with pepper and salt and add into the flour mixture, tossing to coat.
- In a big skillet, melt 1 tablespoon of butter on medium-high heat and add 2 tablespoons of almonds, then sauté for 2 minutes until golden and toasted. Transfer the almonds into a bowl. In the same skillet, melt 2 tablespoons of butter and add the fish, then sauté for 2 minutes on each side until cooked through.
- Arrange the fish on top of the watercress. Add dry white wine into the skillet and whisk on a medium heat until the sauce simmers, then season with pepper and salt. Spoon over the fish and sprinkle with the toasted almonds. Garnish with the lemon wedges then serve.

Nutrition Information

- Calories: 442
- Total Fat: 28 g(43%)
- Saturated Fat: 12 g(62%)
- Sodium: 96 mg(4%)
- Fiber: 3 g(12%)
- Total Carbohydrate: 17 g(6%)
- Cholesterol: 92 mg(31%)
- Protein: 27 g(55%)

254. Sea Bass With Tomatoes And Onions

Serving: Makes 4 servings | Prep: | Ready in:

Ingredients

- 7 tablespoons olive oil
- 4 4x2x1/2-inch French bread slices
- 3 cups thinly sliced onions
- 1/2 cup chopped fresh parsley
- 2 tablespoons chopped canned anchovies (from one 2-ounce can)
- 1 1/2 tablespoons minced garlic
- 1/4 teaspoon dried crushed red pepper
- 1 1/4 pounds plum tomatoes, seeded, finely chopped
- 3/4 cup dry white wine
- 4 8-ounce sea bass fillets (about 1 inch thick)

Direction

- Preheat the oven to 350°F. Brush each side of bread slices with 2 tablespoons of oil. Put on the baking sheet; bake for 12 minutes, till toasted a bit. Put aside.
- Raise the oven heat to 500°F. In ovenproof, big skillet, heat 5 tablespoons of oil on moderately-high heat. Put in the red pepper, garlic, anchovies, 1/4 cup parsley and onions. Sauté for 5 minutes, till onions start to become tender. Mix in wine and tomatoes. Scatter pepper and salt on fish. In the same skillet, put the fish. Scoop the vegetables on top of fish. Simmer. Put cover; bake for 12 minutes, till fish turn opaque in middle. Turn the fish onto plates.
- Into sauce, mix leftover cup of parsley. Let sauce boil for 2 minutes till cooked down a bit. Season with pepper and salt to taste. Scoop the sauce on top of fish. Serve along with croutons.

Nutrition Information

- Calories: 559
- Sodium: 452 mg(19%)
- Fiber: 4 g(15%)
- Total Carbohydrate: 21 g(7%)
- Cholesterol: 98 mg(33%)
- Protein: 47 g(95%)
- Total Fat: 29 g(45%)
- Saturated Fat: 5 g(23%)

255. Sea Bream With Artichokes And Caper Dressing

Serving: Makes 4 servings | Prep: | Ready in:

Ingredients

- 3 1/3 cups low-salt chicken broth
- 1 onion, sliced
- 3/4 cup dry white wine
- 2 tablespoons fresh lemon juice
- 3 fresh thyme sprigs
- 2 large garlic cloves, crushed
- 1 fresh rosemary sprig
- 4 whole artichokes
- 5 tablespoons olive oil
- 5 tablespoons balsamic vinegar
- 1 teaspoon grated lemon peel
- 2 tablespoons drained capers
- 2 pounds russet potatoes, peeled, cut into 1-inch cubes
- 3 tablespoons butter
- 3 tablespoons extra-virgin olive oil

- 4 5- to 6-ounce sea bream, striped bass, or whitefish fillets
- 3 tablespoons butter
- 3 tablespoons olive oil

Direction

- For artichokes: In a heavy large saucepan, mix the first 7 ingredients. Trim off stems and take off all leaves, working with 1 artichoke at a time. Clean out chokes, cut edges of hearts then put to the saucepan; dust with pepper and salt to taste. Bring to a boil over medium-high heat. Simmer for about 35 minutes, covering the pan. Place hearts onto a plate using a slotted spoon. Slice hearts into a thickness of 1/3-inch cuts. (You can prepare 1 day in advance. Chill it covered.)
- To make the dressing: In a small bowl, mix lemon peel, vinegar, and oil; mix in capers. Add pepper and salt to the dressing to taste.
- To prepare potatoes: In a large saucepan with boiling salted water, add potatoes and cook for about 15 minutes just until tender. Drain the potatoes; bring back to the same pan. Add oil and butter; mash until smooth. Add pepper and salt to the potatoes to taste. (You can prepare 2 hours in advance. Allow them to stand at room temperature. Warm them again before serving.)
- For the fish: Dust fish with pepper and salt. In a heavy large skillet over medium-high heat, put oil and butter to melt. Put artichoke slices to the skillet. Stir-fry for about 5 minutes until heated through. Take away from the heat. In each center of 4 plates, arrange artichokes using a slotted spoon; set the skillet aside. Place 3/4 of warm potatoes atop artichokes on each plate; use foil to tent them with to keep warm.
- Set the reserved skillet with butter mixture over medium-high heat. Put in fish and stir-fry each side for about 4 minutes until just opaque in the center. Arrange fish over potatoes on each plate. Scoop the dressing over the fish then serve.

Nutrition Information

- Calories: 5625
- Saturated Fat: 42 g(210%)
- Sodium: 3674 mg(153%)
- Fiber: 7 g(26%)
- Total Carbohydrate: 57 g(19%)
- Cholesterol: 4046 mg(1349%)
- Protein: 898 g(1796%)
- Total Fat: 173 g(265%)

256. Sea Scallops With Ham Braised Cabbage And Kale

Serving: Makes 6 servings | Prep: 1hours | Ready in:

Ingredients

- 1 large onion, chopped (2 cups)
- 5 tablespoons extra-virgin olive oil
- 1 Turkish or 1/2 California bay leaf
- 1 tablespoon finely chopped garlic (2 cloves)
- 1 large head Savoy cabbage (2 to 2 1/2 pounds), quartered, cored, and coarsely chopped (12 cups loosely packed)
- Ham stock including meat
- 1 1/4 pounds tender green kale (1 large bunch), stems and center ribs cut out and discarded and leaves coarsely chopped (12 cups loosely packed)
- 1 teaspoon salt
- 1/2 teaspoon black pepper
- 30 large sea scallops (2 to 2 1/2 pounds total), tough muscle removed from side of each if necessary
- 1 cup dry white wine
- 1 teaspoon fresh lemon juice, or to taste
- Accompaniment: creamy stone-ground grits

Direction

- Cook onion and bay leaf in 3 tbsp. oil for 3 minutes till starting to soften in 6-8-qt. heavy pot on medium heat, occasionally mixing. Add garlic; cook for 1 minute, occasionally mixing.

- Add cabbage; put heat on medium high. Sauté for 5 minutes till cabbage starts to wilt, occasionally mixing. Add stock with the meat from ham hocks; simmer for 30 minutes till cabbage is tender, occasionally mixing, partially covered.
- Mix in 1/4 tsp. pepper, 1/2 tsp. salt and kale; simmer for 15 minutes till kale is tender, occasionally mixing, partially covered.
- Preheat an oven to 200°F.
- Pat dry scallops; sprinkle 1/4 tsp. pepper and leftover 1/2 tsp. salt total on both sides. Heat leftover 2 tbsp. oil till hot yet not smoking in 12-in. heavy nonstick skillet on medium high heat; sauté scallops, in 2 batches if needed, without crowding for 5 minutes in total per batch till cooked through and golden, flipping once. Put scallops onto shallow baking dish; in oven, keep warm.
- Put wine in skillet; boil to deglaze till liquid reduces to 2/3 cup, scraping brown bits up from bottom of skillet, mixing. Mix in 1 tsp. lemon juice. Put sauce in cabbage mixture; season with extra lemon juice (optional), pepper and salt. Put accumulated scallop juices in baking dish in the cabbage mixture; serve mixture over grits with scallops on top.
- You can make cabbage mixture 1 day ahead, fully cooled, uncovered then cover and chill. Reheat; before serving, add the pan juices from scallops.

Nutrition Information

- Calories: 592
- Saturated Fat: 9 g(45%)
- Sodium: 1300 mg(54%)
- Fiber: 6 g(26%)
- Total Carbohydrate: 24 g(8%)
- Cholesterol: 124 mg(41%)
- Protein: 43 g(86%)
- Total Fat: 35 g(53%)

257. Seafood Cannelloni

Serving: Makes 6 servings | Prep: 1.75hours | Ready in:

Ingredients

- 1/3 cup finely chopped shallot
- 2 tablespoons finely chopped carrot
- 2 tablespoons finely chopped celery
- 1 lb medium shrimp in shells (31 to 35 per lb), peeled, reserving shells, and deveined
- 1 lb sea scallops, tough muscle removed from side of each and reserved
- 5 tablespoons unsalted butter, softened
- 1 teaspoon tomato paste
- 1 cup dry white wine
- 3 cups water
- 1 tablespoon seafood glaze* (optional)
- 2 fresh flat-leaf parsley sprigs
- 3 tablespoons all-purpose flour
- 1 cup heavy cream
- 1/2 teaspoon fresh lemon juice, or to taste
- 1 1/2 teaspoons salt
- 1/2 teaspoon black pepper
- 2 tablespoons Cognac
- 1/2 cup finely chopped fresh chives
- 14 (6- by 3-inch) flat fresh or no-boil lasagne noodles (without curly edges)
- a 3-quart flameproof rectangular casserole dish (about 13 by 9 inches; not glass)

Direction

- For the sauce, cook the carrot, reserved scallop muscles, reserved shrimp shells, celery, and shallot in a 2-3-qt heavy saucepan with 3 tbsp. of butter over moderately low heat for 5 minutes, uncovered and stirring for some time until the vegetables are pale golden and softened. Add the tomato paste. Cook and stir the mixture for 1 minute. Add the wine. Boil the mixture over high heat for 6-8 minutes while occasionally stirring it until it is reduced to 1/4 cup. Add the water, parsley sprigs, and seafood glaze, if using. Cover the mixture and simmer for 30 minutes.

- Discard the parsley. Working in 2 batches, puree the stock and shrimp shells in a blender (be careful in blending hot liquids). Transfer the mixture into a bowl through the fine-mesh sieve. Make sure to press the solids and discard it after.
- In a clean saucepan, melt leftover 2 tbsp. of butter over moderately low heat. Add the flour and cook and stir over low heat for 3 minutes. Add all the warm seafood stock while stirring the mixture. Bring the mixture to a boil while stirring it. Add 1/2 cup of the cream. Simmer the sauce gently for 10 minutes, stirring it for some time. Mix in 1/4 tsp. of pepper, 1/2 tsp. of salt, and lemon juice.
- Pour 1/2 cup of the sauce into a bowl that is set over a larger bowl. Fill the larger bowl with ice and cold water to cool the filling.
- For the seafood filling, get 1/3 of the scallops and 1/3 of the shrimp. Slice them into 1/4-inch pieces. Toss the slices with 1/4 tsp. of salt. In a food processor, puree the remaining scallops and shrimp together with the cooled 1/2 cup of sauce, Cognac, leftover 1/4 tsp. of pepper, and leftover 3/4 tsp. of salt. Pour in 1/2 cup of cream. Pulse the mixture until just combined. Pour the mousse into a large bowl. Mix in chives and shrimp and scallop slices.
- Cook the pasta and start assembling the cannelloni. Set the oven to 375°F for preheating.
- In a large pot, boil the lasagna noodles, a few at a time, together with salted water for 2 minutes for fresh noodles while 6 minutes for no-boil, stirring the noodles to separate until al dente. Use tongs and a slotted spatula to transfer the noodles into a large bowl with cold water. Allow the noodles to stop cooking. Lift the noodles out, shaking off any excess water, and then lay the noodles flat onto the dry kitchen towels (do not use terry cloth). Drizzle each noodle with 1/3 cup of the mousse. Make sure to leave a 1/2-inch border on all of the short ends. Roll each noodle up loosely, starting from the short end.
- Pour 1/2 cup of the sauce onto the bottom of the casserole dish. Arrange the cannelloni onto the dish snugly in 1 layer, seam-sides down. Drizzle over the remaining sauce. Cover the cannelloni with foil and bake it inside the middle of the oven for 25-30 minutes until the filling is cooked through and the sauce is bubbling. (To test the doneness of the filling, insert a metal skewer into the cannelloni and let it stay there for 5 seconds. Remove the skewer and bring it against your bottom lip, pressing it to your lip of bottom. If the metal is already warm, the filling is already cooked and the casserole is heated through.)
- Set the broiler to preheating.
- Remove the foil and position the cannelloni inside the broiler 3-inches away from the heat. Broil for 3-5 minutes until brown spots appear. Allow it to stand for 10 minutes; serve.
- Note: Ingredients are available in some specialty foods shops or supermarkets.
- Also, the casserole can be assembled 4 hours ahead (not yet baked or broiled). Just let it chilled and covered with a foil. Before baking the casserole, let it stand first at room temperature for 20 minutes.

Nutrition Information

- Calories: 598
- Total Fat: 26 g(41%)
- Saturated Fat: 16 g(78%)
- Sodium: 1003 mg(42%)
- Fiber: 3 g(10%)
- Total Carbohydrate: 54 g(18%)
- Cholesterol: 193 mg(64%)
- Protein: 29 g(58%)

258. Seafood Stew With Fennel And Thyme

Serving: Makes 6 servings | Prep: | Ready in:

Ingredients

- 1 1/2 pounds mussels, scrubbed, debearded

- 2 1/2 cups chopped onions
- 1 cup dry white wine
- 12 parsley sprigs plus 1/2 cup chopped parsley
- 2 tablespoons (1/4 stick) butter
- 2 cups finely chopped leeks (white and pale green parts only)
- 2 cups diced trimmed fennel bulb
- 4 8-ounce bottles clam juice
- 4 large fresh thyme sprigs
- 2 bay leaves
- 1 3/4 pounds thick halibut fillets, cut into 1 1/2-inch pieces
- 10 ounces sea scallops
- 1 cup crème fraîche*
- 2 large egg yolks

Direction

- In big pot, mix 8 parsley sprigs, wine, 1 1/4 cups onions and mussels; boil. Cook with cover for 5 minutes, till mussels open, shake pot frequently. Turn the mussels into a big bowl to cool down with slotted spoon, throw mussels that remain closed. Into a big measuring cup, drain the cooking liquid; Throw the vegetables in strainer. Pour in cooking liquid with sufficient water to reach 2 cups. Take mussels from shells if wished.
- Use the same big pot to liquify butter on moderate heat. Put in leeks, fennel and leftover 1 1/4 cups of onions, and sauté for 7 minutes, till leeks soften, mixing often. Put in bay leaves, thyme sprigs, clam juice, 4 parsley sprigs and reserved cooking liquid of mussel. Simmer with no cover for 25 minutes, till liquid has cooked down by 1/3 and vegetables become tender. Put into broth with scallops and halibut and simmer for 4 minutes, till just opaque in the middle. Turn the scallops and halibut into bowl with slotted spoon. Throw thyme sprigs, bay leaves and parsley sprigs.
- In medium a bowl, mix egg yolks and crème fraîche to incorporate. Mix in half cup of hot cooking liquid from the pot. Slowly mix mixture of yolk into stew. Cook on moderate heat till liquid partially thickens, mixing continuously, for 5 minutes, prevent mixture from boiling. Put scallops, mussels and halibut back to pan. Cook for 5 minutes, till halibut is heated completely, mixing frequently. Mix in half cup of chopped parsley. Add pepper and salt to season. Put in heated shallow bowls to serve.
- In case crème fraîche is not available, heat a cup of whipping cream to 85°F or lukewarm. Take off heat and stir 2 tablespoons of buttermilk in. Rest in draft-free, warm place with cover till partially thickened, for a day to 2 days, will vary on heat of room. Chill till set to use.

Nutrition Information

- Calories: 562
- Total Carbohydrate: 45 g(15%)
- Cholesterol: 156 mg(52%)
- Protein: 48 g(97%)
- Total Fat: 31 g(48%)
- Saturated Fat: 12 g(59%)
- Sodium: 2185 mg(91%)
- Fiber: 3 g(13%)

259. Seared Scallops With Tarragon Butter Sauce

Serving: Makes 4 servings | Prep: 20mins | Ready in:

Ingredients

- 1 1/4 pounds large sea scallops, tough ligament from side of each discarded
- 7 tablespoons unsalted butter, cut into tablespoons, divided
- 2 tablespoons finely chopped shallot
- 1/4 cup dry white wine
- 1/4 cup white-wine vinegar
- 1 tablespoon finely chopped tarragon

Direction

- Blot dry the scallops and scatter a total of quarter teaspoon of salt and quarter teaspoon of pepper over.
- In a nonstick, 12-inch skillet, heat a tablespoon of butter on moderately-high heat till froth settles, then sear the scallops for a total of 5 minutes, flipping one time, till just cooked completely and golden brown. Turn onto platter.
- Put to skillet with the wine, vinegar and shallot, and boil, scratching brown bits up, till cooked down to 2 tablespoons. Put in the juices from the platter and boil, if need be, till liquid is cooked down to roughly quarter cup. Lower heat to low and put in 3 tablespoons of butter, mixing till nearly liquified, then put in leftover 3 tablespoons of butter and tilt till blended and sauce is creamy. Mix salt to taste and tarragon in; top scallops with sauce.

Nutrition Information

- Calories: 291
- Saturated Fat: 13 g(65%)
- Sodium: 560 mg(23%)
- Fiber: 0 g(1%)
- Total Carbohydrate: 6 g(2%)
- Cholesterol: 87 mg(29%)
- Protein: 18 g(35%)
- Total Fat: 21 g(32%)

260. Seared Sea Scallops With Lemongrass Sauce And Basil, Mint And Cilantro Salad

Serving: | Prep: | Ready in:

Ingredients

- 2 teaspoons canola oil
- 1 onion, chopped
- 6 stalks lemongrass, dry leaves removed, stems pounded; cut into 3-inch lengths
- 4 cloves garlic, finely chopped
- 3 red Thai bird chiles, finely chopped (found in grocery stores' Asian section)
- 2 cups dry white wine
- 1 can (28 ounce) whole tomatoes, plus juice
- 1/2 cup Thai basil
- 1/2 cup fresh mint
- 1/2 cup cilantro sprigs
- Juice from 1/2 lime
- 2 teaspoon canola oil
- 24 jumbo sea scallops
- 1 tablespoon canola oil

Direction

- Over low heat, heat oil in a large, nonstick pan, add onion along with a pinch of salt and cook for about 12 minutes until translucent. Mix in chiles, garlic and lemon grass. Pour in wine. Increase the heat to high, and then let simmer for 5 minutes. Pour in the tomatoes and juice and break tomatoes apart. Simmer for about 20 minutes until the sauce is thick. Press the sauce through a colander and get rid of solids. Season with pepper and salt.
- For the salad: in a bowl, combine all the ingredients and then season with pepper and salt.
- For the scallops: Add pepper and salt to taste. Over high heat, heat a large nonstick pan for a minute and pour in oil. Cook eight scallops for one minute. Lower the heat to medium-high and then cook undisturbed for about 4 minutes until turned golden. Flip the scallops over and cook for three minutes longer. Take out from the heat. Repeat this process. Divide the sauce and scallops in between 8 bowls and then add salad on top.

Nutrition Information

261. Seckel Pear Tart With Poire William Cream

Serving: Makes 8 servings | Prep: 1.5hours | Ready in:

Ingredients

- Sweet pastry dough
- 1 cup dry white wine
- 2 ripe Bartlett pears
- 3/4 cup sugar
- 2 pounds Seckel pears (24 very small or 16 small)
- 3 large egg yolks
- 1 1/2 tablespoons cornstarch
- 1/2 vanilla bean, split lengthwise
- 2 tablespoons poire William (pear eau-de-vie)
- 1/2 tablespoon unsalted butter
- 1 tablespoon poire William
- 3/4 teaspoon unflavored gelatin (from a 1/4-ounce envelope)
- Equipment: a 13-by 4-inch rectangular fluted tart pan with removable side; pie weights or dried beans; a flour sack or linen cloth

Direction

- Prepare shell: on a floured counter, unroll dough, using a rolling pin dusted with flour, to make a rectangle, 20-inch by 8-inch in size, flouring the surface again as need to be. Turn onto tart pan, softly suiting dough into pan but no stretching it. Clip overhang into three fourths-inch, slicing corners off. Fold overhang toward inside to enhance the side, then clip flush with pan edge. Put extra pastry aside for other use if wished. Puncture tart bottom shell entirely using fork and refrigerate for half an hour, till firm.
- Preheat the oven, with rack in the center, to 375°F.
- Line foil on shell and fill using pie weights, then bake for 20 minutes, till sides are firm. Take weights and foil and let shell bake for an additional of 15 to 20 minutes, till golden brown entirely. Cool fully in pan.
- Poach the pears: in a 4-quart, wide pot, add the wine and place a dampened flour sack cloth-lined-sieve on top of it. Use box grater big holes to grate the Bartlett pears with skin right into cloth, then collect cloth around the mixture and press as much clear juice as there is through the cloth right into the pan of wine. Throw leftover solids in cloth. Turn the mixture of wine onto a 2-cup measure and pour in sufficient water, if need be, to measure 2 cups of liquid, then put back to pan and mix sugar in.
- Peel Seckel pears cautiously, keep the stems attach, then use a small knife or tip of vegetable peeler to core through base to get rid of the seeds.
- Boil the wine mixture, mixing till sugar dissolves, then put in pears, in single pile if can be. Covered tightly and simmer for 20 minutes, flipping from time to time, till tender. Cautiously turn the pears onto rack place on 4-sided sheet pan using slotted spoon to let drain and let cool while standing upright. Turn the syrup of pear into a clean 2-cup measure, putting in any pan juices beneath pears, to measure 1 1/4 to 1 1/2 cups of syrup, and put aside for glaze and pastry cream.
- Prepare pastry cream: mix in small bowl with cornstarch and egg yolks, then mix a cup of pear syrup in. Turn onto a heavy, small saucepan and scoop in vanilla bean seeds, saving pod for other use. Boil on moderate heat, mixing, then cook for 2 minutes, mixing. Take off heat and mix in butter and poire William. Turn onto bowl, cover the surface and cool fully.
- Prepare glaze: in an extremely small bowl, mix gelatin and poire William and rest for a minute.
- In a heavy and extremely small saucepan, boil the rest of the pear syrup, then let boil, if need be, till cooked down to roughly 1/3 cup. Mix in mixture of gelatin till dissolves. Take off heat.
- Take the tart pan side. Mix the cooled pastry cream till loosen, then smear in the shell. Let

pears stand upright on the pastry cream, placing in 8 rows of 2 to 3.
- Once glaze is cool and slightly thick, place the pan in ice bath for a speedy cooling, brush pears with it. Reheat the glaze very quickly in case it gels in pan.
- Notes: Tart shell may be baked a day in advance; keep at room temperature, put cover when cool.
- Seckel pears may be poached a day in advance and cover loosely then refrigerate.
- Pastry cream may be done a day in advance and cover the surface then refrigerate.
- Assembled tart may be stored for an hour at room temperature or refrigerate for 4 hours.

Nutrition Information

262. Set It And Forget It Roast Pork Shoulder

Serving: 8 servings | Prep: | Ready in:

Ingredients

- 1/4 cup black peppercorns
- 3 tablespoons juniper berries
- 1 tablespoons coriander seeds
- 1/2 cup Diamond Crystal or 1/4 cup plus 1 1/2 tsp. Morton kosher salt
- 3 tablespoons sugar
- 1 (8–10-pound) skin-on, bone-in pork shoulder (Boston butt)
- 5 sprigs rosemary
- 10 garlic cloves, unpeeled, lightly crushed
- 2 cups dry white wine
- Cranberry sauce, cornichons, and whole grain mustard (for serving)
- A spice mill or mortar and pestle

Direction

- Prepare a mortar and pestle or a spice mill. Using either one, grind the coriander seeds, juniper berries and peppercorns until they are fine. Move them into a tiny bowl to be combined with sugar and salt.
- Get an X-Acto knife or an extremely sharp paring knife or a box cutter with a 1/3"-blade. Use either one to slice parallel lines into the skin on the pork shoulder. Keep the spacing about 3/4" away from each other.
- Make sure to slice all the way across the fat to get near as possible to the meat without cutting into it. Form a diamond shaped pattern by cutting in between the rows with a pair of kitchen shears, making sure they are 3/4" away from one another. The purpose of slicing until a crosshatch design into the fat is to allow the spices and salt to seep into the meat and for the insides to be cooked.
- Massage the spice mixture into the whole shoulder and through the cuts in fats, covering any exposed meat Try to get the spices into the fatty layer and not on the surface of the skin, where they may burn as the shoulder roasts. Utilise every single bit of the abundant spices, even though it may seem like a lot Use plastic to cover the shoulder up securely. Leave it chilling for a minimum of 3 hours up to 3 days.
- Preheat the oven to 225°F and put a rack on the lower third section. Use 2 layers of durable foil to generously line a rimmed baking sheet (be generous with the foil unless you really enjoy scrubbing pots and pans after Thanksgiving dinner).
- On the centre of the baking sheet, set the garlic and rosemary sprigs followed by a wire rack atop. Place the pork shoulder down on the rack and move it into the oven. Insert 2 cups of water and wine onto baking sheet and roast the shoulder for a 9 or 10 hours or even through the night. The ideal meat should have a very dark skin and appear to be detaching from bone.
- Without any cover at room temperature, leave the pork shoulder to rest for a minimum of 30 minutes to 5 hours or just until serving time.

- Set the oven in between the range of 350°F to 400°F and heat the roast up again for 5 to 10 minutes before serving. Let the top of the meat warm up and let the fat turn soft, but do not let it turn any more color. Place it with mustard, cornichons and cranberry sauce. Serve the dish warm.

Nutrition Information

- Calories: 973
- Protein: 67 g(133%)
- Total Fat: 69 g(107%)
- Saturated Fat: 24 g(120%)
- Sodium: 1310 mg(55%)
- Fiber: 2 g(7%)
- Total Carbohydrate: 10 g(3%)
- Cholesterol: 272 mg(91%)

263. Shellfish With Carrot Ginger Purée

Serving: Makes 4 servings | Prep: | Ready in:

Ingredients

- 1/2 pound carrots
- 3/4 teaspoon grated peeled fresh gingerroot
- 1/4 teaspoon ground cumin, or to taste
- 20 littleneck clams (about 1 3/4 pounds)
- 20 mussels (preferably cultivated; about 3/4 pound)
- 3/4 pound medium shrimp (20 to 24)
- 1/2 cup dry white wine
- 1/4 cup chopped shallot
- 1 tablespoon unsalted butter, cut into pieces
- Garnish: chopped fresh chives
- Accompaniment: 3/4 pound no-fat country-style bread, cut into 8 slices and toasted

Direction

- Peel the carrots and cut into 1/2-inch pieces crosswise.
- Boil 4 cups of salted water in a large saucepan and cook carrots for 7 minutes until tender. Reserve 2 cups of the cooking liquid and use a colander to drain the carrots. Puree the hot carrots in batches with cumin, ginger root, the cooking liquid that was reserved, and pepper and salt for the seasoning. Be careful when blending hot liquids.
- Scrub the mussels and clams and pull the beards from the mussels, if needed. If you want, you can shell and devein the shrimp.
- Boil the shallots with the wine in a 6 quart heavy kettle that has a tight-fitting lid until the wine reduces by 1/2. Turn the heat down to low and add in the butter with half the carrot puree while stirring. Add in the clams and simmer while covered, stirring, on moderate heat for 5 - 10 minutes. After 5 minutes, check every minute to transfer the open ones using a slotted spoon onto a bowl. Discard unopened clams after 10 minutes of simmering.
- Add the mussels onto the wine mixture and simmer, stirring, while covered for 3 - 8 minutes, and check on them every minute after about 3 minutes to transfer the open ones with a slotted spoon onto a bowl. Throw away any unopened mussels after 8 minutes.
- Add in the shrimp and the rest of the carrot puree onto the wine mixture and simmer while stirring, uncovered, for 3 minutes until the shrimp are just cooked through. Return the mussels and clams onto the kettle and gently stir until heated thoroughly.
- Divide the sauce and the shellfish onto 4 bowls, garnishing with chives. Serve with toast.

Nutrition Information

264. Shrimp Risotto

Serving: 10 | Prep: 15mins | Ready in:

Ingredients

- 2 pounds large shrimp in their shells
- 6 cups chicken stock
- 4 tablespoons olive oil, divided
- 3 cloves garlic, minced
- 4 tablespoons butter, divided
- 2 (12 ounce) packages Arborio rice
- 2 large shallots, diced
- 1/2 cup dry white wine
- 1 tablespoon chopped fresh rosemary
- 6 saffron threads, crumbled
- 2 cups grated Parmesan cheese
- 1 teaspoon lemon zest
- 1 teaspoon red pepper flakes

Direction

- Peel, then devein shrimp; keep shells. Heat stock in big saucepan; add shells. Cover; simmer for 30 minutes.
- Chop shrimp to bite-sized morsels. Toss with garlic and olive oil; cover, refrigerate.
- Strain stock; discard shells. On low heat, keep warm.
- Melt 2 tbsp. olive oil and 2 tbsp. butter in heavy saucepan on low heat. Add shallots; cook for 4 minutes till soft yet not brown. Add dry rice; mix for 3 minutes till every grain gets coated and begins to be translucent. Put heat on medium. Add wine; simmer and mix for 3-5 minutes till mostly evaporated.
- Put 1/2 cup warm stock into rice mixture; constantly mix for 3-5 minutes till stock is absorbed. Add saffron, another 1/2 cup stock and rosemary; mix for 3 minutes till absorbed. Repeat for 10-15 minutes with 4 extra cups of stock. Add marinated shrimp to leftover 1 cup stock, mix for 1 minute; put mixture into rice. Mix and cook for 6-8 minutes till risotto is tender but al dente.
- Mix leftover 2 tbsp. butter, red pepper flakes, lemon zest and parmesan cheese into risotto. Mix till creamy. Immediately serve in warmed bowls.

Nutrition Information

- Calories: 494 calories;
- Total Fat: 15.8
- Sodium: 850
- Total Carbohydrate: 57.9
- Cholesterol: 165
- Protein: 26.3

265. Shrimp And Leek Linguine In White Wine Sauce

Serving: Makes 4 to 6 servings | Prep: | Ready in:

Ingredients

- 1 pound small uncooked shrimp, peeled, deveined, shells reserved
- 1 3/4 cups water
- 6 tablespoons olive oil
- 2 large garlic cloves, minced
- 2 1/2 cups thinly sliced leeks (white and pale green parts only from about 2 large)
- 1/4 cup thinly sliced stemmed drained peperoncini (about 4 whole)
- 3 tablespoons chopped fresh oregano
- 2 teaspoons minced lemon peel
- 1/4 cup dry white wine
- 2 tablespoons fresh lemon juice
- 1 pound linguine
- Chopped fresh parsley

Direction

- In a medium saucepan, put shrimp shells. Mix in a liberal pinch of salt and 1 3/4 cups water. Boil on medium high heat; put a cover on and lower heat to medium low. Simmer for 15 minutes till it reduces to 1 cup liquid. Strain into a measuring cup; press on shells to remove as much liquid as you can.
- Meanwhile, heat 3 tbsp. oil on medium high heat in big heavy skillet. Add shrimp; sauté for 2 minutes till opaque. Put into medium bowl using slotted spoon. Lower heat to low. Put

leftover 3 tbsp. oil in same skillet. Add garlic; sauté for 1 minute till soft. Mix in lemon peel, oregano, pepperoncini and leeks; cover. Cook for 3 minutes till leeks are soft. Uncover; add shrimp-shell liquid, lemon juice and wine. Put heat on high; boil for 2 minutes till reduced by half. Take off from heat.

- Cook pasta, occasionally mixing, in a big pot with boiling salted water till tender yet firm to chew. Drain; keep 1 cup of cooking liquid. Put shrimp and pasta in skillet with sauce; toss to coat. If needed, add sufficient amount of reserved cooking liquid to moisten. Season with pepper and salt to taste. Put into big bowl; use parsley to garnish.

Nutrition Information

- Calories: 743
- Total Carbohydrate: 99 g(33%)
- Cholesterol: 143 mg(48%)
- Protein: 32 g(64%)
- Total Fat: 24 g(36%)
- Saturated Fat: 4 g(18%)
- Sodium: 789 mg(33%)
- Fiber: 7 g(28%)

266. Shrimp And Mushroom Quinoa Risotto

Serving: Makes 8 main-course servings | Prep: | Ready in:

Ingredients

- 8 cups cold water
- 2 lb small hard-shell clams (2 to 2 1/2 inches in diameter)
- 1 celery rib, coarsely chopped
- 1 large carrot, coarsely chopped
- 1/2 large red onion, coarsely chopped
- 1 Turkish or 1/2 California bay leaf
- 1/4 teaspoon black pepper
- 2 cups quinoa (12 ounces)
- 2 lb medium shrimp in shell (31 to 35 per pound), peeled and deveined
- 1 1/2 teaspoons salt
- 1/3 cup vegetable oil
- 1 tablespoon achiote (annatto) seeds
- 1/2 stick (1/4 cup) unsalted butter
- 1/2 teaspoon black pepper
- 1/2 lb cremini or button mushrooms, trimmed and sliced (3/4 inch thick; 3 cups)
- 1/2 lb oyster mushrooms, trimmed and large caps halved lengthwise (2 3/4 cups)
- 1 (5- to 6-oz) portabella mushroom cap, sliced (1/4 inch thick)
- 2 tablespoons olive oil
- 1/2 large red onion, thinly sliced
- 2 garlic cloves, thinly sliced
- 2 tablespoons bottled aj amarillo purée
- 1 cup dry white wine
- 3/4 teaspoon crumbled saffron threads
- 1/2 cup heavy cream
- 1/4 lb finely grated Parmigiano-Reggiano (2 cups)
- 3 tablespoons chopped fresh basil

Direction

- Clam broth: Simmer all broth ingredients in 4-6-qt. heavy pot, partially covered, for 30 minutes. Through fine-mesh sieve, pour; discard solids. Put broth into 3-qt. heavy saucepan; cover.
- Quinoa: In 3 changes of the cold water in bowl, wash quinoa; drain between changes of water in fine-mesh sieve. Put quinoa in bowl.
- Pat dry shrimp; sprinkle 1 tsp. salt.
- Heat achiote seeds and vegetable oil in 1 1/2-2-qt. heavy saucepan on low heat for 10 minutes till oil is bright yellow. Through sieve, put oil into 4-6-qt. cleaned heavy pot; discard seeds.
- Put 1 tbsp. butter in oil in pot; heat till foam subsides on medium high heat. Cook 1/4 tsp. pepper and shrimp, mixing, for 3-5 minutes till shrimp nearly cook through. Use a slotted spoon to put into big bowl; don't clean pot.
- Heat 2 tbsp. butter till foam subsides in pot on medium heat; cook 1/2 tsp. salt, leftover 1/4

tsp. pepper and mushrooms, mixing, scraping browned bits up from bottom of pot, for 5 minutes till mushrooms exude liquid and soften. Add 1/2 cup water if mushrooms don't exude liquid to aid scraping brown bits up. Put mushrooms with liquid in shrimp. Don't clean pot.

- Heat leftover 1 tbsp. butter and olive oil till foam subsides in pot on medium heat; cook leftover 1/2 tsp. salt, garlic and onion, occasionally mixing, for 5 minutes till onion is soft. Add aj Amarillo and quinoa; cook, mixing, for 5 minutes. Add saffron and wine; simmer briskly, constantly mixing, for 5 minutes till wine is absorbed.
- Meanwhile, simmer clam broth; mix. Keep at bare simmer.
- Put 1/2 cup broth in quinoa; briskly simmer, constantly mixing, till broth is absorbed. Keep simmering, adding 1/2 cup hot broth at a time, frequently mixing quinoa, letting every addition get absorbed before adding next, for 30 minutes total till germs separate from grains and quinoa is tender. You'll have leftover broth.
- Mix cream into risotto; simmer on medium heat. Add shrimp mixture with juice; cook, mixing, for 1-2 minutes till shrimp just cook through. Take off heat. Mix in 2 tbsp. basil and cheese; season with pepper and salt. Sprinkle leftover 1 tbsp. basil; serve.

Nutrition Information

- Calories: 710
- Cholesterol: 232 mg(77%)
- Protein: 51 g(103%)
- Total Fat: 36 g(56%)
- Saturated Fat: 14 g(68%)
- Sodium: 1750 mg(73%)
- Fiber: 5 g(20%)
- Total Carbohydrate: 41 g(14%)

267. Shrimp And Pea Risotto

Serving: Makes 4 main-course servings | Prep: | Ready in:

Ingredients

- 3/4 lb medium shrimp in shell (31 to 35 per lb), peeled, deveined, and shells reserved
- 7 cups water
- 1 1/4 teaspoons salt
- 1 cup thawed frozen baby peas (5 oz)
- 1/4 cup chopped fresh chives
- 1 teaspoon finely grated fresh lemon zest
- 1/2 teaspoon black pepper
- 1 medium onion, finely chopped
- 3 tablespoons unsalted butter
- 1 1/3 cups Arborio rice (9 oz)
- 3/4 cup dry white wine

Direction

- Simmer 7 cups water and shrimp shells; keep, covered, at bare simmer.
- Toss 1/2 tsp. salt and shrimp; chill, covered.
- Toss pepper, zest, chives and peas in a bowl.
- Cook the onion with 3/4 tsp. salt in butter in 4-5-qt. wide heavy pot on medium low heat, mixing, for 3-5 minutes till soft.
- Add rice; cook, mixing, for 2 minutes. Put heat on medium. Add wine; cook, mixing, for 1 minute. Mix in 1/2 cup of simmering shrimp broth (put through sieve then throw shells); cook, constantly mixing, keeping at strong simmer, till most broth is absorbed. Keep cooking, add 1/2 cup broth at a time, constantly mixing and letting every addition get absorbed before adding next, for 18 minutes total till rice looks creamy and is tender yet till al dente. Add pea mixture and shrimp; cook, mixing, adding more broth as needed, for 3-5 minutes till shrimp cooks through. You might have leftover broth. Season with salt; immediately serve.

Nutrition Information

- Calories: 425
- Fiber: 4 g(17%)
- Total Carbohydrate: 59 g(20%)
- Cholesterol: 130 mg(43%)
- Protein: 18 g(36%)
- Total Fat: 10 g(16%)
- Saturated Fat: 6 g(29%)
- Sodium: 1326 mg(55%)

268. Shrimp With Orange Dust

Serving: Makes 4 first-course servings | Prep: | Ready in:

Ingredients

- 3/4 cup loosely packed fresh basil leaves plus 1/2 cup micro-basil or small basil leaves
- 1/4 cup grapeseed oil
- 1 lemon, halved
- 4 large artichokes (12 ounces each)
- 1 medium onion, thinly sliced
- 2 tablespoons olive oil
- 1 1/2 cups dry white wine
- 16 extra-large (16 to 20 per pound) shrimp in shell without heads, peeled and deveined
- 1/4 teaspoon salt
- 1/8 teaspoon cayenne
- 1 tablespoon plus 2 teaspoons orange dust plus additional to taste
- 3 tablespoons unsalted butter
- 8 ounces arugula, coarse stems discarded
- 1 1/2 tablespoons fresh lemon juice

Direction

- Prepare basil oil: in 2-quart saucepan with salted boiling water, let 3/4 cup basil blanch for 2 minutes, then use sieve to strain and dunk in a bowl with ice water to halt the cooking. Let basil drain once more and squeeze out extra liquid. Use blender to purée grapeseed oil and basil for 2 minutes. Put the mixture in airtight container and refrigerate for 8 hours to half a day. Pass through an extremely fine sieve right to small bowl, avoid pressing on solids.
- Prep artichokes: juice a half of lemon into big bowl with water, then put the squeezed half into water.
- Using a serrated knife, slice off an-inch top of an artichoke, at opposing end, keeping the stem intact. Lean the outer leaves back till they snap off near to the base, then get rid of a few additional layers in exactly the same manner till you reach light yellow leaves that has light green tips.
- Use sharp knife to slice the rest of the leaves flush with top of artichoke base, then cut off fibrous, dark green potions from sides and base of artichoke. Rub the rest of lemon half on cut surfaces. Slice quarter-inch off stem to reveal the inner core. Clip stem sides, keep intact, down into light inner core. Rub same lemon half on cut surfaces. Slice artichoke making four wedges, then trim any left fuzzy choke and purple leaves and put wedges of artichoke to lemon water. Prep leftover 3 artichokes in exactly the same manner.
- In a heavy, 12-inch skillet, cook onion in olive oil on medium heat for 5 minutes, mixing from time to time, till softened. Strain the artichokes and use paper towels to blot dry. Place artichokes on top of onion, then pour in wine and simmer with cover for 30 to 40 minutes, till artichokes become tender. Use a slotted spoon to turn the mixture onto a big bowl and cover to retain warmth.
- Cook the shrimp and put the dish together: blot dry the shrimp and scatter cayenne, a tablespoon of orange dust and salt over. In cleaned skillet, heat the butter on medium high heat till froth settles, then let shrimp cook for 2 minutes per side, till just cooked completely.
- Toss leftover 2 teaspoons of orange dust, lemon juice, leftover half cup of micro-basil and arugula along with mixture of artichoke and add salt to season. Distribute mixture between 4 plates and surround salad with shrimp. Sprinkle some basil oil on every serving and scatter more orange dust over.

Nutrition Information

- Calories: 414
- Protein: 10 g(20%)
- Total Fat: 30 g(46%)
- Saturated Fat: 8 g(39%)
- Sodium: 430 mg(18%)
- Fiber: 9 g(37%)
- Total Carbohydrate: 22 g(7%)
- Cholesterol: 53 mg(18%)

269. Skillet Stuffing With Italian Sausage And Wild Mushrooms

Serving: 8 servings | Prep: 30mins | Ready in:

Ingredients

- 2 crusty white demi baguettes (about 10 1/2 ounces), cut into 3/4" cubes (about 8 cups cubes)
- 2 tablespoons extra-virgin olive oil, divided
- 1/2 pound hot or sweet Italian sausage, casings removed
- 1 medium onion, chopped
- 8 ounces wild mushrooms, cut into large pieces
- 2 tablespoons finely chopped sage
- 1 cup dry white wine
- 2 large eggs
- 1 1/4 cups low-sodium chicken broth
- 1 1/2 ounces finely grated Parmesan or Pecorino (about 1/2 cup)
- 1 tablespoon Dijon mustard
- 1 1/4 teaspoons kosher salt
- 1 teaspoon freshly ground black pepper

Direction

- Preheat an oven to 425°F. On the rimmed baking sheet, toast bread for 10 minutes till dry; cool. Lower oven temperature to about 375°F.
- Meanwhile, in a 12-in. cast-iron skillet, heat 1 tbsp. oil over medium high heat. Add sausage; cook for 7 minutes till brown, using a spatula to break into pieces. Add sage, mushrooms and onion; cook for 8-10 minutes till well browned, occasionally mixing. Add wine; cook till reduced by half, occasionally mixing. Slightly cool.
- Whisk pepper, salt, mustard, cheese, broth and eggs in a big bowl. Add sausage mixture; put aside skillet and bread. Toss to mix. Allow to sit for 5 minutes; toss. Pack into the skillet.
- Bake stuffing for 20 minutes till cooked through and lightly browned on top.
- Demi baguettes are best for this recipe, but you may use 1 white baguette with a weight of 10 1/2-oz.

Nutrition Information

- Calories: 299
- Cholesterol: 60 mg(20%)
- Protein: 16 g(31%)
- Total Fat: 11 g(16%)
- Saturated Fat: 3 g(17%)
- Sodium: 614 mg(26%)
- Fiber: 3 g(13%)
- Total Carbohydrate: 33 g(11%)

270. Slow Cooked Pork Shoulder With Braised White Beans

Serving: 4 servings | Prep: | Ready in:

Ingredients

- 1 (6-lb.) bone-in pork shoulder (Boston butt), fat cap trimmed to 1/4 inch
- 3 tablespoons Diamond Crystal or 5 teaspoons Morton kosher salt, plus more
- 8 fresh bay leaves, divided

- 1/4 cup sage leaves, plus 4 large sprigs
- 4 tablespoons olive oil, divided
- 1 head of garlic, halved crosswise
- 9 juniper berries
- 4 black peppercorns
- 3 cups dry white wine
- 1/4 cup best-quality red wine vinegar
- 1 large beefsteak tomato, halved crosswise
- 1 head of garlic, halved crosswise
- 4 large sprigs sage
- 2 cups coco nano or cannellini (white kidney) beans, soaked overnight, drained
- 2 tablespoons plus 1/4 cup olive oil
- Kosher salt
- 2 bunches mature spinach, tough stems removed
- Kosher salt
- 2 tablespoons olive oil, plus more for drizzling
- 4 garlic cloves, thinly sliced
- Flaky sea salt

Direction

- Pork: Sprinkle 3 tablespoons or 5 teaspoons salt on the entire pork. Tear apart quarter cup of sage leaves and four bay leaves to make small pieces and spread on pork. Put pork on wire rack place in a rimmed baking sheet and use plastic wrap to loosely cover; refrigerate for 12 hours.
- Rest pork for an hour at room temperature, for an even cooking.
- Preheat the oven to 450°F. Heat in a heavy, big pot 2 tablespoons of oil on moderately-high. Let pork cook for 15 to 20 minutes, flipping from time to time, till browned on each side. Turn pork onto a big plate.
- Take pot off heat and drain any fat. Throw any leaves in pot and fat; wipe clean the pot. Put to pot the leftover 2 tablespoons oil including leftover 4 bay leaves, sage sprigs, peppercorns, juniper berries and garlic. Cook for a minute on low heat till garlic barely begins to brown on edges. Add in vinegar and wine. Put pork back to pot, fat side facing up, and use parchment paper to cover, folding edges down surrounding pork sides, this will keep it from drying. Use a lid to cover the pot, turn onto oven, and let pork cook for half an hour. Lower oven heat to 300° and cook for 2 1/2 to 3 hours, flipping pork after every half an hour or longer and putting in a splash of water in case braising liquid is cooking down too fast, till meat is extremely tender and falling off bone.
- Rest pork till cool enough to hold. Take bones; throw. Pull meat apart to make 2-inch-3-inch pieces, getting rid of any extra fat, it must shred very effortlessly yet remain together in pieces. Turn the meat onto a big saucepan and drain braising liquid on top; throw the solids. Keep warm with cover on as low heat as possible till set to serve.
- Beans: mix in a big pot the 2 tablespoons oil, beans, sage, garlic and tomato. Add in cold water to soak by 1 1/2 inches and simmer on moderate heat, scooping froth from top as necessary. Lower the heat, making liquid at an extremely slow simmer; cook for 35 to 45 minutes, till beans are nearly tender yet remain starchy a bit in middles, cooked approximately 75 percent. While beans are cooking, preheat the oven to 300°F.
- Take beans off heat; add a few liberal pinches of salt to season and put in leftover quarter cup of oil. Turn into oven and bake for 15 to 25 minutes, without moving the beans for a film to form on top, till tender. Complete the beans cooking in oven to guarantee an even cooking and creaminess. Switch oven off and keep beans in oven to retain warmth till set to serve.
- Greens and assembly: in a big pot with salted boiling water, let spinach cook in 2 batches for 2 minutes, till no bite left and tender. Use colander to strain and cool a bit, then press out extra water.
- In medium size skillet, heat 2 tablespoons of oil on moderate and let garlic cook for a minute, mixing, till soft and just golden. Put in the spinach and mix till leaves are barely coated with oil and warm completely.
- To serve, scoop a bit cooking liquid and beans to plates. Top beans with a few pork pieces

and spinach on. Sprinkle oil and scatter sea salt over.
- Beans may be done a day in advance. Cool down in liquid; chill with cover. Rewarm slowly prior to serving.

Nutrition Information

- Calories: 2157
- Cholesterol: 362 mg(121%)
- Protein: 120 g(240%)
- Total Fat: 138 g(213%)
- Saturated Fat: 40 g(200%)
- Sodium: 2826 mg(118%)
- Fiber: 41 g(164%)
- Total Carbohydrate: 95 g(32%)

271. Sluggers' Strawberry Slushies

Serving: Makes 6 servings | Prep: 10mins | Ready in:

Ingredients

- 2 cups hulled strawberries
- 1 750 milliliter bottle dry Riesling
- 1 tablespoon fresh lemon juice
- 2 tablespoons sugar

Direction

- In a food processor, blend lemon juice, sugar, Riesling, and strawberries until liquefied. Follow the manufacturer's directions on how to process the ice cream. Distribute among cups and serve it immediately with straws. You can also transfer it into a container and let it freeze.

Nutrition Information

272. Smoked Salmon Benedict

Serving: Makes 6 servings | Prep: | Ready in:

Ingredients

- 3 tablespoons minced shallots
- 2 teaspoons dry mustard
- 1 1/2 cups dry white wine
- 3/4 cup whipping cream
- 3 tablespoons white wine vinegar
- 12 large eggs
- 6 3/4-inch-thick slices brioche loaf or egg bread, lightly toasted, each slice cut in half on diagonal
- 8 ounces thinly sliced smoked salmon (not lox)
- 3 large egg yolks
- 3 tablespoons chopped fresh dill
- Fresh dill sprigs (optional)

Direction

- In medium saucepan, mix mustard and shallots. Whisk wine in gradually; boil on high heat for 10 minutes, whisking often, till mixture reduces to 1/2 cup. Whisk cream in. Season with pepper and salt. You can make this a day ahead, chilled and covered.
- Use cold water to fill a big bowl. Boil a big skillet with water; add vinegar. Lower heat to medium low. 6 whole eggs at one time, crack eggs open. Put into simmering water. Cook for 3 minutes till whites set. 1 at a time, transfer 1 egg with a slotted spoon into cold water. Put skillet with vinegar water aside. You can make this an hour ahead, standing at room temperature.
- On each of the 6 plates, put 2 toast triangles. Put salmon on top. Simmer vinegar water. Put cream sauce to the double broiler's top above simmering water. In cream sauce, whisk 3 raw egg yolks in. Constantly whisk till an inserted instant-read thermometer into sauce reads 160°F and sauce thickens for 4 minutes. Take off heat. Put chopped dill in; whisk for a minute. 1 at a time, gently put poached eggs with a slotted spoon from bowl with cold water into skillet with simmering vinegar

water. Cook eggs for 30 seconds till warm. Transfer a poached egg with a slotted spoon onto every toast triangle. Spoon the sauce on top. If desired, garnish with dill sprigs.

Nutrition Information

- Calories: 456
- Fiber: 1 g(5%)
- Total Carbohydrate: 23 g(8%)
- Cholesterol: 526 mg(175%)
- Protein: 26 g(51%)
- Total Fat: 25 g(39%)
- Saturated Fat: 11 g(54%)
- Sodium: 566 mg(24%)

273. Smoked Salmon Pasta Verde

Serving: Makes 4 to 6 servings | Prep: | Ready in:

Ingredients

- 1 1/2 cups dry white wine
- 3/4 cup crème fraîche or sour cream
- 12 ounces dried fettuccine
- 8 ounces small sugar snap peas (about 2 cups), strings removed, or thawed frozen shelled edamame
- 1 cup thinly sliced green onions (about 5)
- 1/3 cup chopped fresh Italian parsley
- 2 tablespoons chopped fresh thyme
- 4 ounces smoked salmon, cut crosswise into 1/4-inch strips

Direction

- In medium size saucepan, boil the wine for 8 minutes, till cooked down to 3/4 cup. Take wine off heat and mix crème fraîche in.
- Meantime, in big pot with salted boiling water, let pasta cook till nearly tender yet remain firm to bite, mixing from time to time. Put to same pot with the edamame or sugar snap peas and cook for 2 minutes, till peas are tender-crisp. Strain peas and pasta, then put back to pot.
- Top peas and pasta with crème fraîche mixture. Put in the parsley, thyme and green onions; toss till coated. Put in salmon; toss once more. Add pepper and salt to season the pasta. Distribute pasta between plates to serve.

Nutrition Information

- Calories: 558
- Sodium: 229 mg(10%)
- Fiber: 7 g(28%)
- Total Carbohydrate: 75 g(25%)
- Cholesterol: 28 mg(9%)
- Protein: 24 g(48%)
- Total Fat: 14 g(21%)
- Saturated Fat: 6 g(29%)

274. Sole Piccata With Grapes And Capers

Serving: Makes 4 servings | Prep: | Ready in:

Ingredients

- 2 tablespoons olive oil
- 4 Dover sole or petrale sole fillets
- All purpose flour
- 1/2 cup seedless red grapes, cut in half
- 1/4 cup white grape juice
- 1/4 cup dry white wine
- 2 tablespoons (1/4 stick) butter
- 1 tablespoon drained capers
- 1 tablespoon chopped fresh parsley

Direction

- In nonstick, big skillet, heat the oil on moderately-high heat. Scatter pepper and salt on fish; flour each side. Put into skillet; cook for 2 minutes on each side, till browned and barely opaque in the middle. Turn the fish onto a platter. Put to same skillet with butter, wine, grape juice and grapes. Boil the mixture, mixing up some browned bits. Put in parsley and capers. Let sauce simmer for 3 minutes, till thickened partially. Season with pepper and salt to taste. Top fish with sauce.

Nutrition Information

275. Spaghetti With Chorizo And Almonds

Serving: Makes 4 servings | Prep: 30mins | Ready in:

Ingredients

- 1 1/2 cups reduced-sodium chicken broth
- 1 1/2 cups water
- 1/2 cup dry white wine
- 1/2 teaspoon crumbled saffron thoureads
- 2 tablespoons extra-virgin olive oil plus additional for drizzling
- 6 garlic cloves, thinly sliced
- 4 ounces Spanish chorizo (cured spiced pork sausage; not hot), cut into 1/2-inch pieces
- 2 tablespoons unsalted butter, cut into pieces
- 1 medium onion, finely chopped
- 12 ounces fideos (dried coiled vermicelli noodles) or angel-hair pasta or thin spaghetti, broken into 2-inch lengths
- 1 (14- to 19-ounce) can chickpeas, rinsed and drained
- 1/2 cup chopped flat-leaf parsley
- 1/2 cup sliced almonds with skins, toasted

Direction

- Preparation: In a small saucepan, combine 1/2 teaspoon salt, saffron, wine, water, and broth then bring to a boil and lower the heat then maintain at a bare simmer.
- In a 5- to 6-qt heavy pot over medium-high heat, put oil until it shimmers then add garlic and stir-fry for about 30 seconds until pale golden. Use a slotted spoon to move and drain onto paper towels. Put in chorizo and stir-fry for about 3 minutes until golden brown. Use a slotted spoon to place onto paper towels with the garlic. Put butter to the pot and add onion then stir-fry for about 5 minutes until golden, and put in pasta then stir-fry for about 4 minutes, using a wooden spoon to break up fideos, until golden. Pour in broth mixture then cook for about 6 minutes, covered, until all liquid is soaked up. Mix in pepper and salt to taste, parsley, garlic, chorizo, and chickpeas.
- Sprinkle almonds over the pasta and dot with oil to serve.

Nutrition Information

- Calories: 826
- Total Carbohydrate: 98 g(33%)
- Cholesterol: 40 mg(13%)
- Protein: 31 g(61%)
- Total Fat: 34 g(52%)
- Saturated Fat: 10 g(48%)
- Sodium: 862 mg(36%)
- Fiber: 12 g(50%)

276. Spaghetti With Fresh Clams, Parsley, And Lemon

Serving: Makes 4 servings | Prep: | Ready in:

Ingredients

- 1/2 cup extra-virgin olive oil
- 8 garlic cloves, thinly sliced
- 3 pounds fresh Manila clams or small littleneck clams, scrubbed
- 1/4 cup plus 2 tablespoons chopped fresh Italian parsley
- 1/2 cup dry white wine
- 1/4 cup fresh lemon juice
- 1 pound spaghetti

Direction

- In big, heavy pot, heat the oil on moderately-high heat. Put in and sauté sliced garlic for a minute, till pale brown. Put in quarter cup of chopped Italian parsley and clams; mix for 2 minutes. Pour in wine; let simmer for 2 minutes. Put in fresh lemon juice. Simmer with cover for 6 minutes, till clams open, throw any that remain closed.
- Meantime, in big pot with salted boiling water, let pasta cook till just tender yet remain firm to bite. Strain. Put to mixture of clam with pasta and toss till coated. Season with pepper and salt to taste. Turn onto a big bowl. Scatter with leftover 2 tablespoons of parsley to serve.

Nutrition Information

- Calories: 981
- Sodium: 2057 mg(86%)
- Fiber: 4 g(16%)
- Total Carbohydrate: 101 g(34%)
- Cholesterol: 102 mg(34%)
- Protein: 65 g(131%)
- Total Fat: 32 g(49%)
- Saturated Fat: 5 g(23%)

277. Spaghetti With Lobster And Mussels

Serving: Serves 12 | Prep: | Ready in:

Ingredients

- 1 cup dry white wine
- 1 cup water
- two 1 1/2-pound live lobsters
- 1 pound spaghetti
- 4 cups spicy tomato sauce
- 1 pound mussels (preferably cultivated), scrubbed well and beards pulled off
- 2 tablespoons minced fresh parsley leaves (wash and dry before mincing)

Direction

- Boil water and wine in a big kettle. Put in lobsters and cook for 3 minutes, with cover. They will be cooked slightly. Use tongs to turn the lobsters onto a big bowl and let cooking liquid boil till cooked down to approximately 1/3 cup.
- Remove the claws and break claws on a side using heavy knife flat side. Slice tails off and slice every tail crosswise to make 4 portions, slicing through the shell and throwing the dark intestinal vein. Cut the body sections in half and throw the head sacs. Put any roe and tomalley aside if wished. Lobsters can be prepped up to this portion 4 hours in advance and refrigerate with cover.
- Boil 5 quarts of salted water in 6-quart kettle for spaghetti.
- Simmer reserved roe and tomalley if using, cooking liquid of lobster and tomato sauce in a heavy, 5-quart kettle, mixing. Put in bodies and claws and simmer for 5 minutes, with cover, or till meat from claw is barely cooked completely. Turn the claws onto big bowl using tongs and cover to retain warmth.
- Put the pieces of tail into sauce and simmer for 3 to 4 minutes, with cover, or till barely cooked completely. Turn pieces of tail onto bowl using tongs and cover to retain warmth. Take the lobster bodies and throw.
- Put mussels into sauce and simmer for 3 to 8 minutes, with cover, monitoring mussels every minute or longer and turning once opened onto bowl using tongs. Cover to retain mussels' warmth. Throw any mussels that remain closed 8 minutes after. Add pepper and salt to season sauce and cover to retain warmth.
- Meanwhile, in boiling water, let spaghetti cook till al dente and strain using colander. Put lobster, mussels and spaghetti into sauce and heat on medium heat till heated completely, mixing and tossing till spaghetti is thoroughly coated in sauce.
- Turn the seafood and spaghetti on a big large platter and scatter parsley over.

Nutrition Information

- Calories: 290
- Protein: 29 g(58%)
- Total Fat: 3 g(4%)
- Saturated Fat: 1 g(3%)
- Sodium: 979 mg(41%)
- Fiber: 2 g(10%)
- Total Carbohydrate: 34 g(11%)
- Cholesterol: 155 mg(52%)

278. Spanish Style Rice With Chicken And Seafood (Riz À La Valencienne)

Serving: Makes 6 servings | Prep: | Ready in:

Ingredients

- 1 lemon, halved
- 3 medium artichokes or 1 (10-ounce) box frozen artichoke hearts, thawed
- pound green beans, trimmed and cut into 3-inch pieces
- 1 1/2 dozen littleneck clams (1 1/2 to 2 inches in diameter), scrubbed
- 1 1/2 dozen mussels (preferably cultivated), scrubbed and beards removed
- 1/2 cup dry white wine
- 1 (3- to 3 1/2-pound) chicken, cut into 12 pieces
- 4 tablespoons olive oil
- 1 large onion, chopped
- 2 garlic cloves, minced
- 2 tablespoons paprika (preferably Spanish)
- 2 cups medium-grain rice
- 1 (14 1/2-ounce) can diced tomatoes, drained
- 1 3/4 cups chicken broth
- 2 red bell peppers, cut into 1/4-inch-thick strips
- a 15 3/4- by 2 3/4-inch paella pan

Direction

- Into a bowl of cold water, juice 1 half of lemon. Slice off and throw stems of a whole artichoke and slice off top 1 1/2 inches of the leaves. Lean back outside leaves till they detached close to base and get rid of few additional layers of leaves in exactly the same way till showing leaves are light green at top and yellow at bottom. Using a sharp paring knife, clip fibrous deep green areas from sides and base, then slice artichoke in 4 portions lengthwise. Rub another half of lemon on cut surfaces, and into the water, put the artichoke. Clip leftover artichokes in exactly the same way.
- Boil a big pot of salted water and let fresh artichokes simmer for 10 to 12 minutes till just soft. Avoid cooking thawed artichokes. Using a slotted spoon, put to paper towels to let drain. Once cool enough to handle, using a spoon, scoop out choke.
- In same pot of boiling salted water, let the beans cook for 4 minutes till crisp-tender. Let drain in colander, then to end cooking, wash under running cold water. Pat dry.
- In a big heavy pot over moderately -high heat, cook mussels and clams in wine with cover for 4 to 10 minutes, mixing from time to time, monitoring shellfish often 4 minutes later and putting to bowl as they open, mussels will open first then the clams. Throw any mussels that remain closed 8 minutes later and any close clams 10 minutes after. Cover to retain warmth. Through a fine paper-towel-lined sieve, pour the shellfish cooking liquid into a big measure glass and put sufficient water to measure 2 cups.
- Pat dry the chicken and put pepper and salt to season. In paella pan over moderately -high heat, heat 1 1/2 tablespoons of oil till hot yet not smoking, then thoroughly brown chicken on all sides for 15 minutes. Put to plate using slotted spoon.
- Preheat the oven to 400°F.
- In pan over moderate heat, let the onion cook in 1 1/2 tablespoons of oil for 6 minutes,

mixing, till softened. Put paprika and garlic and let cook for 2 minutes till aromatic. Put rice and allow to cook for a minute, mixing, then mix in the tomatoes.
- Mix in chicken with juices, chicken broth and seafood cooking liquid and boil over high heat. Let boil for 15 minutes, slowly mixing and often rotating the pan, till rice has soaked in majority of the liquid and spoon leaves a hollow showing base of pan once pulled through the rice.
- Take off pan from the heat and into the rice, push mussels and clams. Let the riz bake in center of the oven without cover for 10 minutes, till chicken is cooked completely, liquid is soaked in and a crust creates surrounding edge of pan.
- Meanwhile, in a big nonstick skillet over moderately-high heat, heat leftover tablespoon of oil till hot yet not smoking, then sauté bell peppers for 5 minutes till crisp-tender. Put artichokes cooked fresh or thawed and green beans and sauté just till heated through. Add pepper and salt to season.
- Into riz, insert the vegetables and let sit for 10 minutes prior serving.

Nutrition Information

- Calories: 828
- Cholesterol: 153 mg(51%)
- Protein: 52 g(105%)
- Total Fat: 37 g(57%)
- Saturated Fat: 9 g(45%)
- Sodium: 645 mg(27%)
- Fiber: 7 g(27%)
- Total Carbohydrate: 67 g(22%)

279. Spice Rubbed Chicken Breasts With Lemon Shallot Sauce

Serving: Makes 8 servings | Prep: | Ready in:

Ingredients

- 1 teaspoon salt
- 1 teaspoon ground black pepper
- 3/4 teaspoon ground allspice
- 8 skinless boneless chicken breast halves
- 8 tablespoons olive oil
- 1/2 cup dry white wine
- 1 cup canned low-salt chicken broth
- 3 tablespoons fresh lemon juice
- 2 teaspoons grated lemon peel
- 2 tablespoons minced shallots
- 1 teaspoon chopped fresh thyme
- 4 tablespoons chopped fresh parsley

Direction

- In a small bowl, mix 1/2 tsp. of allspice, salt, and pepper. Rub both sides of the chicken using this spice mixture. Put 1 tbsp. of oil in each of the 2 large nonstick skillets and heat each over medium-high. Distribute the chicken among the 2 skillets. Cook each side for 4 minutes until cooked through. Transfer the cooked chicken into the work surface. Use a foil to tent to keep them warm. Pour 1/4 cup of wine into each skillet. Let them boil while scraping all the browned bits up. Mix the wine from the other skillet in one. Mix in 1 tbsp. of lemon juice, lemon peel, and broth. Boil the mixture for 5 minutes until the mixture is reduced to 1/2 cup. Mix in 6 tbsp. of oil, 1/4 tsp. of allspice, 2 tbsp. of lemon juice, shallots, and thyme. Season the mixture with salt and pepper. Slice the chicken crosswise into 1/2-inch thick pieces.
- Distribute the chicken among the plates and drizzle each with sauce. Sprinkle them with parsley.

Nutrition Information

- Calories: 241
- Total Fat: 16 g(25%)
- Saturated Fat: 2 g(12%)
- Sodium: 341 mg(14%)
- Fiber: 0 g(1%)

- Total Carbohydrate: 2 g(1%)
- Cholesterol: 64 mg(21%)
- Protein: 20 g(41%)

280. Spiced Fruit Compote

Serving: Makes 8 servings | Prep: | Ready in:

Ingredients

- 1 750-ml bottle Vin du Glacier wine or Essencia (orange Muscat wine)
- 2/3 cup sugar
- 1/2 cup water
- 1 cinnamon stick, broken in half
- 5 whole cloves
- 2 8-ounce firm but ripe pears, peeled, halved, cored, each half cut into 4 wedges
- 18 dried Calimyrna figs, quartered
- 3/4 cup dried apricots, halved
- 8 dried pear halves, each cut into 3 wedges

Direction

- In a big saucepan, stir the first five ingredients together on moderate heat until sugar is dissolved. Put in remaining ingredients and simmer for 15 minutes, until fruit is softened. Turn fruit to bowl with a slotted spoon. Boil syrup in pan for 7 minutes, until reduced to 1/2 cup, then pour over fruit. Allow to cool, then cover and refrigerate for 3 hours, until cold. (Can be prepared 3 days in advance, keep chilled.)

Nutrition Information

- Calories: 335
- Saturated Fat: 0 g(0%)
- Sodium: 10 mg(0%)
- Fiber: 7 g(30%)
- Total Carbohydrate: 70 g(23%)
- Protein: 2 g(4%)
- Total Fat: 1 g(1%)

281. Spiced Orange Wine

Serving: Makes 2 (750-ml) bottles | Prep: 15mins | Ready in:

Ingredients

- 2 (750-ml) bottles dry white wine
- 1/2 cup sugar
- 1/4 cup orange liqueur such as Grand Marnier
- 1/4 cup Pernod
- 2 whole cloves
- 4 Turkish or 2 California bay leaves
- 2 navel oranges

Direction

- Boil all ingredients but oranges, mixing till sugar dissolves. Put corks and wine bottles aside.
- In a continuous spiral with vegetable peeler, remove zest from orange; use a paring knife to cut off white pith. Put oranges aside for another time; divide zest to empty wine bottles.
- Use orange wine to fill bottles; cool for 1 hour, uncorked.
- Cork bottles; chill for 4 hours.

Nutrition Information

- Calories: 1006
- Total Fat: 0 g(1%)
- Saturated Fat: 0 g(0%)
- Sodium: 40 mg(2%)
- Fiber: 3 g(14%)
- Total Carbohydrate: 88 g(29%)
- Protein: 2 g(4%)

282. Spiced Pear Butter

Serving: 40 | Prep: 30mins | Ready in:

Ingredients

- 4 pounds ripe pears - unpeeled, quartered, and cored
- 1/2 cup water
- 1 1/2 cups agave nectar
- 1/3 cup fresh lemon juice
- 1 tablespoon orange zest
- 1 teaspoon vanilla extract
- 1/2 teaspoon ground cinnamon
- 1/4 teaspoon ground nutmeg
- 1/8 teaspoon ground cloves
- 1/8 teaspoon allspice

Direction

- In a big saucepan on medium heat, place 1/2 cup water and pears. Cook 20 minutes until softened. Move pears to a food processor or a blender and puree until smooth yet not liquefied.
- Bring the pear puree back to saucepan. Put in allspice, cloves, nutmeg, cinnamon, vanilla extract, orange zest, lemon juice, and agave nectar. Decrease to medium-low heat. Allow pear butter to simmer 70-90 minutes, mixing occasionally, until thickened.
- Rinse and wash six 1/2-pint jars and their rings and lids; place rings and jars on a rack to dry. Submerge lids into a dish of boiling water.
- Fill water in a big canning pot. Heat to a boil; cover the pot and keep simmering.
- With a canning funnel and ladle, pour hot pear butter into the dry jars to fill 1/2 in. from their top. Clean rims. Use tongs to pick up lids; cover jars with lids, then screw on the rings. With canning tongs, entirely submerge jars into the pot filled with boiling water. Put cover on pot and allow jars to boil 10 minutes.
- Use tongs to take jars out. Allow to cool 24 hours. Check seals to ensure that lids have sucked down; hear a popping sound. Affix labels to jars and store.

Nutrition Information

- Calories: 64 calories;
- Total Carbohydrate: 16.9
- Cholesterol: 0
- Protein: 0.2
- Total Fat: 0.1
- Sodium: 1

283. Spicy Mussels In White Wine

Serving: 6 Appetizer Servings | Prep: | Ready in:

Ingredients

- 1/3 cup olive oil
- 1/2 onion, thinly sliced
- 4 large garlic cloves, chopped
- 2 teaspoons fennel seeds
- 1 teaspoon dried crushed red pepper
- 1/2 teaspoon salt
- 1 cup dry white wine
- 2 1/4-inch-thick lemon slices
- 1/2 cup chopped fresh parsley
- 2 1/2 pounds fresh mussels, scrubbed, debearded
- 1/2 cup chopped seeded tomatoes

Direction

- In heavy big pot, heat the oil over medium-high heat. Put salt, crushed red pepper, fennel seeds, garlic and onion; sauté for 4 minutes till onion turned slightly brown. Put 1/4 cup parsley, lemon slices and wine; boil. Put the mussels. Cover the pot and let cook for 6 minutes till shells of mussels open, mixing one time to reset mussels; throw any mussels that remain closed. Put mussels to big shallow bowl with slotted spoon. In pot, boil the broth for 3 minutes till reduced to a cup; season with pepper to taste. Put broth on top of the mussels. Scatter the rest of the parsley and the tomatoes on top.

Nutrition Information

- Calories: 311
- Saturated Fat: 2 g(12%)
- Sodium: 644 mg(27%)
- Fiber: 1 g(6%)
- Total Carbohydrate: 13 g(4%)
- Cholesterol: 53 mg(18%)
- Protein: 23 g(47%)
- Total Fat: 17 g(25%)

284. Spicy Tomato Basil Sauce

Serving: Makes about 4 1/2 cups | Prep: | Ready in:

Ingredients

- 4 1/2 cups canned crushed tomatoes with added puree (from two 28-ounce cans), divided
- 1/4 cup pine nuts
- 4 1/2 tablespoons extra-virgin olive oil
- 3/4 cup finely chopped onion
- 4 large garlic cloves, minced
- 1 teaspoon fennel seeds (finely crushed in plastic bag)
- 3/8 teaspoon (or more) dried crushed red pepper
- 1/2 cup finely chopped fresh basil, divided
- 1/3 cup dry white wine
- 1 teaspoon dried oregano

Direction

- Blend pine nuts, 1 cup of crushed tomatoes and freshly ground black pepper for 1 minute till really smooth in a blender.
- Heat oil in big heavy pot on medium low heat then add 3/8 tsp. of dried crushed red pepper, fennel seeds, garlic and onion; sauté for 5 minutes till onion is soft. Add oregano, wine, 2 tbsp. of chopped basil and leftover crushed tomatoes. Scrape in tomato mixture from the blender; mix to combine. Simmer the sauce for 5-6 minutes till flavors blend; season with extra dried crushed red pepper (optional), pepper and salt to taste. You can make this 1 day ahead and cool, cover then chill.
- Rewarm the sauce; mix in leftover chopped basil.

Nutrition Information

285. Spiked Blackberry Coulis

Serving: Makes about 2 cups | Prep: | Ready in:

Ingredients

- 1 1-pound bag frozen unsweetened blackberries, thawed
- 1 cup plus 2 tablespoons semidry white wine (such as Chenin Blanc)
- 6 tablespoons (about) sugar, divided
- 3 whole cloves
- 2 Turkish bay leaves
- 1/4 teaspoon ground allspice
- 1 teaspoon brandy

Direction

- Put 4 tablespoons sugar, wine and berries in blender and then puree. Transfer to medium saucepan. Add allspice, bay leaves and cloves. Heat to simmer while stirring sometimes. Lower the heat, then cover and Let simmer for 8 minutes.
- Strain into a medium bowl. Get rid of the solids in the strainer. Then whisk in brandy and sweeten with the remaining sugar if you like. (You can make 5 days ahead. Then cover and chill. Whisk again prior to using.)

Nutrition Information

- Calories: 162
- Fiber: 6 g(25%)
- Total Carbohydrate: 31 g(10%)
- Protein: 2 g(3%)
- Total Fat: 1 g(1%)
- Saturated Fat: 0 g(0%)
- Sodium: 4 mg(0%)

286. Spinach, Pear And Green Bean Salad With Riesling Dressing

Serving: Serves 6 | Prep: | Ready in:

Ingredients

- 1/2 cup diced peeled cored ripe Bartlett pear
- 6 tablespoons medium-dry Riesling
- 3 tablespoons fresh lemon juice
- 1 tablespoon chopped shallot
- 1 teaspoon Dijon mustard
- 1/2 cup vegetable oil
- 1/2 pound haricots verts or small green beans, trimmed
- 6 cups (packed) baby spinach leaves (about 6 ounces)
- 3 ripe Bartlett pears, quartered, cored, cut into 1/4-inch-thick slices
- 3/4 cup crumbled blue cheese
- 3/4 cup walnuts, toasted

Direction

- In a food processor, puree the Dijon mustard, Riesling, diced pear, shallot, and lemon juice until smooth. While the machine is still running, add the vegetable oil through the feed tube gradually. Blend the mixture until smooth. Transfer the mixture into a bowl and season it with salt and pepper to taste.
- In a large pot filled with boiling salted water, cook the green beans until just tender yet firm to the bite. Drain the beans and transfer them into the medium bowl filled with ice water. Let the beans cool thoroughly. (The dressing and beans can be prepared a day in advance. Just cover them separately, and then chill.)
- In a large bowl, mix the sliced pears, spinach, and green beans and coat them with enough Riesling dressing. Distribute the salad among the plates and sprinkle each with toasted walnuts and crumbled blue cheese.

Nutrition Information

- Calories: 347
- Total Carbohydrate: 22 g(7%)
- Cholesterol: 13 mg(4%)
- Protein: 6 g(12%)
- Total Fat: 26 g(40%)
- Saturated Fat: 5 g(23%)
- Sodium: 229 mg(10%)
- Fiber: 5 g(21%)

287. Spring Onion Soup With Garlic Croutons

Serving: Makes about 12 cups, serving 8 | Prep: | Ready in:

Ingredients

- 1 loaf of Italian bread
- 4 garlic cloves, sliced
- 1/3 cup olive oil
- 2 pounds large onions (preferably white), chopped fine
- 3 tablespoons unsalted butter
- 2 tablespoons vegetables oil
- 4 large garlic cloves, minced
- 3/4 cup dry vermouth or dry white wine
- 7 cups chicken broth
- 1 1/2 tablespoons Angostura bitters
- 3 cups finely chopped scallion (about 3 bunches)

Direction

- Prep garlic croutons: Preheat an oven to 325°F. Take crust from bread using serrated knife, throwing it, and slice bread to make cubes, about 3/4-inch. Place bread cubes in shallow baking pan in single pile; for 10 to 15 minutes, bake in the center of oven, mixing from time to time, or till golden, and turn croutons onto a big bowl. Let garlic cook in oil in skillet on medium low heat, mixing, till golden and get rid of garlic using slotted spoon. Sprinkle all over croutons with oil, tossing till coated thoroughly, and scatter salt on croutons to taste.
- Prepare soup: let onions cook in oil and butter in kettle on medium heat, mixing from time to time, for 25 minutes to half an hour, or till light golden and soft, put in garlic, and let the mixture cook for three minutes. Mix vermouth in and let the mixture boil till most of liquid is vaporized. Put in bitters, pepper and salt to taste and broth, and allow soup to simmer for five minutes. Soup can be done up to this portion 2 days ahead, keep in refrigerator with cover, and rewarmed. Mix scallion in.
- Put croutons on top of soup and serve.

Nutrition Information

- Calories: 421
- Protein: 11 g(22%)
- Total Fat: 21 g(32%)
- Saturated Fat: 5 g(26%)
- Sodium: 559 mg(23%)
- Fiber: 4 g(17%)
- Total Carbohydrate: 43 g(14%)
- Cholesterol: 18 mg(6%)

288. Spring Vegetable Risotto With Poached Eggs

Serving: Makes 6 servings | Prep: | Ready in:

Ingredients

- 2 cups shelled fresh (or frozen, thawed) fava beans or peas (from about 2 pounds pods)
- Kosher salt
- 1 tablespoon distilled white vinegar
- 6 large eggs
- 8 cups low-sodium chicken broth
- 2 tablespoons unsalted butter, divided
- 1/4 pound chanterelles or crimini (baby bella) mushrooms, halved or quartered if large
- 2 tablespoons olive oil
- 2 large leeks, whites and pale greens only, chopped
- 1 fennel bulb, chopped
- 4 garlic cloves, finely chopped
- 2 cups arborio rice
- 1 cup dry white wine
- 1 bunch flat-leaf spinach, trimmed, leaves torn
- 2 tablespoons crème fraîche or sour cream
- 1 1/2 cups finely grated Pecorino or Parmesan (about 3 ounces) plus more for shaving
- 1/4 cup chopped fresh chives plus more for serving
- Freshly ground black pepper

Direction

- In big saucepan with salted boiling water, cook fresh fava beans for a minute in case using. Strain; turn onto bowl with ice water and cool down. Remove favas peel and turn onto small bowl.
- Let salted water in a big skillet come to bare simmer on moderately-low heat. Pour in vinegar. Break an egg in small bowl, then slip in the simmering water. Redo with 2 additional eggs. Cook for 3 minutes, till whites are done yet yolks are still liquid. Cautiously turn the eggs onto bowl with ice water using slotted spoon. Redo with leftover 3 eggs.
- In a big saucepan, simmer broth on moderate heat. Lower the heat to low; retain warmth with cover.
- Meantime, in a wide, big heavy pot, liquify a tablespoon of butter on moderate heat. Put in and cook mushrooms for 5 minutes, mixing frequently, till tender. Turn onto bowl of favas with slotted spoon.

- Using the same pot, heat leftover 1 tablespoon of butter and oil on moderate heat. Put in fennel, garlic and leeks. Cook for 4 minutes, mixing frequently, till vegetables soften.
- Put in rice and mix for 2 minutes, till coated. Pour in wine and cook for 4 minutes, mixing from time to time, till vaporized. Put in a cup of broth. Cook, mixing frequently, no need to mix continuously, till broth is nearly soaked in. Put in leftover cupfuls of broth, letting broth be soaked in prior putting in additional, mixing frequently, till mixture becomes creamy and rice is tender yet remain firm to bite, for a total of 20 minutes.
- Put reserved mushrooms and fava beans, quarter cup of chives, 1 1/2 cups of grated Pecorino, crème fraîche and spinach to risotto. Cook for 2 minutes, mixing from time to time, till cheese melts and spinach wilts. Use salt to season risotto.
- Several minutes prior to risotto is finished, in big skillet with simmering water, rewarm poached eggs for a minute. Distribute risotto between bowls and put pepper, chives, shaved Pecorino and eggs on top.

Nutrition Information

- Calories: 617
- Total Carbohydrate: 78 g(26%)
- Cholesterol: 213 mg(71%)
- Protein: 29 g(57%)
- Total Fat: 21 g(32%)
- Saturated Fat: 8 g(42%)
- Sodium: 1608 mg(67%)
- Fiber: 9 g(36%)

289. Steamed Cod With Cauliflower And Saffron

Serving: | Prep: 25mins | Ready in:

Ingredients

- 1 large pinch of saffron threads, crumbled
- 1 cup lukewarm water
- 1 2-pound head cauliflower
- 1 tablespoon olive oil
- 1 garlic clove, crushed
- 1 small carrot, cut into 1/4-inch dice (1/3 cup)
- 1/2 cup dry white wine
- 1 cup fat-free reduced-sodium chicken broth
- 1 1/4 teaspoons salt
- 1/2 teaspoon white pepper
- 1 1/2 pounds small to medium mussels (preferably cultivated; 3 dozen), scrubbed and beards removed
- 6 1/4-pound pieces cod or scrod fillet (1 inch thick), skinned and pin bones removed
- 3 scallions, chopped (2/3 cup)
- 2 tablespoons chopped fresh parsley

Direction

- In a small bowl, put in saffron threads and stir with lukewarm water then allow to stand.
- Trim a cauliflower stalk flushed to the crown base, throwing the stalk away, then cut into quarters lengthwise. Cut every quarter lengthwise into slices that are 1/2-inch thick. Set aside the large slices and reserve the stemless small pieces for another use.
- In a 12-inch deep, heavy skillet, swirl oil with the garlic to coat and heat on moderately high heat until the oil just smokes, discarding the garlic. Arrange the cauliflower slices carefully into one layer on the skillet and cook for 2 minutes until the underside is browned lightly. Use tongs to turn them over and cook the other sides for 2 minutes until lightly browned.
- Add wine and carrots, swirling the skillet to blend, then boil for 30 seconds until the liquid reduces by 1/2. Add 1/4 teaspoon white pepper, 3/4 teaspoon salt, broth and saffron water, then simmer while covered for 5 - 8 minutes until the carrots and cauliflower are tender-crisp.
- While the vegetables simmer, pat the fish dry and sprinkle each side with the remaining 1/4 teaspoon white pepper and 1/2 teaspoon salt.

- Turn the heat up to moderately high and add mussels onto the skillet, then steam while covered, frequently checking after 3 - 4 minutes, until all mussels open wide. Discard mussels that don't open after 8 minutes. Divide the mussels into 6 shallow serving bowls with the use of a slotted spoon.
- Place the cod on top of the cauliflower, arranging the fillets in one layer. Sprinkle with parsley and scallions, then steam while covered on moderately high heat for 7 - 10 minutes until the fish cooks through.
- Transfer some of the cauliflower with 1 piece of cod onto each bowl with the use of a slotted spoon. Season the broth with white pepper and salt, then ladle the broth with the carrots over each of the servings.

Nutrition Information

290. Steamed Fingerling Potatoes In White Wine

Serving: Makes 6 servings | Prep: 25mins | Ready in:

Ingredients

- 3 pound (2- to 4-inch-long) fingerling potatoes, scrubbed well
- 1/3 cup dry white wine
- 2 tablespoons olive oil

Direction

- Remove potatoes peel, once peeled, place in bowl with cold water to avoid discoloration. Strain the potatoes, then in steamer place on top of boiling water, steam with cover for 18 to 20 minutes, till soft.
- Toss in big bowl with the wine and hot potatoes, then put in a teaspoon of salt, half teaspoon of pepper and oil, and toss once more. Let come to room temperature.

- Note: Potatoes may be done a day in advance and refrigerate with cover.

Nutrition Information

- Calories: 233
- Total Carbohydrate: 40 g(13%)
- Protein: 5 g(11%)
- Total Fat: 5 g(7%)
- Saturated Fat: 1 g(3%)
- Sodium: 14 mg(1%)
- Fiber: 3 g(11%)

291. Steamed Mussels In White Wine

Serving: Makes 4 servings | Prep: 30mins | Ready in:

Ingredients

- 1 large shallot, finely chopped
- 1/4 onion, finely chopped (about 1/3 cup)
- 1/4 cup dry white wine
- 3 1/2 tablespoons unsalted butter, cut into 1/2" cubes
- 1 tablespoon white wine vinegar
- 4 1/2 pounds mussels, scrubbed, debearded
- Freshly ground black pepper
- 2 tablespoons chopped flat-leaf parsley
- Cheesecloth

Direction

- In a big heavy pot, place in vinegar, butter, wine, onion, and shallots. Add the mussels and boil while covered. Cook while shaking the pot gently once or twice for 3 - 5 minutes until the mussels have opened. Throw away any that haven't.
- Line a strainer with double layers of cheesecloth over a bowl and put aside. Use a slotted spoon to move the mussels onto a big bowl. Pour the mixture from the pot onto the

lined strainer and season with pepper. Pour it over the mussels and sprinkle with parsley.

Nutrition Information

- Calories: 274
- Fiber: 1 g(3%)
- Total Carbohydrate: 5 g(2%)
- Cholesterol: 89 mg(30%)
- Protein: 2 g(3%)
- Total Fat: 25 g(39%)
- Saturated Fat: 16 g(78%)
- Sodium: 33 mg(1%)

292. Steamed Mussels With Curry And Lemongrass

Serving: Makes 4 servings | Prep: | Ready in:

Ingredients

- 1 cup dry white wine
- 1 cup heavy cream
- 2 garlic cloves, minced
- 1 tablespoon minced shallot
- 1 stalk fresh lemongrass* (lower 6 inches only), outer leaves discarded and root ends trimmed, cut into 1-inch pieces
- 2 teaspoons curry powder
- 1 1/2 pounds black mussels (preferably cultivated), scrubbed well in several changes of water and beards pulled off
- 1 tablespoon thinly sliced scallion
- 1 tablespoon unsalted butter
- *available at Asian markets and some specialty foods shops

Direction

- Boil curry powder, lemongrass, shallot, garlic, cream and wine in a heavy, 5- to 6-quart kettle. Put in mussels and cook for 4 to 6 minutes, with cover, on medium high heat, or till opened, throw any that remain closed, and lemongrass. Distribute mussels between 4 bowls with a slotted spoon.
- Put to liquid left in kettle with butter, pepper and salt to taste and scallion, mixing till butter is blended, and scoop on top of mussels.

Nutrition Information

293. Steamed Mussels With Lemon Saffron Sauce

Serving: Makes 4 servings | Prep: | Ready in:

Ingredients

- 1/2 cup crème fraîche*
- 2 large egg yolks
- 1 1/2 tablespoons butter
- 2 large shallots, finely chopped
- 2 tablespoons Cognac or brandy
- 3 tablespoons fresh lemon juice
- 1 generous pinch of saffron threads
- 40 mussels, scrubbed, debearded
- 1 cup dry white wine
- Fresh chives

Direction

- In a medium bowl, whisk together egg yolks and crème fraiche to combine. In a medium heavy skillet, melt butter over medium heat and add shallots, then sauté for 3 minutes until soft. Take skillet away from heat. Add the Cognac and light up with a match. Let the flames burn out and whisk in saffron and lemon juice, then set the mixtures aside.
- In a large heavy pot, place the mussels and pour wine, then boil over a medium-high heat. Cook while covered for 6 minutes until the mussels open and take away from the heat. Use tongs to transfer the mussels to a baking sheet, discarding the ones that don't open. Remove top half of each shell and divide

mussels in bottom shells among 4 bowls, then tent with foil.
- With a sieve lined with a damp paper towel, strain the mussel cooking liquid into the skillet with the shallot mixture. Boil over a medium-high heat for 3 minutes until it reduces to 1 cup. Whisk the hot liquid very slowly into the crème fraiche mixture and return to the same skillet. Stir over a low heat for 2 minutes until the sauce is thick enough to coat a spoon. Take away from heat and season with pepper and salt. Spoon the sauce over the mussels and garnish with chives.
- If you can't find crème fraiche, you can heat 1 cup whipping cream until lukewarm or 85 degrees F. Take away from heat and mix in 2 tablespoons buttermilk. Let stand while covered in a draft-free and warm area for 24 - 48 hours, depending on the room temperature, until slightly thick. Keep refrigerated until ready to be used.

Nutrition Information

- Calories: 325
- Saturated Fat: 7 g(37%)
- Sodium: 457 mg(19%)
- Fiber: 1 g(5%)
- Total Carbohydrate: 15 g(5%)
- Cholesterol: 161 mg(54%)
- Protein: 21 g(42%)
- Total Fat: 16 g(24%)

294. Steamed Mussels With Orange, Fennel, And Garlic

Serving: Serves 4 as an hors d'oeuvre | Prep: | Ready in:

Ingredients

- 1 navel orange
- 2 large garlic cloves, minced and mashed to a paste with 1/2 teaspoon salt
- 2 shallots, chopped fine (about 1/3 cup)
- 1/2 cup finely chopped fennel bulb (sometimes called anise)
- 1 teaspoon fennel seeds
- 2 tablespoons unsalted butter
- 1/4 cup dry white wine
- 1/2 cup chicken broth
- 1 pound mussels (preferably cultivated), scrubbed well and beards pulled off
- 1 tablespoon chopped fresh parsley leaves

Direction

- Take 3 orange zest strips, about 3-by-1/2-inch, using vegetable peeler. Use a sharp knife to slice the rest of the peel including pith from orange and throw. Cut through sections of fruit between the membranes, throwing membranes, and finely chop sufficient fruit to get a third cup, putting aside the rest of the fruit for other use.
- Cook fennel seeds, chopped fennel, shallots and garlic paste in butter in a big saucepan on medium heat for 5 minutes, mixing, till chopped fennel softens. Mix zest and wine in and let boil or a minute. Pour in broth and bring back to boil. Put in mussels and cook on high heat for 3 to 8 minutes, use a tight-fitting lid to cover, check them after every minute, use a slotted spoon to turn them once they open into a serving bowl. Throw any mussels remain closed 8 minutes after.
- Mix chopped orange, pepper and salt to taste and parsley into broth and scoop on top of mussels.

Nutrition Information

- Calories: 202
- Protein: 15 g(31%)
- Total Fat: 9 g(14%)
- Saturated Fat: 4 g(21%)
- Sodium: 377 mg(16%)
- Fiber: 2 g(7%)
- Total Carbohydrate: 14 g(5%)
- Cholesterol: 48 mg(16%)

295. Steamed Mussels With Sausages And Fennel

Serving: Makes 8 servings | Prep: | Ready in:

Ingredients

- 2 pounds sweet or hot Italian link sausages, divided
- 2 large onions, sliced (about 6 cups), divided
- 2 large fresh fennel bulbs, sliced (about 6 cups), divided
- 6 garlic cloves, crushed, divided
- 1 teaspoon dried crushed red pepper, divided
- 3 cups dry white wine (about one 750-ml bottle), divided
- 6 pounds mussels, scrubbed, debearded
- 1 16-ounce crusty French or sourdough baguette, cut into 1/2-inch-thick slices, divided
- Extra-virgin olive oil (for drizzling)
- Chopped fresh Italian parsley

Direction

- Set oven to 450 degrees F. Use a fork to pierce all over the sausages. Heat 2 big cast-iron skillets or other ovenproof pans on medium-high heat. Add 1/2 of the sausages onto each skillet and cook, occasionally turning, for 5 minutes until browned. Add onto each skillet half the dried crushed red pepper, half the garlic, half the fennel, and half the onions. Add 1 cup white wine onto each skillet and boil. Simmer while covered for 12 minutes until vegetables and sausages are cooked thoroughly. Add 1/2 of the mussels and 1/2 cup white wine onto each of the skillets and move them into the oven, roasting while uncovered for 5 minutes. Remove the skillets carefully from the oven and top each one with slices of baguettes to completely cover. Place them back in the oven and bake while uncovered for another 5 minutes until the mussels have opened and the bread starts to brown. Throw away any mussels that didn't open.
- Drizzle all the bread with extra-virgin olive oil then sprinkle with the chopped parsley. Serve sausages and mussels straight from the skillet.

Nutrition Information

- Calories: 1036
- Protein: 67 g(134%)
- Total Fat: 49 g(75%)
- Saturated Fat: 12 g(61%)
- Sodium: 2211 mg(92%)
- Fiber: 6 g(26%)
- Total Carbohydrate: 65 g(22%)
- Cholesterol: 175 mg(58%)

296. Strawberry Mosel Cup

Serving: Makes 10 cups | Prep: | Ready in:

Ingredients

- 2 bottles chilled Mosel (a medium dry German white wine)
- 2/3 cup cognac
- 1/2 cup Grand Marnier
- 2 cups chilled seltzer or club soda
- 1 pint strawberries, hulled (and quartered if large)

Direction

- Mix cognac, Grand Marnier and Mosel in punch bowl. Put in ice cubes or one ice block. Mix till extremely cold, then mix seltzer in. Jazz punch up with strawberries.

Nutrition Information

- Calories: 486
- Saturated Fat: 0 g(0%)
- Sodium: 45 mg(2%)
- Fiber: 2 g(7%)

- Total Carbohydrate: 17 g(6%)
- Protein: 1 g(2%)
- Total Fat: 0 g(0%)

297. Strawberry And Cream Cake With Cardamom Syrup

Serving: Makes 10 servings | Prep: | Ready in:

Ingredients

- 8 large egg yolks
- 1 1/2 cups sugar
- 1/4 cup whole milk
- 1 teaspoon vanilla
- 1/2 teaspoon finely grated fresh lemon zest
- 1 cup all-purpose flour
- 1/2 teaspoon salt
- 4 large egg whites
- 1 1/2 cups Muscat de Beaumes-de-Venise or Essensia (orange-flavored Muscat wine)
- 1/4 cup sugar
- 3/4 teaspoon ground cardamom
- 2 cups chilled heavy cream
- 1/2 cup sour cream
- 2 tablespoons sugar
- 1 teaspoon vanilla
- 1 1/2 pound strawberries, 5 left whole and remainder trimmed and cut lengthwise into 1/4-inch-thick slices
- 3 (9- by 2-inch) round cake pans; parchment paper

Direction

- For the cake layers: Position the racks in lower and upper thirds of the oven; turn on to 350 degrees F to preheat. Coat cake pans with butter. Use a round parchment paper to line the bottom of each pan; butter the parchment, add a dust of flour and remove excess.
- In a large bowl, combine zest, vanilla, milk, 1 cup of sugar and yolks until smooth. Stir in salt and flour until mixed (it will form a thick batter).
- In a bowl, use an electric mixer to beat a pinch of salt and whites at medium-high speed until soft peaks form. Beat in leftover 1/2 cup of sugar at medium speed, a little at a time; beat for another 2 minutes until stiff glossy peaks form.
- Add 1/3 of whites into batter, fold to lighten; fold in the remaining whites thoroughly but gently.
- Distribute batter into cake pans and put into the oven to bake for 20-25 minutes until a skewer or a wooden pick comes out clean when inserted into the center and the cake springs back when touched, switch the position halfway through. Allow to cool for 10 minutes in pans on racks, then flip over onto racks. Remove parchment carefully; allow to cool completely.
- While waiting for the cakes to cool, make the syrup: In a 1-quart heavy saucepan, boil cardamom, sugar and wine for 6-8 minutes while stirring to dissolve the sugar; let it boil until it is reduced to 1 cup. Run syrup through a fine-mesh sieve; allow to cool completely.
- Make the filling when the syrup and cakes are cool: In a bowl, use cleaned beaters to beat vanilla, sugar, sour cream and heavy cream together until stiff peaks form.
- To assemble cake: Use a skewer or wooden pick to prick cake layers all over; pour or brush the syrup, little by little, over each layer evenly; allow the syrup to be absorbed before adding more.
- On a plate or a cake stand, place 1 layer, flat side up; add a rounded cup of cream and spread. Place some sliced strawberries over cream in 1 layer. Turn the second layer over; add a thin layer of cream on top and spread, then use a spatula to position it onto the layer of strawberries, cream side down. Continue with the layers using cake, strawberries and cream. Use the remaining cream to spread on top and use the remaining strawberries to decorate.

Nutrition Information

- Calories: 486
- Cholesterol: 219 mg(73%)
- Protein: 7 g(14%)
- Total Fat: 24 g(37%)
- Saturated Fat: 14 g(69%)
- Sodium: 174 mg(7%)
- Fiber: 2 g(7%)
- Total Carbohydrate: 56 g(19%)

298. Strawberry And Peach Sangria

Serving: Makes 8 servings | Prep: | Ready in:

Ingredients

- 1 750-ml bottle dry white wine
- 1 1/2 cups Essensia (orange Muscat, a sweet dessert wine)
- 1 1/2 cups sliced strawberries
- 1 cup peach liqueur
- 3 peaches, each cut into 12 slices
- 1 large orange, cut crosswise into 6 slices
- 1 large lemon, cut crosswise into 6 slices
- 1/4 cup strawberry syrup (optional)
- 3 to 4 cups ice cubes

Direction

- In big pitcher, combine strawberry syrup, lemon slices, orange slices, peaches, peach liqueur, strawberries, Essensia and white wine, slightly crushing slices of citrus. Rest for not less than 2 hours at room temperature or refrigerate for up to 4 hours. Serve the sangria over ice.

Nutrition Information

- Calories: 305
- Total Carbohydrate: 42 g(14%)
- Protein: 1 g(3%)
- Total Fat: 0 g(0%)
- Saturated Fat: 0 g(0%)
- Sodium: 14 mg(1%)
- Fiber: 3 g(11%)

299. Summer Fruit Terrine

Serving: Serves 4 to 6 | Prep: | Ready in:

Ingredients

- 1 cup dry white wine
- 1/2 cup sugar
- 3 tablespoons fresh lemon juice
- 4 large peaches (about 2 pounds)
- 2 envelopes (about 2 tablespoons) unflavored gelatin
- 16 to 18 small strawberries, hulled and halved lengthwise
- 1/2 cup raspberries
- 1/2 cup blueberries
- 1/2 cup seedless green grapes, halved lengthwise
- 2 1/4 cups raspberry peach sauce
- 1/4 cup sugar
- 3 tablespoons fresh lemon juice
- 2 large peaches (about 1 pound)
- 1-1/2 cups raspberries
- mint sprigs for garnish if desired

Direction

- Prepare summer fruit terrine: mix half cup water, lemon juice, sugar, and wine in saucepan, boil the mixture, mixing till sugar dissolves, and put in 2 of peaches, peel removed, sliced in half, and pitted, cut sides facing down. Let peaches simmer till extremely tender, for 10 to 15 minutes, and turn onto blender using slotted spoon. Pour a cup cooking liquid and process mixture till smooth. Scatter gelatin on top of a third cup of cold water in small saucepan, soften for five minutes, and let the mixture heat on low heat, mixing, till gelatin dissolves. Put to peach mixture the gelatin mixture in stream while machine is running till blended thoroughly.

You should have approximately 2-1/2 cups of peach purée.

- Line plastic wrap on a loaf pan or 5- to 6-cup terrine and put in approximately quarter cup of peach purée, or sufficient to barely cover the base. Place 1/2 of strawberries in single layer, cut sides facing down, on peach purée and add sufficient peach purée on top of layer of strawberry to barley cover. Peel leftover 2 peaches, slice in half, and pit, then thinly slice, and toss them in bowl along with quarter cup peach purée. Place half the slices of peach, overlap them a bit, on top of layer of strawberry and add sufficient of leftover peach purée on top of peach layer to barely cover.
- Toss blueberries and raspberries in small bowl with quarter cup peach purée and place berries on top of peaches in single layer. Add sufficient of leftover peach purée to terrine till berries are barely covered, toss grapes in bowl along with approximately 2 tablespoons of leftover purée, and place them on top of berries in single layer. Add sufficient of leftover purée in terrine till grape layer is just covered, place leftover peaches on top of grapes in single layer, overlap them a bit, and add sufficient of leftover purée on top of peaches to barely cover. Place the leftover strawberries on top of peaches, cut sides facing up, in single layer and top with leftover purée to cover them. Refrigerate terrine till just set, for an hour, use plastic wrap to cover it, and refrigerate overnight.
- Uncover the top of terrine, flip onto serving plate, and cautiously remove plastic wrap. Use serrated knife to slice terrine to make 3/4-inch pieces and serve along with mint sprigs and sauce.
- Prepare raspberry peach sauce: mix lemon juice, quarter cup of water and sugar in saucepan and boil the mixture, mixing till sugar dissolves. Purée raspberries and peaches, peel removed, pitted, and chopped in blender along with sugar syrup till mixture becomes smooth and use a fine sieve placed on top of bowl to pass mixture of puree through, throwing solids. Refrigerate sauce with cover, for not less than an hour to overnight. Yields 2-1/4 cups.

Nutrition Information

- Calories: 418
- Total Fat: 2 g(3%)
- Saturated Fat: 0 g(1%)
- Sodium: 11 mg(0%)
- Fiber: 11 g(46%)
- Total Carbohydrate: 95 g(32%)
- Protein: 8 g(16%)

300. Summer Punch

Serving: Makes about 20 servings | Prep: | Ready in:

Ingredients

- 1 block ice
- 3 bottles dry white wine
- 1 1/2 cups crème de cassis
- 12 orange slices, halved
- 1 pint strawberries

Direction

- In a punch bowl, place block of ice. Stir in cassis and wine. Let strawberries and orange slice float on top. Pour into 4-ounch punch glasses to serve.

Nutrition Information

301. Sun Dried Tomato Onion Jam

Serving: Makes about 2 cups | Prep: | Ready in:

Ingredients

- 3 medium onions, halved lengthwise and thinly sliced crosswise
- 3 tablespoons unsalted butter
- 1/3 cup sugar
- 1/2 teaspoon salt
- 1/4 teaspoon black pepper
- 1/8 teaspoon dried hot red pepper flakes
- 1/2 cup dry white wine
- 1 tablespoon red-wine vinegar
- 1/4 cup packed dried apricots, thinly sliced
- 3/4 cup drained oil-packed sun-dried tomatoes, chopped

Direction

- In a heavy, 10-inch skillet, cook red pepper flakes, pepper, salt, sugar, butter and onions on low heat, with cover, mixing from time to time, till onions turn light golden and soften, for half an hour. Put in tomatoes, apricots, vinegar and wine, and simmer, with no cover, mixing from time to time, till thick, for 20 minutes to half an hour. Let come to room temperature and serve.

Nutrition Information

- Calories: 169
- Total Fat: 8 g(12%)
- Saturated Fat: 4 g(20%)
- Sodium: 235 mg(10%)
- Fiber: 2 g(9%)
- Total Carbohydrate: 23 g(8%)
- Cholesterol: 15 mg(5%)
- Protein: 2 g(3%)

302. Sunflower Seed "Risotto" With Squash And Mushrooms

Serving: Serves 4 | Prep: 1hours | Ready in:

Ingredients

- 4 cups raw sunflower seeds
- 2/3 cup heavy cream
- 2/3 cup freshly grated Parmesan (about 1 ounce), plus more for serving
- 4 tablespoons olive oil, divided
- 1/2 large onion, finely chopped
- 4 garlic cloves, finely chopped, divided
- 6 thyme sprigs, divided, plus more for serving
- 2 cups vegetable broth
- 2 tablespoons dry white wine
- 3 cups 1/2" cubed butternut squash (about 1 pound squash)
- 3 1/2 ounces shiitake or cremini mushrooms, trimmed, coarsely chopped
- 1 1/2 teaspoons kosher salt, plus more
- 1/2 teaspoon freshly ground black pepper, plus more

Direction

- In a Dutch oven or medium-sized, heavy, wide pot, put the sunflower seeds and submerge in water. Place pot cover and boil, then lower to simmer and cook for 45 to 55 minutes, till al dente.
- Use a fine-mesh sieve to drain seeds into a big bowl, saving cooking water. Put a cup of seeds and a cup cooking water and onto blender; put aside the rest of seeds and throw the leftover liquid. Put in 2/3 cup of Parmesan and cream and blend till extremely smooth.
- Wipe pot clean. Heat in pot with 2 tablespoons of oil on moderate. Put in 1/2 of the garlic, 4 thyme sprigs and onion. Cook for 4 minutes, mixing, till garlic is aromatic and onion starts to turn clear. Put reserved sunflower seeds in and cook for a minute, till seeds toast. Pour in wine and broth and simmer on moderate heat for 15 to 20 minutes, till liquid is nearly completely cooked down and seeds are soft.
- Meantime, in a big skillet, heat a tablespoon of oil on moderately-high. Put in and cook squash for 5 to 7 minutes, mixing from time to time, till just starting to brown. Put in 2 thyme sprigs, mushrooms, and leftover 1 tablespoon of oil and garlic and keep cooking for 5 minutes, till squash and mushrooms are soft.

213

Add 1/4 teaspoon pepper and 1/2 teaspoon salt to season and turn onto plate.
- Once broth is nearly fully vaporized, pour in blended seed mixture and cook for 5 to 8 minutes, till sauce is thick. Throw thyme sprigs and mix in 1/4 teaspoon pepper and 1 teaspoon salt; check for taste and fix seasonings. Distribute "risotto" between bowls and put sautéed thyme sprigs, pepper, Parmesan and vegetables on top.

Nutrition Information

- Calories: 633
- Total Carbohydrate: 29 g(10%)
- Cholesterol: 59 mg(20%)
- Protein: 15 g(31%)
- Total Fat: 54 g(83%)
- Saturated Fat: 14 g(71%)
- Sodium: 849 mg(35%)
- Fiber: 8 g(30%)

303. Swiss Cheese And Porcini Fondue

Serving: Serves 6 | Prep: | Ready in:

Ingredients

- 1 ounce dried porcini mushrooms*
- 1 1/2 cups hot water
- 1/2 pound Emmenthal cheese, grated
- 1/2 pound Swiss Gruyère cheese, grated
- 1 tablespoon cornstarch
- 1 cup dry white wine
- 1 garlic clove, halved
- 2 teaspoons minced fresh thyme
- Fresh thyme leaves
- Day-old French bread, cut into 1-inch cubes
- *Porcini are available at Italian markets and specialty foods stores.

Direction

- Let porcini mushrooms submerge for 20 minutes in 1 1/2 cups of hot water till soft. Strain, saving soaking water. Squeeze dry. Chop the mushrooms.
- Combine in big bowl cornstarch and Gruyère and Emmenthal cheese. In medium, heavy saucepan or fondue pot, mix white wine, garlic and a cup reserved of the mushroom soaking water. Simmer for two minutes. Throw the garlic. Fix the heat to keep liquid at a barely simmers. Put in cheese by handfuls and mix till every increment melt prior to putting in next.
- Once all cheese has been put in, stir till smooth. Stir in 2 teaspoons of the minced fresh thyme and mushrooms. Liberally season with pepper. May be prepped a day in advance. Cool down. Push a plastic on top of fondue and chill. Refrigerate the leftover mushroom soaking water with cover. Prior to proceeding, reheat fondue on low heat, mixing often and putting in reserved mushroom soaking water as need be in case fondue turns very thick. Turn the mixture onto a 2-quart, flame-safe casserole in case not using pot for fondue. Scatter fresh thyme leaves over. Place above gas table burner or alcohol burner and serve, letting diners skewer bread using fork and dunk in cheese fondue.

Nutrition Information

304. Swiss Fondue

Serving: Serves 4 to 6 | Prep: | Ready in:

Ingredients

- 1/2 garlic clove
- 1 2/3 cups dry white wine
- 1 pound Gruyère, grated coarse
- 2 teaspoons cornstarch

- 1/4 cup kirsch plus additional for thinning the fondue if necessary
- freshly grated nutmeg to taste
- 2 loaves of crusty French bread, cut into 1-inch cubes

Direction

- Rub garlic on the inner part of heavy saucepan, pour in wine, and heat on medium low heat till mixture is hot and cheese melts. Put in handfuls of Gruyère, mixing, till cheese melts and mixture is thoroughly incorporated, and maintain the mixture barely under the simmering point. Mix thoroughly the 1/4 cup kirsch and cornstarch in small bowl, put mixture to mixture of Gruyère including pepper to taste and nutmeg, and let the fondue heat up till it just starts to bubble, mixing continuously, however do not allow it to boil. Turn fondue onto a warm pot of fondue and maintain it hot one low flame. In case fondue turns very thick, put in some extra kirsch. Use long-handled forks to spear the bread cubes and dunk into fondue.

Nutrition Information

---

305. Swordfish Kebabs

Serving: Makes 3 servings | Prep: | Ready in:

Ingredients

- 1/2 cup dry white wine
- 1/4 cup olive oil
- 1/4 cup lemon juice
- 1/4 cup Worcestershire sauce
- 2 garlic cloves, minced
- 1/4 teaspoon pepper
- 1 pound swordfish, cut into 1-inch cubes
- 12 bamboo skewers
- 6 small boiling onions, peeled
- 1 green bell pepper, cut into 1-inch pieces
- 1 red bell pepper, cut into 1-inch pieces
- 12 mushrooms

Direction

- In medium bowl, mix the initial 6 ingredients to incorporate. Put in fish and chill for not less than an hour to 4 hours maximum.
- Preheat the broiler or have barbecue ready for moderate heat. Let fish drain, saving marinade. Use skewers to thread fish alternating with green and bell peppers, mushrooms and onions. Place skewers on a grill. Grill for 5 minutes, till swordfish is barely cooked completely, brush skewers often using marinade.

Nutrition Information

- Calories: 559
- Sodium: 366 mg(15%)
- Fiber: 7 g(27%)
- Total Carbohydrate: 37 g(12%)
- Cholesterol: 100 mg(33%)
- Protein: 36 g(71%)
- Total Fat: 29 g(44%)
- Saturated Fat: 5 g(25%)

---

306. Tagliatelle With Mussels, Clams And Pesto

Serving: Makes 2 servings; can be doubled | Prep: | Ready in:

Ingredients

- 12 littleneck clams, scrubbed
- 12 mussels, scrubbed, debearded
- 1 cup dry white wine
- 8 ounces tagliatelle or linguine
- 6 tablespoons purchased pesto
- 1/4 cup sliced drained oil-packed sun-dried tomatoes
- 1/4 teaspoon dried crushed red pepper

Direction

- Mix in big, heavy pot the mussels, wine and clams; boil on moderately-high heat. Place pot cover; cook for 7 minutes, till shellfish open, throw any that remain closed. Turn the shellfish onto bowl with tongs; use foil to cover to retain warmth. Put shellfish juices aside.
- Meantime, in medium size pot with salted boiling water, let pasta cook till just tender yet remain firm to bite
- Strain the pasta; put back to same pot. Put in the crushed red pepper, sun-dried tomatoes, pesto, and reserved shellfish juices. Toss on moderate heat barely till pasta is coated in sauce. Add pepper and salt to season. Distribute the pasta among 2 bowls; put shellfish on top to serve.

Nutrition Information

- Calories: 833
- Fiber: 5 g(21%)
- Total Carbohydrate: 100 g(33%)
- Cholesterol: 55 mg(18%)
- Protein: 42 g(83%)
- Total Fat: 23 g(35%)
- Saturated Fat: 3 g(16%)
- Sodium: 1339 mg(56%)

307. Taglierini With Morels, Asparagus, And Nasturtiums

Serving: Serves 8 (first course) | Prep: 1.25hours | Ready in:

Ingredients

- 3/4 pound fresh taglierini or 1/2 pound dried 1/8-inch-wide flat egg noodles
- 1 ounce small dried morels
- 3/4 pound thin asparagus stalks
- 1 cup dry white wine
- 3 tablespoons fresh lemon juice
- 1/4 cup finely chopped shallots
- 1/3 cup heavy cream
- 1 cup chicken broth
- 1 1/2 sticks (3/4 cup) cold unsalted butter, cut into pieces
- 50 nontoxic and organic nasturtiums, halved if large

Direction

- Prep fresh pasta in case using.
- Let dried morels submerge for 20 minutes in a cup of warm water. Agitate morels to remove the grit, then take out of water, pressing mushrooms to return liquid back to bowl. Put the liquid aside. Cautiously pour liquid from mushroom to small bowl once grit has sink, keeping sediment behind, if need be, drain liquid using a moistened cheesecloth or coffee filter. Get rid of any tough stems from morels.
- Cut off tough asparagus ends and throw. Slice 2-inch from top tips and slice tips in half lengthwise. Slice the rest of asparagus to make long diagonal pieces roughly quarter-inch thick.
- In a heavy, big skillet, simmer lemon juice, shallots and wine till liquid is cooked down to roughly 2 tablespoons. Put in cream and simmer for a minute. Put in mushroom soaking liquid, broth and morels, then simmer for five minutes. Put in butter, all together, and let sauce cook on medium-low heat, mixing continuously, barely till creamy and butter blends. Prevent sauce from becoming too hot for butter will separate and sauce will lose its creaminess. Take skillet off heat and add pepper and salt to season sauce. Cover to retain warmth.
- Shake excess flour off in case using fresh taglierini. In 6-quart pot with salted boiling water, cook asparagus and fresh taglierini for a minute, till pasta becomes al dente. Follow packaging directions for dried pasta and put in asparagus on final minute of cooking time. Put half cup of cooking water aside and use a colander to strain asparagus and pasta.

- In a big bowl, toss asparagus and pasta with 1/3 of nasturtiums, cup of sauce, with no morels and sufficient reserved pasta liquid to maintain them moist. Mix into sauce the rest of nasturtiums.
- To serve, wind every taglierini portion surrounding a carving fork and turn onto the middle of soup plate. Place morels, sauce and asparagus around.
- Note: toss asparagus mixture and pasta along with nasturtiums and sauce, putting in more pasta liquid if need be for simpler presentation.

Nutrition Information

- Calories: 390
- Fiber: 3 g(10%)
- Total Carbohydrate: 35 g(12%)
- Cholesterol: 96 mg(32%)
- Protein: 8 g(17%)
- Total Fat: 23 g(36%)
- Saturated Fat: 14 g(69%)
- Sodium: 61 mg(3%)

308. Tamarind Mango Sangria

Serving: Makes 10 to 12 drinks | Prep: 15mins | Ready in:

Ingredients

- 3/4 cup thawed frozen unsweetened tamarind purée
- 2 cups water
- 3/4 cup sugar, or to taste
- 2 1/2 cups diced fresh mangoes (from 2 large)
- 1 (750-ml) bottle chilled dry white wine
- 1/3 cup tequila (preferably reposado)
- 1 cup halved green and red seedless grapes

Direction

- In a blender, purée 1 1/2 cup mangoes, tamarind, sugar, and water until smooth. Filter through a sieve with medium mesh on a pitcher. Mix in the remaining cup of mangoes, wine, grapes, and tequila; cover. Refrigerate up to a day until ready to serve with ice.

Nutrition Information

- Calories: 194
- Saturated Fat: 0 g(0%)
- Sodium: 17 mg(1%)
- Fiber: 1 g(5%)
- Total Carbohydrate: 32 g(11%)
- Protein: 1 g(2%)
- Total Fat: 0 g(0%)

309. Ten Minute Ravioli With Tomato Cream Sauce

Serving: Makes 4 servings | Prep: | Ready in:

Ingredients

- 9 ounces purchased 4-cheese ravioli
- 3 tablespoons extra-virgin olive oil
- 6 garlic cloves, minced
- 2 pounds ripe tomatoes (red, yellow, and/or orange), seeded, chopped
- 1 cup dry white wine
- 1/3 cup whipping cream
- 2 tablespoons chopped fresh tarragon
- 1/2 cup grated Parmesan cheese

Direction

- Follow package directions to cook pasta; drain.
- Meanwhile, heat oil in a big heavy skillet on medium high heat. Add the garlic; sauté for 30 seconds. Add tomatoes; simmer for approximately 5 minutes till juicy. Mix in wine; simmer for 3 minutes. Mix in tarragon and cream; simmer for about 2 minutes till slightly thickened. Mix in cheese; season sauce

with pepper and sauce. In serving bowl, put ravioli; scoop sauce on top.

Nutrition Information

- Calories: 479
- Total Carbohydrate: 43 g(14%)
- Cholesterol: 59 mg(20%)
- Protein: 17 g(33%)
- Total Fat: 25 g(39%)
- Saturated Fat: 10 g(50%)
- Sodium: 475 mg(20%)
- Fiber: 4 g(16%)

310. Thanksgiving Dinner For One

Serving: 1 serving | Prep: 45mins | Ready in:

Ingredients

- 1 sweet potato
- 1 teaspoon finely grated orange zest
- 1 teaspoon finely chopped thyme, plus 1 sprig
- Kosher salt, freshly ground pepper
- 1 turkey breast tenderloin (about 10 ounces)
- 1 tablespoon canola or vegetable oil
- 1 large egg yolk
- 5 tablespoons unsalted butter, divided
- 2 tablespoons fresh orange juice, divided
- 2 tablespoons coarsely chopped pecans
- 2 tablespoons mini marshmallows
- 1 shallot, thinly sliced
- 4 ounces green beans, trimmed
- 1/2 cup dry white wine

Direction

- Preheat an oven to 375°F; roast the sweet potato for 45-55 minutes till tender on a foil-lined rimmed baking sheet; sit till cool enough to handle.
- Meanwhile, mix 1/4 tsp. pepper, 1/2 tsp. salt, chopped thyme and orange zest in a small bowl; rub zest mixture all over turkey tenderloin. Sit for 15 minutes at room temperature.
- Heat oil in a big ovenproof skillet on medium high heat till shimmering; sear turkey for 5 minutes till all sides are lightly browned, occasionally turning. Put skillet in oven; roast turkey for 8-10 minutes till inserted instant-read thermometer in the middle reads 165°F, turning once halfway through. Put turkey on a cutting board; before slicing, sit for 5 minutes. Keep drippings in the skillet.
- Lengthwise halve potato; scoop flesh out from 1 halve above medium bowl, leaving 1/2-in. thick flesh layer inside the skin to be your boat. Put boat onto same foil-lined sheet. Scoop all flesh out from leftover half in bowl; throw skin. Use whisk to mash flesh. Add 1/2 tsp. salt, 1 tbsp. orange juice, 1 tbsp. butter and egg yolk; whisk till as smooth as possible. Taste; adjust seasoning if you want. Put filling in prepped boat; Top with pecans and marshmallows. Bake potato boat for 15 minutes till golden brown and top is lightly puffed.
- Meanwhile, in a small skillet, heat 1 tbsp. butter on medium heat till melted. Add shallot; cook for 1 minute, mixing. Add green beans and cover; cook for 3-4 minutes till shallot is caramelized lightly and beans are crisp-tender, occasionally mixing. Season with pinch of pepper and 1/8 tsp. salt.
- Heat turkey drippings in skillet on high heat. Add wine; use wooden spoon to scrape browned bits up. Add thyme sprig; cook for 5 minutes till liquid reduces by half, mixing. Mix leftover 1 tbsp. orange juice in; take off heat. Discard thyme sprig. Cut leftover 3 tbsp. butter to cubes; one by one, add to skillet, mixing till emulsified and melted prior to adding next. Season with pepper and salt.
- Put sliced turkey on a plate; put sauce on top. Serve with stuffed sweet potato and green beans on the side.

Nutrition Information

- Calories: 1516
- Sodium: 1903 mg(79%)
- Fiber: 11 g(44%)
- Total Carbohydrate: 58 g(19%)
- Cholesterol: 521 mg(174%)
- Protein: 73 g(146%)
- Total Fat: 106 g(164%)
- Saturated Fat: 45 g(227%)

311. Tom Valenti's Lamb Shanks

Serving: Makes 6 servings | Prep: | Ready in:

Ingredients

- 6 lamb foreshanks
- Coarse salt and pepper, to taste
- 3 tablespoons plus 1/4 cup olive oil
- 2 ribs of celery, roughly chopped
- 1 carrot, roughly chopped
- 1 onion, roughly chopped
- 1/3 cup tomato paste
- 5 sprigs of fresh thyme
- 1 bay leaf
- 8 whole black peppercorns
- 3 anchovy fillets
- 1 whole head of garlic, cut in half crosswise
- 2 cups red wine
- 1 cup white wine
- 1/3 cup white-wine vinegar
- 1 teaspoon sugar
- 2 cups beef broth and 2 cups chicken broth
- White Bean Puree, for serving

Direction

- Preheat an oven to 325°F; season lamb with pepper and salt.
- Heat 3 tablespoons oil in pot on medium high heat. Add onion, carrot and celery; cook for 8-10 minutes till very soft.
- Add tomato paste; cook for 1-2 minutes. Add garlic, anchovies, peppercorns, bay leaf and thyme; cook for 3 minutes.
- Add sugar, vinegar and wines; put heat on high. Boil; reduce heat to medium. Add broths; leave on medium heat while browning lamb shanks.
- Put leftover 1/4 cup olive oil in sauté pan; brown lamb shanks on medium high heat well on all sides; flip over using tongs.
- Put lamb shanks in roasting pan; put braising liquid over. Use aluminum foil to cover; in preheated oven, cook for 1 hour. Remove foil; cook, turning shanks every half hour till meat is very soft, for 2 1/2-3 hours.
- Take shanks from braising liquid; strain liquid. Skim fat that rises to surface; use liquid for sauce. Serve inside shallow bowls over white bean puree.

Nutrition Information

312. Tomato Mushroom Bisque

Serving: Serves 8 | Prep: | Ready in:

Ingredients

- 3 tablespoons olive oil
- 2 celery stalks, trimmed, chopped
- 1 small onion, chopped
- 1 leek (white and light green parts only), chopped
- 1 large shallot, chopped
- 1 garlic clove, chopped
- 3/4 pound fresh shiitake mushrooms,* stemmed, thinly sliced
- 2 1/2 pounds tomatoes, peeled, seeded, chopped
- 2 cups chicken stock or canned broth
- 3/4 cup dry white wine
- 1/2 cup whipping cream

- 1 tablespoon fresh lemon juice
- 1 teaspoon dried thyme, crumbled
- 1 small bay leaf
- Pinch of saffron threads
- *If unavailable, three ounces dried shiitake mushrooms can be substituted. Cover with hot water and soak 30 minutes. Drain. Squeeze out water; cut out stems.

Direction

- In big, heavy saucepan, heat 2 tablespoons of oil on moderately-high heat. Put in garlic, shallot, leek, onion and celery. Cook for 7 minutes, till vegetables are clear, mixing from time to time. Put in and sauté half pound of mushrooms for 5 minutes. Put in saffron, bay leaf, thyme, lemon juice, cream, wine, chicken stock and tomatoes. Boil. Lower the heat and simmer for half an hour. Throw the bay leaf. Use processor to puree soup till smooth. Season with pepper and salt to taste. May be prepped a day in advance. Chill. Rewarm prior to serving.
- In small, heavy skillet, heat leftover 1 tablespoon of oil on moderately-high heat. Put in and sauté leftover quarter-pound mushrooms for 5 minutes. Season with pepper and salt to taste. Scoop bisque to serving bowls and jazz up using sautéed mushrooms.

Nutrition Information

- Calories: 182
- Total Carbohydrate: 16 g(5%)
- Cholesterol: 18 mg(6%)
- Protein: 5 g(9%)
- Total Fat: 11 g(17%)
- Saturated Fat: 4 g(19%)
- Sodium: 115 mg(5%)
- Fiber: 4 g(15%)

313. Tortelloni With Mushroom Sage Sauce

Serving: Makes 6 servings | Prep: | Ready in:

Ingredients

- 2 packages (about 9 ounces each) mushroom and cheese tortelloni
- 1/4 cup (1/2 stick) butter
- 1/2 cup chopped shallots
- 12 ounces fresh shiitake mushrooms, stemmed, caps thickly sliced
- 1 1/4 cups dry vermouth or dry white wine
- 3/4 cup whipping cream
- 1 1/2 tablespoons chopped fresh sage

Direction

- In pot with salted boiling water, cook the pasta following packaging instructions; strain.
- In big, heavy skillet, liquify butter on moderately-high heat. Put in shallots; sauté for a minute. Put in and sauté mushrooms, for 7 minutes till brown. Put in cream and vermouth. Boil for 5 minutes, till sauce is thick and coats the spoon. Mix sage in. Add pepper and salt to season. Put in pasta; toss till heated completely to serve.

Nutrition Information

- Calories: 608
- Cholesterol: 105 mg(35%)
- Protein: 19 g(38%)
- Total Fat: 26 g(40%)
- Saturated Fat: 15 g(76%)
- Sodium: 519 mg(22%)
- Fiber: 5 g(20%)
- Total Carbohydrate: 67 g(22%)

314. Triple Whammy Saffroned Tomato Fennel Soup

Serving: Makes 2 servings | Prep: | Ready in:

Ingredients

- 1 1/2 tbsp olive oil
- 1 medium onion, diced
- 1 fennel bulb, trimmed and diced, fronds reserved for garnish
- 1 clove garlic, minced
- 1/2 to 1 tsp saffron threads
- 1/4 cup dry white wine
- 1/4 cup fresh basil, finely shredded
- 1 can (28 oz) chopped tomatoes
- 1/4 cup roughly chopped fresh basil

Direction

- Heat oil in a big saucepan on moderately-low. Put in fennel, garlic and onion; cook with cover for 10 minutes. Heat saffron in a small pan or metal, big spoon for 10 seconds on low heat till dry. Use the back of spoon to grind into powder and steep for a minute in a tablespoon boiling water to render the flavor. Put spoonful of saffron and wine into pan, then mix shredded basil in. Boil on moderately-high heat; lower the heat to low and simmer for a minute to two. Put in a cup water, tomatoes and their juice. Bring back to boil on high heat; lower the heat to low and cover slightly to simmer for half an hour. Jazz up using chopped basil and fennel fronds.

Nutrition Information

315. Tropical Fruit Compote With Mango Sorbet

Serving: Serves 6 | Prep: | Ready in:

Ingredients

- 3/4 cup water
- 1/2 cup dry white wine
- 1/2 cup sugar
- 1/2 pineapple, peeled, cored, cut into 3/4-inch pieces (about 2 cups)
- 3 kiwis, peeled, halved crosswise, each half quartered
- 1 mango, peeled, pitted, cut into 3/4-inch pieces
- 1 1/2 tablespoons fresh lime juice
- 1 teaspoon grated lime peel
- 1 1/2 pints mango sorbet

Direction

- Preparation: In a small pan, mix wine, sugar, and 3/4 cup of water; boil. Stir the mixture until the sugar dissolves. Let the syrup cool until cold.
- In a large bowl, mix pineapple, lime peel, mango, lime juice, and kiwis well with the chilled syrup. Cover the bowl of fruit mixture and keep refrigerated for at least an hour or overnight.
- Serve half a cup of the mango sorbet in each of the 6 compote dishes or wine glasses. Place the prepared fruit mixture around the sorbet.

Nutrition Information

- Calories: 306
- Fiber: 4 g(17%)
- Total Carbohydrate: 76 g(25%)
- Protein: 1 g(3%)
- Total Fat: 0 g(1%)
- Saturated Fat: 0 g(0%)
- Sodium: 10 mg(0%)

316. Tropical Sparkling Sangria

Serving: Makes about 2 1/2 quarts. | Prep: | Ready in:

Ingredients

- 2 limes, sliced thin
- 2 small carambolas (star fruit, available at specialty produce markets), sliced thin crosswise
- 1 chilled 750-ml. bottle dry white wine
- 1 chilled 12-ounce can mango nectar
- 1 mango, cut into 1/2-inch cubes
- 1 chilled 12-ounce can ginger ale
- 1 chilled 750-ml. bottle champagne

Direction

- Reserve and prepare carambola slices and some of the limes for garnish. Mix the carambola slices, leftover of the lime, mango, mango nectar and the white wine together in a big pitcher. Up to this point, the sangria may be prepared, kept covered and chilled a day in advance. Mix in the ice cubes, the champagne, and the ginger ale before serving. Garnish the sangria with the reserved carambola slices and lime and serve.

Nutrition Information

- Calories: 427
- Saturated Fat: 0 g(1%)
- Sodium: 22 mg(1%)
- Fiber: 4 g(17%)
- Total Carbohydrate: 40 g(13%)
- Protein: 2 g(4%)
- Total Fat: 1 g(1%)

317. Trout In Riesling

Serving: Makes 4 main-course servings | Prep: 50mins | Ready in:

Ingredients

- 2 tablespoons (1 oz) unsalted butter plus additional for greasing
- 1 medium carrot
- 1 celery rib
- 4 (6- to 8-oz) trout fillets with skin
- 1 1/2 teaspoons salt
- 1 teaspoon black pepper
- 4 medium shallots, cut lengthwise into 1/8-inch-thick slices (1 cup)
- 2 fresh parsley sprigs
- 5 black peppercorns
- 1 1/2 cups water
- 1 1/2 cups dry Riesling
- 3/4 cup heavy cream
- 2 teaspoons cornstarch
- 2 teaspoons chopped fresh tarragon
- 1/2 teaspoon fresh lemon juice
- an adjustable-blade slicer; tweezers or needlenose pliers

Direction

- Preparation: Set oven rack in the center position and prepare the oven by preheating to 375 degrees F. Prepare buttered sides and bottom glass baking dish (13x9-inch).
- Use a slicer to slice celery and carrot lengthwise into very thin matchsticks (2 1/2-inches long and less than 1/8-inch wide).
- Wash trout and use needlenose pliers or tweezers to discard any pin bones. Pat dry then dust each with 1/2 teaspoon pepper and salt on fish (flesh sides only). Arrange fillets in the baking dish, overlapping slightly, skin sides down.
- In a 12-inch heavy skillet over moderate heat, put 2 tablespoons butter until foam subsides, add shallots and cook for about 3 minutes, until softened (do not brown), mixing. Put in peppercorns, parsley, celery, and carrot then cook for about 5 minutes, stirring, until vegetables are crisp-tender. Add 1/2 teaspoon salt, wine, and water then boil for 1 minute. Take the skillet away from the heat and place liquid over the fish and place vegetables in the baking dish and spread evenly. Reserve the skillet. Use foil to cover the dish tightly and bake for 6-8 minutes until fish is just cooked through.

- Place fish (topped with vegetables) onto a platter and use foil to cover it and keep warm. Put cooking liquid with any left vegetables through a sieve set over a bowl. Dust vegetables from sieve over the fish (get rid of peppercorns) and cover again with foil.
- Pour 1 cup of the strained cooking liquid into the cleaned skillet. Boil for about 2 minutes over high heat, until reduced to about 1/2 cup. Mix the cream into cornstarch until smooth, then stir into the sauce and boil for about 1 minute, stirring, until thickened. Mix in the rest 1/2 teaspoons each of pepper and salt, lemon juice, and tarragon.
- Take off the foil from the fish and use paper towels to blot any liquid accumulated on the platter. Put sauce over the fish.

Nutrition Information

- Calories: 616
- Saturated Fat: 17 g(84%)
- Sodium: 1021 mg(43%)
- Fiber: 3 g(11%)
- Total Carbohydrate: 19 g(6%)
- Cholesterol: 193 mg(64%)
- Protein: 43 g(85%)
- Total Fat: 35 g(53%)

318. Turkey Breast Braciola

Serving: Serves 12 as part of a buffet | Prep: | Ready in:

Ingredients

- 1 large head escarole (about 1 1/2 pounds), washed well and drained
- 3 tablespoons olive oil
- 1 large onion, chopped
- 1/2 cup raisins
- 1 1/2 cups low-salt chicken broth
- 1/3 cup freshly grated Parmesan cheese
- 1/4 cup pine nuts, toasted
- 1 slice homemade-type white bread, minced (about 1/2 cup coarse bread crumbs)
- 1 skinless boneless turkey breast half (2 to 2 1/2 pounds)
- 1/4 pound thinly sliced prosciutto
- 1/2 cup dry white wine
- 2 teaspoons fresh lemon juice

Direction

- Chop enough escarole coarsely to get 7 loosely packed cups; put leftover escarole aside. Heat 2 tbsp. oil in 12-in. skillet on medium high heat till hot yet not smoking; sauté onion till it starts to brown, occasionally mixing. Add chopped escarole to onion; cook till wilted, frequently mixing. Mix 1/2 cup broth and raisins in; cook on high heat till most liquid evaporates. Take the pan off from the heat; mix bread, pine nuts and parmesan into the filling.
- On a long plastic wrap sheet, put turkey. Butterfly turkey breast: Starting from long side, create lengthwise horizontal cut nearly yet not all the way through the turkey. Spread open turkey to create thinner, bigger meat piece. Put another plastic wrap sheet over turkey; use meat mallet/bottom of heavy skillet to pound till meat is 12x8-in. Don't create any holes in meat.
- Discard top plastic wrap sheet; put prosciutto in one layer on turkey, slightly overlapping. Spread 1/2-in. thick layer filling on prosciutto; leave 1/2-in. border all round. Put aside any leftover filling. Starting at long side, roll turkey up using plastic wrap for guide; flip seam side down then throw plastic wrap. Use kitchen string to tie rolled turkey lengthwise then at 1-in. intervals crosswise. Season with pepper and salt.
- Heat leftover tbsp. oil in 12-in. deep skillet on medium high heat till hot yet not smoking; brown turkey, flipping it. Add any leftover filling, leftover cup broth and wine; braise on medium low heat for 35 minutes, flipping turkey halfway through cooking, covered. Put turkey on a cutting board; cool. Through a

sieve, strain braising liquid into a small saucepan. Boil the liquid till reduced to 1/2 cup; skim foam off. Mix lemon juice in; fully cool sauce. You can make sauce and turkey 2 days ahead; covered with plastic wrap, separately chilled.
- Discard string from turkey; crosswise cut turkey to 1/2-in. thick slices. Shred leftover escarole; toss with 1/2 sauce in a bowl. Put escarole on a platter with the turkey slices; drizzle leftover sauce on turkey.

Nutrition Information

- Calories: 245
- Saturated Fat: 3 g(14%)
- Sodium: 357 mg(15%)
- Fiber: 2 g(10%)
- Total Carbohydrate: 10 g(3%)
- Cholesterol: 59 mg(20%)
- Protein: 22 g(45%)
- Total Fat: 12 g(19%)

319. Turkey Cutlets With Springtime Vegetables

Serving: Makes 2 servings | Prep: | Ready in:

Ingredients

- 8 ounces turkey cutlets or breast slices, cut crosswise into
- 1 1/2 teaspoons dried tarragon
- 2 tablespoons olive oil
- 1 cup thinly sliced leeks (white and pale green parts only)
- 3/4 cup peeled baby carrots (about 3 ounces), halved lengthwise
- 1 tablespoon all purpose flour
- 1 1/4 cups canned low-salt chicken broth
- 1/4 cup dry white wine
- 3/4 cup frozen petite peas

Direction

- Sprinkle pepper, salt, and 1 teaspoon tarragon over the turkey. In a big, heavy frying pan, heat oil over high heat. Put in turkey and sauté for 2 minutes until no pink remains. Bring the turkey to a dish with a slotted spoon. Lower the heat to medium. Put in the leftover 1/2 teaspoon tarragon, carrots, and leeks to the frying pan with the drippings. Cook for 3 minutes the leeks start to get tender. Stir flour into the vegetables and cook for 1 minute. Slowly stir in wine and broth. Simmer without a cover for 10 minutes until the sauce is thick and the carrots are nearly soft, mixing sometimes. Add turkey and peas. Simmer for another 2 minutes until the turkey has been fully cooked and the vegetables are soft. Use pepper and salt to season to taste and enjoy.

Nutrition Information

- Calories: 438
- Total Fat: 23 g(35%)
- Saturated Fat: 4 g(22%)
- Sodium: 158 mg(7%)
- Fiber: 5 g(20%)
- Total Carbohydrate: 23 g(8%)
- Cholesterol: 74 mg(25%)
- Protein: 32 g(64%)

320. Turkey Giblet Stock

Serving: 4 | Prep: | Ready in:

Ingredients

- Neck and giblets from a 10- to 12-pound turkey
- 6 cups water
- 1 medium onion, peeled and quartered
- 1 medium carrot, chopped
- 1 stalk celery, chopped
- 1 bay leaf
- 1 sprig fresh thyme
- 1 teaspoon whole black peppercorns

Direction

- In a big saucepan, mix together celery, carrot, onion, water, neck, and giblets excluding liver; boil. Put the peppercorns, thyme, and bay leaf in. Lower heat and let it simmer for an hour while skimming and removing any foam from surface.
- Use a fine-mesh sieve to strain the stock in a bowl. Cool and dispose of any solids.

Nutrition Information

- Calories: 79 calories;
- Saturated Fat: 1
- Sodium: 105
- Fiber: 2
- Total Carbohydrate: 7
- Sugar: 3
- Total Fat: 2
- Cholesterol: 148
- Protein: 8

321. Turkey Tonnato

Serving: Makes 6 to 8 (main-course) servings | Prep: 30mins | Ready in:

Ingredients

- 3 tablespoons black-olive tapenade
- 1 tablespoon finely grated fresh lemon zest
- 1 tablespoon finely chopped garlic
- 2 teaspoons finely chopped fresh rosemary
- 1 (4- to 4 1/2-lb) boneless turkey breast half with skin
- 2 teaspoons salt
- 1 teaspoon black pepper
- 2 tablespoons extra-virgin olive oil
- 1 cup dry white wine
- 1 (6-oz) can chunk light tuna in olive oil (do not drain)
- 1/2 cup extra-virgin olive oil
- 2 tablespoons water
- 1 tablespoon fresh lemon juice
- 2 teaspoons anchovy paste
- Accompaniments: lemon wedges; capers; chopped fresh flat-leaf parsley
- kitchen string; an instant-read thermometer

Direction

- Filling and roast: Place oven rack in center position. Preheat the oven to 350°F.
- In a small bowl, mix rosemary, garlic, zest and tapenade.
- On a work surface, put turkey with pointed, narrower end near you, skin side up. Choose which breast's long side is thickest. Starting from the thickest side, hold a knife parallel to work surface, horizontally cutting breast nearly in half, halting an inch from the other side. Open the breast up like a book. Season 1/2 tsp. pepper and 1 tsp. salt on breast. Evenly spread tapenade mixture on breast using a spoon's back. On all sides, leave an inch border. Beginning with side without the skin, roll turkey up sideways, finishing with the seam side down. The skin should be outside the rolled breast. At 1-in. intervals, use kitchen string to tie the turkey breast crosswise. Pat dry roast. Sprinkle leftover 1 tsp. salt and 1/2 tsp. pepper outside all over the roast.
- Cooking: In a 12-in. heavy skillet, heat 2 tbsp. olive oil till hot yet not smoking. Brown turkey, 8 minutes total, occasionally turning. Put into a 13x9-in. roasting pan. Put wine into pan. Roast turkey for 1 hour till an inserted thermometer diagonally 2-in. into the thickest part reads 160°F.
- On platter, put roast; cool. Keep pan juices. Completely cool roast. Chill, uncovered, wrapped tightly in plastic wrap for 2 hours.
- Sauce: In a blender, puree 4 tbsp. reserved pan juices, anchovy paste, lemon juice, water, 1/2 cup olive oil and tuna and its oil in a blender. Stop to scrape down sides if needed till very smooth. Put into a bowl. Season with pepper and salt. Use a plastic wrap to cover bowl. Chill for 1 hour till cold.

- Turkey tonnato assembly: Slice chilled turkey roast to 1/4-in. thick slices. Throw strings. Put chilled sauce on top. Bring sauce and turkey to room temperature for an hour. Serve with parsley, capers and lemon wedges.
- You can make sauce and turkey roast chilled, separately, for up to 2 days.

Nutrition Information

- Calories: 742
- Fiber: 0 g(2%)
- Total Carbohydrate: 2 g(1%)
- Cholesterol: 194 mg(65%)
- Protein: 72 g(144%)
- Total Fat: 46 g(71%)
- Saturated Fat: 9 g(46%)
- Sodium: 959 mg(40%)

322. Twelve Fruit Compote

Serving: Serves 12 | Prep: | Ready in:

Ingredients

- 3 cups water
- 1 cup sugar
- 1 pound mixed dried fruits (such as prunes, pears, apricots, peaches, apples and figs), cut into 1/2-inch pieces
- 1 cup sweet white wine (such as Johannisberg Riesling)
- 1 orange, unpeeled, thinly sliced
- 1 lemon, unpeeled, thinly sliced
- 1/2 cup raisins
- 1/2 cup dried cherries, cranberries or currants
- 8 whole cloves
- 4 cinnamon sticks
- 1 cup seedless grapes

Direction

- In big, heavy saucepan, mix sugar and 3 cups of water. Mix on moderate heat till sugar is dissolved. Put in cinnamon sticks, cloves, dried cherries, raisins, lemon, orange, white wine and mixed dried fruits. Let compote simmer for 20 minutes till fruits become tender and liquid is cooked down into syrup, mixing from time to time. Stir grapes in. Let compote cool to room temperature; tightly cover and chill. May be prepped 3 days maximum advance. Keep in refrigerator. Scoop compote to stemmed goblets to serve.

Nutrition Information

- Calories: 223
- Saturated Fat: 0 g(0%)
- Sodium: 8 mg(0%)
- Fiber: 4 g(18%)
- Total Carbohydrate: 55 g(18%)
- Protein: 2 g(4%)
- Total Fat: 0 g(1%)

323. Vanilla Panna Cotta With Mixed Berry Compote

Serving: Makes 8 servings | Prep: | Ready in:

Ingredients

- 1/4 cup cold water
- 2 1/2 teaspoons unflavored gelatin (from 2 packages)
- 3 cups whipping cream
- 1 cup sugar
- 1 1/2 teaspoons vanilla extract
- 4 1/2-pint baskets assorted fresh berries (such as raspberries, blueberries, blackberries, and strawberries)
- 1/3 cup sweet white wine (such as Moscato)

Direction

- To small custard cup, add quarter cup cold water. Scatter gelatin on top. Rest for 15 minutes till gelatin is soft. Boil an-inch water

in small skillet. Pour cup of gelatin into water. Mix for 2 minutes, till gelatin is dissolved. Take off heat.
- In medium, heavy saucepan, mix 2/3 cup sugar and cream. Mix on moderate heat barely till sugar is dissolved. Take off heat. Stir in gelatin and vanilla. Distribute pudding mixture between 8 glasses of wine. Chill with cover till set, not less than 6 hours to maximum of a day.
- In medium bowl, mix leftover 1/3 cup sugar and berries. Slightly mash the berries using back of a spoon. Stir wine in. Rest compote till sugar and berry juices form syrup, mixing frequently, for not less than an hour to no longer than 2 hours.
- Top puddings with scoop of compote.

Nutrition Information

- Calories: 438
- Saturated Fat: 17 g(87%)
- Sodium: 34 mg(1%)
- Fiber: 9 g(34%)
- Total Carbohydrate: 43 g(14%)
- Cholesterol: 99 mg(33%)
- Protein: 5 g(10%)
- Total Fat: 28 g(44%)

324. Vanilla Pear Clafoutis

Serving: Makes 6 servings | Prep: | Ready in:

Ingredients

- 3/4 cup sweet white wine (such as Riesling)
- 3 large pears, peeled, cored, cut lengthwise into 1/2-inch-thick slices
- 4 large eggs
- 1/2 cup sugar
- Pinch of salt
- 6 tablespoons all purpose flour
- 1 cup milk (do not use low-fat or nonfat)
- 1/4 cup (1/2 stick) butter, melted
- 1 tablespoon vanilla extract
- Powdered sugar

Direction

- Preheat the oven to 325°F. Mix pears and wine in big bowl; rest for 10 minutes. Strain the pears, putting aside quarter cup of wine.
- Use butter to grease glass pie dish, 9-inch in diameter. Whip in medium bowl with sugar, salt and eggs to incorporate. Mix flour in. Put in reserved 1/4 cup wine, vanilla, butter and milk; mix till smooth. Place pears in prepped dish. Top pears with batter.
- Let clafoutis bake for 55 minutes, till middle is set and surface turn golden. Allow to cool for 10 minutes. Liberally sift powdered sugar on top. Slice to make wedges; serve while warm.

Nutrition Information

- Calories: 331
- Total Carbohydrate: 46 g(15%)
- Cholesterol: 148 mg(49%)
- Protein: 7 g(14%)
- Total Fat: 12 g(19%)
- Saturated Fat: 7 g(33%)
- Sodium: 117 mg(5%)
- Fiber: 4 g(15%)

325. Vanilla Poached Pineapple

Serving: Makes 8 servings | Prep: 30mins | Ready in:

Ingredients

- 1 large extra-sweet pineapple
- 1 vanilla bean, split lengthwise
- 4 cups dry white wine
- 1/3 cup Grand Marnier
- 1/3 cup packed light brown sugar
- 1 (2-to 3-inch) piece of cinnamon stick
- 1 Turkish or 1/2 California bay leaf

- 2 cloves
- 1 1/2 tablespoons granulated sugar
- Accompaniment: vanilla ice cream

Direction

- Peel pineapple; quarter lengthwise. Cut core out. Cut every quarter lengthwise to 4 pieces to get 16.
- From vanilla bean, scrape seeds into a heavy 12-in. skillet using a paring knife's tip. Add a big pinch of salt, cloves, bay leaf, cinnamon stick, brown sugar, Grand Marnier, wine and pod. Boil, mixing till sugar melts.
- Put pineapple into wine mixture; boil. Take off heat. In liquid, cool pineapple for an hour. Use a slotted spoon to transfer pineapple onto a 4-sided sheet pan. Boil liquid for 35 minutes till reduced to 2/3 cup.
- Preheat the broiler.
- Sprinkle granulated sugar on pineapple. Broil 3-4-in. away from heat for 10-15 minutes till lightly charred in spots and slightly caramelized. Carefully watch and remove pineapples that quickly color. Serve it drizzled with syrup.
- You can poach pineapple and reduce liquid 1 day ahead, chilled separately. Sprinkle sugar on then broil prior to serving.

Nutrition Information

- Calories: 185
- Saturated Fat: 0 g(0%)
- Sodium: 8 mg(0%)
- Fiber: 2 g(7%)
- Total Carbohydrate: 29 g(10%)
- Protein: 1 g(1%)
- Total Fat: 0 g(0%)

---

326. Veal Piccata With Capers And Pine Nuts

Serving: Serves 2 | Prep: | Ready in:

Ingredients

- 2 bacon slices, chopped
- 6 ounces veal scallops (about 6 scallops), pounded very thin
- All purpose flour (for dredging)
- 4 tablespoons (1/2 stick) unsalted butter
- 1/2 cup dry white wine
- 3 tablespoons toasted pine nuts
- 1 tablespoon drained capers
- 2 teaspoons minced fresh sage or 1/2 teaspoon dried rubbed sage
- Fresh sage leaves (optional)

Direction

- Cook bacon till crisp in big heavy skillet on medium high heat; use slotted spoon to put in bowl. Season veal with pepper and salt. Dredge in flour; shake excess off. Put 1 tablespoon butter into pan drippings in skillet; melt on medium high heat then add veal. Sauté for 1 minute per side till just cooked through. To 2 plates, divide veal; to keep warm, tent with foil. Boil wine in same skillet, scraping browned bits up. Boil for 2 minutes till liquid reduces to 3 cups. Whisk leftover 3 tablespoon butter in; mix bacon, minced sage, capers and pine nuts in. Season with pepper; scoop sauce on veal. If desired, garnish with sage leaves and serve.

Nutrition Information

- Calories: 503
- Saturated Fat: 19 g(96%)
- Sodium: 586 mg(24%)
- Fiber: 2 g(7%)
- Total Carbohydrate: 8 g(3%)
- Cholesterol: 98 mg(33%)
- Protein: 15 g(30%)
- Total Fat: 44 g(67%)

327. Veal Scallops With Creamy Mushroom Sauce

Serving: Makes 4 main-course servings | Prep: | Ready in:

Ingredients

- 1/2 cup all purpose flour
- 1 1/4 pounds large veal scallops (each about 1/4 inch thick)
- 5 tablespoons butter
- 8 ounces crimini mushrooms, sliced
- 2 large shallots, finely chopped (about 1/2 cup)
- 3/4 cup dry white wine
- 1 cup whipping cream
- 2 tablespoons chopped fresh parsley

Direction

- In shallow dish, put flour. Sprinkle pepper and salt on veal scallops. Melt 2 tablespoons butter in big heavy skillet on high heat. In flour, coat veal; shake excess off. Put veal in skillet in batches; sauté for 1 minute per side till starting to brown. Put on plate; to keep warm, tent with foil.
- In same skillet, melt leftover 3 tablespoons butter on medium high heat then add shallots and mushrooms; sauté for 7 minutes till mushrooms are tender and brown. Add wine; simmer till liquid reduces to 1/4 cup. Add cream and simmer for 3 minutes till reduced to sauce consistency; season with pepper and salt. Put veal back in skillet; simmer for 1 minute till just heated through. Put veal on plates; scoop sauce on top. Sprinkle parsley and serve.

Nutrition Information

- Calories: 508
- Total Carbohydrate: 25 g(8%)
- Cholesterol: 139 mg(46%)
- Protein: 22 g(44%)
- Total Fat: 34 g(52%)
- Saturated Fat: 21 g(104%)
- Sodium: 587 mg(24%)
- Fiber: 2 g(6%)

328. Veal Scallops With Lemon And Capers

Serving: Serves 2 | Prep: | Ready in:

Ingredients

- 1/4 cup all-purpose flour
- 1/2 teaspoon salt
- four 3-ounce veal scallops, each about 1/8 inch thick
- 1 tablespoon olive oil
- 1/2 cup dry white wine
- three 1/4-inch lemon slices, halved
- 1 teaspoon drained bottled capers
- 1 tablespoon unsalted butter
- 1 teaspoon minced fresh parsley leaves

Direction

- Mix salt and flour in shallow dish and dip veal in flour mixture, 1 by 1, shake excess off. Heat oil in a non-stick, big skillet on medium high heat till hot yet not smoking and sauté veal in it till light golden, for a minute. Flip veal and sauté for an additional of 30 seconds, or till light golden and just bouncy to touch. Turn veal onto platter and cover to retain warmth. Put lemon, capers and wine to skillet and let mixture simmer for a minute. Tilt in parsley and butter and put sauce on top of veal.

Nutrition Information

- Calories: 341
- Total Fat: 14 g(21%)
- Saturated Fat: 5 g(24%)
- Sodium: 756 mg(32%)
- Fiber: 3 g(12%)
- Total Carbohydrate: 26 g(9%)

- Cholesterol: 56 mg(19%)
- Protein: 23 g(46%)

329. Veal And Tomato Ragoût With Potatoes, Cinnamon, And Cream

Serving: Makes 6 servings | Prep: | Ready in:

Ingredients

- 2 pounds 1-inch pieces trimmed boneless veal stew meat
- 1/4 cup all purpose flour
- 3 tablespoons butter
- 1 tablespoon olive oil
- 2 medium onions, finely chopped
- 2 celery stalks, finely chopped
- 1 1/4 cups dry white wine
- 2 cups tomato sauce
- 1 cup (or more) water
- 3 tablespoons chopped fresh parsley
- 2 cinnamon sticks
- 1 1/4 pounds white-skinned potatoes, peeled, cut into 1/2-inch pieces
- 1/2 cup whipping cream

Direction

- Sprinkle flour on veal in medium bowl; toss to coat. Shake excess off; sprinkle pepper and salt on veal. Melt butter along with oil in heavy big pot on high heat; sauté veal in batches for 6 minutes per side till all sides are brown. Put in bowl. Add celery and onions to pot; sauté for 5 minutes till veggies start to soften. Put veal in pot. Add wine; boil, scraping browned bits up. Boil for 3 minutes till liquid reduces by half. Mix cinnamon sticks, parsley, 1 cup water and tomato sauce in; boil. Lower heat to low and cover; simmer for 1 hour 15 minutes, occasionally mixing.
- Mix cream and potatoes into stew; season with pepper and salt. Cover; simmer for 1 hour till potatoes and veal are very tender, mixing often and, if needed, thin with extra water. Discard cinnamon sticks and serve.

Nutrition Information

- Calories: 482
- Cholesterol: 133 mg(44%)
- Protein: 37 g(74%)
- Total Fat: 22 g(34%)
- Saturated Fat: 11 g(55%)
- Sodium: 536 mg(22%)
- Fiber: 5 g(19%)
- Total Carbohydrate: 31 g(10%)

330. Vegan "Tofurkey" With Mushroom Stuffing And Gravy

Serving: 8 servings | Prep: 1hours20mins | Ready in:

Ingredients

- 4 tablespoons vegetable oil, divided, plus more for pan
- 1 French demi baguette (about 4 1/2 ounces), cut into 1/4"cubes (about 3 cups)
- 1/2 cup raw pecans, coarsely chopped
- 1/2 medium onion, chopped
- 1 garlic clove, finely chopped
- 5 sprigs thyme
- 8 ounces crimini mushrooms, coarsely chopped
- 1 large celery stalk, sliced crosswise into 1/4"-thick pieces (about 3/4 cup)
- 1 cup homemade vegetable stock or low-sodium vegetable broth
- 1/3 cup dry white wine
- 1 3/4 teaspoons kosher salt, divided
- 1 1/4 teaspoons freshly ground black pepper, divided
- 2 tablespoons soy sauce
- 1 tablespoon pure maple syrup
- 1/2 teaspoon smoked paprika

- 1/8 teaspoon cayenne pepper
- 3 (14-ounce) packages extra-firm tofu
- 3 tablespoons white miso paste
- 2 tablespoons cornstarch
- 1 teaspoon garlic powder
- 1 tablespoon chopped parsley
- 3 tablespoons vegetable oil, divided
- 12 ounces crimini mushrooms, coarsely chopped
- 2 shallots, quartered
- 1 garlic clove, crushed
- 5 sprigs thyme
- 2 fresh bay leaves
- 4 cups homemade vegetable stock or low-sodium vegetable broth
- 2 tablespoons all-purpose flour
- 1/2 cup dry white wine
- 1 tablespoon coarsely chopped parsley
- 1 1/2 teaspoons kosher salt, plus more
- 1/4 teaspoon freshly ground black pepper, plus more
- A 1 1/2-quart oval loaf pan or 9x5" loaf pan

Direction

- To prepare the tofurkey: Turn the oven to 425°F to preheat. Oil an oval pan, and in the middle of the pan, put a 12-inch parchment strip lengthwise, leaving 1-inch overhang.
- On a rimmed baking tray, arrange 1 layer of pecans and bread and bake for 8 minutes until the bread is dry and turns pale golden brown.
- In a big skillet, heat 2 tablespoons of oil over medium heat. Stir and cook thyme, garlic, and onion for 3 minutes until the onion is translucent. Add mushrooms and cook for 5 minutes until barely turning brown. Add celery and cook for another 3 minutes until the mushrooms have been fully cooked, tossing frequently. Remove the mixture to a big bowl; discard the thyme sprigs. Add pecans and bread, then mix to blend and put aside.
- In the hot skillet, pour wine and stock and heat on medium-high, using a spoon to scrape up browned pieces; use 1/2 teaspoon black pepper and 1 teaspoon salt to season. Cook for 1 minute until barely blended, tossing. Add to the bread mixture, and then mix to blend.
- In a medium-sized bowl, combine 1/2 teaspoon salt, 2 tablespoons oil, cayenne, paprika, maple syrup, and soy sauce.
- Crumble tofu into big chunks. Crumble the tofu by hands, in batches, and press down into a colander lined with a towel to strain as much liquid as you can. Assemble the ends of the towel to gather the tofu into the center, squeezing the towel into a ball to release as much liquid as you can. Remove the tofu to a food processor. Add 1/2 teaspoon black pepper, the leftover 2 teaspoons salt, garlic powder, cornstarch, and miso. Process for 30 seconds until smooth.
- With a greased spatula, line 2/3 of the tofu mixture into the interior sides and bottom of the prepared pan, firmly pressing to make tight 3/4-in. high walls. Put the mushroom mixture into the middle and firmly press down. Put on the leftover tofu mixture to cover and even out the surface. (If you have any stuffing left, bake, covered in a dish, individually and enjoy as a side dish). Generously brush the soy-maple glaze over the top with a pastry brush.
- Remove the pan to a rimmed baking sheet and bake the tofurkey for 30 minutes, brushing the glaze over the top halfway through, until the loaf is light brown and set. Line parchment into a separate rimmed baking sheet and set onto the oval pan. Swiftly and gently flip the pan to turn out the tofurkey onto the sheet, carefully taking out of the pan by using the parchment. Brush the leftover glaze over the entire loaf.
- Turn on the broiler and broil for 6-7 minutes until forming a pale brown crust. Let cool for a minimum of 10 minutes. Put parsley on top and enjoy with the gravy on the side.
- To prepare the gravy: In a medium-sized saucepan, heat 1 tablespoon oil over medium-low for 30 seconds until aromatic and starting to turn brown. Cook bay leaves, thyme, garlic, shallot, and mushrooms, stirring sometimes, for 5 minutes until starting to turn brown and

- soft. Pour in the stock, let come to a simmer, and cook for 30 minutes until decreased by 1/2, tossing sometimes.
- Pour the mushroom mixture through a fine-mesh sieve to drain into a big bowl, then clean the pot. In the pot, cook the leftover 2 tablespoons of oil and flour over medium heat for 5-7 minutes until thickened and browned, whisking continually.
- Pour in the wine and cook for 30 seconds, whisking to blend. Mix in 1/4 teaspoon pepper, 1 1/2 teaspoon salt, parsley, and mushroom broth and simmer over medium-low heat. Cook for 10 minutes until thickened and partially decreased, whisking sometimes. Use pepper and salt to season.
- You can prepare the stuffing 1 day in advance; use plastic to wrap tightly and refrigerate. You can prepare the gravy for 3 days in advance; remove to an airtight container and refrigerate. Heat over medium in a small pot for 5 minutes until smooth, stirring continually and if necessary, adding stock or warm water by 1 tablespoon each time.

Nutrition Information

- Calories: 479
- Protein: 22 g(44%)
- Total Fat: 25 g(39%)
- Saturated Fat: 3 g(15%)
- Sodium: 1158 mg(48%)
- Fiber: 6 g(24%)
- Total Carbohydrate: 44 g(15%)

331. Vin D'orange (Orange Wine)

Serving: Makes about 2-1/2 quarts vin d'orange | Prep: | Ready in:

Ingredients

- The skin and the pith from 10 large oranges
- 8 cups dry white wine, such as Sauvignon Blanc
- 2 cups vodka
- 1/4 cup coffee beans
- 2 vanilla beans
- 2 cups sugar

Direction

- Preparation:
- 1. In a non-reactive bowl, lay vanilla beans, coffee beans, vodka, wine, and orange skins. Add half the sugar and mix well.
- 2. In a small and heavy-bottomed saucepan, lay the remaining half of sugar and allow it to caramelize over medium heat to a deep golden, to make sure all of the sugar evenly caramelizes, rotate the pan from time to time. Remove the pan from the heat. In the bowl with the oranges and the liquid, slowly pour the caramel, be careful not to let the caramel get on your skin. The caramelized sugar will get hard immediately, but don't be concerned. It will melt into the liquid eventually.
- 3. Cover the bowl and allow to rest for 6 days, stirring several times a day.
- 4. Use 3 thicknesses of cheesecloth to drain the wine and decant into bottles. Cover the bottles with a cork and allow to rest for at least a month and up to a year before opening.

Nutrition Information

332. Walnut Risotto With Roasted Asparagus

Serving: Serves 4 | Prep: | Ready in:

Ingredients

- 4 1/2 to 5 cups canned low-salt chicken broth
- 3 teaspoons olive oil (preferably extra virgin)
- 1/3 cup chopped onion

- 1-1/4 cups arborio rice or medium-grain white rice
- 1/2 cup dry white wine
- 1 pound asparagus, tough ends trimmed
- 1 large garlic clove, thinly sliced
- 1/4 cup finely chopped toasted walnuts
- 2 tablespoons freshly grated Parmesan cheese

Direction

- Preheat the oven to 450 degrees F. Simmer broth in a medium pot; cover and take off heat. On medium-high heat, heat 1 1/2 tsp olive oil in a heavy medium pot. Sauté onion for 4mins until light golden; put in rice and mix for a minute. Pour in wine and mix for 2mins until it evaporates. Pour in half cup hot broth; cook and stir frequently until the rice absorbs the liquid. Keep on adding half cup of broth at a time until the rice is creamy and tender. Mix regularly to let the rice absorb broth then add more, 25mins.
- In a shallow baking dish, arrange garlic and asparagus. Pour in leftover 1 1/2 tsp oil; season with pepper and salt. Mix the asparagus and garlic to coat. Bake for 16mins until tender, flip from time to time.
- Stir grated Parmesan and walnuts into the risotto; sprinkle pepper and salt. Place roasted asparagus in the middle of four plates then add risotto on top.

Nutrition Information

333. Watermelon Sorbet With Wine Basil Gelée

Serving: Makes 6 to 8 dessert servings | Prep: | Ready in:

Ingredients

- 3/4 cup sugar
- 1/4 cup water
- 1 teaspoon finely grated fresh lemon zest
- 5 cups coarsely chopped seeded watermelon (from a 4-lb piece, rind discarded)
- 2 tablespoons fresh lemon juice, or to taste
- 1/4 cup packed fresh basil leaves
- 1 1/2 cups dry white wine
- 1/2 cup sugar
- 1 teaspoon finely grated fresh lemon zest
- 1/2 cup plus 2 tablespoons water
- 2 teaspoons unflavored gelatin (from 1 envelope)
- 2 tablespoons fresh lemon juice, or to taste
- an ice cream maker

Direction

- Prepare sorbet: in a heavy, 2-quart saucepan, boil water, zest and sugar, mixing till sugar dissolves, then lower the heat and simmer for 2 minutes, without mixing, brushing down any crystals of sugar on pan side using pastry brush dunked in cold water.
- Place watermelon in blender, then put in lemon juice and syrup and process till smooth. Pass through a sieve with fine-mesh right into a big bowl, forcing on pulp and throwing any leftover solids.
- Use an ice cream maker to freeze, then turn onto airtight container and place in freezer till set.
- Meanwhile, prepare gelée: in 3-quart pot with salted boiling water, let basil blanch for 5 seconds, then strain and turn onto bowl with cold water and ice to halt the cooking. Strain the basil and press dry.
- In a cleaned heavy, 2-quart saucepan, boil half cup of water, zest, sugar and wine, mixing till sugar dissolves, then simmer for two minutes.
- Meanwhile, in a big metal bowl, scatter gelatin on top of leftover 2 tablespoons of water and soften for a minute.
- Pass approximately half cup of wine syrup through a dampened paper towel-lined-medium-mesh sieve right into the mixture of gelatin, put the lined sieve aside, then mix till gelatin dissolves.

- Use a cleaned blender to process the rest of the syrup along with lemon juice and basil till smooth, be careful once processing hot liquids, then pass through the lined sieve right into the mixture of gelatin. Place bowl in a bigger bowl with cold water and ice and rest for 15 minutes, mixing from time to time, till cold, then refrigerate to chill, with no cover, till set, for not less than 2 hours.
- Mix gelée slowly to break into small portions and serve base for sorbet scoops.
- Notes: Sorbet may be done a day in advance. Gelée, unbroken, may be put in refrigerator for maximum of 8 hours. Put on cover 2 hours after.

Nutrition Information

- Calories: 270
- Cholesterol: 7 mg(2%)
- Protein: 2 g(4%)
- Total Fat: 2 g(3%)
- Saturated Fat: 1 g(6%)
- Sodium: 20 mg(1%)
- Fiber: 1 g(3%)
- Total Carbohydrate: 57 g(19%)

334. White Chocolate Tiramisu Trifle With Spiced Pears

Serving: Makes 10 to 12 servings | Prep: | Ready in:

Ingredients

- 1 750-ml bottle dry white wine
- 2 cups pear juice or pear nectar
- 1 1/4 cups sugar
- 12 whole green cardamom pods, crushed in resealable plastic bag with mallet
- 4 1-inch-diameter rounds peeled fresh ginger (each about 1/8 inch thick)
- 2 cinnamon sticks, broken in half
- 5 large firm but ripe Anjou pears (3 to 31/4 pounds), peeled
- 7 ounces high-quality white chocolate (such as Lindt or Perugina), finely chopped
- 1/3 cup poire Williams (clear pear brandy)
- 1/4 cup water
- 1/2 vanilla bean, split lengthwise
- 1 8- to 8.8-ounce container mascarpone cheese*
- 1 cup chilled heavy whipping cream
- 3 3-ounce packages soft ladyfingers,** separated
- 2 cups chilled heavy whipping cream
- 1/4 cup minced crystallized ginger
- White chocolate curls
- 1 tablespoon powdered sugar

Direction

- Spiced pears: mix in big saucepan the initial 6 ingredients. Mix on moderately-high heat till sugar is dissolved. Put in pears and boil. Lower the heat to moderate, put cover, and simmer for 35 minutes, till pears are barely soft once pricked using. Turn the liquid including pears onto a big bowl and chill for 3 hours, till cold.
- Turn the pears onto plate with slotted spoon. In big, heavy saucepan, let poaching liquid boil for 15 minutes on moderately-high heat till partially thickened and cooked down to liberal 1 1/2 cups. Drain in a 2-cup measuring cup; throw the spices in the strainer. Cool down. Refrigerate pear syrup and pears with cover till cold.
- Mousse: in double boiler top place above simmering water, mix pear brandy, quarter cup water and white chocolate. Mix till smooth, mixture will become extremely liquidy in consistency. Scoop in vanilla bean seeds; throw the bean. Turn the mixture of white chocolate onto big bowl; slowly put in mascarpone, mixing till mixture become smooth. Let mascarpone mixture cool to just lukewarm.
- In medium size bowl, whip a cup of cream with electric mixer to peaks. Fold into mixture of mascarpone with the whipped cream in 4

increments. Refrigerate white chocolate mousse with cover for 3 hours, till firm. Mousse and pears may be done a day in advance. Keep refrigerated.
- Trifle assembly: halve pears lengthwise and take stems and cores; slice halves lengthwise to make quarter-inch-thick pieces.
- In the base of 12-cup trifle dish, approximately 8-inch-diameter and 5-inch-deep, place the ladyfingers in one pile, rounded sides facing down, completely covering the base, with roughly 15 ladyfingers. Evenly drizzle ladyfingers with 5 tablespoons of pear syrup. Smear a third white chocolate mousse on top of ladyfingers with offset, small spatula, creating layer a bit thicker around the outer dish edges, letting mousse be more noticeable, middle of layer of mousse will become thin. Beginning at the outer dish edges, put slices of pear in one-layer on top of mousse, curved edges against dish sides, fully covering. Redo piling of pears, mousse, syrup, and ladyfingers twice more. Put 4th pile of ladyfingers to cover, there might have some remaining pear slices and ladyfingers. Evenly sprinkle 5 tablespoons of syrup on ladyfingers. May be done a day in advance. Put cover and separately chill leftover pear syrup and trifle.
- In big bowl, whip 2 cups of whipping cream with electric mixer to soft peak. Put in quarter cup of pear syrup and whip to forming stiff peak. Turn the cream into a big pastry bag equipped with big star tip, do it in batches. Pipe rosettes on the entire top of trifle, piling a bit in the middle. Scatter crystallized ginger over. Jazz up using chocolate curls. May be done 6 hours in advance. Keep in refrigerator.
- Sift powdered sugar on top of trifle barely prior to serving.
- Tip: To create chocolate curls, put a 3 1/2-ounce bar of top-quality white chocolate like Perugina or Lindt on plate and microwave at after every 5-second on high barely till softened a bit, yet not hot or starting to liquify. Beginning at a long chocolate bar edge, shave the white chocolate to make curls with vegetable peeler. Chocolate is not soft enough in case it breaks into small shards, so return in microwave for several seconds. Rest chocolate at room temperature or refrigerate in short while till it firms up slightly in case chocolate turns overly soft.

Nutrition Information

- Calories: 1184
- Total Carbohydrate: 109 g(36%)
- Cholesterol: 303 mg(101%)
- Protein: 11 g(22%)
- Total Fat: 75 g(115%)
- Saturated Fat: 43 g(214%)
- Sodium: 205 mg(9%)
- Fiber: 8 g(31%)

335. White Clam Sauce Dip

Serving: Makes about 1 1/2 cups | Prep: 20mins | Ready in:

Ingredients

- 3/4 cup chopped flat-leaf parsley
- 1 tablespoon fine dry bread crumbs
- 6 tablespoons extra-virgin olive oil, divided
- 1/3 cup finely chopped onion
- 5 garlic cloves, finely chopped
- 1/4 teaspoon hot red pepper flakes
- 1/4 cup dry white wine
- 1/4 cup bottled clam juice
- 3 (6 1/2-ounces) cans chopped clams, drained
- 1 to 2 teaspoons fresh lemon juice

Direction

- Puree 1/4 cup oil, breadcrumbs and parsley in a food processor.
- Cook red pepper flakes, garlic and onion in leftover 2 tbsp. oil on medium heat in a medium skillet for 5 minutes till pale golden, mixing. Add clam juice and wine; boil for 1-2 minutes till slightly reduced, mixing. Mix in

clams; cook till heated through. Mix in parsley puree; take off heat. Season with salt and lemon juice.

Nutrition Information

- Calories: 545
- Fiber: 1 g(4%)
- Total Carbohydrate: 17 g(6%)
- Cholesterol: 92 mg(31%)
- Protein: 47 g(94%)
- Total Fat: 30 g(47%)
- Saturated Fat: 4 g(22%)
- Sodium: 360 mg(15%)

336. White Wine And Peach Sangria

Serving: Makes 6 cups. | Prep: | Ready in:

Ingredients

- 1 750-ml bottle dry white wine
- 3/4 cup peach brandy
- 6 tablespoons frozen lemonade concentrate, thawed
- 1/4 cup sugar
- 1/2 16-ounce package frozen unsweetened sliced peaches
- 3/4 cup seedless green grapes, halved
- 3/4 cup seedless red grapes, halved

Direction

- Mix in big pitcher with the initial 4 ingredients till sugar dissolves. Put in all grapes and peaches. Chill sangría for 2 hours, till thoroughly chilled. Pour over ice and serve.

Nutrition Information

- Calories: 389
- Fiber: 1 g(5%)
- Total Carbohydrate: 34 g(11%)

- Protein: 1 g(2%)
- Total Fat: 0 g(0%)
- Saturated Fat: 0 g(0%)
- Sodium: 12 mg(1%)

337. White Zinfandel Sangria

Serving: Serves 6 | Prep: | Ready in:

Ingredients

- 1 750-ml bottle of chilled White Zinfandel
- 1/2 cup peach schnapps
- 2 tablespoons Cointreau or other orange liqueur
- 2 tablespoons sugar
- 2 cinnamon sticks, broken in half
- 1 lemon, sliced
- 1 orange, sliced
- 1 peach, sliced into wedges
- 1 10-ounce bottle of chilled club soda
- Ice cubes

Direction

- In a tall pitcher, combine the first 8 ingredients. For at least 30 minutes, keep it refrigerated to let the flavors blend together before adding club soda. To serve, insert ice cubes into 6 wineglasses before pouring the sangria over it.

Nutrition Information

- Calories: 174
- Saturated Fat: 0 g(0%)
- Sodium: 11 mg(0%)
- Fiber: 2 g(7%)
- Total Carbohydrate: 17 g(6%)
- Protein: 1 g(2%)
- Total Fat: 0 g(0%)

338. Whole Snapper

Serving: Makes 10 to 12 servings | Prep: | Ready in:

Ingredients

- 1/4 cup olive oil
- 2 Spanish onions, peeled and thinly sliced
- 2 large cloves garlic, peeled and chopped, plus 4 cloves whole garlic, peeled
- 1 cup dry white wine
- 2 bay leaves
- 6 tablespoons unsalted butter
- Juice of 2 lemons
- 2 (4-pound) whole red snappers, cleaned, with head and tail intact
- 1 small tomato, sliced
- 2 ribs celery, halved crosswise
- Juice of 10 Key limes or small thin-skinned limes, plus 4 limes cut into quarters for serving
- 1/2 cup coarsely chopped fresh cilantro
- 1 (12- by 18-inch or larger) roasting pan

Direction

- Preheat an oven to 400°F.
- Heat oil on medium heat in a big sauté pan. Put and sauté onions for 5 minutes, mixing from time to time, till soft. Put and sauté chopped garlic for a minute, mixing from time to time. Put in bay leaves and 3/4 cup of wine and simmer. Keep simmering for 3 minutes till wine is cooked down a bit and onions become tender. Mix butter in then take pan off heat and mix lemon juice in.
- Place snappers, nest to each other, in 12- inch by 18-inch roasting pan or bigger. Stuff celery, tomato slices, whole garlic and quarter cup of onion mixture inside the cavity of every fish. Season with pepper and salt to taste. Scoop the leftover onion mixture on top of fish then add 1/2 of lime juice on top and on surrounding of the fish and to pan, pour in 2 cups water. Use foil to snugly encase the pan and roast, about 25 minutes. Take foil and keep roasting for an additional of 20 to 25 minutes, till fish is cooked completely. Take the onion from fish top then cautiously turn the fish onto a big serving platter, keep onion or juices left in pan. Sprinkle the rest of the lime juice on top of the fish and use foil to loosely cover to retain warmth.
- Transfer onion including the juices from roasting pan to medium saucepan. Pour in quarter cup of water and leftover quarter cup of white wine, and simmer. Keep simmering till partially cooked down, then pass through a strainer with fine-mesh.
- Serve: jazz fish up using cilantro and serve including lime wedges and reduced sauce from pan.
- Note: To grill snapper, preheat a grill to moderately-high, approximately 375° and grill for 40 minutes, till barely cooked completely.

Nutrition Information

339. Wild Mushroom Ravioli In Porcini Broth

Serving: Makes 6 servings | Prep: | Ready in:

Ingredients

- 3 cups water
- 2 ounces dried porcini mushrooms (about 3 cups)
- Cheesecloth
- 2 tablespoons olive oil
- 2 large shallots, minced (about 3/4 cup)
- 4 1/2 cups low-salt chicken broth
- 1/2 cup dry white wine
- 3 tablespoons dry Sherry
- 1 1/2 teaspoons coarse kosher salt
- 1/2 teaspoon ground black pepper
- 8 ounces purchased fresh or frozen wild mushroom ravioli
- 3/4 cup thinly sliced green onion tops

Direction

- In medium saucepan, boil 3 cups water. Put in porcini. Take off heat; submerge for 20 minutes, till mushrooms soften. Put the strainer on top of medium bowl; line cheesecloth on strainer. Drain the mushroom soaking liquid, put mushrooms aside for other use.
- In big saucepan, heat the oil on moderate heat. Put in shallots; lower the heat to moderately-low and sauté for 5 minutes, till shallots are soft. Put in mushroom soaking liquid, then pepper, salt, Sherry, wine and chicken broth; boil. Lower the heat and simmer with cover for 5 minutes. May be done a day in advance. Refrigerate with cover. Simmer prior to using.
- In big saucepan with salted boiling water, cook ravioli till just tender yet remain firm to bite. Strain. Put into hot mushroom broth with ravioli; scoop to bowls. Scatter green onion tops over to serve.

Nutrition Information

- Calories: 436
- Saturated Fat: 2 g(12%)
- Sodium: 724 mg(30%)
- Fiber: 10 g(41%)
- Total Carbohydrate: 81 g(27%)
- Cholesterol: 16 mg(5%)
- Protein: 17 g(33%)
- Total Fat: 9 g(14%)

340. Wild Mushroom Soup With Sherry

Serving: Makes 8 to 10 servings | Prep: | Ready in:

Ingredients

- 8 tablespoons (1 stick) butter, room temperature
- 2 cups sliced celery
- 1 cup sliced shallots
- 3/4 cup chopped onion
- 3 garlic cloves, minced
- 3 cups sliced stemmed fresh shiitake mushrooms (about 6 ounces)
- 3 cups sliced crimini mushrooms (about 6 ounces)
- 3 cups sliced oyster mushrooms (about 4 1/2 ounces)
- 1/2 cup dry white wine
- 1/2 cup dry Sherry
- 1/4 cup all purpose flour
- 8 cups chicken stock or canned low-salt chicken broth
- 1/2 cup whipping cream

Direction

- On medium-high heat, add 6 tablespoons of butter in a big pot to melt. Toss in onion, celery, garlic, and shallots; stir-fry until onion turns opaque for about 8 minutes. Toss in all of the mushrooms; stir-fry until starts to soften for about 4 minutes. Pour in Sherry and white wine, allow boiling until the liquid turns to glaze for about 6 minutes.
- In a small sized bowl, combine the 1/4 cup of flour and the rest of 2 tablespoons butter until mixture turns to smooth paste. Add the flour paste into the mushroom mixture in the pot, mixing until dissolved and the vegetables are coated. Slowly stir in the stock. Allow boiling while frequently stirring. Lower heat to medium-low; simmer until mushroom tenderized, mixing often for about 10 minutes. Add in cream; stir. Sprinkle pepper and salt over to season.
- Using a processor or blender, work in batches to mash the soup until smooth. Transfer soup into the pot. (Soup can be done 1 day ahead. Keep in the refrigerator with cover. To use: On medium-low heat, reheat stock. Serve.) Scoop soup using a ladle into the bowls. Serve.

Nutrition Information

- Calories: 298
- Total Fat: 19 g(30%)
- Saturated Fat: 11 g(55%)

- Sodium: 433 mg(18%)
- Fiber: 2 g(10%)
- Total Carbohydrate: 22 g(7%)
- Cholesterol: 54 mg(18%)
- Protein: 9 g(19%)

341. Wild Striped Bass With Charred Leeks And Squid Vinaigrette

Serving: Makes 4 servings | Prep: | Ready in:

Ingredients

- 1 pound cleaned calamari tentacles or cuttlefish tentacles
- 4 large leeks, whites only, cleaned and cut into 5-inch lengths
- 9 tablespoons extra-virgin olive oil
- Kosher salt and freshly ground black pepper
- 4 6-ounce wild striped bass fillets, skinned
- 1/4 cup dry white wine
- Juice and zest of 1 lemon
- 2 packets (2 tablespoons) of squid ink
- 1 teaspoon Dijon mustard

Direction

- Boil 3 quarts of water with an ice bath nearby. Place calamari in boiling water. Cook for 30 seconds. Take out calamari using a strainer or slotted spoon. Plunge immediately into ice bath. Let it cool for 1 minute. Drain and put aside. Blanch leeks for 8-9 minutes in the same water until just tender. Refresh in ice bath. Cut, lengthwise, in half.
- Preheat broiler or grill. Brush 2 tablespoons olive oil on leek halves and season with pepper and salt. Broil or grill leeks for 8-10 minutes, cut side toward heat, until charred. Only move them 1 time.
- Heat 3 tablespoons oil in a 12 to 14-inch sauté pan on high heat until it smokes. Season fish fillets with pepper and salt. Cook for 5-7 minutes, skin side down, until it easily moves without tearing and flesh is crispy.
- As fish cooks, boil squid ink, lemon juice, and wine in a separate sauté pan. Turn heat off. Mix in mustard then leftover 4 tablespoons of olive oil. Season with pepper and salt. Add calamari. Retain warmth.
- Flip fish and add leeks to the pan. Cook the other side of fish for 2-3 minutes, heating leeks through. Put 2 leeks in the middle of each of the 4 warmed plates. Put 1 fillet on every bed of leeks with the flesh side up. Drizzle some squid vinaigrette on every fillet. Garnish with lemon zest and tentacles. Immediately serve.

Nutrition Information

- Calories: 611
- Saturated Fat: 5 g(26%)
- Sodium: 1061 mg(44%)
- Fiber: 3 g(11%)
- Total Carbohydrate: 19 g(6%)
- Cholesterol: 275 mg(92%)
- Protein: 51 g(103%)
- Total Fat: 36 g(55%)

342. Wine Baked Halibut Steaks With Mustard Fennel Butter

Serving: Makes 4 servings | Prep: | Ready in:

Ingredients

- 2 teaspoons fennel seeds
- 6 tablespoons (3/4 stick) unsalted butter, room temperature
- 1/4 cup chopped fresh parsley
- 3 tablespoons Dijon mustard
- 4 6- to 8-ounce halibut steaks
- 1 cup dry white wine

Direction

- Place rack in center of the oven and preheat to 400°F. In small, heavy skillet, let fennel seeds toast on moderate heat for 5 minutes, till aromatic, mixing from time to time. Take the skillet; let cool. Chop the fennel seeds finely.
- Mix in small bowl with fennel seeds, mustard, parsley and butter. Use rubber spatula to crush till combined thoroughly and smooth. Season the fennel butter with pepper and salt to taste. Fennel butter may be done 4 days in advance and chilled. Let come to room temperature prior to using. Scatter pepper and salt on fish. Put fish in a glass baking dish, 8x8-inch in size. Add wine on top of fish. Bake for 15 minutes, till opaque in middle, basting from time to time with juices in dish and wine.
- Distribute fish between 4 plates. Smear fish with all of fennel butter.

Nutrition Information

- Calories: 375
- Total Fat: 20 g(31%)
- Saturated Fat: 12 g(58%)
- Sodium: 266 mg(11%)
- Fiber: 1 g(4%)
- Total Carbohydrate: 2 g(1%)
- Cholesterol: 143 mg(48%)
- Protein: 38 g(75%)

343. Wine Baked Onions With Herbed Crumb Topping

Serving: Serves 4 | Prep: | Ready in:

Ingredients

- 2 medium onions, peeled, halved crosswise
- 2/3 cup dry white wine
- 2 tablespoons (1/4 stick) butter
- 1 cup fresh French breadcrumbs
- 2 tablespoons chopped fresh parsley
- 1 tablespoon fresh thyme leaves or 1 teaspoon dried

Direction

- Preheat the oven to 350°F. Clip onions end to level. Put onions in small baking dish, flat side facing up. Add pepper and salt to season the onions. Pour to baking dish with wine. Use foil to cover and bake for 55 minutes, till onions become tender, baste with wine from time to time.
- Meantime, in nonstick, medium skillet, liquify butter on moderate heat. Put in parsley, thyme and breadcrumbs and sauté for 4 minutes, till breadcrumbs turn pale golden brown.
- Take onions out of pan. Evenly scoop breadcrumb mixture to onions. Lightly force breadcrumbs to stick. Keep baking the onions for 15 minutes, with no cover, till breadcrumbs turn golden brown and crisp. May be done 6 hours in advance. Rest at room temperature. Reheat the onions in oven at 350 °F. for 15 minutes, till topping crisp.

Nutrition Information

344. Yellow Tomato Soup

Serving: Makes 6 (first-course) servings | Prep: | Ready in:

Ingredients

- 1 large onion, chopped (about 2 1/2 cups)
- 6 bacon slices (about 5 ounces), chopped
- 5 cups chopped yellow tomatoes (about 2 pounds)
- 2 garlic cloves, minced
- 1/2 cup dry Sherry
- 1/2 cup dry white wine
- 4 cups chicken stock or canned low-salt chicken broth
- 2 teaspoons minced canned chipotle chilies*
- 1 tablespoon fresh chopped oregano leaves
- 1/2 cup whipping cream

Direction

- In heavy large pot, sauté bacon and onion over medium heat for 15 minutes or until onion is starting to brown and tender. Put in garlic and tomatoes. Simmer for 20 minutes, stirring occasionally, until the tomatoes are juicy and tender. Put in wine and Sherry and simmer for 5 minutes. Put in stock, simmer for 15 minutes or until the mixture is reduced to six and a half cup. Stir in oregano and chipotle chilies. In blender, puree soup in batches. Put back into pot. Put in cream, then stir until they are heated through. Season with pepper and salt to taste. Then enjoy.

Nutrition Information

- Calories: 283
- Protein: 10 g(20%)
- Total Fat: 18 g(28%)
- Saturated Fat: 8 g(38%)
- Sodium: 520 mg(22%)
- Fiber: 3 g(11%)
- Total Carbohydrate: 20 g(7%)
- Cholesterol: 42 mg(14%)

345. Ziti With Kielbasa And Sauerkraut

Serving: Makes 6 servings | Prep: | Ready in:

Ingredients

- 3 tablespoons extra-virgin olive oil
- 1 medium onion, chopped (about 1 cup)
- 1 medium-size red bell pepper, thinly sliced
- 1 pound kielbasa sausage or smoked sausage, cut into 1/4-inch-thick slices
- 12 ounces sauerkraut (about 3 cups), rinsed, well drained
- 2 tablespoons Dijon mustard
- 1 teaspoon caraway seeds
- Pinch of cayenne pepper
- 1/4 cup dry white wine
- 2 tablespoons chopped fresh parsley
- 12 ounces ziti pasta

Direction

- In big, heavy skillet, heat the olive oil on moderate heat. Put in and sauté red bell pepper and onion for 7 minutes, till nearly tender. Put in and sauté sausage for 8 minutes, till starting to brown. Stir in cayenne pepper, caraway seeds, mustard and sauerkraut. Sauté for 4 minutes, till heated completely. Mix in parsley and wine. Let mixture cook for an additional of 2 minutes.
- Meantime, in big pot with salted boiling water, cook the pasta till tender yet remain firm to bite, mixing from time to time. Strain the pasta and put back to pot.
- Put to pasta with sausage mixture and toss till coated. Add pepper and salt to season.

Nutrition Information

- Calories: 526
- Sodium: 1090 mg(45%)
- Fiber: 5 g(20%)
- Total Carbohydrate: 50 g(17%)
- Cholesterol: 53 mg(18%)
- Protein: 20 g(41%)
- Total Fat: 27 g(41%)
- Saturated Fat: 7 g(35%)

Index

A

Almond 7,196

Angostura bitters 203

Anise 3,5,10,131

Apple 3,6,11,50,171

Apricot 4,58

Arborio rice 93,164,188,190

Artichoke 3,4,5,6,39,56,57,130,172,179

Asparagus 5,6,7,8,129,156,216,232

B

Bacon 3,4,12,32,72

Baking 17

Basil 3,5,7,8,34,43,119,184,202,233

Beans 4,7,67,75,93,192,193,194

Beef 6,151,154

Beer 3,33

Berry 7,226

Biscotti 127

Blackberry 7,202

Blood orange 16

Blueberry 3,5,46,101,117

Bouquet garni 53

Bran 3,27

Brazil nut 156

Bread 4,53,75

Brie 3,27,28

Brioche 3,16

Brisket 3,31

Broth 5,8,99,111,237

Burger 6,167

Butter 3,4,5,6,7,8,24,29,30,62,73,78,87,113,127,144,183,201,223,239

C

Cabbage 5,6,103,180

Cake 3,4,7,29,30,67,210

Capers 4,5,6,7,8,76,125,167,195,228,229

Caramel 3,31,49

Cardamom 5,7,127,210

Carrot 6,7,147,187

Cauliflower 3,7,32,205

Cayenne pepper 57

Celery 4,57

Champ 11

Chard 6,70,105,173,174

Cheddar 4,74,168

Cheese 3,4,5,7,16,33,34,43,69,71,76,118,206,214,237

Chicken 3,4,5,6,7,19,20,21,34,35,36,37,38,39,40,41,42,43,44,45,58,59,69,86,91,99,101,122,152,153,154,157,166,167,172,198,199

Chives 4,67

Chocolate 5,8,133,234,235

Chorizo 7,196

Cider 3,50

Cinnamon 5,8,127,230

Clams 4,6,7,93,100,144,196,215

Clementine 4,61

Coconut 4,52

Cod 7,205

Coffee 113

Cognac 181,182,207

Coriander 6,161

Coulis 7,202

Crab 4,6,55,57,143

Cranberry 4,55,56,186

Crayfish 173

Cream 3,4,5,7,8,10,20,43,46,56,57,94,95,115,128,130,155,185,210,217,229,230

Crumble 231

Curry 4,7,52,207

Custard 3,13

D

Dijon mustard 27,65,115,135,139,140,155,192,203,239,241

Dill 3,4,40,92

Dover sole 195

Duck 3,4,5,21,61,107

Dumplings 3,44

E

Egg 7,204

Elderflower 5,130

F

Farfalle 4,63

Fat 9,10,11,12,13,14,15,17,18,19,20,21,22,23,24,26,27,28,29,30,32,33,34,35,36,37,38,39,40,41,42,43,44,45,46,47,48,50,51,53,54,55,56,57,58,59,60,61,62,63,64,65,67,68,69,70,71,72,73,74,75,76,77,78,79,80,81,82,83,84,85,86,87,89,90,92,93,95,96,97,99,100,101,102,103,104,105,106,107,108,109,110,111,112,113,114,116,117,118,119,120,121,122,123,124,125,126,127,128,129,130,131,132,133,135,136,137,138,139,140,142,143,144,145,146,147,149,150,151,152,153,154,155,156,157,158,159,161,163,164,165,166,167,168,169,170,171,172,173,174,175,176,177,178,179,180,181,182,183,184,187,188,189,190,191,192,194,195,196,197,198,199,200,201,202,203,204,205,206,207,208,209,210,211,212,213,214,215,216,217,218,219,220,221,222,223,224,225,226,227,228,229,230,232,234,235,236,238,239,240,241

Fennel 3,4,5,6,7,8,9,87,89,113,122,138,152,158,159,161,182,208,209,221,239,240

Feta 74

Fig 3,4,16,18,61

Fish 4,6,63,64,65,66,81,86,142,163

Flatbread 51

Flour 37

Fontina cheese 67

French bread 27,65,69,104,179,214,215,240

Fruit 3,4,5,6,7,10,60,118,131,155,200,211,221,226

G

Garlic 3,4,5,6,7,20,45,62,69,70,71,91,113,138,152,203,208

Gin 3,4,5,6,7,18,72,73,131,170,187

Gnocchi 6,140,141

Goose 5,130

Gorgonzola 5,139,140

Grapefruit 4,63

Grapes 4,6,7,81,141,195

Gratin 4,74

Gravy 5,8,99,230

H

Halibut 4,8,76,77,239

Ham 4,6,78,82,180

Hazelnut 3,4,32,77

Herbs 4,6,88,153

Honey 4,5,83,126

Horseradish 3,4,29,83,84

I

Ice cream 128

J

Jam 7,212

Jelly 4,55

Jerusalem artichoke 56

John Dory 4,87

Jus 4,14,22,23,79,114,182,203

K

Kale 4,6,58,180

L

Lamb 3,4,6,7,22,79,88,89,91,143,148,150,159,219

Langoustine 6,173,174

Leek 3,5,6,7,8,21,108,147,188,239

Lemon 3,4,6,7,8,18,38,66,91,92,93,153,161,167,168,172,178,184,196,199,207,229

Lettuce 167

Lime 3,46

Ling 4,7,94,188

Lobster 5,6,7,95,96,97,175,197

M

Madeira 5,6,132,133,134,166,167

Madeleines 13

Mango 5,7,99,217,221

Mascarpone 4,43,83

Mayonnaise 5,109,167

Meat 5,104,176

Melon 5,101

Mince 18,70,107,148

Mint 3,5,7,48,74,101,184

Monkfish 5,105,123

Morel 3,5,7,21,136,216

Mushroom 3,4,5,6,7,8,14,26,27,28,63,76,77,86,93,104,108,137,140,156,177,189,192,213,219,220,229,230,237,238

Mussels 3,4,5,7,9,94,109,110,111,112,113,114,115,197,201,206,207,208,209,215

Mustard 3,4,5,6,8,19,40,82,109,115,116,139,155,239

N

Nasturtium 7,216

Nectarine 5,117

Nut 6,7,9,10,11,12,13,14,15,16,17,18,19,20,21,22,23,24,25,26,27,28,29,30,31,32,33,34,35,36,37,38,39,40,41,42,43,44,45,46,47,48,49,50,51,52,53,54,55,56,57,58,59,60,61,62,63,64,65,66,67,68,69,70,71,72,73,74,75,76,77,78,79,80,81,82,83,84,85,86,87,88,89,90,91,92,93,94,95,96,97,99,100,101,102,103,104,105,106,107,108,109,110,111,112,113,114,115,116,117,118,119,120,121,122,123,124,125,126,127,128,129,130,131,132,133,135,136,137,138,139,140,141,142,143,144,145,146,147,148,149,150,151,152,153,154,155,156,157,158,159,160,161,162,163,164,165,166,167,168,169,170,171,172,173,174,175,176,177,178,179,180,181,182,183,184,186,187,188,189,190,192,194,195,196,197,198,199,200,201,202,203,204,205,206,207,208,209,210,211,212,213,214,215,216,217,218,219,220,221,222,223,224,225,226,227,228,229,230,232,233,234,235,236,237,238,239,240,241

O

Oil 43,140,231

Olive 3,4,6,21,43,58,64,76,80,118,161,172

Onion 3,4,5,6,7,8,27,31,50,66,121,179,203,212,240

Orange 3,4,5,6,7,8,15,60,69,118,119,131,158,159,170,191,200,208,232

Oregano 4,64

P

Pancetta 6,154

Pappardelle 5,122

Parmesan 5,14,23,30,67,73,92,103,105,112,120,122,123,129,137,141,150,151,165,177,188,192,204,213,214,217,223,233

Parsley 3,4,5,7,44,62,63,124,196

Pasta 5,6,7,95,123,125,175,195

Pastry 5,126,186

Peach 5,7,8,127,130,211,236

Pear 3,4,5,6,7,8,13,49,50,83,127,128,131,132,133,165,185,201,203,227,234

Peas 4,5,63,71,122,136

Pecorino 125,164,192,204,205

Peel 13,16,41,57,84,98,100,102,113,130,131,135,143,145,163,165,174,185,187,188,212,228

Penne 5,43,129

Pepper 3,4,5,6,12,15,43,71,110,113,165,176

Pesto 3,5,7,9,43,112,215

Pheasant 3,50

Pie 5,96

Pineapple 5,7,129,227

Pizza 4,52

Plum 6,160

Pomegranate 5,107,136

Porcini 3,5,7,8,26,137,214,237

Pork 3,4,5,6,7,15,18,26,69,137,138,139,140,155,160,162,176,186,192,193

Port 118,132,173

Potato 4,5,6,7,8,54,68,74,114,118,135,140,141,157,206,230

Poussin 4,90

Prosciutto 3,26,42

Prune 6,176

Pulse 182

Pumpkin 6,144,145,146

Q

Quince 6,147

Quinoa 7,189

R

Rabbit 5,6,119,147

Radish 6,164

Raisins 3,51

Raspberry 6,149

Rhubarb 6,149,150

Rice 7,74,198

Rigatoni 3,6,14,23,150

Risotto 4,5,6,7,8,67,72,92,93,104,137,151,164,187,189,190,204,213,232

Roast chicken 70

Roast lamb 149

Roast pork 26,138,163

Roast turkey 225

Roquefort 3,28

Rosemary 3,4,5,22,42,51,55,77,119

Rouille 6,142

S

Saffron 5,6,7,104,111,142,170,205,207,221

Sage 3,4,6,7,30,34,77,144,166,220

Salad 4,7,68,89,184,203

Salmon 3,4,5,6,7,29,83,94,115,134,135,136,167,168,169,170,194,195

Salsify 174

Salt 21,24,31,34,35,37,45,53,74,101,151,176

Sardine 3,15

Satsuma 160

Sausage 3,4,7,14,34,37,45,77,103,192,209

Savoy cabbage 180

Scallop 6,8,176,177,180,183,184,229

Seafood 5,6,7,100,181,182,198

Shallot 5,7,122,199

Shellfish 5,6,7,120,161,174,187

Sherry 8,113,149,237,238,240,241

Snapper 6,8,161,237

Sole 5,7,116,195

Sorbet 7,8,221,233,234

Soup 3,4,5,6,7,8,27,32,46,47,48,56,57,58,65,86,87,108,124,130,142,145,163,203,204,221,238,240

Spaghetti 7,196,197

Spinach 5,6,7,103,165,203

Squash 3,7,19,30,213

Squid 4,5,8,70,120,239

Steak 3,4,5,8,29,80,122,239

Stew 3,6,39,40,45,154,182

Stock 3,4,5,7,38,65,84,97,167,224

Strawberry 7,194,209,210,211

Stuffing 3,4,6,7,8,34,77,78,84,85,155,192,230

Sugar 5,126,225

Swordfish 5,7,122,215

Syrup 3,5,7,16,119,210

T

Tagliatelle 7,215

Tamari 7,217

Tarragon 4,5,6,63,74,135,154,183

Tea 77,193

Terrine 7,211

Thai basil 184

Thyme 4,6,90,150,168,182

Tofu 8,230

Tomato 3,4,5,6,7,8,12,20,22,43,47,54,66,72,76,77,88,119,120,129,167,172,179,202,212,217,219,221,230,240

Trout 5,6,7,121,146,150,169,222

Truffle 3,24,174

Turkey 3,7,24,223,224,225,226

V

Veal 3,6,7,8,24,25,26,158,228,229,230

Vegan 8,230

Vegetable oil 171

Vegetables 3,4,6,7,24,28,31,44,59,79,162,174,224

W

Walnut 3,8,16,232

Watercress 5,6,116,178

Watermelon 3,8,48,233

White chocolate 234

White wine 24,75

Wine 1,3,4,5,6,7,8,9,20,31,37,42,45,55,60,81,86,91,99,101,107,111,127,148,169,172,177,188,200,201,206,232,233,236,239,240

Worcestershire sauce 215

Z

Zest 5,131

L

lasagna 182

Conclusion

Thank you again for downloading this book!

I hope you enjoyed reading about my book!

If you enjoyed this book, please take the time to share your thoughts and post a review on Amazon. It'd be greatly appreciated!

Write me an honest review about the book – I truly value your opinion and thoughts and I will incorporate them into my next book, which is already underway.

Thank you!

If you have any questions, **feel free to contact at:** *author@rutabagarecipes.com*

Mary Walter

rutabagarecipes.com

Made in United States
Orlando, FL
17 June 2023